E.L. Frothingham, A. L. Frothingham

Philosophy as Absolute Science founded in The Universal Laws of being

And decoding Ontology, Theology, and Psychology made one, as spirit, soul, and body

E.L. Frothingham, A. L. Frothingham

Philosophy as Absolute Science founded in The Universal Laws of being
And decoding Ontology, Theology, and Psychology made one, as spirit,soul, and body

ISBN/EAN: 9783741179662

Manufactured in Europe, USA, Canada, Australia, Japa

Cover: Foto ©Andreas Hilbeck / pixelio.de

Manufactured and distributed by brebook publishing software (www.brebook.com)

E.L. Frothingham, A. L. Frothingham

Philosophy as Absolute Science founded in The Universal Laws of being

PHILOSOPHY

AS

ABSOLUTE SCIENCE,

FOUNDED IN

The Universal Laws of Being,

AND INCLUDING

ONTOLOGY, THEOLOGY, AND PSYCHOLOGY

MADE ONE,

AS SPIRIT, SOUL, AND BODY.

By E. L. & A. L. FROTHINGHAM.

"ABSOLUTE SCIENCE is the pure self-consciousness of the Reason,—the conviction that it has of itself,—which assures to every special science its value and right import, and is at the same time versed in them all, and combines into a whole their various branches. Its object is the eternal truth,—the unchangeable, unborn, imperishable,—of which all that can be truly said is, that IT IS. This eternal and unchangeable Being we call God."—PLATO.

VOLUME I.

BOSTON:
WALKER, WISE, AND COMPANY,
245, WASHINGTON STREET.
1864.

Entered, according to Act of Congress, in the year 1864,
BY EPHRAIM L. FROTHINGHAM,
In the Clerk's Office of the District Court of the District of Massachusetts.

BOSTON:
STEREOTYPED AND PRINTED BY JOHN WILSON AND SON,
5, WATER STREET.

INTRODUCTION.

That Truth is One, and that Philosophy must therefore be realized as Absolute Science, through the conception and application of the Universal Laws of Existence in its construction, in order that it should be legitimate, reliable, and permanent, has always been acknowledged; and the realization of this universal form has therefore been the principal object in all Ontological and Eclectical speculations. M. Chalybäus, in his "Historical Survey of Experimental Philosophy," says, "The chief business of human thought is, and must be, to discover and comprehend principle, means, and end, both in singular and in the whole. All three moments ought to be one or united; but they must also be distinguished, and, each in its own place, must necessarily be that to which, by this place, it is entitled or justified. To find the true formula for this relation, has been, as the whole history of Philosophy teaches us, the problem from Pythagoras down to Hegel: incessantly has the human mind labored with this intention, and without having in itself a distinct consciousness of the fact, worked within the pale of this formula, in order to obtain possession of it for itself." Cicero recognized the necessity for this universal form, and defined Philosophy to be "The Science of things Divine, and of things Human." By Plato, "Absolute Science" was demanded as the condition of true knowledge, and was defined in the following words: "Absolute Science is the pure self-consciousness of the Reason, — the conviction that it has of itself, — which assures to every special science its value and right import, and is, at the same time, versed in them all, and combines into a whole their various branches. Its object is the eternal truth,—the unchangeable, unborn, and imperishable,—of which all that can be truly said is, that IT IS. This eternal and unchangeable being we call God."

A demand for Absolute Science has been made in all Ontological systems, because Ontology is "The Science of Being," and it must therefore attempt to define the nature of Absolute and of Phenomenal Being, and to show the relationship that exists between them; and this demand has been made in all Eclectical systems of Philosophy, because these are constructed for the purpose of uniting opposite ontological and psychological systems. This demand was made even by the Speculative School founded by Kant, who commenced an inquiry into the nature of subjective and objective experiences, and into the relationship between Absolute Being and the facts of the human consciousness. Kant, however, came to the conclusion, that neither the Subjective nor the Absolute could be conceived; and that natural appearances, which have their ground in sensible experience, constitute both the form and the substance of all possible knowledge: while all the writers of this school not only came to the pantheistic conclusion that Absolute and Phenomenal—Subjective and Objective —Being and Nought—are one and the same, but ended in realizing a form of Anthropomorphism, or a conception of God founded upon the facts of the human consciousness. Kant commenced this by saying, "From the cognition of Self to the cognition of the World, and through these to the Supreme Being, the progression is so natural, that it seems to resemble the logical march of Reason from the premises to the conclusion:" and his followers ended in asserting, that God first arrives at a definite self-consciousness in human nature, or through the consciousness of individual men; and thus accepted the theory of Spinoza, that all things of which we become conscious are simply modes of manifestation in the Infinite Substance, outside of which nothing can exist.

The possibility of realizing Absolute Science has always been denied by the moral and sensualistic schools in Philosophy; and the reason for this is, that they are purely psychological, and therefore are constructed from, or are founded entirely upon, the facts of the natural consciousness, which present the most discordant collection of phenomena that can possibly be conceived; these being external and deceptive in character, and realized in a region of the mind which cannot become receptive either of laws from the Reason, by which absolute rationality is demanded, or of analogies from the Imagination, corresponding with these, by which it is represented; but is dependent for all its knowledge upon generalizations and classifications of these discordant phenomena by the "Fancy," under the laws of "Contrast" and "Resemblance," in a form of Unity in Diversity, by which a fictitious representation is produced that is an inversion of the real condition and relationships of things. This possibility has also been denied by the Theologians and by the Church, for the reason that the religious mind can believe in nothing higher than theological truth, and supposes the religious to be the spiritual condition of the individual: while, as we shall clearly demonstrate, Religion and Rationality are, in the natural, necessarily antagonized and destructive to each other; and the religious and the spiritual conditions of the soul are not only antagonized, but are the farthest removed from each other in the order of production. As an introduction to the present work, therefore, we will consider the grounds upon which this opposition to Absolute Science is founded; why this position has been taken, and why it cannot be sustained; and then show the ground that we have for a belief in the possibility of Absolute Science for man, and the reasons we have for believing that such a science has been realized in this work.

The sensualistic philosophers have sought to obtain a ground for their opposition to Absolute Science by assuming two premises which are palpably unphilosophical: these are, the identity of the Absolute, the Spiritual, and the Infinite, — which they characterize as Invisible; and the identity of Creation and the Finite, — which they characterize as Visible. By thus identifying the Absolute with the Infinite, — which is a universal indefinite principle, — the possibility is excluded of obtaining any statement of Absolute Law, any definite conception of Absolute Creating Cause, or any recognition of an Infinite, and thus Vital, ground for Creation; and Philosophy is confined to a knowledge of phenomenal appearances and relationships, which are discordant, deceptive, and the opposite of what they seem; so that neither truth nor consistency is possible for it. By thus identifying Creation with the Finite, the possibility is excluded of recognizing this principle as one of the two Universal Causes of all Existence, or Definite Being; both of which causes, together with the manner in which they become united in production, must be conceived before a single phenomenon can really be comprehended, for the reason that all phenomena are representative of the union of Infinite and Finite Absolute Laws in the realization of Absolute Existence. In the following extract from Sir William Hamilton, who is one of the last and most popular of the English exponents of the sensualistic schools of Philosophy, this denial of any cognition by the mind of either the Absolute or the Universal, and this assertion of the purely relative character of knowledge, is so broadly stated as to approach caricature. He says, "All our knowledge is relative; that is to say, we know unity only as it is defined by plurality. It is therefore contradictory and false to say that we know the one as undefined by the many; that is, as universal. Hence I insist that the Absolute represents no substantial cognition, but only our ignorance of the irrelative. When we wish to indicate something beyond the sphere of our knowledge, we call up the Absolute to represent that unknown something. For example, we have a relative knowledge of man; that is, of the good man as defined by the bad man, and *vice versa*; or of John as defined by Joseph, by Charles, by all the not Johns. When, then, we wish to deny that we are speaking of the good man, or of the bad man, or the John, we say that we are speaking of man absolutely; that is, not any man specifically defined, but freed from definition; that is, the man universal. We do not mean to say that we know this undefined universal man; because, in that case, our knowledge would be contradictory. For if it be true that we know the specific man, or the man limited by other men, it necessarily follows that the absolute man, or the man unlimited by other men, is the man we do not know."

Mr. Field, who, in imitation of the German Eclectics, attempted the construction of a universal science by the individualization of natural phenomena as internal, external, and medial, has taken the same position; although, being expressed in a more scientific manner, the absurdity of the statement does not so readily appear. He says, "As there is nothing known that cannot be resolved into correlative elements, all knowledge consists of relations; and the absolute and the privative, as extremes, are equally excluded from the sphere of knowledge or philosophy. We hold, therefore, that the whole universe is, to human cognizance, a universe of relations or of analogy; and that all true analogy springs from universal relation;—that the primary relations of things are invariable and eternal, whence all knowledge is systematic and constant, inasmuch as it partakes of those universal relations, or first principles;—and, therefore, that all certainty is certainty of relation only, and not absolute; for of the absolute we have only indication, but not knowledge or comprehension."

Now, it is of course true, that "the whole Universe is, to human cognizance, a universe of relations or of analogy," and that from this human and natural point of view "the absolute and the privative, as extremes, are excluded;" because the opposite universal laws which constitute the opposite poles of existence, or definite being, cannot be conceived from a natural, but only from a spiritual, point of view. This not only excludes from the natural consciousness the recognition of these opposite universal causes, but prevents the recognition of any thing that is spiritual and real, and confines it to the apprehensive recognition of the relative and representative, the nature of which it cannot comprehend, and even the existence of which it cannot demonstrate. All philosophical difficulties have arisen in this very fact, "that the Universe is to human cognizance a universe of relations," while the universal laws which must govern these relations were excluded from the consciousness; because the consequence of this has been, that the mind was obliged to seek for the spiritual law in the natural phenomenon, which contradicts while it represents it, and is the opposite of what it seems. This task has been particularly hopeless, for three reasons: first, because all natural phenomena are representative of two opposite absolute causes, while the laws which constitute their life are representative of one, and the laws which govern their production are representative of the other; next, because these phenomena are unreal appearances, which are opposite to real causes; and, finally, because, while representing laws or causes which are absolutely antagonistic, they have to be explained from a unitarian point of view, or to be regarded as harmonious or homogeneous, and explained by the application of the natural law of existence, which is Unity in Diversity, and the natural classifying law of Tri-Unity, by which opposite things are confounded, and nothing real can be known. It is true that ideas and laws, derived from the Reason and from the Sentiment, representative of vital spiritual ideas and laws, have been discordantly combined with these unreal natural appearances which are opposite to them, and have communicated to them a natural vitality, by which some of the mischievous effects that they are calculated to produce have been counteracted; but when these ideas and laws come to be repudiated, — as they must be in the development of the mind from within outwards, — in consequence of a demand by the natural understanding for consistency and for a belief in appearances, a sceptical materialism is the necessary result; and, when they come to be inverted, — as we shall show that they must be in the course of this development, — not only is supernatural truth repudiated, but supernatural falsehood is substituted in its place.

But although Absolute Law has thus been excluded from the human consciousness, and the mind has, consequently, been unable to realize the Absolute Science which the Reason has always demanded, we are not for this reason to suppose its realization to be impossible; because this would be to suppose that man is always to be confined to a natural sphere of consciousness, and can never ascend into heaven, where "flesh and blood," which constitute the natural man, can never come. Although it is undeniably true that the realization of Absolute Science is impossible so long as the soul is confined to a natural sphere of consciousness, it is equally true, that, after the development of the natural has been completed, the individual must necessarily be brought into a spiritual sphere of consciousness, where every thing will become one in a universal form, and the realization of Absolute Science is inevitable. The fact that this science has been demanded and represented would be sufficient to prove not only its possibility, but the necessity for its realization: but the most conclusive evidence of this is found in the fact, that Spiritual Life and Absolute Truth are inseparable; and that, as the condition of realizing this life, after a natural development of the soul has been completed, its spiritual development must commence under the operation of Absolute Law. It becomes, therefore, simply a question of time; because the advent of the Spiritual must follow the close of this natural development, which we shall show has now come to an end. It is true that the possibility of realizing Philosophy as Absolute Science is more emphatically denied at the present time than ever before; but this is because the mind becomes developed from within outwards, and thus the lowest forms of thought are the last in the order of production, and the greatest despair of absolute truth must immediately precede its presentation to the mind: and, although it will here be demonstrated that Philosophy has, for the third time, exhausted all the forms of the human consciousness which constitute a complete circle of philosophical experience from a natural point of view, instead of concluding from this that nothing more can be known, from this very fact we are to conclude that a new order of thought and of experience is now to be commenced, and that Absolute

Truth is now to be placed within our reach; because we shall show, that, in this threefold form, the natural development of the consciousness is completed.

The realization of Absolute Truth, which is, as Plato says, the recognition of God Himself in the consciousness, has been supposed by some to be impossible under any circumstances, upon the ground, that, to *know* God, we must *be* God. M. Chalybäus, in commenting upon the demand for Absolute Science made by the German Eclectics, says, "Must we not, in order to cognize God *a priori*, transport ourselves into the place of God, or, in order to find him within ourselves, be in ourselves God Himself, or, at all events, Divine? Now, to invite Philosophy to such an undertaking, would imply nothing else than to entice her cunningly to the verge of some dizzy precipice in order that she might more certainly topple over, break her neck, and leave once and for ever a free field open to the empirical belief upon authority." Now, to assert that we must be God, in order that we should know God, is simply absurd, because upon this ground we could not know any thing without being it, and the idea of knowledge would be destroyed. It is true that "the things of God knoweth no man, but the Spirit of God;" and therefore, to know God, we must become conscious through a spiritual or divine-human principle, in which the divine and the human have become harmoniously at-one, by which we become "partakers of the divine nature." But as even St. Peter, the founder of the Catholic Church, has affirmed the competency of man so to become; as the marriage of the soul to God, which is based upon this fact, is taught in the Scriptures, from Genesis to Revelation; and as we could not love God, as we are there commanded, without knowing him, — this idea ought not certainly to be regarded as a subject for ridicule. Instead of this, it should be regarded as the great end of Creation; all other experiences being only the preparation for its realization. Man is therefore created "in the Image of God;" and the forms and modes of Divine Existence are impressed upon him, — an impression that will finally become realized to him in a spiritual consciousness through the Reason, which is the spiritual region of the mind; when the Universal Laws of Being, and their operation in realizing spheres of Absolute and of Phenomenal Existence, will be revealed to his Consciousness. "The natural man receiveth not the things of the Spirit of God; for they are foolishness unto him: neither can he know them, because they are spiritually discerned. But he that is spiritual judgeth all things; yet he himself is judged of no man."

It is because these universal laws have not been conceived by the mind, that such a variety of philosophical and theological systems, opposite to each other and inconsistent in themselves, have successively been produced; these being the discordant products of the human consciousness which have been realized in the course of its natural development. These systems of Theology have therefore been separated from and antagonized to Philosophy, and these philosophical systems have failed to give that explanation of the phenomena of life and of the consciousness which Reason demands, and which it is the particular business of Philosophy to give; and they have therefore been confined for the most part to the attention of the learned, instead of being generally applied as practical guides to the knowledge of truth and of good. From its highest point, however, Philosophy has always demanded the realization of Absolute Science as the condition of real knowledge. It is only from its lowest psychological point that the possibility of its realization has been denied by the philosophers: and, upon the sensualistic ground of appearances taken by them, these psychologists not only deny the possibility of realizing Philosophy as Absolute Science, but deny the possibility of any philosophy; because, by repudiating Intuition, through which we obtain a knowledge of the laws which govern phenomena, they confine knowledge to the generalization of sensible experiences; setting up individual notions, and the most superficial, discordant, and deceptive appearances, not only as guides in the search after truth, but as the highest standard of truth, by which every thing else is to be measured; an abrogation of Law that must be productive of a philosophical chaos, — lead to the destruction of all that is ideal and vital in the consciousness, and corresponds with the realities of things, — and end in the establishment of materialism and scepticism. So far as Philosophy is concerned, therefore, we have every support for the position here taken, — that no real or permanent knowledge can be obtained by the mind, except through the realization of Philosophy as Absolute Science.

We have said that the reason why the possibility of Absolute Science is denied by the Theologians and by the Church is, that the religious mind can believe in nothing higher than theological truth, and supposes the religious to be the spiritual condition of the individual: while Religion and Rationality are, in the natural, necessarily antagonistic and destructive to each other; and the religious and the spiritual conditions of the soul are not only antagonized, but are the furthest removed from each other in the order of production. It is true, that Philosophy has always taken its departure from Religion, or from the Church, and has been at its commencement little more than a defence of her theological statements, for the reason that Religion is the natural representative of the Spiritual, which it is the province of Philosophy to state in the form of a universal science; and it therefore becomes suggestive in the realization of natural intuitions from the Reason, which are symbolized by the Imagination in its construction of ontological systems representative of Philosophy as Absolute Science. But, while Religion has thus determined the character of Philosophy, nothing could be more opposite in their construction than Theology and Philosophy have been; because the latter necessarily demands perspicuity, reality, and consistency, while the former has been characterized as poetical, unreal, and inconsistent: and the reason for this is, that, while the theology of Religion is founded in ideas representative of spiritual phenomena, these necessarily become incarnated in natural experiences of the most external description, by which the most violent contrasts and the most extreme opposition to consistency and rationality are produced. This is why Philosophy always becomes particularly antagonistic to the Church when released from subjection to her; why the latter has never depended upon intellectual but always upon sentimental recognition, where thought is made subservient to feeling; why she has never adopted the religious ideas which are embodied in her theological statements as a ground for philosophy, but has regarded these systems as superstructures of truth that were to be supported by all intellectual statements, whether of Christian or of Pagan origin, that could be made useful for this purpose: and this is why she has been especially hostile to all efforts for the realization of Absolute Science. Three principal positions have been taken by her, antagonistic to such a realization: the first being, that feeling, and not thought, is the guide to spiritual truth; the second being, that the Bible is the only revelation of this truth separate from the traditions of the Church, and that it is therefore only here that spiritual truth is to be found; and the third being, that as the truths of the Bible are spiritual, while the human understanding is natural, no scientific conception of spiritual truth is possible, but only a sentimental apprehension in the form of religious faith, which is a contradiction to the natural understanding and the natural consciousness.

To illustrate the first of these positions, we will quote from the writings of Frederic Schlegel, who came out on the side of the Church, in opposition to the attempt made by the speculative school of philosophy founded by Kant to realize a universal science: "True human science is founded on experience, and on tradition, language, and revelation. But, on the contrary, that false, or, as I termed it at the outset, that unhuman and absolute knowledge, as it pretends to embrace all at once, and by one step to place us in full possession of the whole sum of human knowledge; so, ever fluctuating between being and non-being, it soon dissolves into thin air, and leaves nothing behind but a baseless void of absolute non-knowing. Feeling is every thing: in words only does there lie a possibility of misconception. When philosophy sets out from the false semblance of necessary thought, it must always have a similar result. It cannot extricate itself from its own subtle web of scientific delusion." Now, we may admit, that, in this search after "unhuman and absolute knowledge," the philosophers of this school were led into conclusions which are liable to the severest criticism, and which, so far as the representation of truth and the practical uses of life are concerned, fall far below that human knowledge, founded in experience, tradition, and revelation, to which Schlegel applies the name of human science; although science is the last term that should be applied to such a heterogeneous compound. Their intellectual position was, however, much higher than that of Schlegel, whose hostility to absolute science evidently grew out of the irrational character of his own mind, which did not seem to comprehend the meaning of consistency, or the idea of science; for nothing can be more external and recklessly contradictory than the assertions of this writer, or more simply dogmatical, and destitute of proof. By antagonizing some of his principal statements with regard to the nature of Philosophy, this will at once be seen. He says, "Philosophy is the science of the Consciousness alone." "It is common enough to speak of the facts of the Consciousness; but the only fact that really deserves to be so named is its internal dissension: for the whole human consciousness is filled with unmitigated discord and division." Again: "Philosophy must, in every case, take God for the basis of its speculations, — set out from Him, and draw in every instance from this divine source." "The highest and loftiest language would fail us were it our purpose to speak of the inmost essence of the Godhead, since He is that which no thought or conception can comprehend, and which no words are sufficient completely to describe, or adequately to express." The external character of his mind is sufficiently evident, from the fact that he regards feeling instead of thought as the guide to truth, and denies any internal information to the mind. With regard to the first, we have already quoted his words: with regard to the second, he says, "Man, as at present constituted, does possess one, but only one, species of inborn ideas; viz., an innate idea of death." This is a fair specimen of the consistency and the credibility of those who affirm that truth is to be apprehended by the sentiment through feeling and external reception, and cannot be comprehended as scientific thought through the intuition and internal conception of its laws.

The second position to be noticed is, that the Bible is the only revelation of spiritual truth that can be made to mankind, and that the Church is its only authorized interpreter; for although the claim to a private interpretation of the Scriptures through individual inspiration was necessarily set up by the Protestant Church to secure a separation from the Church of Rome, and must indeed be asserted by her as an internal church, no church can tolerate a departure from its creed, or recognize any other interpretations of the Bible than its own. Now, there could not be any thing more indefensible than such a position as this; because it is an undeniable philosophical fact, which is demanded by a universal law of Being, and will be demonstrated in a thousand ways in the course of this work, that all consciousness, whether of sensation, thought, feeling, or emotion, is produced by the union in the mind of phenomena with the laws by which they are governed: so that no revelation can possibly be made to the mind from without, except as it corresponds with a revelation made to it from within. This cannot well be denied, because it is evidently impossible that what is external to the mind, and must therefore be made known to it through sensation or by physical contact, should ever be any thing more to it than suggestive; so that something in the mind may be furnished with material for production, and be excited to incarnate itself in form. We cannot but see, therefore, that, although the presentation and exposition of the Scriptures are the conditions, they can never be the cause, of their recognition and reception,—this cause being necessarily something in the mind itself, with which this presentation corresponds. Admitting, then, that the Bible constitutes a threefold representation of Divine Truth, even the letter or most external form of which is divinely inspired, — which is all that can possibly be claimed for it, — these questions immediately arise: How is this representation to be recognized by the mind? By what power of the mind is it to be interpreted? What are the mental processes through which it is made to affect the individual? Now, we shall show that there are three legitimate points of view from which the Bible is contemplated, and that it is made to affect the individual in three legitimate modes, which succeed each other in the growth and development of the Consciousness; and that these correspond with the external and unconscious, the internal and self-conscious, and the spiritual, conditions of the soul. The first is the point of religious feeling, which arises in a receptive condition of the religious sentiment, in which the individual experiences are characterized as unconscious and emotional, — these being produced through symbolic representations of the most external character, constituting the most external form or letter of the Scriptures, which is relatively natural; neither the supernatural significance of which, nor the manner in which it produces its effects, are comprehended either by the individual or by the Church: the second is the point of religious conception, which arises in a conceptive condition of the religious sentiment, in which the individual becomes productive of self-conscious experiences, which obtain a legitimate expression in the form of prayer, — these being produced through representations of religious truth, constituting the internal form of the Scriptures which is relatively supernatural, and susceptible of incarnation in natural thought, and in individual natural experiences, from a self-conscious point of view: the third is the point of spiritual insight; from which the Bible is comprehended through scientific thought by the realization and application of the Universal Laws of Being, and, instead of being simply a discordant representative of the Supernatural, becomes a Universal Representative. Now, the first of these is peculiar to the Catholic, while the second is peculiar to the Protestant Church, and are the only legitimate points of view from which the Scriptures have yet been contemplated; and we shall demonstrate that these do no: communicate the Spiritual, but only represent the Supernatural, — that, although supernatural or religious truth is thus represented from an external, it is contradicted from an internal, point of view, — and that these natural and supernatural representations are realized in harmony with vital natural institutions, and supernatural forms of thought; are the means through which vital individual experiences are realized, and a natural development is secured; and will furnish suggestive material in the incarnation of Spiritual Truth, when the individual shall be brought out of a natural into a spiritual sphere of consciousness.

After the human consciousness has been fully developed from this supernatural point of view, a natural order of thought, founded in appearances, usurps the place of these representatives of supernatural truth, and a full development of the consciousness from a natural point of view ensues; in which these supernatural representations are repudiated and destroyed by the establishment of Unitarianism, and Natural Good, instead of representations of supernatural truth, is adopted as the governing principle of the individual life: and, finally, these external natural experiences are succeeded by an inverted supernaturalism, through which Spiritual Falsehood, instead of Spiritual Truth, is represented, and the consciousness becomes developed from what is termed a transcendental point of view; completing the natural experiences of the soul, and preparing it for a birth into the spiritual. It is only after all these experiences have been realized, and the individual has been brought into a spiritual sphere of consciousness, that Spiritual Truth can really be communicated to him; and it becomes realized by him through the intuition of the Universal Laws of Being, and their application in the construction of Philosophy as Absolute Science, in which Theology constitutes the mediating principle as the Science of Christianity,—when all natural, supernatural, and spiritual things will be comprehended and explained by being included in this universal form: for although these conceptions of universal law could not be realized in the consciousness without the intervention of a suggestive principle in spiritual phenomena communicated through the sentimental principles, in the conception of which the supernatural representative forms furnished by the Scriptures and by the Church furnish suggestive material, being realized, all the spiritual phenomena of which the Scriptures and the Church are only the discordant natural representatives must be at once conceived as the consecutive production of Spiritual Law, and the representative character of all natural things must be revealed.

It will be seen, that, according to this statement,—the truth of which will be demonstrated in this work,—the Bible, instead of being interpreted from a spiritual point of view, or from the point of Absolute Science, has, up to the present time, been interpreted from a supernatural point of view, or through the means of religious sentimentalism, so far as it has been interpreted in a legitimate manner; and, therefore, that the truths there contained, instead of being realized as harmonious and comprehensible, have been realized in discordant natural representative forms that must necessarily contradict the supernatural ideas which they represent: so that nothing can be further from the truth than this supposition, that spiritual truth is not conceived by the individual, but is communicated by the Bible as interpreted by the Church. The statement here made is confirmed by the fact, that the beliefs of the Church, instead of being comprehensible, rational, and philosophical, and founded in universal spiritual laws, have been confined to a discordant representation of supernatural phenomena; and that these correspond with natural thought and individual natural experiences of the most external description, are addressed to the selfish motives of hope and of fear, and are realized in the greatest diversity and discord. If no other recognition and realization of Christianity than these of the Church were possible, its promulgation would be nothing but a mockery; because, as spiritual truth could really never be recognized, received, or submitted to, by the Soul, in a spiritual "baptism of the Holy Ghost and of Fire," this religious substitute — the only object of which is to prepare the Soul for these spiritual experiences, and which is simply the natural, preparatory baptism of Water — would have to be regarded as a cruel and unnecessary infliction. As the Church has failed to give to Theology that rationality, permanency, and universality which must characterize every form of Spiritual Truth, we are compelled to look for a revelation of this truth, not from the Church, but through Individual Inspiration, or through the conception and application of Universal Spiritual Laws; by which Truth will be realized as Absolute Science, in which Theology constitutes the mediating principle by which spiritual laws are connected with the individual experiences. To doubt the possibility of such a realization would be to doubt the promises and the goodness of God, as well as the highest intuitions of the Reason; because such a revelation is promised in the Scriptures, and has always been demanded by the rational powers of the mind: and, in giving an account of the development of the human consciousness, — the measure of which is to be found in the history of Philosophy, —

we shall show that this is precisely the time when we ought to expect it.

We have next to consider the third position of the Church: that, as the truths of the Bible are spiritual while the human understanding is natural, no scientific conception of Spiritual Truth is possible, but only a sentimental apprehension in the form of religious faith, which is a contradiction to the natural understanding and the natural consciousness. Now, we admit, that, so far as the natural understanding becomes the interpreter of the Scriptures, this interpretation must be destructive to all supernatural representation; because we find, that as the religious sentiment, upon which the mind is dependent for the recognition of religious truth, becomes inactive, and the Bible consequently comes to be interpreted from intellectual and affectional points of view, the symbolism and the doctrines of the Church, which constitute this representation, are repudiated,—the first being regarded as "mummery," and the second as a detestable incubus of superstition, to be rid of which is a happy release. The giving of the Bible to the people by the Protestant Church has therefore ended in its extensive repudiation and perversion; for, although it was at first read in the light of a religious sentiment that is harmonious with the teaching of this Church, as the power of this sentiment declined, as it necessarily must in the development of the mind from within outwards, the Bible came to be interpreted by the natural instead of the supernatural powers of the mind, and its significance as a representative of the Spiritual was destroyed. But this destruction of supernatural forms by the natural understanding is necessary as a preparation for the production of spiritual forms by the divine-human principle; it being therefore that the Saviour said, "Destroy this Temple, and in three days I will raise it up." Though it is true that the natural understanding is destructive to supernatural truth, it is also true that the spiritual understanding is productive of spiritual truth (of which the supernatural is only the discordant and unreal representative), and constitutes the medium through which it becomes realized in the consciousness. This spiritual understanding is realized in a spiritual sphere of consciousness, where alone any spiritual knowledge is possible, through the union of the Understanding with the Reason, which constitutes the spiritual region of the mind. Through the Reason, we then obtain intuitions of the Universal Laws of Being in both Absolute and Phenomenal Spheres of Existence, and the relationship that exists between them; by which all natural, supernatural, and spiritual phenomena are explained, — a spiritual knowledge that is termed, in the Old Testament, "The Wisdom of God," and, in the New Testament, "The Spirit of Truth." For it will be demonstrated in this Philosophy, as the most exact and scientific truth, that Man is created with a capacity for realizing this knowledge that he may become united to God in a spiritual consciousness, and become a medium through which he can manifest His Divine Perfections through a phenomenal sphere of existence. This will be sustained by describing the principles in the Human Constitution through which, in a spiritual sphere of consciousness, this knowledge is communicated, and these perfections become manifested, — through which the individual becomes intuitive, or receptive from within, and conceptive, of Universal Spiritual Causes, — of the nature and form of God as Absolute Creator, — of the nature and form of Creation, with Man as its head, — of the nature and form of Christ, the God-Man, as the Mediator, — and of the natural and spiritual relationships which exist between them; and also through which Man becomes a medium for the manifestation of the Will of God.

This is the fulfilment of a prophecy of the Scriptures, which is contained in the command given to Man upon Mount Sinai, and also by Christ, that he should love God with all his Heart, with all his Soul, and with all his Mind. This command carries with it a perfect assurance that this knowledge of the Absolute will be realized by the soul. For, if Man was not endowed with a capacity for knowing God, — which must, of course, include a capacity for the realization of Spiritual Knowledge, through the intuition and definite conception of Universal Spiritual Laws, — he could not possibly know any thing of God, and, consequently, could not love Him, — the realization of Christianity, which must be based upon the Spiritual Love of God, would be impossible to man, — and his love would have to be confined to natural images which correspond with natural selfish want, and exist in diversity and discord; a state of idolatry, or division of worship between a multiplicity of different gods, being a necessity of natural experience. This is plainly taught in the Scriptures; and is as distinctly illustrated in what are called Christian as it is in what are really Pagan communities, though the latter are the legitimate representatives of this fact. The facts which have here been stated are specifically represented in the Scriptures. We say that man has been endowed with Reason, through which, in a spiritual sphere of consciousness, he obtains intuitions of the Universal Laws of Being, and that, through the union of the Understanding with these laws, he will construct a Universal Spiritual Science; and this fact is thus represented in the Scriptures: "He gave them counsel, and a tongue, and eyes, and ears, and a heart to devise; and he filled them with the knowledge of understanding. He created in them the Science of the Spirit, he filled their heart with wisdom, and showed them both Good and Evil." We say that the Spiritual Science which man is to realize through the intuition of the Universal Laws of Being includes a conception of the manner in which both Absolute and Phenomenal Existence become realized through the union of opposite indefinite, universal laws, and in which the form of God and the modes of His existence and manifestation are represented in all the forms of Creation; and this fact is thus represented in the Scriptures: "For the invisible things of Him from the creation of the world are clearly seen, being understood by the things that are made; even his eternal Power and Godhead." He who asserts that the invisible things of God, or "His eternal Power and Godhead," cannot be clearly seen, or that a Universal Spiritual Science by which all things are explained cannot be realized, denies the most express declarations of the Scriptures, as well as the most constant demand of the Reason.

And, now, what reasons have we for supposing that this Universal Spiritual Science, which we term "Philosophy as Absolute Science," has here been realized? What can we say that will give to the reader any assurance that the promise here made will be redeemed in the following pages, and that his labor will not be wasted, or his time unprofitably employed, in making the investigation for himself? We can safely say, that, if this promise has been redeemed, any amount of labor and time will be well bestowed, because Absolute Truth is the "one pearl of great price," which, when a man finds, he will sell all that he hath to purchase; but we can also confidently say that it has been realized, and will give our reasons for this assertion. The most prominent reason that we have for claiming that Philosophy as Absolute Science has here been realized is, that Ontology, Theology, and Psychology — the three great departments of thought which include the sum of Truth, and which have heretofore been separated and antagonized, while each one of these has been realized in the greatest diversity and discord — are here realized in universal forms which are perfectly harmonious, mutually dependent, and inseparably one as Spirit, Soul, and Body; all being founded in, and governed by, the same laws, which are thus proved to be universal spiritual laws; so that these three departments of thought, which have heretofore been only partially and discordantly *represented*, are here fully and harmoniously *realized*, and constitute universal, indestructible systems: and, in saying this, we fully mean what we say. The Ontological System is an entire and complete system, in which are stated the Laws of Absolute Being, and their operation in realizing God as Tri-personal Creating Cause, — the Laws of Phenomenal Being, and the nature of the phenomenal substances which furnish material for Creation, by which the nature of this Creation and its relation to Absolute and to Phenomenal Causes are explained, — and also the manner in which these Causes are represented in Creation, and the laws which govern the structure, growth, development, and manifestations of the Human Constitution. The Theological System is an entire and complete system, in which, in addition to the conception of God as Absolute Being, and Man as Phenomenal Being, already realized, the Soul as a Natural Creation is described from a strictly Theological point of view; in which description all its natural manifestations are separated from, and antagonized to, the Spiritual, — the necessity is shown for the Incarnation of God in this Atmosphere, as the consequence of Creation and as the condition of Salvation to Man through the realization of Spiritual Life, and the nature of Christ as Divine-Human Being is described, — and, finally, a full conception of the Soul as a Spiritual Creation is realized, including the phenomena which accompany its Spiritual Birth, and the consequences which necessarily follow in the phenomena of Salvation upon the one hand, and of Reprobation upon the other; by which all the symbolism of the Bible and of the Church, representative of these, is explained, and a Spiritual Form of Christianity is realized. The Psychological System is an entire and complete system, in which all the primitive elements of the Human Constitution are enumerated, classified, analyzed, and illustrated, and the sources and character of every possible mental manifestation that can be referred to man are shown. Believing what we have here stated, we cannot but affirm that our claim has been abundantly sustained; because nothing but a Universal Spiritual Science could produce such results, — although every one must decide for himself whether he is willing or not to allow this claim.

With regard to the usefulness of such a science, and to the

probability of its recognition and acceptance, it is not, of course, possible that a system of Absolute Truth should be generally accepted, because the number of those who have been endowed with the requisite perceptive power is limited, and because it is contrary to the natural conceptions of the mind, to the facts of the natural consciousness, and to the inclinations of the natural heart. But, although it cannot be generally adopted, there is every reason to suppose that it will be generally useful; because it must furnish an indestructible scientific form, that will, from its strict rationality, and applicability to use in explaining the phenomena of life and of the consciousness, exert a powerful influence in modifying the partial natural views of those who cannot comprehend or accept it as a whole; so that the cause of truth and of good will be advanced, even when the truth itself is not recognized: and because it will furnish support to all those impressions, aspirations, and apprehensive recognitions of the mind which constitute the ideal and supernatural side of human nature, and which, however much they may be buried up and overpowered by external and natural things, are realized to some extent by every mind, and are those which most need to be nourished, encouraged, and supported. We all live, at the same time, in two worlds which are perfectly opposite in character; that is, in an ideal and in a practical world, — one a world of realities, and the other a world of illusive appearances: and, although the practical may command our most constant attention and belief, the ideal and real must always exercise more or less influence over us in modifying and correcting these impressions of the world of sense by which we are surrounded, and in which we labor. The Ideal must always be an important element in the consciousness, and must even constitute the life of all other things; and the more completely it is elevated from out of the region of poetic impression into that of rational conviction, the higher must be the effect produced upon our minds, our hearts, and our lives. To those who have been prepared for the reception of Absolute Truth, its importance is incalculable; because to them it ushers in the end of the world, and the day of judgment, — when opposite Absolute Laws are presented to their consciousness, and they are called upon to choose Light instead of Darkness, that they may not perish everlastingly. With many, this preparation has been completed through the experiences of Transcendentalism. Already we hear the cry, "Watchman, what of the night? Watchman, what of the night? And the Watchman replieth,

The morning cometh, and also the night: if ye will inquire, inquire ye: return, come." The morn of an everlasting day, of which God Himself is the light, will dawn upon those who choose Life; while, upon those who choose Death, an eternal night will close in, separating them for ever from God as outcasts from His Kingdom: for of these elect it is written, "See, I have set before thee this day Life and Good, and Death and Evil:" "choose life, that both thou and thy seed may live."

SYSTEM OF ONTOLOGICAL SCIENCE;

IN WHICH ARE STATED

THE

LAWS OF ABSOLUTE BEING,

AND THE FORM AND NATURE OF

The Tri-Personal God as Absolute Creating Cause.

THE

LAWS OF PHENOMENAL BEING,

AND THE FORM AND NATURE OF

The Creation as a Phenomenal Receptive Medium.

THE

LAW OF TRI-PERSONALITY,

AND ITS APPLICATION IN ANALYZING

The Structure, Nature, and Manifestation of the Universe.

CONTENTS OF VOLUME I.

PRELIMINARY STATEMENT.

	PAGE.
The nature of Philosophy considered	1
Why it must be founded in the Universal Laws of Being	2
Its failure for the want of this foundation	2
Why Philosophy must take its departure from the Church	3
Correspondence between Philosophy and Religion	3
How the antagonism between them arises	8
Why the development of Philosophy is confined to the Caucasian race	4
Why the Indian and Ethiopian races are excluded	5
Why the Malay and Mongolian races are excluded	6
Description of the Hindoo Nation as the highest of the Malay race	7
Statement of the ground upon which three spheres of philosophical development, related as Ontological, Psychological, and Eclectical, are demanded	11
This demand responded to, according to the history of Philosophy, as follows :	

THE ONTOLOGICAL SPHERE.

Departure of Philosophy from Religion in Egypt	14
Development of Philosophy in Egypt as Material Ontology	15
Character of the Egyptians considered	16
Departure of Philosophy from Religion in Persia	17
Development of Philosophy in Persia as Spiritual Ontology	18
Character of the Persians considered	18
Eclectical development of Philosophy by the Hebrews in the form of Religious Symbolism	19

THE PSYCHOLOGICAL SPHERE.

Departure of Philosophy from Religion in Greece	21
Development of Philosophy as Material Ontology by the Ionians in the physiological systems of Thales, Anaximander, and Anaxagoras	22
Development of Philosophy as Spiritual Ontology by the Ionians in the dynamical systems of Anaximenes, Diogenes of Appolonia, and Heraclitus	24
Why both internal and external schools are demanded in this sphere	28

xxvi   CONTENTS.

	PAGE
Description of the Italic School founded by Pythagoras as a more internal form of Material Ontology	29
Description of the Eleatic School founded by Xenophanes as a more internal form of Spiritual Ontology	30
Development of this Philosophy by Parmanides and Zeno	31
Description of the difference between the Ontological and Psychological forms of Philosophy	31
Preparation by the Sophists for a psychological development of Philosophy	32
The character of the Sophists considered	32
Establishment by Socrates of the Psychological Method	33
The nature of Psychology considered, showing why it must be realized in Intellectual and Moral forms, each being antagonized as Internal and External	34
Development of Moral Philosophy in its Internal form by Antisthenes	35
Development of Moral Philosophy in its external form by Aristippus	36
The antagonism between these forms described	37
Development of Intellectual Philosophy in its Internal form by Plato, and in its external form by Aristotle	38
The antagonism between these forms described	39
The destruction of these schools by Stoicism and Epicureanism	41
The philosophy of Epicurus and of the Stoics considered	42
The Eclectical development of Philosophy in Gnosticism and in the school of Alexandria	44

THE ECLECTICAL SPHERE.

Departure of Philosophy from Religion in Christian Europe	46
The Scholastics, or the Religious School of Philosophy, described	46
Its dependence upon the Pagan systems explained	46
Development of Material Ontology in Nominalism and Realism	48
Improvement in the philosophical position of the human mind described	48
Development of Spiritual Ontology by the Mystics as Religious Philosophy	49
Preparation for a psychological development of Philosophy in the Sixteenth Century	50
Establishment by Lord Bacon of the modern Psychological Method	51
Development of Moral Philosophy in its Internal form by Hobbes, and in its external form by Gassendi	51
The antagonism between these forms described	51
Development of Intellectual Philosophy in its Internal form by Descartes, and in its external form by Locke	53
The theories of Spinoza and Malebranche, the disciples of Descartes	56
Preparation by the Sceptics for the introduction of Eclecticism	58
Development of Eclecticism in its Mystical form	58
Establishment of Eclectical Philosophy in its Intellectual form by Leibnitz	59
The system of Eclectical Philosophy by Emanuel Kant described	62
,, ,, ,, ,, ,, by Reinhold ,,	64
,, ,, ,, ,, ,, by Fichte ,,	64
,, ,, ,, ,, ,, by Schelling ,,	65
,, ,, ,, ,, ,, by Hegel ,,	66
,, ,, ,, ,, ,, by Cousin ,,	69

	PAGE
Completion of the philosophical development	73
Why Philosophy has not been realized as legitimate Science	73
The destruction of Philosophy by the establishment of Materialism, under the name of "Positive Philosophy," by Auguste Comte	73
Why a new ground for Philosophy is now demanded	74

THE UNIVERSAL LAWS OF BEING.

Posit of the Infinite — Life Itself — The Infinite Sphere in God — as a Universal Spiritual Cause	81
Why the subsistence of an Opposite to the Infinite is necessitated	82
Posit of the Finite — Death Itself — The Spirit of Evil — as a Universal Spiritual Cause	84
Necessity for opposite Universal Spiritual Causes as the Condition of Existence	84
The union of Infinite and Finite in One Consciousness the Condition of Definite Being	85
Conception of the realization of Definite Absolute Individuality	86
Why this must first be realized in a Natural Condition	87
Definition of a Natural Condition	87
The realization of Spiritual Consciousness in an Absolute Sphere	88
Conception of the formation of the Divine Sphere in God	89
Christianity a representation of these Absolute Phenomena	90
Necessity for a Third Person in God	90
Conception of the formation of the Spiritual Sphere in God	91
Statement of Tri-Personality in God	92
The relationship between Holy Ghost, Father, and Son	92
Illustration of this relationship in the Spheres of the Universe, of the Mind, and of Universal Law	94

THE LAWS OF PHENOMENAL BEING,

AND THE NATURE OF PHENOMENAL SUBSTANCE WHICH FURNISHES TO GOD THE MATERIAL FOR CREATION.

The manner in which these Phenomenal Laws come into the consciousness of God as Material for Creation	97
The nature of Infinite and Finite Phenomenal Substances	98
The manner in which these are combined in Creation	99
The nature of Creation, and its relation to Absolute Causes	100
The nature of the Soul as Created Existence	100
The nature of Human Substance as the Sphere of Phenomenal Life	102
The necessity for recognizing a Phenomenal Sphere of Subsistence	103
Comparison of this statement with the theories of Philosophy	104
The nature of Matter considered and explained	105
Statement of the Laws of Unity, Duality, and Trinity, which constitute the Law of Tri-Personality, and which we posit as the external ground of Absolute Science	107

THE LAW OF UNITY.

	PAGE
The destructive character of its natural representatives considered	109
How these are destructive in Ontological Philosophy	110
„ „ „ „ „ Psychological Philosophy	114
„ „ „ „ „ Eclectical Philosophy	115
„ „ „ „ „ Unitarianism and Transcendentalism	116
Division of Unitarianism into Pantheism and Naturalism	116
„ „ Pantheism into Spiritualism and Materialism	116
„ „ Naturalism into Transcendentalism and Moralism	116
Comparison of Transcendentalism and Unitarianism	116
The destructive character of these forms of Naturalism	116
The natural law of Unity as it operates in the Church	120
The antagonism between Philosophy and the Church accounted for	121

THE LAW OF DUALITY.

How this is represented in Philosophy	124
Dualistic theories of the Egyptians, Ionians, Pythagoreans, and Persians	124
The dualistic theory of Plato	125
The theories of Zoroaster and of Plato compared	126
The theories of the Marcionites and Manicheans described	127
The celebrated theory of Plutarch examined	129
The theory of the Hebrews as embodied in their Scriptures	131
„ „ „ Christian Church	132
„ „ „ Modern Eclectical Philosophers	132

THE LAW OF TRINITY.

How this is represented in Philosophy, Society, and the Church	134
Triune theories of the Egyptians, Persians, and Hindoos	136
The theory of Plato, and other similar theories, described	137
„ „ „ St. Augustine, and other psychological conceptions, described	139
„ „ „ the German Eclectics described	140
„ „ „ Böhme and Swedenborg described	141
„ „ „ the Christian Church examined, and its origin shown	142

THE LAWS OF CORRESPONDENCE, OR OF REPRESENTATION.

Conception of these through the application of the Law of Tri-Personality	151
Importance of Analogy as a Philosophical Form	152
Definition of Correspondence, and division into three spheres	153
Correspondences of the Fancy, which are destructive	154
„ „ Imagination, which are representative	155
„ „ Reason, which are vital and productive	157
Obstacles which the mind will encounter in the reception of the Spiritual Science of Correspondence	157

CONTENTS.   xxix

	PAGE
Those which arise in the natural consciousness and previous experience	158
" " " in the fact of Opposition in Creation	159
" " " in the unreal character of the Natural	159
" " " in its development under the law of Contrariety	160
The Law of Tri-Personality, the Universal Law of Correspondence which includes the laws of Opposition, Attraction, and Marriage	162
THE LAW OF OPPOSITION, — the ground of this law	163
Illustration of this law by the principles of Truth and Good	164
The ground of our conception of Truth and Good	164
The relationship between Truth and Good described	164
How this is represented in the Human Constitution	164
How this is represented in all Individual Manifestations	166
The separation of Truth from Good in the consciousness of Man	166
THE LAW OF ATTRACTION, — the ground of this law	170
The different kinds of attraction which are to be recognized	171
THE LAW OF MARRIAGE, — the ground of this law	172
Spiritual Marriage in Absolute and Divine-Human Spheres of Being	173
Necessity for the representation of Marriage in the Natural, as the condition of life	173
Religious Faith, its highest representative	174
Representation of Marriage in the structure and manifestations of the Human Constitution	175
The Supernatural manifestations of the Human Constitution considered	176
The Institution of Matrimony as a representative of Marriage	180
The subjection of the Female to the Male principles necessary to all natural production	181
Representation of this fact by the Hebrews	182
The manner in which the Law of Tri-Personality, as the Universal Law of Correspondence, is to be applied in classifying and analyzing the forms, relationships, and manifestations of Creation	183

THE GENERAL FORMS OF THE UNIVERSE
WHICH ILLUSTRATE THE LAWS OF CORRESPONDENCE.

Construction of the Universe in Spiritual, Ethereal, and Material Spheres	184
Conception of the principles of the Material Universe	185
How the Material Sphere illustrates the Laws of Correspondence	186
How the Ethereal Sphere illustrates the Laws of Correspondence	187
How this statement agrees with the theories of Philosophy	188

THE GENERAL FORMS OF THE HUMAN RACE
WHICH ILLUSTRATE THE LAWS OF CORRESPONDENCE.

How divided into three spheres related as soul, body, and spirit	191
The Indian and Ethiopian races contrasted as representing internal and external principles in the most external sphere	192
Description of the Ethiopian race as the representative of Affectionalism	196

CONTENTS.

	PAGE.
Description of the Caucasian race as universally representative	201
Comparison of the French and English Nations as the representatives of Democracy and Aristocracy	202

THE STRUCTURE OF THE HUMAN CONSTITUTION

WHICH ILLUSTRATES THE LAWS OF CORRESPONDENCE.

Division of the Human Constitution into general and personal spheres	206
General description of the Mind, or sphere of General Consciousness	207
FORM OF THE GENERAL CONSCIOUSNESS, CONSTITUTING THE HUMAN MIND	208
"Perfection" and "Imperfection," which constitute the roots of the Mind	209
The "Reason," as the Spiritual region of the Mind	209
The Supernatural Region of the Mind, which is constituted by the Religious and Moral Sentiments	209
The manner in which these illustrate the Laws of Correspondence	211
The Natural region of the Mind, which is constituted by the Understanding and the Instinct	212
The manner in which these illustrate the Laws of Correspondence	212
Description of the nature of the Human Understanding	213
Its division into Perceptive, Receptive, and Reflective Faculties	214
Enumeration and classification of the principles of the Understanding	218
The manner in which these illustrate the Laws of Correspondence	219
Description of the nature of the Human Instinct	220
Enumeration and classification of the instinctive or affectional principles	221
The manner in which these illustrate the Laws of Correspondence	221
Necessity shown for a sphere of Personal Consciousness as the condition and ground of Individual manifestation	224
The character of this form of Consciousness	226
FORM OF THE PERSONAL CONSCIOUSNESS, CONSTITUTING THE HUMAN SOUL	228
Illustration of this by the forms of the Mind	229
Description of the Personifying Principles, which constitute the most concentrated form of the Individual	230
The manner in which these have been recognized in other systems	230
Description of the Will, as a tri-personal form of spirit, soul, and body	232
The character of "Direction," the Body of the Will	233
The character of "Relation," the Soul of the Will	234
The character of "Consciousness," the Spirit of the Will	236
The relationship between these spheres of the Will	237
The manner in which the Will has been regarded in other systems	237
Statement of the relationship between the general divisions of the Human Constitution	239

FORM OF THE HUMAN CONSTITUTION,

INCLUDING ALL THE PRINCIPLES OF HUMAN NATURE.

	PAGE
How far these have been recognized	244
Difference between spheres of the Mind, spheres of the Will, and spheres of Consciousness	245

THE STRUCTURE OF SOCIETY

WHICH ILLUSTRATES THE LAWS OF CORRESPONDENCE.

The elements which constitute Society described and classified	249
Democracy and Aristocracy, as internal and external, constitute the State, as the external sphere of Society	252
The imperfect conceptions entertained with regard to these principles	252
The sources of Democracy and Aristocracy	254
Description of Aristocracy, and the aristocratic Class	257
Description of Democracy, and the democratic Class	264
Why these must be combined in legitimate social production	268
The manner in which the Laws of Correspondence are illustrated in Society	269

THE LAWS OF SUCCESSION, OR NATURAL GROWTH AND DEVELOPMENT.

Statement of the Ontological ground for these laws, which we name "Contrariety" and "Circularity"	273
THE LAW OF CONTRARIETY,—its necessity, nature, and ground	276
Illustration of this law in the State	279
" " " " Philosophy	281
" " " " the Church	282
" " " " Catholicism	286
" " " " Protestantism	287
" " " " Unitarianism	290
" " " " Transcendentalism	291
THE LAW OF CIRCULARITY	293
How this law is represented in Philosophy and in the Scriptures	293
How this law is regarded by the Moderns	294
Necessity for this law in the nature of Creation	295
How this law is illustrated by Geological formations	299

THE MANIFESTATIONS OF THE SENTIMENTAL NATURE

WHICH ILLUSTRATE THE LAW OF CIRCULARITY.

Illustrations of this law in Catholicism	301
" " " " Protestantism	308
" " " " Unitarianism	309
" " " " Transcendentalism	311

THE HISTORY OF THE STATE

WHICH ILLUSTRATES THE LAW OF CIRCULARITY.

	PAGE
The opposite elements which constitute the State, described	814
Theories of Philosophy upon the subject of social development	817
How these agree with the statement here made	818
Statement of the Causes which produce the development of Society	819
Why a just government of the people by the people is impossible	822
The manner in which the State is destroyed	824

THE HISTORY OF ART

WHICH ILLUSTRATES THE LAW OF CIRCULARITY.

The opposition between Ancient and Modern Art described	828
The degradation, the elevation, and the use, of Modern Art	829
The representative and ideal character of Ancient Art	329
The causes which produced its destruction	831
The inverted Idealism of Modern Art	831
The causes by which this inversion is produced	832
The character of true Art as a representative of Spiritual Beauty	833
The character of false Art as a representative of Spiritual Deformity	834
The ground and the sources of these in the Mind	834
Construction of the Body of Art by the Fancy	834
Construction of the Soul of Art by the Imagination	835
Relation of these as Natural and Supernatural	836
Explanation of Idealism in Art	839
Illustrated by the representative forms of Architecture	339
Description of the degradation that has taken place in Art	842
The degradation in Architecture described	842
,, ,, in Sculpture described	843
,, ,, in Philosophy described	845
,, ,, in Music and Painting described	848
Definition of the True Picturesque in Art	850
Definition of the False Picturesque in Art	852
Degradation in the Unitarian School of Modern Art	852
Degradation in the Transcendental School of Modern Art	853
Illustrations from the writings of John Ruskin	853
His repudiation of Idealism and defence of Naturalism in Art	854
Illustration of this in his definition of Art	855
Inversion of Idealism in his definition of " Vital Beauty "	856
Illustration of this inversion in his statement of Idealism as " Purist, Naturalist, and Grotesque "	857
Illustration in his statement of " Purist Idealism "	858
,, in his statement of " Naturalist Idealism "	858
,, in his description of " Vital Beauty "	859
,, in his comparison of Turner and Georgione	861
,, in his comparison of Shakspeare and Dante	862
Ground of this inversion in the destructive sentimental laws	863

CONTENTS.   xxxiii

                                                                   PAGE.
Illustration of this inversion in Ruskin's description of "Ideal Beauty"   . 363
    "   "   "   in his repudiation of Christian Art   365
    "   "   "   in his statement of "Grotesque Idealism" .   366
    "   "   "   in his defence of the Comic as a true Ideal in
                                Art   366
General result of the development of the Mind from within outwards   .   . 367

TRANSCENDENTALISM
WHICH ILLUSTRATES THE LAW OF CIRCULARITY.

Why Transcendentalism is not adapted to this atmosphere   371
Its anti-practical character explained   372
Illustration of this from the writings of Emerson   372
His definition of Transcendentalism examined   374
In what Transcendentalism really consists   374
Why it cannot be known from an external point of view   375
How it comes to be combined with the grossest externalism   376
The point of departure and ground of Transcendentalism   377
The laws which govern it, and how they become realized   380
Manifestation of these in producing the supremacy of Feeling   381
The consequences which result from this supremacy   382
Manifestations of Transcendental laws in the inversion of Rationality   . 383
Illustration of this inversion from the writings of Henry James   383
The falsity of Externalism detected by the Transcendentalists   384
Why Transcendentalism is still more false   385
The uses of Transcendentalism described   385
Ground for its claim to be the true Christianity examined   386
The transcendental manifestations of the Reason   387
Consequent assertion of Personal Want as Good   388
Consequent worship of Natural Perfection   389
The transcendental manifestations of the Religious Sentiments   390
The transcendental manifestations of the Moral Sentiments   393
Illustrations from the writings of Emerson   395
The transcendental manifestations of the Intellectual Faculties   396
The transcendental manifestations of the Affectional Powers   398
Origin of its demand for Communism explained   398
     "   of its perverted manifestations of Friendship   400
     "   of its perverted Domestic manifestations   401
     "   of its perverted Individual manifestations   403
The transcendental manifestations of the Personifying Principles   .   .   . 404
The vital individual condition of Transcendentalism described   405
The destructive personal manifestations of Transcendentalism described   . 405
The transcendental manifestations of the Will   406
The necessity for a realization of simple Individualism   410
The combination of vital and destructive forces in Transcendentalism   .   . 412
Its uses as a preparation for the Spiritual Birth   414
Individual experiences of the Transcendentalist described   414

APPENDIX.

INTERPRETATIONS OF THE SYMBOLISM OF THE BIBLE AND OF HEATHEN MYTHOLOGY.

	PAGE
Illustration of the opposition between spiritual and natural spheres from the Grecian Mythology	419
Illustration of the relation between Truth and Good from the Mosaic account of the creation of the female from the male	420
Illustration of this relation in the myth of the Garden of Hesperus	421
Illustration of the principles of the Human Constitution from an account of the creation of man in "Ecclesiasticus"	421
Illustration of the development of the Sentimental Nature —	
By the parable of "the Lost Sheep"	425
By the parable of "the Prodigal Son"	429
By the history of "Job"	436
By the myth of "Cupid and Psyche"	449
Illustration of the Spiritual Birth of the Soul by "the Conversion of Saul."	452

PRELIMINARY STATEMENT.

IN WHICH

THE NATURAL DEVELOPMENT OF PHILOSOPHY

IS TRACED

FROM ITS COMMENCEMENT TO THE PRESENT TIME;

SHOWING

THE LAWS WHICH GOVERN IT,

AND

THE CAUSES OF ITS DESTRUCTION.

HISTORY OF PHILOSOPHY.

BEFORE making a statement of the Laws upon which we purpose to construct our system of Philosophy, we will consider the nature of Philosophy, and briefly examine the causes and the character of its development; and we shall do this for the purpose of showing how it is that all attempts have heretofore failed to realize Philosophy in the form of Absolute Science, which is its spiritual form. The necessity for such a realization in order that Philosophy should exist, or that any thing should be understood or truly known, has always been most distinctly recognized; and it has been acknowledged that what we call Philosophy is simply the result of the strivings of the human mind after the truth, and is not the Truth Itself, which has never been conceived, but only its natural substitute. No single department of knowledge can be dignified with the name of Philosophy, even in a popular sense, except as it furnishes material in the construction of the Universal Science which must constitute it, and which must be realized through the union of the Reason and Understanding in a spiritual consciousness; a union of opposites that can be realized only by the discovery and application of the universal laws which underlie both spiritual and natural existence, or which govern the Spiritual and are represented in the Natural, and by the application of which all natural phenomena can therefore be explained. And, because these universal laws have never been conceived and applied as philosophical formulas, all the various systems of philosophy have been characterized by partiality, diversity, and discord, while they have entirely failed to explain the phenomena of existence and the facts of the Consciousness, or to account for, define, and reconcile the opposite things which are there found to be combined. These natural substitutes for philosophy have thus been without vitality, because the natural mind is necessarily governed by the law of diversity, which includes discord; because the phenomena which are recognized by it are false and deceptive, being the opposite of what they seem; and because the laws which are conceived and applied in the construction of these substitutes for philosophy are simply generalizations of these phenomena, and must therefore partake of the same partial, discordant, and deceptive character. Philosophy can be realized only by the conception and application of Absolute Truth, which is nothing less than a revelation of God Himself in the Consciousness; and the necessity for this may be seen from the fact, that all things are created to represent the Universal Laws of Being, and their operation in the realization of God as a Tri-Personality. It is therefore that "the invisible things of Him from the foundation of the world are clearly seen, being understood by the things which are made, even his eternal Power and Godhead." We may, therefore, see that the realization of Truth, or of Philosophy, is possible to man only because he includes a capacity for becoming conscious of Universal Spiritual Causes as well as of the laws and phenomena of the universe; and of the form of God as well as of the form of Nature; it being only upon this condition that Philosophy can be realized in its legitimate form as Absolute Science, including ontological, theological, and psychological Truth in one harmonious form as spirit, soul, and body, realized by the conception and application of the universal laws of Being. To show that these laws could not before have been conceived, we will briefly consider the history of Philosophy from its commencement to the present time, show the laws which have governed it, and the causes which have led to its destruction.

There is one prominent and important fact that presents itself at the commencement of this investigation; which is, that Philosophy has, in each sphere of its development, taken its departure from Religion; being at its commencement simply a defence from the point of the Understanding of the religious conceptions of the Church: and this is an important fact, because it shows that the ground of both must be the same, and that the legitimate demand of both is the realization of Absolute Truth. This will account for the pertinacity and consistency with which Philosophy has always sought for a rational ground for thought, instead of the sentimental and irrational one that has been occupied by the Church, notwithstanding that in its development it has been brought into a natural region of thought, which is antagonized to spiritual and real knowledge. We can understand why this intimate relation should originally exist between Philosophy and the Church, because we can see that the foundation of both is constituted by ideas derived from the Reason, which are natural forms of universal laws from which conceptions of the nature of God, of man, and of the relationship that exists between them, are derived; the principal difference between them being, that in the first these are contemplated from a universal, and in the second from a personal, point of view. We can also understand how it is that they become divided and antagonized, and that they invariably become hostile to each other, as soon as Philosophy throws off its subjection to the Church, and assumes an independent attitude. Philosophy takes its departure from the Church, because, as the mind is developed from within outwards, in the incarnation of these ideas a sentimental and religious form, that is addressed to feeling rather than to thought, must precede the intellectual and philosophic form in the order of realization, because it is relatively internal; but when Philosophy leaves this internal ground and descends into the intellectual region, or when the intellectual instead of the sentimental becomes the ruling power, she necessarily becomes antagonized to the Church, because this intellectualism belongs to the natural region of the mind, while the religion of the Church belongs to the supernatural region, and these are opposite and antagonistic. Although these sentimental developments of Philosophy are the most internal and vital, they have usually been excluded from the pale of philosophic thought. Some historians of Philosophy, among whom Ritter is conspicuous, have for this reason ruled out the philosophemes of Arabia, Judæa, Persia, and Egypt, as not coming within the limits of philosophical investigation; while they have recognized as philosophical the writings of the Hindoos, because this nation constitutes among the races the representative of the intellectual principle, and their writings are therefore characterized as intellectual; although, as the productions of an imperfect, unimprovable race, they cannot belong to a real development of philosophy, but must be regarded simply as poetical and representative. We will therefore first clear the ground of obstructions by showing what are and what are not the legitimate sources of philosophy, or by whom it has been developed.

If the reader refers to our illustration of the laws of Correspondence, he will find that the most general division of the human family, and the one that has been most generally recognized, is to be found in the Indian, Ethiopian, Malay, Mongolian, and Caucasian races, — that the Indian and Ethiopian races represent the intellectual and affectional principles, and constitute an external and destructive social sphere which is Savage, — that the Malay and Mongolian races represent the intellective and affective principles, and constitute an internal and representative social sphere which is Barbarous, — and that the Caucasian race represents the active and constructive principle, and constitutes a vital and real social sphere which is Universal and Supernatural; to which alone, therefore, the realization of Christianity and Philosophy is possible, and to which a progress that includes all the possibilities of human experience is to be attributed, the other races being partial, imperfect, stationary, and unimprovable; and these races are thus related because these five principles constitute, under the universal law of Existence, the form of every department of life. The reason why the Caucasian is the only race that can be instrumental in accomplishing the development of Philosophy, is the same that determines this race to be the only one capable of realizing Christianity; it being the only one which is capable of progress or of development, and of realizing Spiritual Life through Marriage, or the union of opposites through sacrifice, both of which are essential in the realization of Christianity and Philosophy, while the first is essential even to their natural representation. This makes the Caucasian the only philosophic race, because philosophy is developed as a consequence of the development of the human constitution, and is only a record of the changes through which the human consciousness has passed in the search after truth; for, in the development of Philosophy, it is not sufficient that truth should be partially and artificially represented, as we find it to be in the imperfect and stationary races, but particularly in the Malay as the representative of the intellectual principle: it is necessary that it should be lived, or really experienced in the consciousness by actual production from its sources in the mind, before it can be converted into material for Philosophy. It makes the Caucasian the only Christian race, because, as the only universal race, it is the only one capable of realizing a full development of the opposite sides of the human consciousness, as a preparation for the presentation to the individual of opposite spiritual laws between which a choice must be made, — a presentation and choice which are indispensable to the realization of Christianity: for until the individual has passed through every variety of natural experience in the process of his natural regeneration, constituting his birth by blood and by water, his birth into the spiritual cannot take place; and consequently he cannot experience Christianity, which is the marriage of the soul to God, through the spiritual act of Faith. If this natural development is really necessary to the realization of Christianity and of Philosophy, — and that it is so we shall clearly demonstrate in the course of this work, — it must be at once conceded, that the Caucasian race is the only race that is capable of their realization. Let us, however, consider what claims the imperfect races have to be included among those to whom the development of Philosophy has been intrusted, that we may add the evidence of facts to that of theory, by which all but the Caucasian race have been excluded.

A philosophic capacity will not probably be claimed either for the Indian or the Ethiopian race, even by the most inveterate abolitionist; for it is impossible to point to even the most insignificant contribution that has been made by either of them to Philosophy. With regard to the Chinese, which is the most important nation of the Mongolian race, even the cautious Ritter acknowledges that "they have never been able to realize any philosophical doctrine;" while Hegel represents them as being totally unconscious of any moral as well as of any philosophical principles, unable to distinguish between what is real and what is accidental, and entirely dependent upon instruction, or external direction, for the performance of all domestic as well as of all social duties; both of which, carried out into the most minute particulars and pervading the whole life of the individual, are perpetuated by record and by tradition through the legitimate mediums. With regard to the Hindoo nation, however, which is the highest of the Malay race, this philosophic incapacity has not so readily been acknowledged. Indeed, by some of the leading transcendentalists, the Hindoo writings have been considered as containing the highest and most spiritual of all philosophies. We will therefore state some of the leading facts with reference to the mental manifestations of this people, that we may show that this race has been correctly classified in our science, and consequently that it is a partial and imperfect race, representative of an internal-intellectual principle alone; is destitute of that rationality, derived from the Reason, which antagonizes those things which are opposite, while it demands their union by the subjection of the lower to the higher; is a representative of the principle of Naturalism, and is therefore governed by the law of diversity, by which opposites are confounded, and life becomes dissipated; and is destitute both of that self-consciousness which constitutes a philosophic capacity, and of that variety of individual experiences which constitutes the material for Philosophy.

That the Hindoos belong to a partial and imperfect race may be known, because they exist isolated from all other nations; because they are stationary, and unimprovable in their condition; and because they are divided into castes, — this being similar to the division of the North-American Indians into tribes, and including an antagonism so extreme, that nothing is recognized as belonging to them in common. Thus, with them, " every caste has its especial duties and rights. Duties and rights, therefore, are not recognized as pertaining to mankind generally, but as those of a particular caste. While we say bravery is a virtue, the Hindoo says bravery is the virtue of the Cshatryas." * That they represent an internal-intellectual sphere of thought may be known, because an internal contemplative state, combined with external fixedness or repose, constitutes, according to them, the highest position of the soul; and because an extreme asceticism prevails among them, destructive to the bodily wants and to the affectional tendencies, which, as external and affectional, are antagonistic to an internal and intellectual principle and state. That they represent the principle of Naturalism, and that the law of diversity governs all the manifestations of Hindoo thought, may be known, because we find in this thought a complete inversion of Spiritualism, and a confounding of opposite things, which brings it into a chaotic condition; and because the highest condition conceived by them is that of Annihilation. To such an extent is this naturalism carried, that they not only do not distinguish between the natural and the spiritual in the experiences of the human soul, but do not even distinguish between gods and men; indeed, between the supreme god and the meanest form of material existence: for Naturalism, while it always commences with the belief in one principle, and therefore with confounding together spiritual and natural things which are opposite, always ends in the greatest diversity and discord. We therefore find that both

---

* Hegel's Philosophy of History.

Monotheism and the extreme of Polytheism are to be attributed to the Hindoos; that the utmost diversity of opinion prevails among them as to which of the various deities worshipped by them is to be regarded as supreme; and that they entertain the belief, that any man may, by a series of external mortifications, elevate himself to be a god, and even to be the supreme ruler of gods; or, as Ritter says, "that a man, freeing himself by holiness of conduct from the obstacles of nature, may deliver his fellow-men from the corruption of the times, and become a benefactor of his race, and also supreme god, a Buddha."

One proof of the correctness of the position here assumed is the strong affinity that exists among the sect of Transcendentalists for forms of Hindoo thought, which they dignify with the name of philosophy; an affinity which arises in the fact, that, while Transcendentalism is the realization of the internal-natural experiences of the soul which are governed by Naturalism and Individualism, the Hindoo is the representative of Naturalism and of an internal-natural order of thought, and thus becomes a legitimate representative of transcendentalism intellectually considered. A great similarity may therefore be seen in the intellectual manifestations referable to them; and so powerfully are transcendentalists attracted towards the forms of Hindoo thought, that many seem to have become identified with them, and even to believe with them in the final absorption of all individuals into one original Cause. The transcendentalists, looking exclusively from an internal-natural point of view, suppose the internal-natural to be a vital spiritual condition, when it is in fact completely opposite to this; and they are the more readily led into this mistake with regard to the Hindoos, because of that asceticism and great show of internal contemplation for which they are so remarkable. We may see, however, that this appearance of internalism is not a real self-conscious condition, but only represents that internal contemplation in the consciousness which is realized in transcendentalism; and that this sacrifice of external things, while it represents, has no relation, except one of opposition, to that sacrifice of the individual which is demanded by Christianity, and is legitimately represented by self-conscious natural experiences in the Church. The Naturalism of the Hindoo may be seen in the facts, that the sacrifice of animal life, even in the meanest of its forms, is by them scrupulously avoided; that a great proportion of their writings is materialistic or atheistic, while all include the grossest kind of pantheism and fatalism; and that their asceticism is combined with the grossest sensuality, or gratification of animal appetite, plainly showing that it is simply representative, and not real.

As the Hindoos are the legitimate representatives of an internal-intellectual sphere, many forms of philosophy are represented by them, but particularly that inverted metaphysical form which is governed by the destructive laws of the Reason, and is realized in transcendentalism. A form of religious mysticism is also realized by them, which appears to represent the religious ideas of the Christian Church, including the great doctrine of justification by faith without works; and even to represent the Sabbath, which is founded upon the prohibition of works. But we are not to mistake these appearances for real self-conscious experiences, or even for legitimate representations. What appears in them to be a state of internal contemplation is a perfectly inactive state of the body and of the mind: and even their highest state of religious ecstasy is produced by artificial means; and directions are given in their religious books for its production, one of these being to hold the breath. Although representing an internal-natural condition and principle from an intellectual point of view, this representation is not a legitimate natural, but an illegitimate artificial one, which represents an inversion of rationality, and is realized through emotion, and not through thought; or through a perfectly passive instead of an active mental state, by which the individual is brought into an abnormal condition corresponding with somnambulism. This passive state of the subject is always the first step to the realization of a receptive somnambulic or entranced condition; and we therefore find that the Hindoos and also the Gypsy tribes, which belong to the same race, have always extensively practised the arts of somnambulism and necromancy.

The following extract from Hegel's "Philosophy of History," which came to the writer's notice after he had made the foregoing statement, although pervaded by the fanciful and pantheistic theories of this writer, completely confirms the view that has here been taken:—

"India, like China, is a phenomenon antique as well as modern; one which has remained stationary and fixed, and has received a most perfect home-sprung development. It has always been the land of imaginative aspiration, and appears to us still like a fairy region, an enchanted world. In contrast with the Chinese State, which presents only the most prosaic understanding, India is the region of phantasy and sensibility. The point of advance in principle which it exhibits to us may be generally stated as follows: In China, the patriarchal principle rules a people in the condition of nonage, the part of whose moral resolution is occupied by the regulating law, and the moral oversight of the Emperor. Now, it is the interest of Spirit, that external conditions should become internal ones; that the natural and the spiritual world should be recognized in the subjective aspect belonging to intelligence; by which process the unity of Subjectivity and positive Being generally, or the Idealism of Existence, is established. This Idealism, then, is found in India, but only as an idealism of imagination, without distinct conceptions, — one which does, indeed, free existence from Beginning and Matter (liberates it from temporal limitations and gross materiality), but changes every thing into the merely imaginative; for although the latter appears interwoven with definite conceptions, and thought presents itself as an occasional concomitant, this happens only through accidental combinations. Since, however, it is the abstract and absolute Thought itself that enters into these dreams as their material, we may say that Absolute Being is presented here as in the ecstatic state of a dreaming condition. For we have not the dreaming of an actual Individual, possessing distinct personality, and simply unfettering the latter from limitation; but we have the dreaming of the unlimited absolute spirit.

"There is a beauty of a peculiar kind in women during the magnetic somnambulic sleep, connecting them with a world of super-terrestrial beauty. A great artist (Schoreel) has given this tone to the dying Mary, whose spirit is already rising to the regions of the blessed, but once more, as it were, lights up her dying countenance for a farewell kiss. Such a beauty we find also in its loveliest form in the Indian world; a beauty of enervation, in which all that is rough, rigid, and contradictory, is dissolved, and we have only the soul in a state of emotion, — a soul, however, in which the death of free, self-reliant spirit is perceptible. For, should we approach the charm of this flower-life; should we look at it more closely, and examine it in the light of human dignity and freedom, — the more attractive the first sight of it had been, so much the more unworthy shall we ultimately find it in every respect.

"The dreaming Indian is all that we call finite and individual; and at the same time, as infinitely universal and unlimited, a something intrinsically divine. The Indian view of things is a

Universal Pantheism; a pantheism, however, of Imagination, not of Thought. One substance pervades the Whole of things, and all individualizations are directly vitalized and animated into particular powers. The sensuous matter and content is in each case simply and in the rough taken up, and carried over into the sphere of the Universal and Immeasurable. It is not liberated by the free power of Spirit into a beautiful form, and idealized in the spirit, so that the sensuous might be a merely subservient and compliant expression of the spiritual; but the sensuous object itself is expanded into the immeasurable and undefined, and the Divine is thereby made bizarre, confused, and ridiculous. These dreams are not mere fables, — a play of the imagination, in which the soul only revels in fantastic gambols: it is lost in them; hurried to and fro by these reveries, as something that exists really and seriously for it. It is delivered over to these limited objects as to its lords and gods. Every thing, therefore, — sun, moon, stars, the Ganges, the Indus, beasts, flowers, — every thing is a God to it; and while, in this deification, the finite loses its consistency and substantiality, intelligent conception of it is impossible. Conversely, the Divine, regarded as essentially changeable and unfixed, is also, by the base from which it assumes, defiled and made absurd. In this universal deification of all finite existence, and consequent degradation of the Divine, the idea of Theanthropy, the incarnation of God, is not a particularly important conception. The parrot, the cow, the ape, &c., are likewise incarnations of God, yet are not therefore elevated above their nature. The Divine is not individualized to a subject, to concrete Spirit, but degraded to vulgarity and senselessness. This gives us a general idea of the Indian view of the Universe. Things are as much stripped of rationality, of finite consistent stability of cause and effect, as man is of steadfastness, of individuality, of personality and freedom.

"By the fact, that in India, as already observed, differences extend not only to the objectivity of the spirit, but also to its subjectivity, and thus exhaust all its relations, neither morality nor justice nor religiosity is to be found. Humanity, generally, human duties, human feeling, do not manifest themselves: we find only duties assigned to the several castes. Every thing is petrified into these distinctions, and over this petrifaction a capricious destiny holds sway. Morality and human dignity are unknown; evil passions have their full swing; the spirit wanders in the dream-world; and the highest state is Annihilation."

We see, then, that every characteristic suggested by our science, as belonging to the Malay race, and thus to the Hindoos, has been confirmed, and even intensified, by the reflections of Hegel. To regard such a people, therefore, as connected with the development of Philosophy, would be in the highest degree unreasonable.

We have now shown that the development of Philosophy must be confined to the Caucasian race, and have taken three positions: first, that Philosophy, to be real and spiritual, must have its foundation in a conception of the Universal Laws of Being, and appear in the form of Absolute Science, in which Ontology, Theology, and Psychology are included in one form, as spirit, soul, and body; next, that its natural development, which is only a discordant representation of Philosophy, is all that has yet been realized; and, finally, that, in each sphere of this development, it must take its departure from the Church. We will now proceed to show the forms in which Philosophy has really appeared, and to explain why it has been separated from theology; why its ontological and psychological forms have never been united; why each of these has been divided and antagonized, and each portion realized in a discord that has increased as Philosophy has become developed; and why it has never been realized as a universal science, or as a form of Absolute Truth. So confused and contradictory are the accounts which have come down to us of the Eastern and Grecian philosophical systems, that we could not possibly have accomplished this task, were it not that our science enables us not only to classify all philosophical phenomena under a universal scientific form, and thus to disclose the character of each system by showing the particular position that it occupies in the philosophical circle, but also to conceive the entire development of Philosophy from its commencement to the present time; that is, the general character of its prominent systems, and the order of their production. We are able to conceive this development from an abstract point of view, because every thing grows and becomes developed, exists and becomes manifested, to represent the three great ideas which are developed in the three principal divisions of this science, — the existence of God as a tri-personal Creating Cause; the creation of the Material Universe, with Man as its head; and the salvation and regeneration of the soul through the Incarnation of God. It is by applying the conceptions which we have realized with regard to these subjects that we are able not only to explain all phenomena, but to show how they are produced, because the ideas there developed in a universal form constitute the ground of all production. In order that we should show this, we shall have to anticipate somewhat the statement of our conceptions of these three great ideas, and also some of the results of these conceptions, which will hereafter be explained, illustrated, and demonstrated.

In realizing our conception of Tri-Personality in God, we posit Infinite and Finite as opposite, self-subsisting, Universal Spheres of Indefinite Being, from which we realize a twofold sphere of Definite Being, which with the Infinite constitute God, as a tri-personality of Holy Ghost, Father, and Son, related as Spirit, Soul, and Body. In realizing our conception of Creation, we posit the tri-personal God as Creator, and infinite and finite phenomenal substances as the material for Creation; conceiving that this is first developed in a natural condition, as a dual, discordant, unreal, natural appearance, representing Infinite and Finite Principles, operated upon by infinite and finite material forces in a continuous destruction and reproduction of its forms, and animated by a natural life that is opposite to God. We realize our conception of the salvation and regeneration of the soul through the incarnation of God by conceiving the assumption of Human Nature by the Son of God, and the realization by Him of a mediating principle uniting the divine and the human, through which divine things could be brought down into a form communicable to the soul, and through which it could become inspired with a divine-human principle, and regenerated into a divine-human form. From these conceptions we realize the following facts: that, in Creation, growth is from below, upwards; while development is from within, outwards, — so that the highest forms come to be represented in the lowest sphere of consciousness; that all natural forms which represent Absolute Cause appear in a threefold form, representing the Finite, the Infinite, and the Divine Creator; that all natural forms which represent Creation appear in a discordant dualistic form as "two and two, one against the other," — this being the form of the square, which is the symbol of Nature, first as the internal and external of good, and next as the internal and external of truth; and that all natural representations of Divine Humanity appear in a form representing Marriage, or Spiritual Life through the union of opposites.

In applying these conceptions and facts, in connection with

those already recognized, for the purpose of realizing the form in which Philosophy must be developed, the following demands are made: Philosophy must take its departure from the Church, and become developed successively in three entire spheres; the first being Ontological, as representing Absolute Being, and describing the development of Absolute Substance; the second being Psychological, as representing Creation, and describing the development of Human Nature; and the third being Eclectical, and representing Spiritual Life through Marriage, or the union of opposites through sacrifice, and also representing the realization of Philosophy as Absolute Science. With regard to the ONTOLOGICAL SPHERE, our science demands that it should take its departure from the Church, and represent, first, the production of all things from Finite Substance; next, the production of all things from Infinite Substance; and, finally, the production of all things by a Personal God, or Divine Creator, who, as the Alpha and Omega, combines in Himself both Infinite and Finite as Jehovah God. With regard to the PSYCHOLOGICAL SPHERE, our science demands that it should take its departure from the Church, and become realized, first, as Ontology, commencing with the development of finite substance, and ending with the development of infinite substance, in the forms of the Universe; next, as Psychology, commencing with internal and external moral schools as the exponents of Good, and ending with internal and external intellectual schools as the exponents of Truth, these being divided and antagonized as "two and two, one against the other;" and finally as Eclecticism, first from a supernatural and mystical, and next from a natural and intellectual point of view, by which the representation of spiritual life through marriage shall be realized on the one hand, and the union of opposite philosophical ideas and systems of thought shall be attempted upon the other, by which a chaotic condition of philosophy shall be produced. With regard to the ECLECTICAL SPHERE, our science demands that it should take its departure from the Church, and become developed, first, as Ontological, in opposite forms representative in a more internal and intellectual manner of infinite and finite principles in idealistic and sensualistic systems; next, as Psychological, in opposite moral and in opposite intellectual systems corresponding with those realized in the psychological sphere, and in the same order; and, finally, as Eclectical, in opposite systems, first from the ground of religious mysticism corresponding with a supernatural order of thought and experience, and next from the ground of intellectualism corresponding with a natural order of thought and of experience.

We will now proceed to show, by quotations from the best historians of Philosophy, among whom are Cudworth, Brucker, Ritter, Chalybäus, Hegel, and Cousin, that this is the precise order in which philosophy has been developed; and also to show, from these quotations and in other ways, the character of each system, and the relation that it bears to other systems. With regard to the three spheres of philosophical development demanded by our science, history informs us that the first was realized in the East, and the second in Greece, while the third has been confined to the nations of Christian Europe; and we will therefore describe them in this order.

From the best accounts we have of the philosophy of the East, it appears that it not only took its departure from the Church, but maintained at its commencement an intimate relation with it, the philosophers being at this time the priests; that two opposite developments were there realized,—the first by the Egyptians, and the second by the Persians; and that the philosophical systems of Egypt, where philosophy originated, and which has therefore been termed "the mother of philosophy," represented Creation from a finite absolute substance by describing the development of a feminine substance, which they symbolized by Water; while the Persian systems represented Creation from an infinite absolute substance by describing the development of a masculine substance, which they symbolized by Fire. These are legitimate representatives of Infinite and Finite, because they are opposite substances, which exclude each other; and because they are relatively spiritual and material, which are the ideas associated by the ancient philosophers with Infinite and Finite: and they are used in a manner to represent Creation from opposite absolute substances, because, in one, Creation is realized through development; and, in the other, through emanation. These are the only distinctions that can be made in representing creation from infinite and finite substances in this external sphere; because here every thing must be brought down into the region of sensation, and represented through physical symbols, precisely as the ideas of Christianity must be brought down into physical symbolic forms in being represented by the most external Church. Neither of these theories is to be regarded as simply material, because a vital, intellectual power is recognized by both; by one as being contained in, and by the other as constituting, the substance out of which the Universe is formed.

With regard to the Egyptians, Brucker remarks, "Concerning the esoteric or philosophical doctrine of the Egyptians, it seems evident, in the first place, that they conceived Matter to be the first principle of things; and that, before the regular forms of nature arose, an eternal chaos had existed, which contained, in a state of darkness and confusion, all the materials of future beings. This Chaos, which was also called Night, was, in the most ancient times, worshipped as one of the superior divinities. Aristotle speaks of Chaos and Night as one and the same, and as the first principle, from which, in the ancient cosmogonies, all things are derived. It is probable that the Egyptians worshipped the material principle Chaos, or Night, under the name of Athor; a word which in the Coptic language signifies Night. Besides the material principle, it seems capable of satisfactory proof, that the Egyptians admitted an active principle, or intelligent power, eternally united with the chaotic mass, by whose energy the elements were separated, and bodies were formed; and who continually presides over the universe, and is the efficient cause of all effects."

From this it will be seen that the philosophies of Egypt represented, as we have said, Creation from finite substance through a process of growth from below upwards, or by the evolution of Natural Life from Matter. This was symbolized by the Egyptians in the form of the Sphinx, which was their great national emblem. In his philosophy of history, Hegel says, "The Sphinx may be regarded as a symbol of the Egyptian spirit. The human head looking out from the brute body exhibits Spirit as it begins to emerge from the merely Natural, — to tear itself loose therefrom, and already to look more freely around it; without, however, entirely freeing itself from the fetters Nature had imposed. The innumerable edifices of the Egyptians are half below the ground, and half rise above it into the air. The whole land is divided into a kingdom of life and a kingdom of death. The colossal statue of Memnon resounds at the first glance of the morning sun, though it is not yet the free life of Spirit with which it vibrates. Written language is still a hieroglyphic; and its basis is only the sensuous image, not the letter itself. Thus the memorials of Egypt themselves give us a multitude of forms and images that express its character: we recognize a spirit in them which feels itself compressed; which utters itself, but only in a sensuous mode."

Egypt was not only the exponent of the idea of Creation from finite substance, but represented the Female Principle, and thus the destructive side of the human constitution, from a universal point of view; and she is therefore used in the Scriptures to represent what is destructive, and what is natural, as opposite to the supernatural. She therefore became the great representative of Natural Life; and consequently the natural understanding, combined with the affectional powers, predominated in her mental constitution. It was for this reason that she so much excelled in material science and in the political economics of life; for Hegel informs us, that, "on account of its judicious economy, Egypt was regarded by the ancients as the pattern of a morally regulated condition of things." This feminine condition is strikingly illustrated in the fact, that "the women were engaged in out-door occupations, while the men remained at home to weave:"* and the accompanying devotion to good is shown in the fact, that "the law required that every Egyptian should present himself at a time appointed before the superintendent under whom he lived, and state from what resources he obtained his livelihood; and that, if he could not refer to any, he was punished with death."† It is therefore, also, that the female principle, or the principle of fecundity, was worshipped, not only in the goddess Isis, but under a great variety of animal forms, among which the cat is conspicuous; which if a man killed designedly, he was punished with death. It is for the same reason that oxen were held to be so sacred, that, after death, they were embalmed, and pyramids were erected over their remains; for the ox is the symbol of natural good, as we shall hereafter have occasion to show, as this animal is a very important emblem in the symbolism of the Scriptures.

The Sphinx, however, is not the highest symbol of the Egyptian Idea, which is not simply the evolution of Natural Life from Matter, because it recognized an active power corresponding with Spirit by which this evolution is produced. This threefold idea, which we see represented in their philosophy, was also represented by them in artistic creations, in which the material sublime was a predominant element. These we find in the pyramids, and in those enormous masses of architecture and sculpture with which Egypt is covered. Even in the pyramids, however, the evolution of the natural from the material is the predominant idea represented; for although we have here the form of the triangle,

---

* Hegel. † Ibid.

which is the emblem of Spirit, the pyramid is formed by four lines converging to a point, having their foundation in the square, which, as "two and two, one against the other," is the emblem of natural duality and diversity. This preponderance of material and natural ideas in Egyptian thought made them suitable agents in the construction of Ontology from a material point of view, in which Creation was conceived as an evolution from Matter; thereby representing that "production of all things from a finite substance" which is demanded by our science as the first movement of Philosophy in the first sphere of its development.

While the Egyptians, as we have seen, posited a chaotic material principle or substance as the origin of all things, and worshipped Night as the symbol of Deity; the Persians, on the other hand, worshipped Light, or the element of Fire, as representing the original universal principle from which all things are derived: and from this they supposed to have emanated two opposite and subordinate principles or elements, which they symbolized under the names of Light and Darkness; conceiving these to be the causes of good and of evil, without the combination of which this lower world could never have been produced. Brucker, according to Enfield, says, "If authorities be carefully compared, it will appear probable, that Zoroaster, adopting the principle commonly held by the ancients, — that, from nothing, nothing can be produced, — conceived Light, or those spiritual substances that partake of the active nature of fire, and Darkness, or the impenetrable opaque and passive mass of matter, to be emanations from one eternal Source; that to the derived substances he gave the names already applied by the Magi to the causes of good and evil, — Oromasdes and Arimanius; and that the first fountain of being, or the supreme divinity, he called Mithras. These active and passive principles he conceived to be perpetually at variance; the former tending to produce good; the latter, evil; but, through the mediation or intervention of the Supreme Being, the contest would at last terminate in favor of the good principle."

With regard to the relative position and the characteristics of the Persians, Hegel thus writes: "Asia separates itself into two parts, — Hither and Farther Asia; which are essentially different from each other. While the Chinese and Hindoos — the two great nations of Farther Asia already considered — belong to the strictly Asiatic (namely, the Mongolian) race, and consequently possess a quite peculiar character, discrepant from ours; the nations of Hither Asia belong to the Caucasian, i.e. the European stock. They are related to the West, while the Farther Asiatic peoples are perfectly isolated. The European who goes from Persia to India, observes, therefore, a prodigious contrast. Whereas in the former country he finds himself still somewhat at home, and meets with European dispositions, human virtues, and human passions; as soon as he crosses the Indus (i.e., in the latter region), he encounters the most repellent characteristics pervading every single feature of society.

"The Persians are the first historical people: Persia was the first empire that passed away. While China and India remain stationary, and perpetuate a natural vegetative existence even to the present time, this land has been subject to those developments and revolutions which alone manifest an historical condition. In Persia first arises that Light which shines itself, and illuminates what is around; for Zoroaster's 'Light' belongs to the world of consciousness,— to Spirit, as a relation to something distinct from itself. It holds a position of antithesis to Darkness, and this antithetical relation opens out to us the principle of activity and life. The Universal Essence, which we recognized in Brahm, now becomes perceptible to consciousness,— becomes an object, and acquires a positive import for man. Brahm is not worshipped by the Hindoos: he is nothing more than a condition of the individual, a religious feeling, a non-objective existence,— a relation, which for concrete vitality is that of annihilation. But, in becoming objective, this Universal Essence acquires a positive nature. This form of Universality we see exhibited in Persia, involving a separation of man from the universal essence; while at the same time the individual recognizes himself as a partaker in that essence. In the Chinese and Indian principle, this distinction was not made: we found only a unit of the Spiritual and the Natural. In the Persian principle, Unity first elevates itself to the distinction from the merely natural. This Unity is manifested as Light, which in this case is not simply light as such, the most universal physical element, but at the same time also spiritual purity,— the Good. In contrast with the wretched hebetude of Spirit which we find among the Hindoos, a pure ether— an exhalation of Spirit— meets us in the Persian conception. In it, Spirit emerges from that substantial Unity of Nature, that substantial destitution of import, in which a separation has not yet taken place; in which Spirit has not yet an independent existence in contraposition to its object. This people, namely, attained to the consciousness, that absolute Truth must have the form of Universality, — of Unity. This Universal, Eternal, Infinite Essence is not recognized at first as conditioned in any way: it is Unlimited Identity. This is properly also the character of Brahm. But this Universal Being becomes objective, and their Spirit became the consciousness of this its Essence; while on the contrary, among the Hindoos, this objectivity is only the natural one of the Brahmins, and is recognized as pure Universality only in the destruction of consciousness. Among the Persians, this negative assertion has become a positive one; and man has a relation to Universal Being, of such a kind that he remains positive in sustaining it. This One Universal Being is, indeed, not yet 'worshipped in Spirit and in Truth,' but is still clothed with a form, — that of Light. But Light directly involves an Opposite, — namely, Darkness; just as Evil is the antithesis of Good. As man could not appreciate Good if Evil were not, and as he can be really good only when he has become acquainted with the contrary; so the Light does not exist without Darkness. Among the Persians, Ormuzd and Ahriman present the antithesis in question. Ormuzd is the Lord of the Kingdom of Light. — of Good; Ahriman that of Darkness, — of Evil. But there is a still higher being from which both proceeded, — a Universal Being not affected by this antithesis, called Zeruane, Akrene, the Unlimited All." This account is in perfect correspondence with the demand of our science, because it shows that Ontology was constructed by the Persians from a relatively spiritual point of view, in which Creation was conceived as an emanation from Spirit; thereby representing that "production of all things from an infinite substance," which must, according to this science, constitute the second movement of Philosophy in the first sphere of its development.

The next demand of Absolute Science is, that an eclectical development of Philosophy shall be realized, as "a higher third," in which the two opposite sides of human thought contained in the opposite ontological systems to which we have now alluded shall be combined, and which shall realize a form representative of Spiritual Truth, which includes Marriage, or the union of opposites through the sacrifice of the life of the individual principle; and that Creation should be conceived, not simply from the point of infinite or of finite substance, but as the production of a Tri-Personal God, in whom both infinite and finite are united, — who is Jehovah; the Alpha and Omega; the First and the Last;

and besides whom there is no God, — this Creation being realized, not from his own substance, but from chaotic material substances subsisting outside of his own personality. This development we find to have been realized by the Hebrews, a people prepared and inspired by God to represent by means of historical phenomena, and of symbolic correspondences in a form of Art, this great idea of Marriage, or union of opposites through Sacrifice, — a sacrifice and union that we shall show to have been realized in the sphere of Absolute Existence, and to constitute a type and a prophecy of that which is to be realized in the soul as the condition of its salvation, and resurrection to Spiritual Life; to effect which, God became incarnated, and appeared in this atmosphere in the form of a man; and to aid in the preparation for which is the great design of Art, of Philosophy, and of the Church.

The reason why the eclectical element in Philosophy could not be developed, except through a direct communication from God, was this: although the Egyptian and Persian philosophies, by being founded in legitimate correspondences, were able to represent from partial and opposite points of view the manner in which mundane things were produced, — the dualistic and discordant conditions in which they existed; and also the opposition that existed between Creation and the Creator, — they could not represent the reconciliation and union of these opposite things, because, until after the Incarnation of God, the realization of a divine-human principle, and the construction of a supernatural sphere representative of this, there could not have existed any medium through which the idea of Marriage could be consciously represented to the mind. It was therefore only by direct inspiration from God that this idea could have been represented to man; and this communication could have been made only to minds specially prepared for this purpose, and only then by means of symbolic correspondences realized outside of the individual consciousness. The reason for this is obvious; because it must have been communicated through a natural sphere of life to a corresponding consciousness in man, both of which were antagonistic to the supernatural as the representative of spiritual life through Marriage. These inspirations were communicated to the Hebrews, who may be seen to have been a suitable medium for supernatural representation, because the Hebrew organization was a theocratic one, in which the natural principles were subject to the supernatural; and therefore Hebrew society has always been a theocracy. These communications are contained in the records of the Old Testament, constituting the external form in which is represented to the mind the fact of Christianity or Divine Humanity, which is Spiritual Life through Marriage, or the union of opposites through the voluntary sacrifice of Individual Life. We may therefore see, that although the philosophy of the East is enveloped in much obscurity, owing to the symbolic form in which even its natural ontological systems appeared, and the imperfect accounts which have come down to us, the general idea that we are able to obtain corresponds most perfectly with what was stated at the commencement as the demand of Absolute Science.

Of the development of Philosophy in Greece, although so much more diversified than that of the East on account of the individual character that must belong to its psychological development, we have the most full and reliable accounts. It is true that much dispute has arisen with regard to what were the precise doctrines taught by these philosophies, owing to the individual and consequent heterogeneous and discordant character that must attend such a development, and also to the obscurity in which the theories of philosophers were enveloped for the purpose of concealing their anti-religious character, or that nonconformity with the popular superstitions which made their promulgation dangerous. But as we are able to conceive the course of philosophical development in this sphere, and have a guide which aids us in the classification of systems, this will not prevent our coming to the most accurate conclusions with regard to the general character of these theories; and this is all that it is necessary now to establish.

That Philosophy took its departure from the Church, in commencing its development in this sphere, may be seen, because, at the earliest period of Grecian civilization of which we have any reliable account, we find that Orpheus, who was the founder of the Eleusinian and Panathenæan mysteries and other religious institutions, and Musæus, who continued and improved the rites of Religion which Orpheus established, were also the teachers of Philosophy. The first independent school of philosophy established in Greece, and by which, therefore, the development of philosophy in this sphere was commenced, was that of the Ionic sect, founded by Thales. By this school were realized two distinct and opposite developments or systems, which will be seen to be perfectly analogous to the opposite Egyptian and Persian theories already alluded to. One class of philosophers taught, that all things were evolved or developed out of a material chaotic mass by the separation and recombination, in natural forms, of the opposite material elements contained in this chaotic mass; this separation and recombination being effected by an active force or principle of motion, more or less intellectual in character, which was eternally connected with this mass, but became divorced from it, that it might act upon these material elements in the creation of the world. Two principles were thus recognized by these philosophers, — one corresponding with an active spiritual, and the other with a passive material principle; and Creation was conceived as the result of the operation of the spiritual upon the material: a theory that is similar to the Egyptian theory of birth from Chaos that has already been described. Another class of philosophers taught, that all mundane things are produced by emanation from one simple, pure, ethereal, vital, and active universal substance; or by the transformation of this substance into an infinite variety of phenomenal forms or appearances, which are dualistic and opposite in character: a theory that bears a striking resemblance to the Persian theory, which posited Fire as the universal spiritual and only cause of all mundane things, and conceived this to be productive of the opposite principles of Light and Darkness, which are emanations from this substance, and exist as secondary causes or productive powers. The philosophers who taught the first of these theories were Thales, Anaximander, and Anaxagoras. Those who taught the latter were Anaximenes, Diogenes of Apollonia, and Heraclitus.

THALES taught that the first principle of natural bodies, or the first simple substance from which all things in this world are formed, is Water. Upon this theory, Brucker remarks, "It is probable, that, by the term *water*, Thales meant to express the same idea which the cosmogonists expressed by the word Chaos; the notion annexed to which was, as we have shown, a turbid and muddy mass, from which all things were produced. It has been a subject of much debate, whether Thales, besides the passive principle in nature which he called *water*, admitted an intelligent efficient cause. They who have maintained the affirmative lay great stress upon the testimony of Cicero, who says that Thales taught that water is the first principle of things, and that God is that mind which formed all things out of water. Perhaps the truth is this: that Thales, though he did not expressly maintain an independent mind as the efficient cause of nature, admitted the ancient doctrine concerning God as the animating principle or soul of the world." As he taught that the magnet and amber are endued with a soul, which is the cause of their attracting powers, it is probable, that, like the Egyptians, he recognized a vital principle connected with and operating upon the passive material substance.

ANAXIMANDER taught that all things originated from one infinite substance; although what this philosopher meant by infinity has been a subject of much controversy. According to Brucker, Plutarch asserts this infinity to be nothing but matter. Aristotle explains it in the same manner, and several modern writers adopt the same idea. But this was mere conjecture. It is more probable, that Anaximander, who was a disciple of Thales, would attempt to improve, than that he would entirely reject, the doctrine of his master. If, therefore, the explanation given above of the doctrine of Thales be admitted, there will appear some ground for supposing that Anaximander made use of the term infinity to denote the humid mass of Thales whence all things arose, together with the active intellectual principle by which he supposed it to be animated. Ritter says, "Aristotle and Theophrastus agree in stating, that, by the infinite, Anaximander understood a mixture of multifarious elementary parts, out of which individual things issued by separation. This conjecture would bring us very near to the ancient representations of chaos, out of which all was supposed to be evolved into separate existence. Now, although Aristotle expressly characterizes this infinite as a mixture, we must not, nevertheless, think of it as a mere multiplicity of primary material elements; for to the mind of Anaximander it was a unity, immortal and imperishable, an ever-producing energy. This production of individual things was derived by Anaximander from an eternal motion of the infinite; from which it would appear that he ascribed to it an inherent vital energy."

ANAXAGORAS taught that "all is an aggregation or secretion of pre-existent things: so that all-becoming might more correctly be called becoming-mixed; and all-corruption, becoming-separate." He says, "Together were all things, infinite in number and smallness; and, by reason of its smallness, nothing was distinguishable. Before they were sorted, whiles all was together, then was no quality noticeable; for this was hindered by the commixture of all things, moist and dry, warm and cold, light and dark, and the much earth which was therein, and the multitude of the infinite seeds, in nothing resembling each other." With regard to the moving power by which this separation was effected, it has been supposed that Anaxagoras posited a supreme intellectual principle, entirely distinct and separate from this chaotic mass, by which motion was produced, and creation effected. This, however, is nothing more than the Egyptians did. Both regarded the intellectual principle as originally existing in this mass, as being separated from it, and as operating upon it, after its separation, in the creation of the world. That this was an effort to break loose from the bounds of an unqualified materialism that was but partially successful, we may infer from the following extract from the "Phædo" of Plato. He says, "Hearing one sometimes read out of a book of Anaxagoras, that mind was the order and cause of all things, I was exceedingly pleased herewith; concluding that it must needs follow from thence, that all things were ordered and disposed of as they should, and after the best manner possible. But when afterwards I took Anaxagoras' book into my hand, greedily reading it over, I was exceedingly disappointed of my expectation; finding therein no other causes assigned but only from airs and ethers and waters, and such like physical and material things." Aristotle, in his "Metaphysics," thus expresses a similar opinion: "Anaxagoras useth mind and intellect, that is, God, as a machine in the Cosmopœia; and when he is at a loss to give an account of things by material necessity, then, and never but then, does he draw in mind or God to help him out; but, otherwise, he will rather assign any thing else for a cause than mind." Dr. Cudworth remarks, "From this we may conclude, that though Anaxagoras was so far convinced of Theism as in profession to make one Infinite Mind the cause of all things, matter only excepted, yet he had, notwithstanding, too great a tang of that old material and atheistical philosophy of his predecessors still hanging about him, who resolved all the phenomena of nature into physical, and nothing into mental or final causes."

ANAXIMENES, the first of the emanationists, taught that an infinite substance, which he named Air, was the sole principle from which all things were derived. He says, "The primal substance of all things must be air; for all is produced from it, and is again resolved into it: and in the same way as our soul, which is air, rules us; so, too, air and vapor holds within its compass the entire world." Anaximenes, says Simplicius, taught the unity and immensity of matter, but under a more definite term than Anaximander; calling it air. He held air to be God, because it is diffused through all nature, and is perpetually active. The air of Anaximenes is, then, a subtle ether, animated with a divine principle, whence it becomes the origin of all beings. Brucker says, "In this sense, Lactantius understood his doctrine; for, speaking of Cleanthes as adopting the doctrine of Anaximenes, he adds, the poet assents to it when he sings,—

'Almighty Jove descends in fruitful showers.'"

Ritter says, "The comparison of this doctrine with that of Thales exhibits a considerable step in the philosophical progress, since it regards the world, not after the analogy of an imperfect seed-state, but that of the highest condition of life within our observation,— that of the human soul; and as being in its original state, and from all time, fully evolved and developed. In Anaximenes are the first discovered traces of an attempt to refer to one general law all the transformations of the first simple substance into its successive states. According to Anaximenes, the cause of change is the eternal motion of the air, which was naturally inherent in the primary substance as the principle of life; for transformation is only possible through motion: and, accordingly, he appears to have considered the evolution of the world as one continuous process of life. It was indispensable to such a view of the universe to establish a distinction between the pure idea of the primary substance and its secondary states. Many traces are discoverable of Anaximenes having attempted to determine this problem. Thus he attributed infinitude to the air, as the primary substance; but to the things which issued from it, finitude. Still he does not seem to have made this distinction by any perception of the contrast between the divine and the mundane."

DIOGENES OF APOLLONIA, the scholar of Anaximenes, also taught that air was the sole substance of the universe; understanding by air, not the material element as known by us, but a more refined substance that was conceived by him as a fiery ether. To prove the necessity for one simple substance as the origin of all things, he says, "But, to me, all, whatever is, appears as a continually self-changing form of one and the same, and to be in reality the self-same essence. And this is evident; for if that which is in the world — earth, water, or whatever other phenomenal form it takes — had one part somehow different from another,—different, too, of its proper nature, and not identical,—

and were yet manifoldly to mould and transmute itself, it would be impossible for any reciprocal blending to take place; neither could mutual benefit or injury arise; neither would plants grow out of the earth, nor animals nor aught else be generated; unless these things were so mutually connected and allied as to be identical and the same. But since this is not so, therefore, by the constant changes of the identical, all becomes different at different times, and returns back again into the same."

This idea of a material cause did not prevent Diogenes from attributing to it intelligence as well as motion. From the order of the mundane system, he inferred its origin from an intelligent being, — "a soul which vivifies all and knows all, because it is the First; and which alone could have framed and constituted all, because order could result from intelligence alone." This conception of a compound substance, that was both spiritual and material, was made to constitute a plausible ground for mundane existence, because it recognized a correspondence between the effect and the cause; for, had Diogenes conceived a strictly infinite spiritual cause as the ground of things, he would have been unable, as we shall see that the Eleatæ afterwards were, to imagine the production of a material universe. It is, of course, irrational thus to confound the spiritual with the material, while the greatest difference is at the same time recognized between them, both in the quality and in the character of their life; but it is an irrationality that is universal in philosophy as a natural development, and without which it could not proceed a single step.

HERACLITUS taught that the infinite substance from which all things originated is FIRE: but he would not allow that this fire was flame, which is rather the excess of fire, but defined it to be a warm and dry vapor; therefore a clear, bright fluid, which might be mistaken for a species of air. He says, "The world was, and is, and ever shall be, an ever-living fire, — in due measure self-kindled, and in due measure self-extinguished. All is converted into fire, and fire into All; just as gold is convertible into wares, and wares into gold." Like Anaximenes and Diogenes, he also asserted that this universal cause of all things was the wise and rational intelligence that guides and maintains the development of the whole mundane system. According to Ritter, "Heraclitus supposed a certain longing to be inherent in fire; to gratify which, it constantly transformed itself into some determinate form of being, without, however, any wish to maintain it, but in the mere desire of transmuting itself from one form into another; for any real or definite end of development is not conceivable in the case of the eternal living fire: which notion Heraclitus expressed by rejecting every end and purpose of the mundane existence; and said, in a bold figure, 'To make worlds is Jove's pastime.'"

Notwithstanding that Heraclitus posited this simple infinite substance as the cause of all things, he inconsistently maintained, that, by the swifter or slower motion of this ethereal fire, all the diversities of natural existence were produced, and an antagonistic dualism in all things established: the three great divisions or elementary principles being fire, earth, and water, between which the relation of internal, external, and medial exists; water being the mediating principle between the two extremes, or the mean through which all changes are produced. In this way he conceived a universal antagonistic dualism in creation, effected by means of water, through the agency of which the two extremes of fire and earth became mixed in opposite natural forms. He says, "All is composed of opposites; so that the same is alike good and evil, living and dead, waking and sleeping, young and old. The harmony of the world is of conflicting impulses, like that of the lyre and the bow." "Proceeding with this view, Heraclitus explained all the phenomena of nature by the concurrence of opposite tendencies and efforts in the motion of the eternal living fire."* This was certainly an ingenious way of accounting for the dualistic condition in which it is perceived that nature exists; and has not been improved upon by the moderns, in their attempts to demonstrate that being and non-being are one and the same.

We have now taken notice of all the prominent theories produced by the Ionian School, which was the first independent school of philosophy in Greece; that is, the first in which Philosophy was realized separate from, and independent of, Religion: and we see that the demand of our science, that this development of philosophy should be ontological, and represent Creation first from a finite, and afterwards from an infinite substance, has been fully sustained. We see that this school commenced with a physiological theory corresponding with the Egyptian, and ended with a dynamical theory corresponding with the Persian, and representing in an external manner the same idea which after-

---

* Ritter's History of Philosophy.

wards became realized by the Eleatic School from a more internal and rational point of view: for in coming into a psychological sphere of philosophical development where ontological ideas are connected with the consciousness, although the forms of philosophy become degraded, it obtains a more internal, self-conscious, and intellectual character, by which separate internal and external developments are demanded for each of its departments; and we accordingly find in Greece two distinct national elements, the Ionian and the Dorian, which were related as external and internal; a physiological development of philosophy being demanded by the former, and an intellectual development by the latter. Besides the Ionian, therefore, we have to notice the Italic School, which was founded by Pythagoras, as an intellectual statement of the material side of Ontology, or a representation of Creation from a Finite Substance; and the Eleatic School, founded by Xenophanes, as an intellectual statement of the spiritual side of Ontology, or a representation of Creation from an Infinite Substance. With regard to the first, we find that Pythagoras was ranked among the most eminent founders of scientific mathematics, and that he was chiefly occupied with Astronomy, with the determination of extension, and in measuring ratios of musical tones; and also that the philosophy of this school had its principal foundation in Mathematics and Music. It is true, that little, except tradition, remains to show what was the philosophy of Pythagoras; because, according to the most reliable authority, his school was broken up, while he and most of his disciples were slain; so that "the utmost that even conjecture can hazard is to suppose that the germ of the philosophical view (which was subsequently carried out by his disciples and followers) was pre-existent in the earlier lessons of Pythagoras."* Enough, however, remains to show that his philosophy was characterized as material. Brucker says, "It may be conjectured, that Pythagoras, after the oriental philosophers, conceived of the Deity as a subtle fire, — eternal, active, and intelligent, — of which every human soul is a portion. Though he does not seem to have had the idea of a pure spirit, he nevertheless appears to have conceived of Him as incorporeal; that is, as free from all the properties of gross matter, and as possessing the power of communicating motion, and of forming and directing the universe, with which He is intimately connected as its animating principle. Pythagoras probably did not

---

* Ritter's History of Philosophy.

admit two primary principles, but considered nature, in its original state, as one whole, animated by an intelligent but material principle, which at length separated itself from the chaotic mass, or detached passive matter from itself; after which, the subtle, active fire and the passive matter remained distinct principles." The mode in which this separation was supposed by the Pythagoreans to be effected is thus described by Ritter: "The Pythagoreans describe the origination of the world as a union which came to pass between the opposite principles of the unlimited and the limited, the even and the odd: for they took the ground, that number is the principle of things; that number comprises within itself two species, — the odd and the even; that one or the unit is the odd and the even, or number absolutely, being the union of these two contraries. Now, the Pythagoreans conceived the first one, or the odd, — the genesis of which they did not investigate, — to be surrounded by the infinite void; for with them the infinite is the place of the one. But, at the same time, they supposed a continual effort, on the part of the so-separated contraries, to effect a mutual union. Consequently the limiting one is constantly attracting to and into itself that part of the unlimited which is nearest to itself, and thereby limits it. This effort they call the inhaling of the infinite, or the infinite inspiration, by which the void comes into the world, and thereupon separates things one from another. From this it is evident that the One of the Pythagoreans was supposed primarily to be something perfectly inseparate, — a continuous and indivisible magnitude; in which, however, there was an inherent faculty to dissolve itself, by the mediation of the separative void space, into a multiplicity of things. Thus, then, the Pythagorean doctrine of two opposite first principles appears to be in congruity with the fundamental doctrine, that all issues from one, and is ruled by one Supreme God, or the odd — even — in the primary number." With regard to the theory of the Universe that is peculiar to the Pythagorean school, we think it will be conceded by all who have examined the various and confused accounts which have come down to us of his obscure and symbolic system, that it was nothing more than an attempt to give a mathematical, that is, a geometrical and numerical, form to the ideas of the Ionian physiologists; that the One of the Pythagoreans was nothing more than the Water of Thales, and the Infinite Substance of Anaximander; and that the Odd and the Even, which are included in this One, are nothing but the active spirit and passive matter there recognized, which here take the more intellectual form of Unity, and Diversity or Multiplicity, which they absurdly and arbitrarily refer to the same source; and from the union of which they conceived the world to be produced, under the symbols of the inhalation of the infinite, and the limiting of the unlimited. We may therefore see that the Italic philosophy, so far as it has been made known to us, corresponds completely with the demand made by Absolute Science for an internal and intellectual development of Ontology from a material point of view.

The Eleatic School, which is next in order, was founded by Xenophanes, and his principal followers were Parmenides and Zeno. Of this school, Ritter remarks, " The Eleatic School has in all ages, and not merely in modern times, attracted the attention of philosophers. It is pre-eminently distinguished from the Pythagorean and Ionian schools by the recklessness with which it strove to attain to an exclusive knowledge of the suprasensible; maintaining that the source of all truth was something independent of, and superior to, sense." Of Xenophanes he says, " The conviction had fallen on his mind, that God is One, besides whom no power exists, and in whom all truth and wisdom reside: but being unable to attain to a true knowledge of the Deity, and seeing that man is forced to represent to himself the individual,— which, however, by itself, and separate from God, can have neither permanence nor being,— and being ignorant how the cognition of individual phenomena could lead to a knowledge of the Deity, he found himself in a painful position; desiring, on the one hand, to arrive at a knowledge of God, who is the truth; and, on the other, forced to look to individuals,— in and by themselves, truthless appearances. The Eleatæ believed that they recognized, and could demonstrate, that the truth of all things is one and unchangeable: perceiving, however, that the human faculty of thought is constrained to follow the appearance of things, and to apprehend the changeable and the many, they were forced to confess that we are unable to comprehend the divine truth in its reality; and that to suppose, in conformity with human cognition, that there is actually both a plurality and a change, would be but a cheat, and delusion of the senses." He again says, " Whatever estimate may be formed of the Eleatic doctrine and its results, it cannot be denied, that, as the first attempt to correct the conceptions and representations of sense by the pure notions of reason, it is in the highest degree deserving the attention of the philosopher. By it the pure, speculative element of thought was first abstracted from all that is incidental in its concrete appearance, and consciousness awakened thereby to a true notion of philosophy."

M. Cousin, in alluding to this school, says, " Parmenides, who succeeds Xenophanes, is so much pre-occupied, according to the example of his master, with unity, that, perhaps without denying variety, he neglects it entirely. Zeno goes further: he does not neglect variety; he denies it; consequently he denies movement, consequently the existence of the world; and then you have opposed to each other two schools, both of which, placed upon the exclusive foundation, — one of the evidence of the senses, the other of rational abstraction, — recognizing unity alone without variety, or variety without unity, end in the negation of matter and of the world, or in that of free though: and of God, in an insufficient pantheism, and a chimerical atheism." Nothing, then, can be plainer than the fact, that an intellectual statement of the material side of Ontology by the Pythagorean was succeeded by an intellectual statement of the spiritual side of Ontology by the Eleatic School; because the antagonism between these schools is so extreme, and the opposite positions are so clearly taken, that no room is left for a question.

We have now arrived at the period in which a psychological development of philosophy is demanded. Up to this time, Philosophy has been principally confined to the contemplation of the relationship that exists between Absolute Substance and the phenomena of the Universe; because, as our science demands, and as the history of philosophy shows, the mind is developed from within outwards, so that the highest objects of contemplation are the first to occupy its attention, although the individual is at the same time confined to the lowest or most external and material sphere of consciousness. Philosophy always takes its departure from the Church, and is realized through an apprehensive recognition by the internal or intuitive sentimental powers, and by the principle of "Truth" in the Reason; a natural development of which, as the rational life of these sentimental powers, and of those things representative of the Spiritual which are presented by the Church, is realized at the commencement of the philosophical development; because the highest rational, intellectual, sentimental, and affectional powers are first in the order of development. By this union of internal life with external phenomena, conceptions are formed by the Imagination, which, as the highest constructive power of the Understanding, incarnates the supernatural in physical symbols and in forms of thought; and is thus the exponent of all legitimate Art, and the constructer of Philosophy in its ontological form. The lower powers of the Understanding, therefore, — to which belongs a more external order of thought that is purely intellectual, and is confined to the consideration and generalization of natural phenomena, which are discordant and deceptive natural appearances, — have, up to this time, remained in a comparatively undeveloped state. A psychology, however, is entirely dependent upon these lower powers of the understanding, the development of these, but particularly the development of the reasoning faculty or power of ratiocination, was demanded as a preparatory step, or as the condition of a psychological development of philosophy; because, upon this faculty, Psychology must depend for a form or statement; a development in which Athens, as representing the Ionian or most external element in Greece, appropriately took the lead. This development of the Understanding produced a class of thinkers who were called Sophists. These at first occupied themselves in speculating upon the ideas contained in the Ionian, Eleatic, and Pythagorean theories; Leucippus, Democritus, Protagoras, and Georgias being the most conspicuous among them. They afterwards, however, appeared as Sceptics, or as the open and avowed enemies of Philosophy; it being necessary that these one-sided Ontological systems should be overthrown, by being placed in opposition to those truths of a natural order which are cognizable by the natural understanding and the natural consciousness, as a preparation for the introduction of a new and more external, although more self-conscious, method of philosophizing.

That the Sophists were devoted to the cultivation of the Understanding, or of the intellectual powers of the mind, is shown by the fact, that, with the Greeks, the term Sophist was used to designate a class of men whose occupation was educating the youth of rich and noble families, by which they acquired wealth: and that they were the sceptics of this period is recognized by Ritter, who says, "Scepticism, which has justly been called the vilest dogmatism, had entire possession of the minds of the Sophists; for not only did they confess in their own case that hitherto they had not attained to knowledge, but also denied to men in general the capability of arriving at truth." There is no doubt, however, that the term Sophist was applied to this class, principally for the reason that they had attained to great skill in the art of reasoning, through the cultivation of the external powers of the Understanding; the tendency of which, when excessive, is to what are called sophistical modes of thought, or to the exercise of ingenuity in argumentation for the purpose of confounding the nature of things, including subtlety, insincerity, and unfairness; a tendency which we may discover even in those great philosophers, Socrates and Plato, in whom the ratiocinative faculty was undoubtedly a predominant one.

We have seen, that according to our science, after the complete development of Ontology, Psychology must be established as a philosophical method, and become developed, first as Moral, and afterwards as Intellectual Philosophy, through moral and intellectual schools, each of which is divided and antagonized as internal and external. We accordingly find that Socrates, who had long followed the profession of a teacher of youth, appeared at this time in Greece as the originator of the psychological method in philosophy. Although the originator of this method, Socrates did not construct any philosophical system, or occupy himself so much with the statement of his own opinions as he did with the refutation of the opinions of others from a universal point of view; and the reason for this is, that the originator of a philosophical method must furnish a universal ground for all the systems which can be constructed by its application in the sphere to which he is confined: and as the psychological method is, as we have said, productive of antagonistic systems, — as two and two, one against the other, — which are, therefore, partial and one-sided, no system could possibly be constructed by him. With regard to this period, Cousin remarks, "Greek philosophy was at first a philosophy of nature: arrived at its maturity, it changes character and direction, and becomes moral, social, human philosophy. This does not mean that it has man alone for its object: for it tends, as it always must, to the knowledge of the universal system of things; but it tends to it in starting from a fixed point, — the knowledge of human nature. It was Socrates who opened this new era, and who represented its character in his own person. Socrates, as has been said, made philosophy descend from heaven to earth, in the sense that he wrested it from the physical and astronomical, — the materialistic and the idealistic hypotheses of the Italian and Ionian schools, — and brought it down to the study of human thought; not as the limit, but as the starting-point, of all healthy philosophy. The 'Know thyself,' which had been until then only a wise precept, became a philosophical method. It is enough for the glory of Socrates, that he gave to the world a method, and that he made some happy applications of it to morality and to the theodicea. Behold, then, in modern times, psychology laid down as the basis of all legitimate metaphysics!" Of Socrates, Ritter says, "He chiefly confined himself to questions of morality, referring to the duties of private and public life; not, however, to the exclusion of other topics, both of science and opinion: forasmuch as Socrates made it his peculiar business to expose, in all its nakedness, the pretended wisdom of those who enjoyed a reputation for great talents, as well of politicians and of sophists as of artists and others. By this procedure, he highly gratified the young Athenians by whom he was usually attended, and who strove to acquire the famed Socratic irony; in which he represented himself as one desiring to learn of those whose claim to wisdom it was his purpose to ridicule and expose."

As this is an important epoch in the history of Philosophy, we will here consider the character of this movement, that the consequences which followed this revolution in the philosophical method may be the better understood. Psychology is the science of human nature; and, in the Natural, is produced by analyzing and systematizing the facts of the individual consciousness, upon the ground, that in this consciousness is to be found the law both of truth and of good, by the application of which these phenomena are to be explained. In contemplating the facts of the consciousness, however, it is found that these are made up of a collection of phenomena of the most discordant character; so that it is impossible to conceive any law under which they can be classified and understood, or to adopt any interpretation of one part that is not contradicted by another: and this difficulty has been increased since the introduction of Christianity, from the fact that there now exists in the mind a consciousness of facts belonging to a supernatural order of thought, which are perfectly antagonistic to the great bulk of its experiences, which are, of course, humanitarian and naturalistic in character. By the application of the psychological method to Philosophy, therefore, not only does it become divided and antagonized under the law of dualism as "two and two, one against the other," but even these opposite elements become subdivided, and are made to correspond with the particular individual positions realized by the originators of these more minute divisions of philosophic thought. Thus, although the individual position has been greatly advanced by this movement, inasmuch as a poetical representation has been succeeded by a personal experience in the consciousness, the consequence has been, that all the poetic symbolism upon which the Ontological philosophies were constructed, and which truly represented the absolute science which Philosophy is destined to become, has been discarded; and individual notions of the most discordant character, founded upon naturalistic and materialistic modes of thought, have been substituted in its place.

M. Cousin, who seems to have been astonished that the establishment of this his favorite method should have been productive of such disastrous consequences, instead of being at once productive of the highest results, says, "It seems, at the first glance, that a direction so wise tends to preserve the human mind from the illusions of exclusive systems, and at least that it will be necessary to wait some time in order to find idealistic or sensualistic follies. No: under the very eyes of Socrates, two systems arise, which boast of coming from him, and which in fact do come from him, and of which one already falls into an ultra rigorousness, and the other into an excessive looseness. I speak of the moral philosophy of Antisthenes, or of Cynicism; and of that of Aristippus, or of Cyrenaism."

The reason that the ethical element in Psychology became developed in two opposite systems is, that there are two sides to the human consciousness, one of which is characterized as internal, intellectual, and democratic; and the other as external, affectional, and aristocratic; the first being attended by self-reliance, and the second by self-complacency: and, therefore, that not only society, but every thing else, must take these two opposite forms in its manifestation. In the Cynical school, the ethical element was realized in an internal, intellectual, and democratic form; while, in the Cyrenaian school, it was realized in an external, affectional, and aristocratic form. Antisthenes, the founder of the former, who was a man belonging to the lower orders, therefore taught that the true dignity of man consists in wisdom; and wisdom, in independence of mind. So ultra-democratic was he, and so determined that every thing should be obtained from within, that he resisted education, and asserted that it was pernicious to learn even to read and write; opposed every kind of luxury and external display, assumed the garb of a mendicant, aimed to render his wants as few as possible, and labored to bring men back to an original simplicity in life and manners. He taught that pain is good; and pleasure, on the contrary, evil: and is represented as saying, "I had rather go mad than experience pleasure." This was probably said to express his antagonism to the Cyrenaic doctrine, that pleasure is the only good. He, in fact, only wished to exclude that impure and sensual kind of pleasure which attends the gratification of the lower animal appetites; because we find him commending intellectual pleasures, and even those which spring from the legitimate natural wants and internal relationships of our nature. He taught that the supreme good was a life according to virtue; that we ought to free ourselves from all external influences, and become superior to all the accidents of chance and change. According to Ritter, " In the latter Cynics, all scientific purpose seems to have fallen still further into the background. With them, philosophy was merely the art of living. Diogenes of Sinope, the famous scholar of Antisthenes, sought to restrict philosophy altogether to practice, and to the means which insure the attainment of a pleasant life, which, according to him, consists solely in dispensing with all, even the most simple and necessary wants: on this account, and as carrying to excess the Socratic simplicity of life, he has been called the mad Socrates."

With regard to the Cyrenaic school, founded by Aristippus, a pupil of Socrates, Ritter remarks, "As to the connection between the doctrines of Aristippus and of Socrates, it will be found to lie chiefly in the close resemblance of their views as to the objects of desire and aversion. Socrates, in his inquiries into the true ends of life, proceeded on the supposition, that happiness is the desire and aim of all men; and even his refutation of the votaries of inordinate indulgence and sensuality was mainly directed to show that they mistook the true nature of pleasure, which does not consist in irrational gratifications, but in the prudent and well-regulated life of the soul. Now, pleasure is here apparently admitted to be the end of life: and this may have been the point taken up by Aristippus when he taught that good is pleasure, and pain is evil; referring for proof thereof to the concurrent testimony, not merely of men, but of all living creatures. But as, at the same time, he seems to have maintained, that in true pleasure the soul must still preserve its authority, his true pleasure was consequently nothing more than the Socratic temperance."

Ritter, however, is evidently mistaken in this last remark. The independence and self-control of Socrates arose in that happy blending of self-reliance and self-complacency which characterizes the comprehensive mind and the productive genius; while we cannot but see that the two individuals, whom we have now been considering as the founders of these opposite ethical schools, were partial or one-sided geniuses. The independence and self-control of Antisthenes arose in the principle of self-reliance, the demand of which is freedom from all external control, and thus from all external motives to action, and incentives to sensual enjoyment. The independence of Aristippus, on the contrary, arose in the principle of self-complacency, and included the aristocratic desire, not to resist, but to control, all external things, and thus all external solicitations to enjoyment, that the greatest amount of pleasure might be obtained from them. The desire of pleasure he therefore prohibited, because this makes man the creature of hope and fear; and he taught that a man ought not to desire more than he already possessed. Ritter afterwards correctly remarks, "Opinions like these evidently sprung from the happy, careless, and serene character of the man, who could adapt himself with facility to every situation in life, and trusted less to his good fortune than to his own tact and ability to employ to his own satisfaction all the changes and circumstances of life." It will be seen, then, that this school, although starting from the school of Socrates, must have ended in that of Epicurus.

Having considered the development of psychology with reference to its ethical element, let us now consider it with reference to its intellectual element; which, according to our science, should be the next in order, and should, like the ethical element, become developed in two opposite systems, or according to two opposite methods, which are related to each other as internal and external, and as ideal and sensualistic. Now, upon reference to the history of philosophy, we find that the intellectual department of psychology received its first and its highest development in the systems of Plato and of Aristotle; Plato being the great exponent of the internal and ideal, and Aristotle of the external and sensualistic element. It is not, of course, possible that we should, in the brief space allotted to this general classification of the various philosophical systems of the world, give any thing like a particular description of the systems of these philosophers; nor is it necessary that we should do so, as it is only their general character that we purpose to consider. The only questions to be settled here are these: Are these systems to be regarded as psychological? Do they belong to the intellectual department of psychology? and are they related to each other as internal and external, and as ideal and sensualistic?

M. Cousin, after describing the Cynic and the Cyrenaic schools just alluded to, says, "But let us leave this insignificant commencement of the Socratic philosophy. It is in Plato and in Aristotle that its great and its true development must be sought. These two excellent geniuses knew how to raise the two great systems of dogmatic philosophy to their highest power, and, at the same time, to keep them within the limits of sobriety and Socratic temperance. Neither Plato nor Aristotle fell into the extravagances of idealism and sensualism; but it must be allowed that they might conduct thither those who should follow upon their steps with a judgment less correct and less sure." So far, then, as M. Cousin is authority, these three questions are all answered decidedly in the affirmative, within the limits of this short paragraph. With regard to the internalism and idealism of Plato, and the externalism and sensualism of Aristotle, he says, "Plato is the pupil of Socrates: he is penetrated with his method; he begins with psychology. In applying reflection to consciousness, he encounters in it very different phenomena, — some of which are there on condition of certain others, — which are, as it were, the immutable bases of knowledge; namely, those notions of unity, of substance, &c., which I have already so often enumerated to you, and which have for their character necessity and universality. Plato does not deny the particular, fickle, and changeable notions which enter into human knowledge, and serve it as accidental material; but he distinguishes from them the general notions, without which there is no knowledge; he abstracts them from others, and attaches himself to them as to the true object of the meditations of the philosopher. The constant process of Plato is abstraction, and abstraction gives him an ideal tendency. 'Ideal' is a word which Plato gave the world; and the name has remained attached to his manner as well as his system. This system is an avowed idealism. The glory of Plato, I repeat it, is to have elevated it so high, and to have held it some time on the point whence all idealism falls into extravagance.

"An equal glory of another kind is not wanting in Aristotle. Plato makes use of psychological and logical analysis in order to draw from the depths of human knowledge an element which does not proceed from the senses. This element being found, he makes use of it as a starting-point and a resting-place, in order to pass beyond the visible world. General ideas in the mind conduct him to absolute ideas, and these to God, their proper object.

On the contrary, Aristotle, acknowledging with Plato that there are in the mind ideas which cannot be explained by sensible experience, instead of setting out from these ideas to elevate himself by abstraction to their invisible source, seeks to follow them into reality. The one seems to aspire to go out from the world, the other to plunge into it. Plato is the genius of abstraction; Aristotle, that of classification. The first has more elevation; the second, more extent."

The idealism and internalism of Plato may be seen in his affinity for the theories of the Ionian dynamicists and of the Eleatic school. Ritter says, "From the dynamical physiology, as perfected by Heraclitus, he derived the principal feature of his own theory of the universe, which he regarded as a perfect living or ensouled being, subject to the perpetual flux of becoming, and destined by its order and proportion to be the most perfect representation of the eternal ideas. Still more decided is his bias for Eleatic opinions. The animating principle of this philosophy, that the perfect alone truly and immutably subsists, is rigorously marked out by Plato, who has attempted to illustrate, in a variety of ways, the identity of whatever appears to be different. He accordingly adopts the Eleatic contrariety of the rational knowledge of truth and the sensuous opinion; softening, however, its asperity, in order to do justice to the other elements of Greek philosophy."

The sensualism and externalism of Aristotle may be seen in the sensuous character of his system, in his tendency to subtle argumentation, and in the great diversity and want of scientific coherency which characterize his thought, and which led Brucker to remark, "As the result of the brief survey which we have taken of the philosophy of Aristotle, it may be asserted, that it is rather the philosophy of Words than of Things; and that the study of his writings tends more to perplex the understanding with subtle distinctions, than to enlighten it with real knowledge."

Although both Plato and Aristotle constructed philosophy upon the ground of Psychology, or of the Consciousness, they started from opposite points: Plato from Ideas and from Intuition, and Aristotle from Phenomena and from Sensation; the method of Plato being consequently deductive, while that of Aristotle was inductive. Plato, therefore, arrived at the true idea of science; which is, that phenomena are governed by ideas or general laws; the discovery of which, by the consciousness, enables us to understand all the phenomena to which they are related. It even enabled him to arrive at the idea of Absolute Science, or of a science of sciences in which all things will be explained; although it is true, that he despaired of the attainment of this science by man. Aristotle, on the contrary, arrived at the false idea of science; which is, that we arrive at scientific truth by the generalization of phenomena. Ritter, in his usual cautious, diffuse, and undecided manner, says, " Even upon the most superficial review, we cannot fail to observe that Aristotle is not disposed to open as wide a chasm between the senses, or the sensible, and the understanding of the objects of intellectual cognition, as Plato does, who, at times, seems to regard the sensible as directly foreign to intelligence. On this point, Aristotle differs from his master as widely as it is possible for two men to differ, who agree in making the understanding to be the source of science, and in considering the supra-sensible, and not the sensible, to be its object. As Plato appears to recommend us to get rid of the sensible, so Aristotle would appear to make sense and understanding to merge into each other. He shows that a particular sensation is first produced within us, out of which a sensuous state arises. From the memory of this sensuous state arises distinction; and lastly, by frequent repetition, experience, which now first opens the way to art and science, and to wisdom, or the knowledge of principles. Plato was convinced, that, by the stimulus afforded by a single idea, a man may arrive at the knowledge of all ideas, in consequence of the necessary connection between them. Aristotle, on the other hand, maintained that completeness of knowledge can only be acquired by completeness of experience. He therefore held, that every single idea, or notion, is awakened in us by a particular sensation; and that it is only upon a comparison of the similar and dissimilar, as exhibited in phenomena, that difference results. On this account, Aristotle holds induction to be the only solid basis of science: it alone is the primary source of those higher principles upon which the scientific method of demonstration rests. It is somewhat singular that he did not here observe how, according to this explanation, the formation of science resembles the argument in a circle, — which he elsewhere rejects as invalid, — since it is from the lower notions that the higher are obtained by induction, and yet the higher ideas are again made to legitimate the lower. While Plato, therefore, neglects experience generally, and especially in physical matters, and is but little occupied with the necessary and the particular in phenomena, and regarding them, as it were, but as secondary and accessory matters,—the investigation of which is, at best, but a scientific amusement,— he buries himself in the contemplation of the ideal of the beautiful and good. Aristotle, on the contrary, seeks to derive all possible information, as to the supra-sensible, from the most precise and positive experience; for, in the opinion of Aristotle, reason is not primary, but is gradually formed out of the necessary and natural contingence with which it is invariably associated."

With regard, then, to the three questions proposed for settlement in relation to the philosophical systems of Plato and Aristotle, we think it will be conceded, that they must, according to the evidence, be decided in the affirmative; that is, that they are psychological,—that they belong to the intellectual department of psychology,—and that they are related, as internal and external, and as ideal and sensualistic, and are therefore to be considered as antagonistic systems. This completes the development of psychology in the precise order that is demanded by our science,—first in its ethical and afterwards in its intellectual forms, as "two and two, one against the other." With regard to the degradation that is also demanded by it as the natural consequence of development from within outwards, the evidence is equally convincing; and, to show this, we shall quote again from M. Cousin's "History of Philosophy," for the reason that his statements are more condensed than those of most other writers, and are therefore more suitable for our present purpose.

"Three centuries before the Christian era, the Peripatetic and Platonic schools—debased and degenerated—are replaced by two other schools, which inherit their importance; which continue them, in presenting them under other forms; and which carry on, in an under-ground manner, the quarrel of Peripateticism and Platonism. I speak now of Epicureanism and Stoicism. But here is presented a phenomenon which must be pointed out to you: here begins the dismemberment of Greek philosophy. With Socrates commenced the study of human nature: Aristotle and Plato, in remaining faithful to the spirit of Socrates, in starting from human nature, arrived at a complete System, which embraces with human nature, nature entire, God and the World. Aristotle and Plato gave to philosophy all its parts: they constituted it. But after them, with the debates of their schools, the systematic genius, discouraged, became enfeebled; quitted the heights, thus to speak; descended into the plain; and to the great questions of metaphysics succeeded the interesting but limited researches of moral philosophy. The common character of Stoicism and Epicureanism is to reduce philosophy almost entirely to morality."

With regard to the system of Epicurus, which succeeded the Aristotelian or peripatetic philosophy, as the most external element in Psychology, we need not enlarge, as it is generally understood to be a system of materialism, sensualism, and atheism. Cousin says, "Epicurus concludes that we should guard against introducing trouble into the soul, by allowing in it a place for domestic affections, or for patriotism, which is still more dangerous; and Epicureanism resolves itself into a perfect egotism, adorned by the beautiful name of impassibility. Having set out from Sensation, it arrives first at materialism and at atheism; finally, in morality, at absolute egotism, both public and private,— an egotism which, if it is consistent, and if the soul has energy, would arrive legitimately at iniquity and crime, but which ordinarily limits itself by mere indifference to others. Epicureanism is the last development of Greek sensualism: it places upon the stage of the general history of philosophy the Indian sensualism of Kapila; and I need not ask you to observe how much it surpasses it in extent, in rigor, and in clearness."

With regard to Stoicism, which succeeded Platonism as the internal, intellectual, and ideal side of psychology, he says, " Stoicism is precisely the opposite of Epicureanism, with which it forms a perfect contrast. For Stoicism, as well as for Epicureanism, morality is philosophy *par excellence*. Like Epicureanism, too, it admits physiology and logic as the introduction to morality. But if, in the doctrine of Stoicism, more than one distinct trace of sensualism and often of materialism is found, it is impossible to mistake in it an unequivocal theism; although sometimes it is produced under the form of Pantheism. Since reason is the foundation of humanity, of nature, of God, it follows that the practical law, *par excellence*, is to live conformably to reason. This is the fundamental maxim of Stoic-morality. Behold now the series of consequences derived from this maxim! Pain and pleasure, being neither conformed nor nonconformed to reason, are neither good nor bad; and the physical consequences of actions are as if they did not exist. This must have conducted, and has conducted, Stoicism to a jurisprudence entirely opposite to Epicurean jurisprudence. If we must do what is reasonable, without regard to the consequences, it is not for the utility which results from it, but for the excellence which is in itself. What prevents man from conforming to reason? Passion: Passion, then, is the enemy which it behooves to combat. It is not the struggle against the passions, it is their entire destruction, which it recommends; forgetting that, in extinguishing the flame, its source is destroyed; that is, the principle which alone can put man in conformity with reason and in relation with God. Thus philosophy is only an apprenticeship to death, and not to life: it tends to death by its image, apathy, and ataraxy, and is ultimately resolved into a sublime egotism. You see it is precisely the counterpart of Epicureanism."

There are two things, which, in a particular manner, point to the decline and fall of Psychology in Greece, and which grow out of the fact, that the mind is developed from within outwards. The first is its descent into systems of unqualified moralism; and the second is the development of the sophistical element, which, as we have already seen, attended the destruction of philosophy in the Ontological sphere. On this point, Brucker remarks, "In morals, the principal difference between the Cynics and the Stoics was, that the former disdained the cultivation of nature, the latter affected to rise above it. On the subject of physics, Zeno received his doctrine from Pythagoras and Heraclitus, through the channel of the Platonic school, as will fully appear from a careful comparison of their respective systems. The Stoic philosophy being in this manner of heterogeneous origin, it necessarily partook of the several systems of which it is composed. The idle quibbles, jejune reasonings, and imposing sophisms, which so justly exposed the schools of the dialectic philosophers to ridicule, found their way into the Porch, where much time was wasted, and much ingenuity thrown away, upon questions of no importance. Cicero censures the Stoics for encouraging in their schools a barren kind of disputation, and employing themselves in determining trifling questions, in which the disputants can have no interest, and which, at the close, leaves them neither wiser nor better. It may perhaps be thought surprising, that philosophers who affected so much gravity and wisdom should condescend to such trifling occupations; but it must be considered, that, at this time, a fondness for subtle disputations so generally prevailed in Greece, that excellence in the arts of reasoning and sophistry was a sure path to fame."

As sophistry was followed by scepticism at the close of the ontological period, so we find the same result at the close of the psychological period. Cousin says, " Epicureanism and Stoicism, born nearly together, have been developed with one another and by one another. Their ardent struggle closed only about a century before the Christian era. I ask, if it was possible that scepticism should not have gone forth from the midst of the struggle which they produced. Yes: it did proceed from it, and on all sides. It went forth from idealism: hence the new Academy. But it was reserved for sensualism to produce true scepticism. A century before the Christian era, from a school of natural philosophers and physicians, went forth a new scepticism with Ænesidemus, who made of it a school, which has since had its fixed principles, its method, its history."

The ontological and psychological developments of philosophy in Greece having been completed, and their destruction consummated by the action of Scepticism, a philosophical epoch is demanded by our science, in which the union of these conflicting elements shall be attempted under the form of Eclecticism, as the representative of Absolute Truth: and as this development was characterized as self-conscious, intellectual, and psychological, while spiritual laws could not at this period be conceived, but only represented by supernatural forms, a dualistic natural development of eclectical philosophy was consequently required, including opposite schools; one being supernatural and mystical, and the other natural and intellectual: the first representing Marriage, or the union of opposites through the sacrifice of the individual, from a conscious, internal, supernatural point of view,— the Hebrews having represented it from an unconscious, external, natural point of view; and the second representing the union of opposites from an intellectual point of view by the heterogeneous combination of opposite systems. We therefore find that two developments of eclectical philosophy, corresponding with this demand, were actually realized; Gnosticism being the principal exponent of the first, and the school of Alexandria of the second. Of the first, M. Cousin writes, "The history of Greek philosophy should have had, and did have, a brilliant final movement,—that of religious philosophy. Its first epoch, under Pythagoras and the Ionians, had been consecrated to natural philosophy; its second, under Aristotle and Plato, had been filled by a philosophy, which, without forgetting the Universe and God, had especially a human and moral character; the third and last epoch was that of religious philosophy. On all sides, sects and schools began to appear, whose ruling character was religious, and whose processes were no longer abstraction nor analysis, but inspiration, enthusiasm, illumination. Hence the Cabala of the Jews and Gnosticism." Of the second development, he writes as follows: "But I hasten to reach a system which represents the regular and scientific mysticism of this epoch: I mean the school of Alexandria. Without doubt, the avowed object of the school of Alexandria was Eclecticism. The Alexandrians wished to unite every thing, all the parts of Greek Philosophy among themselves, philosophy and religion, Greece and Asia. They have been accused of having ended in syncretism; in other words, of having left a noble attempt at reconciliation to degenerate into a deplorable confusion. Truly they may be reproached with this; and, with more reason, a contrary reproach may be cast upon them. Alexandria wished to unite the Oriental with the Greek spirit; but, in this fusion, it was the Oriental spirit that prevailed. It wished to unite religion and philosophy; but it was religion that ruled. It wished to unite all the parts of Greek philosophy; but it was Plato that ruled, often indeed Pythagoras. Of the three systems into which we have seen the Greek philosophy resolve itself, Idealism remained alone. But a school which is condemned to a single philosophical element is forced to exaggerate it, in order to draw from it philosophy entire; and the exclusive idealism of the school of Alexandria soon drew it into all the follies of mysticism. Mysticism is the true character of the school of Alexandria: it is that which gives it an elevated and original rank in the history of philosophy. With Alexandrian mysticism, Greek philosophy must have ended, and did end."

Upon this school, Brucker remarks, "The founders of this sect formed the flattering design of selecting from the doctrines of all former philosophers such opinions as seemed to approach nearest the truth, and combining them in one system; but, in attempting to combine the leading tenets of each sect in one common system, these philosophers were obliged, in many cases, to understand them in a sense different from that of their original authors. Finding it impossible to produce an appearance of harmony among systems essentially different from each other, without casting a veil of obscurity over the whole, they exerted their utmost ingenuity in devising fanciful conceptions, subtle distinctions, airy suppositions, and vague terms; combinations of which, infinitely diversified, they attempted, too successfully, to impose upon the world as a system of real and sublime truths."

We now come to the third period in the development of Philosophy, which is the Eclectical sphere, and for which a similar development to that of Greece is demanded; commencing in religion, and becoming afterwards developed, independently of this, in ontological, psychological, and eclectical systems. Upon this subject, M. Cousin remarks, "Hitherto, both in India and in Greece, we have constantly seen philosophy spring from religion; and, at the same time, we have seen that it springs not from it at once, — that a single day is not enough for it to raise itself from the humble submission by which it begins to the absolute independence in which it terminates. Modern philosophy presents the same phenomenon. It is also preceded by an epoch which serves it as an introduction, and, thus to speak, as a vestibule. This epoch is Scholasticism. As the middle age is the cradle of modern society, so scholasticism is that of modern philosophy. What the middle age is to the new society, scholasticism is to the philosophy of the new times. Now, the middle age is nothing else than the absolute reign of ecclesiastical authority, of which the political powers are only the more or less docile instruments. Scholasticism, or the philosophy of the middle age, could not then be any thing else than the labor of thought in the service of faith, and under the inspection of religious authority. Well. here again philosophy is philosophy; and scarcely has it fortified itself by time, scarcely is the hand which was over it removed or become less weighty, when philosophy resumes its natural course, and produces again the four different systems which it has already produced both in India and in Greece."

Although this is relatively the self-conscious period of philosophical development, in which ontological laws are to be conceived from a conscious, intellectual, instead of being represented from an unconscious, rational point of view; in which psychological phenomena are to be realized in a supernatural, instead of a natural, condition of the consciousness; and the conception of Marriage, or the union of opposites, from a supernatural and self-conscious point of view, is the principal object of both Philosophy and Theology, — its foundations were necessarily laid in a condition of society in which the sentimental were the ruling powers of the mind, and the philosophic capacity was consequently made entirely subservient to religious conceptions and recognitions: so that no independent action of the mind, and no philosophic development, were at this time possible. Upon this account, and also because this is relatively the eclectical period of philosophical development in which all previous theories are to be used in the attempt to construct a universal science, both the philosophers and the churchmen were at first compelled to make use of the Eastern and Grecian systems in the establishment of the theories of the Church upon an intellectual basis, notwithstanding these belonged to a natural order of thought and experience antagonistic to the great ideas of Christianity, of which the Church is the representative and natural exponent. We therefore find, that, during the twelve centuries which followed the introduction of Christianity, the old systems of philosophy were used exclusively in the defence and inculcation of the doctrines and precepts of the Church. Brucker says, " Notwithstanding the proofs with which the writings of the Christian fathers abound of their enmity to Pagan philosophy, considered as a system of doctrines opposed to the Christian faith, it is, however, certain that these Christian philosophers did not scruple to avail themselves of all the helps which their learning afforded them in the exercise of the arts of logic and rhetoric. They industriously enriched their writings with the moral doctrines and precepts of the ancients, as far as they would coalesce with the Christian institutes. Without addicting themselves to any sect of heathen philosophers, they selected from each whatever they judged to be consistent with the doctrine of their Divine Master, and capable of forwarding the great end of their office as teachers of Christianity. In fine, from the time that the simplicity of the apostolic age was forsaken, the Christian fathers studied the writings of the ancients, — first, to furnish themselves with weapons against their adversaries; next, to support the Christian doctrine, by maintaining its consonancy to reason, and its superiority to the most perfect systems of Pagan wisdom; and, lastly, to adorn themselves with the embellishments of erudition and eloquence. Basil wrote a distinct treatise upon the benefits which young persons might receive from reading the writings of the heathens. His pupil, Gregory Thaumaturgus, in his panegyric on Origen, insists largely upon the same topic; highly commending him for having, after the example of his preceptor, Clemens Alexandrinus, industriously instructed his pupils in philosophy. And there can be no doubt, that Greek learning of every kind was, at a very early period, admitted into the Christian schools; not, however, without repeated cautions to young persons to distinguish carefully between the true and the false, the useful and the pernicious, in the writings of the ancients; and always to keep human learning in due subordination to Divine wisdom."

Even in the more independent attitudes which philosophy

afterwards assumed, it was principally a revival of old theories, and not the promulgation of new ideas, which occupied the attention of philosophers. The first independent action of the mind upon the subject of philosophy is to be witnessed in the disputes of the Nominalists and the Realists, which continued with great violence during the twelfth and thirteenth centuries, and which furnish the external side of Ontology in the philosophical development of this period. The commencement of this movement is thus described by Cousin: "Everywhere a movement of independence was making itself manifest. This independence was also to be marked in philosophy; and it produced, little by little, the separation of philosophy from theology by the enfeebling and destruction of scholasticism. How did this great event take place? How was war declared between the form and the foundation?—between philosophy and theology, which, until then, had lived in such perfect agreement?—and what was the battle-field? It was the old quarrel of the nominalists and the realists."

Nominalism, which was, as we have seen, the leading idea of the Aristotelian philosophy, was revived by Roscellinus, who maintained that there is no reality, except in individuals. Realism, which was the leading idea of the Platonic philosophy, was revived by Guillaume de Champeaux, who, going to the other extreme, maintained that genera are the only entities that exist. These two schools presented in every possible shape the two opposite sides of the great ontological questions of Being and of Existence from an internal, intellectual, and natural point of contemplation in self-conscious conceptions, instead of the external, representative, and poetical conceptions to which they had before been principally confined. And here we see distinctly the degradation in form, but advance in position, which attended philosophy in this sphere of its development. Although the symbolism by which Creation from infinite and finite substances was represented by the ancient schools has been abandoned, because it could no longer be realized by the mind through a spontaneous production, it has gained, as a substitute, conceptions of these same ideas from an internal, intellectual, and self-conscious point of view, which are more like psychological than ontological experiences. Until this period, nominalism and realism were represented, in the opposite sides of both Ontology and Psychology, as the natural and supernatural sides of thought: but now we find them introduced as internal and external sides of the natural development of ontological thought; while the supernatural side of Ontology is realized as eclectical in a mystical representation of the relations of God to the Soul, or to Creation, not only as its Creator, but as its Saviour and Regenerator. The cause of this great change is, of course, the establishment of Christianity, and the development, in the soul, of supernatural mediums for the representation of Absolute Truth, and for the realization of an order of thought representing Marriage, or the union of opposites through voluntary sacrifice; for, although by the introduction of Christianity the separation between the divine and the human was infinitely increased, the idea of their marriage became at the same time the great idea of the age. It was not the spiritual itself, however, of which the mind at this time became conscious, for the reason that natural forms, first representing, then contradicting, and finally inverting, spiritual ideas, must be realized in the mind before the spiritual itself can be communicated to the Consciousness. It is only a natural form, representing in a discordant and anti-spiritual manner a spiritual order of thought and experience, that first becomes developed in the human constitution; and this is from a supernatural development of the Sentimental Nature, by which man becomes connected with the Church as a Christian Institution. The external and unconscious manifestations of this new sentimental power simply produce the recognition of what the Bible and the Churches teach with regard to the laws and phenomena of spiritual life, and an apprehensive recognition, through feeling, of the external symbolism in which these are represented; but through the internal and conscious manifestations of this sentimental nature are realized supernatural intuitions, which represent the nature of God, the nature of the soul, and the relations existing between the soul and God as its Creator, Redeemer, and Regenerator. The realization of these intuitions constitutes the supernatural side of Ontology in this sphere, where we find Religious Mysticism taking the place corresponding with Eleaticism in the Grecian sphere of philosophical development. According to M. Cousin, " It was in the fourteenth and fifteenth centuries, after the warm debates of nominalism and realism, that Mysticism, separating itself from all other systems, acquired consciousness of itself, was called by its own name, and exposed its theory. According to Gerson, mystic theology is not an abstract science; it is an experimental science: the experience which it invokes is neither the experience of the senses nor that of the reason, but the consciousness of a certain number of sentiments and phenomena which occur in the inmost recesses of the religious soul. True science is, then, that of the religious sentiment, or of the immediate intuition of God through the soul. Immediate intuition is an operation of the soul, whose character is that of being accompanied with knowledge, and at the same time of not proceeding by successive argumentations, and of arriving directly at God, who, being once in contact with the soul, sends to it that light by means of which it discovers truth,— the principles of all truth and all certitude."

We have now come to the close of the ontological development of philosophy in this sphere; and we therefore expect to find, as at the close of the ontological development in Greece, a preparation for the realization of Psychology, in the cultivation of the natural understanding, and the consequent realization of Scepticism. We accordingly find that the sixteenth century was appropriated to this object, and did, in fact, produce these results. M. Cousin says, "At the close of the fifteenth century, ancient philosophy appeared almost entire. Platonism, Peripateticism, Pythagoreanism, Epicureanism, Stoicism, and the philosophy of the Academics and of the Alexandrians, seize equally the mind: Christians are scarcely any longer found, and philosophers are rare enough. The sixteenth century produced scarcely a single great man in philosophy. The entire utility, the mission of this century, was little else than to efface and destroy the middle age under the artificial imitation of antiquity. The philosophy of the revival prepared modern philosophy: it broke the ancient servitude, fruitful servitude, glorious even, so long as it was unobserved, so long as it was in some sort freely borne; but which, once felt, became an insupportable burden, and an obstacle to all progress. In this point of view, the philosophers of the sixteenth century have an importance very superior to that of their works: it is not their writings that interest us, it is their destiny, their life, and especially their death. They have not only been the prophets, but they have more than once been the martyrs, of the new spirit. When Descartes and Leibnitz, the two great philosophers of the seventeenth century, found under their pens the names of those bold thinkers of the sixteenth, they treated them with great disdain: they did not wish to be confounded with these turbulent spirits; and they forgot, that, without them, the liberty of thought which they enjoyed might, perhaps, have never been obtained."

It will be remembered, that in Greece the psychological method was established by Socrates; that he did not himself construct a philosophical system, but only prepared the ground for a psychological development; and that the result of this preparation was, first, two antagonistic Moral schools, related as internal and external, which were founded by Antisthenes and Aristippus; and, next, two antagonistic Intellectual schools, related as ideal and sensualistic, which were founded by Plato and Aristotle. In correspondence with this, and in accordance with the demand of our science, we find a similar series of philosophical phenomena produced by the establishment of Psychology in the seventeenth century. Psychology was established as the form of Philosophy by Lord Bacon, who was born in 1560. Like Socrates, he did not construct a system of philosophy, but only established the psychological method, and prepared the ground for a psychological development. The result of this preparation was the establishment, first, of two antagonistic Moral schools, related as internal and external, — the first founded by Hobbes, who was born in 1588; and the second by Gassendi, who was born in 1592: and, next, the establishment of two antagonistic Intellectual schools, related as ideal and sensualistic, — the first founded by Descartes, who was born in 1596; and the second by Locke, who was born in 1632. To illustrate these facts, and to show that the character of these schools has here been correctly described, we will quote from Cousin's "History of Modern Philosophy;" although his classification of these systems does not exactly correspond with the order of their production, or with the classification presented by our science, in consequence of the different point of view from which they were contemplated by him, and the individual theories he wished to support. He there says, —

"The philosophy of the fifteenth and sixteenth centuries released the human mind from Scholasticism, from slavery to a foreign principle, — authority: at the same time, it prepared it for modern philosophy, for absolute independence; and conducted it from scholasticism to modern philosophy by the intermediation of an epoch wherein authority still reigned, but an authority much more flexible than that of the middle age. — the authority of philosophic antiquity. The philosophy of the fifteenth and sixteenth centuries is, as it were, the education of modern thought by ancient thought. Its character is an ardent and often blind imitation: its necessary result was a universal fermentation, and the want of a definitive revolution. This revolution was consummated in the seventeenth century: it is modern philosophy, properly so called. The most general feature which distinguishes it is an entire independence: it is independent both of the authority which reigned in scholasticism, the ecclesiastical authority, and of the authority which reigned in the fifteenth and sixteenth centuries, the admiration of ancient genius. It breaks with every thing past, thinks only of the future, and feels capable of drawing the future from itself. Bacon and Leibnitz excepted, all the great philosophers of the new era, Descartes, Malebranche, Spinoza, Hobbes, Locke, and their disciples, have no knowledge of and no respect for antiquity: they scarcely read any thing else than what is found in nature and in consciousness. The second characteristic of modern philosophy is, as I have said, the determination of a fixed point of departure, the adoption of a method: and this point of departure, this method, is the study of human nature as the foundation and necessary instrument of all science and of all philosophy; that is, psychology. The chief of a school does not at first perceive all the consequences of his principles: he exhausts his boldness in the invention of principles, and thus overlooks, in a great part, the extravagance of the consequences. Thus Bacon put the modern sensualistic school in the world; but in vain would you seek in Bacon the sad theories at which his school finally arrived. To the school of Bacon immediately attach themselves three men who are his official successors,—Hobbes, Gassendi, Locke. Hobbes was a friend and an avowed disciple of Bacon. And what is the philosophy of this disciple, of this translator, of Bacon? I will tell you in a few words. There is no other certain evidence than that of the senses. The evidence of the senses attests only the existence of bodies: then there is no existence save that of bodies, and philosophy is only the science of bodies. Hobbes' system of physics is that system of which Bacon has spoken with so much eulogium,—that of Democritus, the atomistic and corpuscular philosophy of the Ionian school. Hobbes is completely a nominalist. With him there are no other than contingent ideas: the finite alone can be conceived; the infinite is only a negation of the finite: beyond that, it is a mere word, invented to honor a being whom faith alone can reach. The idea of good and evil has no other foundation than agreeable or disagreeable sensations. Man is capable of enjoying and of suffering: his only law is to suffer as little as possible, and to enjoy as much as possible.

"The life of Gassendi was devoted to the renewal of the philosophy of Epicurus: he took great care, however, in the title of his book, to declare that he rejected from it every thing that was contrary to Christianity. But how could he succeed in this? Principles, processes, results, every thing, in Epicurus, is sensualism, materialism, atheism. The thought of Gassendi must not be sought for in these reserves. It is found in the ardor with which he combated the nascent idealism of Descartes. I ought to call your attention to the success of the philosophy of Gassendi in France. He spread his ideas throughout a small circle of pupils and zealous partisans; among whom, with his biographer Sorbière, we may distinguish the traveller Bernier, Chapelle, Cyrano, and our great Molière. This was the foundation of that society of free-thinkers of the Temple, from which Voltaire drew his first inspirations, before he found in the conversation of Bolingbroke, and in his voyage to England, Epicurean philosophy under a regular and scientific form.

"Locke was the true master of Voltaire. He was the metaphysician of the sensualistic school: he was its most elevated and purest expression in the seventeenth century. Locke assigns two sources of human knowledge, sensation and reflection. Reflection is applied to the operations of the understanding; and is limited to making them known to us, such as they are. These operations are comparison, reasoning, abstraction, composition, association,—all the faculties which separate or combine the elements which are derived from sensation, but add nothing to it. All our knowledge, then, has its first and last root in sensation. Such is the theory of Locke, brought back to its principle. The principle once laid down, you easily guess the consequences. The natural sagacity of Locke has in vain attempted to retain them: they escape him on all sides, and connect him with that chain of sensualistic philosophers, the first link of which is Hobbes. Locke is Hobbes, with all necessary differences. He does not often quote him: he often reproduces him. Such is the sensualistic school of the seventeenth century, in its historical development.

"The founder of the modern idealistic school is Descartes. Descartes seeks the fixed and certain point of departure whereupon philosophy may rest. He finds that thought may question every thing, save itself: whence it follows, that, although we should doubt all things, we could not doubt that we think. This is, then, the firm and certain point of departure sought by Descartes; and, as thought is attested to us through consciousness, behold consciousness taken as the point of departure, and the foundation of all philosophical research!

"Follow out the consequences of this principle. I think, therefore I exist. This is the first consequence: behold the second! What is the character of thought? It is that of being invisible, intangible, imponderable, without dimensions, simple. From this second step, Cartesian philosophy arrives at the spirituality of the soul. But imperfection is one of the manifest characteristics of thought. This notion of the imperfect, of the limited, of the finite, of the contingent, elevates me directly to that of the perfect, of the absolute, of the illimited, of the infinite, of the necessary. Hence the demonstration of the existence of a perfect being; namely, God: so that, from the fact alone that I have the idea of God, it follows that God exists. God is perfection itself; which comprehends both wisdom and veracity: hence, that which appears to exist does then exist, and God is our warrant for the legitimacy of our natural persuasion."

We cannot reflect for a moment upon these three principal notions, which lie at the foundation of the Cartesian philosophy, without perceiving their complete artificiality and absurdity. Descartes takes, as a starting-point for his philosophy, the consciousness of individual existence, which he assumes upon the very superficial and untenable ground, that "*we think.*" This ground is superficial, because the process of thinking is a function even of the most external region of the understanding; and it is untenable, because it is not through this process that the individual obtains an assurance of his existence, but through a recognition of what is presented to his consciousness; and this consists of internal and external appearances, even the reality of which he cannot demonstrate, and the nature of which has always been the great subject of dispute. Even should we allow that the existence of the soul is demonstrated as a conclusion of the understanding, instead of being accepted as a belief of the consciousness, it would be but a barren conclusion; because it could lead to no kind of knowledge whatever concerning the nature of this existence, which is the great question for Philosophy to settle. Philosophy is not called upon to prove that we exist, but to show what Existence is; and this subject cannot even be approached from this phenomenal and material point of view. It is only through a conception of the universal laws of Existence, both Absolute and Phenomenal, that a single phenomenon can be explained. By Descartes, however, this was reversed; and he founded his philosophy upon the ground, that natural appearances, which are in truth the opposite of what they seem, are spiritual realities; that, through a generalization of these deceptive phenomena, we are to arrive at a knowledge of Law; and that, through a contemplation of the facts of the human consciousness, which are thoroughly discordant and utterly false, we arrive at the knowledge of God, who is harmony and truth itself,—a position which must result in the production of Anthropomorphism; as we shall show that it does, by the unconscious confession of one of the deluded adherents to this atheistic system of belief. This atheistic position was taken at the first establishment of the psychological method in modern philosophy; belongs to Psychology, from the very nature of its constitution; and has, therefore, accompanied every form of its development.

The next great step, by which, according to Descartes, we are to be led into a knowledge of the nature of the soul, is this: Thought is invisible; therefore the soul is Spiritual. We may now see why thought, instead of sensation, was assumed as the proof of Existence: it was, that invisibility might be claimed for the soul, and thus its spirituality established; for one of the hypotheses posited by Descartes was, that the great distinction between the natural and the spiritual, and between the finite and the infinite, was that between visibility and invisibility; and we see that he took this superficial, anti-philosophical, and destructive idea as the ground of his system. But, if allowed to reason in this way, we might prove the spirituality even of matter as known to us in this most external atmosphere; because it is well known that all its forms are constituted by the combination of certain laws or forces, which, when separated, become invisible; and that even some of its forms are equally invisible. We do not need to rest the question upon a material ground, however, because we shall demonstrate that the finite is equally invisible with the infinite, and that forms of spiritual and of natural life, although opposite, are equally visible. But the next step by which Descartes proposed to lead us to the knowledge of God, and also to obtain a warrant for and a confirmation of all our natural beliefs, which are founded in appearances, is the most astounding of all, and an appropriate termination to this series of absurd propositions. It is this: Thought, by the means of which our own existence and the spirituality of the soul have been demonstrated, is perceived to be imperfect; therefore we pass, necessarily and at once, to the conception of the perfect, of the infinite, of God; and, as He must be a God of perfect wisdom and veracity, we obtain a warrant that what is apparent is also real, and therefore that all our natural persuasions must be legitimate and true. These conclusions have so little relation to the premises assumed, that they would seem to be nothing more than an unmeaning parade of words, that did not stand for any definite conceptions in the mind, and could not be expressed even in a legitimate logical form; for what can be a greater abuse of logic than the statements, that the recognition of imperfection in natural thought must at once enable us to realize a conception of Absolute Perfection or of God, and that this conception of God must legitimate and verify the imperfect natural perception from which we started? This is not by any means, however, an unmeaning statement, but is an incarnation of ideas in the mind which are a complete inversion of the truth. This statement is an inversion of the truth, for three reasons: first, because it assumes that the original condition of the soul is spiritual and real, — while it is natural and unreal, and the opposite of what it seems; next, because it assumes that a knowledge of natural imperfection must lead to a knowledge of spiritual perfection, — while the truth is, that it is only through a knowledge of spiritual law that a single natural phenomenon can really be explained; and, finally, because it assumes, that, through a knowledge of Perfection or of God, all our natural persuasions will be shown to be real and true, — while such a knowledge will, in truth, show them to be unreal and false. As these positions could not be demonstrated, they had to be assumed; and, as some show of argument was necessary to cover up the assumption, this cloud of metaphysical dust, or of "glittering generalities," had to be raised.

This theory of Descartes was carried out by Spinoza and Malebranche; Spinoza taking the internal and ideal, and Malebranche the external and practical, side. The difference between them, however, is more in form than in substance; for the idealism of Spinoza is merged and lost in natural and material phenomena, which, according to him, are manifestations of the infinite substance, and the only means through which God is made known to us: so that, although purporting to be spiritualistic, we may see that his system is most thoroughly naturalistic and material. On this subject, Cousin says, "Follow Descartes in his two immediate disciples, Spinoza and Malebranche, and you will recognize the fruits of the master's principles. Spinoza sets out with the perfect and infinite being of Descartes: he shows, that, before the infinite being, every thing else has but a phenomenal existence; that a substance being that which possesses existence of itself, and the finite being that which shares existence without possessing it of itself, a finite substance implies two contrary notions. Thus, in the philosophy of Spinoza, man and nature are mere phenomena,— simple attributes of sole and absolute substance, but attributes that are co-eternal with their substance: for as there are no phenomena without a subject, no imperfect without a perfect, no finite without infinite, and as man and nature suppose God; so there is no substance without phenomena, no perfect without imperfect, no infinite without finite, and God implies also humanity and nature.

"The point of departure of Malebranche is the Cartesian theory, that human thought cannot recognize itself as imperfect, and as relative, without conceiving God as perfect and absolute Being. Now, as there is not a single thought that is not accompanied by the feeling of imperfection in itself, it follows that there is not a single thought which is not accompanied by a conception of God, which communicates to it a force and superior authority. Thus the idea of God is contemporaneous with all our ideas, and the basis of their legitimacy. Hence the famous principle of Malebranche, that we see every thing, and the material world itself, in God; which means that our vision and conception of the world is accompanied by a conception of God — of infinite and perfect being — that adds its authority to the uncertain evidence of our senses and our thought. Hence the theory of God as the author and principle of our desires, of our acts, and of our thoughts; hence the theory of occasional causes, founded almost at the same time by Geulinx. The last term of this system is the absorption of man in God. Such is the state in which sensualism and idealism — the schools of Bacon and Descartes — were found at the close of the seventeenth century."

Although there is a want of order in the classification of these psychological systems by M. Cousin, the quotations here made will serve to illustrate the manner in which the demand of our science has been sustained by the development of Psychology in modern philosophy; this being established by Lord Bacon, and developed by Gassendi, Hobbes, Descartes, and Locke. We see that this development was more purely psychological, more strictly confined to the limits of the natural understanding, more thoroughly natural and sensualistic, and thus more destructive in its character, than its first development in Greece, when purely ontological ideas were more readily recognized, and more freely combined with psychological phenomena in the theories of philosophers. But we see that it has retained the same characteristic features, and has ended in the same way; that is, in the two extremes of idealism and sensualism, which are Pantheism and Atheism, of which Spinoza and Voltaire were prominent exponents. We also find, that, out of the struggle which took place between these idealistic and sensualistic schools during the early part of the eighteenth century, the same effect was produced as by the struggle between Platonism and Peripateticism, which resulted in the production of scepticism; and that, in both cases, this was followed by the realization of Eclecticism, which attempted to reconcile and unite these opposite sides of philosophy in a universal system. The scepticism which was the result of this contest, and which is embodied in external and moral, and in internal and intellectual systems, may be studied in the writings of Hartley, Darwin, Priestley, Horne Tooke, Godwin, Bentham, Mandeville, Bayle, Hume, Condillac, Condorcet, Helvetius, Saint Lambert, D'Holbach, and Voltaire. As these need not here be described, we will proceed to examine the establishment and progress of Eclecticism, which, as a legitimate form of philosophy, succeeded them, and concluded its natural development.

Our science demands, as the conclusion of this third sphere of philosophical experience, a twofold development of eclectical philosophy, and that it shall be developed first as mystical, and next as intellectual; and we shall now proceed to show that these developments have been completed,—that these are now being destroyed by Scepticism,—and that nothing remains for philosophy but the realization of Absolute Science. Eclecticism appears first in the form of Mysticism; because it is only through a supernatural and religious experience that the idea of Marriage, or the union of opposites, can be adequately represented, while the individual is confined to a natural sphere of consciousness; and this experience must, therefore, constitute the point of departure in the development of Eclecticism. In this particular form, it may be studied in the writings of Arthur Collier, Henry More, John Pordage, Amos van Helmont, Fénélon, Pierre Poiret, Saint Martin, and others. But as the writings of the mystics are necessarily more dogmatical, sentimental, and poetical than they are philosophical, they would require a more extended notice than our space will allow. We will, therefore, pass to the consideration of the principal philosophical systems, through which was carried on the development of Eclecticism, from a natural and intellectual point of view.

The first movement in this direction was made by Leibnitz, who was born in 1646, and of whose philosophy Wolf is the principal exponent. Of Leibnitz, Cousin writes, "Behold Leibnitz, ther., separating himself equally from the sensualism of Locke and from the idealism of Descartes, and absolutely rejecting neither the one nor the other. This, in my opinion, is the fundamental idea of Leibnitz; and you perceive that I applaud it with all my heart. Why should I not say so? Since precedents are sought to these feeble lectures, I willingly acknowledge that they are found in Leibnitz: for Leibnitz is not only a system, but a method; and a method at the same time theoretical and historical, whose eminent characteristic is to reject nothing, and to comprehend every thing, in order to use every thing. Such is the direction which we strive to follow, and which we shall not cease to recommend, as the only, as the true star on the obscure road of philosophy. But it is necessary to distinguish this general direction of the spirit of Leibnitz from his system; for he also finished by a system, and by a system which, unfortunately, resembles an hypothesis. The basis of all his thoughts is monadology and pre-established harmony. Monadology rests upon this axiom: Every substance is at the same time a cause; and every substance, being a cause, has therefore in itself the principle of its own development: such is the monad. Each monad has relation to all others; it corresponds with the plan of the universe; it is the universe abridged; it is, as Lebnitz says, a living mirror, which reflects the entire universe under its own point of view. But, every monad being simple, there is no immediate action of one monad upon another: there is, however, a natural relation of their respective development, which makes their apparent communication. This natural relation, this harmony, which has its reason in the wisdom of the supreme director, is pre-established harmony. You conceive, then, that the partisans of Locke, far from being arrested by the idealistic hypotheses of Malebranche and Leibnitz, are, on the contrary, authorized by the manifest vices, and, we may say, by the ridiculousness, of these hypotheses, to plunge farther and farther into sensualism, and to push their principles even to the most deplorable consequences."

Ridiculous is not too harsh a word to apply to the ideas of monadology and pre-established harmony, put forth by Leibnitz as the foundation of his system. Indeed, we think they are preëminently and monstrously so. The mind of Leibnitz, although of great power, was external, practical, and naturalistic; he was, therefore, more intellectual than rational; more attached to expedients than to principles; possessed of varied talents and acquirements; and a practical man of the world, rather than a metaphysician. He was, therefore, well qualified to construct a system that should include the greatest variety of discordant elements in the greatest apparent agreement; in short, to be the founder of eclectical philosophy from an intellectual point of view; which requires great ingenuity and boldness, combined with such a degree of superficiality as shall prevent any alarm at contradictions and absurdities. In constructing a system that should harmonize with the principles of common sense,—or with the conclusions of the natural understanding, and with the impressions of the natural consciousness,—it was necessary that he should take a bold stand against the severe metaphysical, pantheistic, and fatalistic position of Spinoza,—that there cannot be any thing else in the universe but the one Infinite Substance, and its modes of manifestation; which, it will be remembered, was the Eleatic position, and one that we cannot, if we are rational, possibly escape from, if we undertake to derive all things from one principle or substance; excepting that even these modes of manifestation are inadmissible, if we reason from a strictly rational ground,—a fact that has always necessitated a dualism of some kind. To escape from this conclusion of Spinoza, he boldly put forth his monstrous doctrine of monadology,—the indefinite divisibility of the infinite substance, or the origination, by "continual fulgurations," or constant emissions from this infinite substance, of innumerable monads; these being minute portions of this substance, each of which is an absolute cause, possessing the power of self-determination, and also that of incarnation, or of assuming a body for itself. As he could not, however, suppose that each monad, although a particle of infinite substance, was equal with the infinite, because this would suppose an indefinite number of infinites,—a degree of absurdity which even he could not admit,—he was obliged to introduce limitation, and thus diversity, into this indefinite number of self-existent, self-directing, independent, and semi-infinite creations. In order that this great diversity of aim and of capacity should be brought into harmony with the one infinite substance and with each other, and also that the manifestations of the mind and the body in each monad should be made to correspond, another theory became necessary, or the positing of some law by which order should be produced among this multitude of independent monads, with their independent minds and bodies; so that they might be made to co-operate towards some general end, and the manifestations of the mind, and those of the body, in each monad, might also be made, although unconsciously, to correspond and to co-operate: for it will be understood that Leibnitz supposed the mind of each monad to be spiritual, and its body to be material, and that no connection whatever could exist between them; although, with a strange inconsistency, he supposed that the latter was produced from the former. This regulator was conceived by him in the doctrine of pre-established harmony, which provided for each monad one series of laws by which the manifestations of its mind, and another by which corresponding manifestations of its body, shall be produced; both series of laws being constructed with reference to all other monads, so that an harmonious manifestation of all may result. And it is a most remarkable fact, that, although each monad is supposed to contain within itself the law of its own development, it is supposed to be at the same time a self-determining power.

It is really surprising that these theories, although they seem to be more like fables invented for the amusement of children than like attempts to state absolute facts upon which philosophy can be based, have found an abundance of supporters and admirers; but particularly among the Unitarians, to whose naturalistic views they furnish a support. One of these,* in alluding to the doctrine of monadology, says, "The philosophic theologian and the Christianizing philosopher will rejoice to find in this proposition a point of reconciliation between the extramundane God of pure theism and the cardinal principle of Spinozism, — the immanence of Deity in creation; a principle as clear to the philosophic mind as that of the extramundane Divinity is to the theologian. The universe of Spinoza is a self-existent unit, divine in itself, but with no Divinity behind it. That of Leibnitz is an endless series of units from a self-existent and divine source. The one is an infinite deep; the other, an everlasting flood." With regard to the doctrine of pre-established harmony, he says, "It is the best solution we know of the old contradiction of free-will and fate, — individual liberty and a necessary world." If

---

* Dr. Hedge. — See "Atlantic Monthly," June, 1858, p. 14.

this is really "the best solution that we know of the old contradiction of free-will and fate, — individual liberty and a necessary world," — is it not quite time that a better solution should be sought?

The next and the most considerable attempt to found Eclectical Philosophy upon an original metaphysical basis was made by Emanuel Kant, who founded a speculative school of philosophy in Germany. It was recognized by the founder of this school, that all objective knowledge must have its ground in internal, subjective laws; and it therefore became the great aim of this school to obtain a conception of these internal and external sides of truth, — the antagonism between which had convulsed the philosophical world from its commencement, — and to produce their reconciliation and union. We will here give a sketch of the principal theories of this school, for the purpose of showing that this attempt resulted in a total failure; inasmuch as all these theories failed to obtain the conception of any subjective law, by the application of which a single phenomenon could be explained, or even accounted for: so that not only did the opposite sides of philosophy remain divorced from and antagonized to each other, but objective phenomena were exclusively relied upon by these philosophers as the laws from which all their conclusions were derived: so that, instead of the subjective, the objective became to them the law of philosophy, and furnished all the materials for its construction. By Kant this attempt to conceive subjective law was finally abandoned; he having come to the conclusion, that nothing but phenomena could be known, and that knowledge must therefore be rigidly confined within the limits of physical science. For this we have the authority of M. Chalybäus, who says, "It has been made out, as the consequence of the 'Critic of Pure Reason,' that the proper objects of metaphysics — namely, God, Universe, and Mind — are wholly inaccessible to our cognition, and lie beyond the limit of all philosophical knowledge." * Although Kant's philosophy recognized two principles, — an idealistic subjective and an empirical objective principle, — the subjective was so limited by the objective, that nothing but the objective ever became visible, and he became as thorough a sensationalist as Locke himself: and, although he undertook to disclose to us the elements of "the Pure Reason," the highest conception that he appears to have

---

* "Historical Survey of Speculative Philosophy from Kant to Hegel."

obtained of it did not rise above the common and superficial one which identifies or confounds it with the power of ratiocination, which is an inferior power even in the Understanding, while he obtained no higher conception of Intuition than the memory of a sensation; theories which have been adopted by most of the philosophers who have succeeded him. Of his conception of the Reason, Chalybäus says, "From all this we readily discern, that the Reason, as Kant comprehended it, is at bottom only a purely formal, logical faculty of reflection in a higher potence or degree; and that it really differs, when reduced to these limits, in no respect from the Understanding." That the position of Kant has here been correctly stated with regard to these two great ideas — Reason and Intuition — may be seen from the following quotations from his great work, "The Critic of Pure Reason:" "There is no proper polemic in the sphere of pure reason. Both parties beat the air, and fight with their own shadows, as they pass beyond the limits of nature, and can find no tangible point of attack, no firm footing for their dogmatical conflict. The whole interest of Reason, speculative as well as practical, is centred in the three following questions: 1. What can I know? 2. What ought I to do? 3. What may I hope? The first question is purely speculative. We have, as I flatter myself, exhausted all the replies of which it is susceptible; and have at last found the reply with which reason must content itself, and with which it ought to be content, so long as it pays no regard to the practical. But, from these two great ends,—to the attainment of which all these efforts of pure reason were in fact directed,— we remain just as far removed as if we had consulted our ease, and declined the task at the outset. So far, then, as knowledge is concerned, thus much, at least, is established, that in regard to these two problems it lies beyond our reach." In the Chapter on "Axioms of Intuition," he says, "The principle of these is, '*All Intuitions are Extensive Quantities.*' An extensive quantity I call that wherein the representation of the parts renders possible (and therefore necessarily antecedes) the representation of the whole. I cannot represent to myself any line, however small, without drawing it in thought; that is, without generating from a point all its parts one after another, and in this way alone producing the intuition. As the pure intuition in all phenomena is either time or space, so is every phenomenon in its character of intuition an extensive quantity, inasmuch as it can only be cognized in our apprehension by successive synthesis from part to part."

Notwithstanding this defection of their leader, however, the followers of Kant were not discouraged, but still continued their search after the subjective, and conceived theory after theory, in the hope of constructing Philosophy upon a truly scientific basis. In a description of these systems, Dr. Murdock says, "The chief aim of most of these systems was to penetrate into the *terra incognita* of Kant; that is, into the region of noumena and of supra-sensible things. The authors were unwilling to believe that we can know so little as Kant had represented. They therefore attempted to rend the veil which conceals the unknowable, or to bridge the impassable gulf of Kant which separates between phenomena and noumena in the material world, and between ideas and the objects of them in the world of thought." How they succeeded in this may be gleaned from the following sketch; the quotations used in which are taken principally from the work of Chalybäus, who is the most highly esteemed critic of German "Speculative Philosophy:" —

Reinhold constructed a system which was based upon this formula: "The Thinker, the Thought, and The act of Thinking;" and he imagined, that, starting from this point, he should be able to discover the subjective and the objective elements of knowledge, and the mediating process through which they become united, by observing the operations of his own mind; because he perceived, that, in the act of thinking, subjective and objective are in some way combined or united. The result of his investigations, however, soon convinced him that this was a barren formula, which could not help him to obtain any knowledge either of the thinker, the thought, or the act of thinking, and it was therefore abandoned by him.

Fichte put forth a system entitled "the Doctrine of Science," in which he undertook to establish a single principle as the ground of all science; and this was, that "I am I," which he supposed to include "the subject, the predicate, and the copula." This, however, was only a new version of the thinker, the thought, and the act of thinking, of Reinhold; except that, in transferring the point of observation from the Understanding to the Consciousness, a wider field was opened from which to select materials for a system. Fichte was thus enabled to select from the facts of his own consciousness, and from the history of mental manifestation, such materials as best suited his purpose in the construction of a system, and corresponded best with his individual position in relation to progress; and as the principle of duty was to him supreme, reasoning anthropomorphically, he came to these conclusions,—that God is simply "the moral order of the Universe;" and that "by striving to realize Duty we approximate to God." Finally, he came to the conclusion, that "the human mind is the only real existence in the Universe; antecedent to which nothing real ever existed, and around and above which nothing real now exists." This extravagant doctrine, however, was not confined to Fichte; for we shall see that it was adopted by Schelling: and of Hegel, Chalybäus writes, "This problem we see Hegel responding to, by assuming a pantheistic identity of the human being and God; in which identity, when regarded from a strictly logical point of view, the Deity itself arrives for the first time, by virtue of human cognition, to a state of consciousness."

Schelling put forth a system purporting to be "the Doctrine of Identity," which maintained the perfect identity of the knowledge of things and the things themselves: so that subjective and objective, spiritual and natural, and absolute and phenomenal, were regarded as one and the same. This was a pantheistic system, which was also called "the doctrine of the All-One," because it maintained that the Universe is God, and God the Universe; or that God, developing Himself in various forms and according to general laws, is the only existence. Of this system, Chalybäus writes, "The Absolute, or that which was called by Spinoza the universal substance, and thus that essence which forms the infinitely numerous things, which is or constitutes the world, was not by Schelling regarded in the light of a dead substance, into which life and motion might be inspired or infused from without as if by some higher spirit, but as being the living, universal, and primordial essence of all things themselves; and then, in order to express at the same time, in this notion, the most general fundamental law,—the archetype or rhythm, which it obeyed in all its moving and living,—he declared the Absolute to be the unlimited, eternal Subject-Object, *i.e.* the living principle, which, in obedience to its own nature, eternally transports itself from the state of subjectivity into that of objectivity, and then returns, as from an elastic tension within itself, to the subjectivity; yet in such wise, that its new state, from being after each return more enriched in internal determinations, as well as in the freedom of determining itself, becomes more elevated in character: so that, *ipso actu*, by its working, *i.e.* the carrying-out of that which lay potentially in it, it becomes gradually for itself that which it had the intrinsic power of becoming. This utterly unconscious but teleologically working life comes at length in Man to itself; *i.e.*, comprehends itself as the absolute rationality." This idea is formally stated by Schelling thus: "The Absolute first attains in Humanity a true self-consciousness; for consciousness presupposes a spiritual transcript, or copy, of what the spirit is in itself; for only in a perfect reflex of its nature does the primordial essence discern or cognize itself." This "Doctrine of Identity," which was maintained by Fichte, Schelling, and Hegel, seems to be the statement of Pantheism from a transcendental point of view; because, by making God to depend upon man for his Consciousness, it virtually substitutes Man for God; that is, makes him to be the incarnation of the Infinite: taking the ground, upon which this statement seems to be founded, that, in the course of his growth and development under the operation of the absolute laws of his nature, Man finally becomes God, it carries out, in this way, the transcendental demand for universal self-assertion to the utmost possible limit. These philosophers were thus carried away from the true objects of philosophy, and realized a complete inversion of philosophic truth. Instead of recognizing the universal opposition in existence, which even their master (Kant) continued to recognize, and which it has always been the great business of philosophy to explain, by showing how this opposition originated, and how these opposites become united in the forms and manifestations of the Universe, they inflexibly closed their eyes, like right loyal unitarians, to every antagonism, and firmly took the position that all things are in essence One.

The system of Hegel, who was the latest and the most important of the writers belonging to this school, was also a pantheistic system similar in character to that of Schelling; although, as Schelling inclined to the real, and Hegel to the ideal side, the former partook more of an atheistic, and the latter more of a pantheistic character. Hegel may have come nearer to the truth than any other philosopher of this school; but if he was convinced, as it is said he was, of his agreement with Schelling in all important points, Truth could never have even dawned upon him, but he must have remained in that deeper night which immediately precedes the day. The following extract from Chalybäus will show the manner in which Hegel undertook to account for the union of infinite and finite in Creation, and attempted to ignore the fact of opposition both in the causes and in the phenomena of the universe: it will also serve to show the obscure and perfectly dogmatic manner in which the subject is treated by these philosophers: " Being does not merely border upon nought, as if the former were here and the latter there, or one were to commence where the other ceases, — each, meanwhile, excluding the other; but no, they are both one and the same, *eodem loco et tempore.* I may speak at one time of being, at another of nought; but by this I do not mean that they are two, but only one and the same. Such, then, is the contradictory contradiction, as posited or existing, which was formerly held in logical works to be an absolute impossibility; namely, that being and non-being are the same. Finitude and Infinitude are, indeed, usually regarded as opposites which fully exclude each other, and enter our thoughts only by turns. But, with this supposition only, an endless chain of position or negation, or a reciprocal line of demarcation between the finite and infinite, would be brought before the intuitive faculty. We may easily convince ourselves, that in this way the true infinity has not been thought of; for we let it cease precisely at the point or moment of time where the finitude begins; so that the former is, as it were, on the other side, the latter on this: for, so soon now as one is bounded off and suppressed by the other, the infinity itself becomes a finitude. What is imperatively required is an identity of the two, like what occurred in the origination or becoming, as the synthesis of being and nought. Thus the true infinity, and, at the same time, the truth of existence, — consequently, of the being also that has been simultaneously resolved into that, — is, that the infinite be regarded as a constant transition into qualitative determinations, and that, indeed, from one to the other: so that it does not therewith pass out of itself, but coalesces in itself together with itself. It is itself this process of self-transformation: for just because it is throughout a determination or a finitude that distinguishes itself from itself, each one of these determinations, when effaced, is by this process the opposite or reverse of itself; *i.e.,* has become different to or is not that which it was before, or has become that which previously it was not, but which previously the other determination external to it was. This other determination was, however, the direct negation of what the first was, thus directly that whereunto the first has now become; so that one has become reciprocally the other: or, regarded *in toto,* — and this is true infinity or change, — the general origination is again present, but with this difference, — that it is a definite, qualitative origination, a determination of itself in itself; or, to use the language of Jacob Böhme, 'a qualification of itself.' In this way the second phase of being is perfected; and its result settles down as a quiescent precipitate, but only to begin the process at the same time anew. This result is the *being per se;* and this being *per se* is that infinite *relation to itself,* which, in the infinite, proved itself to be direct self-determination."

We see, then, that all these theories failed to realize Philosophy, or to realize any law through which the diversity and imperfection in natural existence could be accounted for, or its nature explained; for we cannot suppose that chaotic statements like this of Hegel, which seems to be an attempt to make comprehensible the inverted rationality of Böhme, will be regarded as throwing any light upon this question. All these theories — whatever may have been their point of departure, or whatever may have been their position with regard to subject or to object, to absolute or to phenomenal — ended in the same manner, by becoming immersed in the slough of a discordant objectivism and psychologism; in which the facts of the natural consciousness are assumed as the spiritual laws of the Reason, upon which alone Philosophy can be founded. Not only, therefore, was the conception of spiritual truth impossible, but no consistent natural form could be realized for philosophy; for the reason that the natural consciousness is, as Schlegel asserts, "filled with unmitigated discord and division." In commenting upon the theories of this school, M. Chalybäus says, "The immediate problem of philosophy, subsequent to Kant, was to overcome the subjectivism of his stand-point, and advance to an actual knowledge and willing of objective truth. Fichte, Schelling, and Hegel have grappled with this problem; and the latter has methodically carried it out. While, however, it might seem as though the whole matter was in this way completed, it is evident at once that the passage from subjectivity to objectivity has been effected at the cost of the subjectivity: and thus a third problem presents itself for solution; namely, the concrete union of the two sides." Of Hegel's philosophy, he says, "The same lot befalls Hegel's system as is encountered by every philosophy which, in order that it may justify with positive certainty the empirical element, adopts at once into its principle the empirical dualism of a subjective Ego and an objective world: such a procedure leads to nothing else than to moristic subjectivism; while this again is of such a kind, that, in order to maintain itself, it veers round into immediate objectivism, empiricism, and eudæmonism."

It is said of Hegel, that, just before his death, he became "anxious respecting the fate of his philosophy after his decease; because, among all his disciples, only one understood him, and that one misunderstood him." It is not probable that Hegel understood it himself, because a theory so chaotic is past comprehension: but that he should think his disciple understood him and misunderstood him at the same time, was quite consistent with his philosophy; because this is founded upon the equally absurd hypothesis, that Being and Nought are one and the same thing, and that all apparent opposites are really one. This extravagance, however, was not confined to Hegel, but was shared by all the followers of Kant. The universal opposition that exists in Nature, instead of suggesting to them the spiritual opposition of which it is the representative, only excited them to exercise their ingenuity in attempting to show how two apparently opposite things are really the same, and how the phenomenal and imperfect became realized through the manifestation of the absolute and the perfect.

It is difficult to define distinctly the theories of these philosophers, not only because of the discordant and dogmatical, and hence unphilosophical, character of these theories, but because of the great obscurity and uncouth phraseology in which they are expressed. We shall, however, be able to comment more specifically upon, and show more clearly the absurdity of, the idea upon which these theories rest, — which is the identity of Infinite and Finite, Absolute and Phenomenal, and Subjective and Objective, — as they have been translated into the more practical and scientific forms of the French mind, and have obtained a competent exponent in the celebrated M. Cousin, whose statements we will now consider. Following in the path of these German philosophers, he has attempted to show, by reasoning from appearances, or from the deceptive natural phenomena in which these opposites apparently become united as one, that there is really no opposition between them. He says, "Human reason — whatever may be the mode of its development, however it begin, whatever it consider, whether it stop at the observation of that nature which lies around us, or plunge into the depths of the interior world — conceives all things only under the dominion of two ideas. Reason neither does nor can develop itself but under these two conditions. This division is but a reflection, under a more limited aspect, of that at which I rest; and you may represent it to yourself under the formula of unity and multiplicity, of substance and phenomena, of absolute cause and relative causes, of the perfect and the imperfect, of the finite and the infinite. Each of these has two terms,—one of them necessary, absolute, one, substantial, causal, perfect, infinite; the other imperfect, phenomenal, relative, multiple, finite. A correct analysis identifies all these first terms together, and all these second terms together. It identifies immensity, eternity, absolute substance and absolute cause, perfection, and unity, on the one hand; and, on the other, the multiple, the phenomenal, the relative, the limited, the finite, the bounded, the imperfect. We ought not to say, as is said by two great rival schools, that the human understanding begins either with unity and the infinite, or with the finite and the contingent or multiple. In the order of the acquisition of our knowledge, the one supposes the other. You cannot separate variety from unity, nor unity from variety; neither substance from phenomenon, nor phenomenon from substance: one is anterior to the other, but does not exist without the other; they co-exist necessarily. But how do they co-exist? What is the mystery of this co-existence? Unity is anterior to multiplicity: how, then, can unity admit multiplicity? Human thought is unable to admit one without the other; but, in real order, we have seen that one is anterior to the other: how, then, is this movement from unity to variety made? Here is the fundamental vice of ancient and modern theories; here is the vice of the theory of Kant. It places unity on one side, and multiplicity on the other, and establishes such an opposition between them that all passage from one to the other seems impossible. A higher analysis resolves this contradiction.

"We have identified all the first terms together, and all the second terms together. And what are the first terms? They are immensity, eternity, infinity, unity. We shall hereafter see how the school of Elis—placing itself at this point of view exclusively, at the summit of immensity, eternity, being in itself, and infinite substance—defied all other schools to depart thence, and ever reach relative being, the finite, and multiplicity; and mocked at those who admitted the Existence of the world,—which is only, after all, a great multiplicity. The fundamental error of the school of Elis comes from this source: namely, that, in all the first terms which we have enumerated, it forgot one which equals all the rest in certainty, and is entitled to the same authority as all the rest; and that is the idea of Cause. Unity, or Substance, being an absolute cause, cannot but pass into act, cannot but develop itself. Take away the category of Causality from the other categories, the superficial observer discovers no omission of any importance; but you may now perceive its consequences. It destroys every possible conception of the creation of the world. But Unity in itself, as absolute cause, contains the power of becoming variety and difference.

"What is the road that leads from God to the Universe? It is — creation. And what is creation? What is it — to create? — not according to the hypothetical method, but the method we have followed, — that method which always borrows from human consciousness that which, by a higher induction, it afterwards applies to the Divine Essence. To create, is a thing which it is not difficult to conceive; for it is a thing which we do at every moment: in fact, we create whenever we perform a free action. We create a free action: we create it, I say; for we do not refer it to any principle superior to ourselves: we impute it to ourselves exclusively. It was not: it begins to be, by virtue of that causality which we possess. Thus to cause is to create; but with what? With nothing? Certainly not. Man does not draw forth from nothingness the act which he has not yet done, and is about to do: he draws it forth from the power which he has to do it, — from himself. Here is the type of creation. The divine creation is the same in its nature. God, if he is a Cause, can create; and, if he is an Absolute Cause, he cannot but create; and, in creating the universe, he does not draw it forth from Nothingness, but from Himself."

Although M. Cousin here claims to have abandoned a hypothetical method that is uncertain for a practical method that is sure, because he reasons from facts of the individual consciousness, he has evidently mistaken his own position, both as to its nature and its tendency. He, as well as they, reasons hypothetically; because he assumes that the consciousness of freedom in the individual is equivalent to a conception of the law of Causation, and draws from this hypothetical premise his conclusion: but while they reason legitimately, because they reason from cause to effect, he reasons absurdly, because he reverses the legitimate order of thought, and not only reasons from effect to cause, but substitutes a natural phenomenon for a spiritual law. Now, this is a double absurdity: first, because phenomena can be understood only through a knowledge of law; and, next, because the phenomena of the individual consciousness from which he reasons are natural and fictitious, and therefore completely opposite to spiritual law. M. Cousin is even inconsistent with himself; because, while assuming the false position that the act of self-determination in man, through which he creates from the power inherent in himself, is a type of Causality or of Creation, which is to reveal to us the nature of creation by God, he uses this, as a premise, to prove that God, from Himself, produces the opposite of Himself. The most unfortunate position assumed by this writer is that in which he attempts to obtain a conception of the modes of existence and operation in God by referring to the deceptive appearances presented by the natural consciousness of man. Being unable to obtain any conception of absolute cause, he thought that man infinitely extended might be made to answer the same purpose. He therefore, with the most amusing self-complacency, says, "I wonder at the folly of those, who, in order to understand God better, consider him, as they say, in his pure and absolute essence. I believe I have for ever removed the root of such an extravagance. We must leave vain dialectics, in order to arrive at a real living God. It is the consciousness of ourselves as beings, and at the same time limited beings, which raises us immediately to the conception of a being who is the principle of our being, and who is himself without limits. The being which we possess forces us to recur to a cause which possesses this same being to an infinite degree. Hence God will no longer be simply the infinite, abstract, and indeterminate being which reason and the heart cannot lay hold of: he will be a real and determinate being like ourselves; and psychology will conduct us, without hypothesis, to a theodicy at once sublime and within our reach, free at once from hypothesis and abstraction. Consenting to recognize God only in his signs visible to the eyes, intelligible to the mind, sensible to the soul, it is upon infallible evidences that we have elevated ourselves to God."

Such a theodicy as this is certainly "within our reach," but is as far from being "sublime" as it is from being true. Indeed, the idea, as here set forth in the pompous language of M. Cousin, is rather suggestive of the ridiculous; and is less deserving of serious consideration than the Hindoo theory, that each separate particle of material substance is God. It is somewhat remarkable, that one, who has shown so much sagacity and discrimination in describing and in criticising the philosophic theories of others, should have adopted the worst instead of the best features belonging to them; although this is a good illustration of the fact, that the more intellectual and logical the mind is, the more external and material, and the less rational and consistent, it is. True, that in reasoning, as he has, in a circle, by which process he has invested the discordant and deceptive phenomena of the natural consciousness with all the importance and authority of absolute truth, he has only followed the example of Descartes and his follower Malebranche; but by his greater impetuosity and directness, combined with what may be called a superficial simplicity, he has, though seemingly unconscious of the fact, produced in a much more palpable form than either of these philosophers, not only the worst kind of Pantheism, but the most objectionable kind of Anthropomorphism.

The development of Eclectical Philosophy from an intellectual point of view having been completed, and having come to an end in the labors of M. Cousin, who seems to have been peculiarly well adapted to exhibit all its defects, and thus to close its career, we find Scepticism again appearing, for the purpose of accomplishing the destruction of Philosophy, in the person of M. Comte, whose labors have been seconded by J. Stuart Mill and Henry Buckle in England. To show that this is a correct statement, we will refer to the "Biographical History of Philosophy," by George Henry Lewes, a late English writer, who has undertaken to write the *obituary* of Philosophy, and to introduce us to a substitute in Atheism, as illustrated in the works of Auguste Comte. The following is the statement of Mr. Lewes: "Philosophy is everywhere in Europe fallen into discredit. Once the pride and glory of the greatest intellects, and still forming an important element of liberal culture, its present decadence is attested no less by the complaints of its few followers than by the thronging ranks of its opponents. Few now believe in its large promises: still fewer devote to it that passionate patience which is devoted by thousands to Science. Every day the conviction gains strength, that Philosophy is condemned, by the very nature of its impulses, to wander for ever in one tortuous labyrinth, within whose circumscribed and winding spaces weary seekers are continually finding themselves in the trodden tracts of predecessors, who, they know, could find no exit. Philosophy has been ever in movement; but the movement has been circular. Precisely the same questions are agitated in Germany at the present moment that were agitated in ancient Greece, and with no more certain methods of solving them, with no nearer hopes of ultimate success. The difficulty is impossibility. No progress can be made, because no certainty is possible. To aspire to the knowledge of more than phenomena,—their resemblances, co-existences, and successions,—is to aspire to transcend the inexorable limits of human faculty." Having completed his History of Philosophy, which ends with a description of the development of Eclectical Philosophy, of which M. Cousin was the last exponent, he says, "Having dismissed Eclecticism as a method, we need not waste time in examining M. Cousin's various and constantly shifting opinions. It is enough that he himself has relinquished them. It is enough that France and Europe reject them. This final decision, then, fares no better than the doctrines which preceded it. Philosophy is still in search after its method and its basis; and, wearied out by so many fruitless efforts, it finally gives up the quest, and allows itself to be absorbed by Science. The dogmatic assertion of this position is to be found in Auguste Comte."

The position taken in this new advent of Scepticism, under the name of Positive Philosophy, is correctly stated by Mr. Lewes: It is, that knowledge is necessarily confined to "phenomena,—their resemblances, co-existences, and successions." The method by which these sceptical writers hope to arrive at truth is just the opposite of a true one. According to this method, we must commence our researches in the lowest and most external, which is the material, region of knowledge, and work upwards from this by the application of the law of similarity; the ground being taken by Mr. Buckle, that it is only by exhausting phenomena that we can obtain materials for the highest generalization, and thus make the nearest approach to the truth. "We need not waste time in examining" this new advent of Scepticism. It commences with the old atheistical method of positing a material, finite, natural multiplicity, instead of an infinite, spiritual unity, as a basis for truth; and must, of course, come to the old atheistical end. It is a foundation of sand upon which these builders of a new Babel are expecting to erect a tower that shall reach to heaven, but which must lead, instead, to the confusion of thought and the dissipation of all true knowledge; because the law of similarity, upon which they depend as a guide, is, as we shall demonstrate, an inversion of the law of true relationship, and is a destructive element even in the Fancy.

We have now shown that the natural development of Philosophy in three several spheres has been completed, by which it has been exhausted from a natural point of view; that it has been productive of nothing but Pantheism, Atheism, and Anthropomorphism; and that its results are now being repudiated and destroyed, and a materialistic and atheistic scepticism substituted in their place. The questions which naturally arise are, therefore, these: What are the causes which have produced these results, and prevented the realization of Philosophy in its legitimate form as Absolute Science? and what are the conditions which seem to be demanded, in order that Philosophy should be so realized? The first cause to be mentioned is, that the Consciousness must be fully developed in its natural form, from a natural point of view, before its spiritual form can be developed; and, therefore, that Philosophy must be developed as a natural production in three spheres, before it can be realized as a Universal Spiritual Science. The second cause of the results and of the failure here mentioned is, that universal spiritual cause has been conceived from a pagan, unitarian, and naturalistic point of view; and it has therefore been demanded that every thing should be realized from One Universal Cause or Substance: because, in consequence of this, Philosophy has failed to recognize the difference between absolute and phenomenal spheres of being, and so has failed to explain the difference between the nature of God and the nature of man from any rational point of view; and has also failed to recognize the antagonism of Infinite and Finite in the original causes of things, and so has failed to realize a ground for individual Freedom, and for Marriage as the universal law of Life. It has therefore failed to obtain any conception of those finite laws which constitute the natural life of Creation,—are antagonistic to those of the Infinite Life,—and the knowledge of which is necessary to the explanation of natural existence, by showing the origin and nature of diversity, imperfection, and evil. In consequence of this, Philosophy has been obliged to recognize Necessity as the universal law of Life, and to conceive the production of the phenomenal from the absolute,—therefore of Man from God; and also the production of the finite from the infinite,—therefore of diversity from unity, of evil from good, and of death from life; which is the greatest violation of rationality that can possibly be supposed. It has, therefore, not only failed to supply the legitimate demand of the Reason for a universal science, but has realized substitutes for this which are inversions of rationality and universality, and which fail to explain permanently and satisfactorily a single fact of the consciousness, or a single phenomenon of natural life. The most legitimate point of departure for Philosophy has been the point of Infinite Substance; but as the ideas of infinite unity and universality are perfectly antagonistic to those of diversity and partiality, which are the most palpably presented to the observation in the phenomena of natural existence, it has not been possible, in any legitimate way, to pass from this perfect Infinite Cause to the imperfect multiplicity of Creation; and this passage had, therefore, to be effected in an illegitimate and irrational manner, which could not stand the test of critical investigation: so that one system after another appeared only to be soon destroyed from its incapacity to account for the phenomena of life and the facts of the consciousness. As effects could not be referred to their real causes, because nothing but infinite perfection could be recognized in the universal absolute cause, phenomena had to be explained by referring them to inadequate, imaginary causes, or to psychological phenomena, which are the opposite of what they seem: so that Philosophy, instead of being the exponent of truth, became fanciful and fabulous, and antagonized to the representations of spiritual truth contained in the Scriptures and taught by the Church.

To this assertion, that philosophy has been confined to the recognition of one universal cause or substance as the origin of things, it may be objected that a diversity was recognized in the causes and in the ruling powers of the Universe by both the Eastern and the Grecian philosophers, and especially in the writings of the Hindoos, which are remarkable for their recognition of a multiplicity of gods: but this objection cannot be sustained, because this diversity was, in all cases, referred to one Supreme Cause; which was regarded as the only original, self-subsisting substance, from which all things were derived. It is a notorious as well as a remarkable fact, that although Naturalism, Paganism, and Unitarianism are always polytheistic, idolatrous, or worshippers of many gods, they are always, at the same time, pantheistic, or believers in only one principle or substance. This Infinite One, however, is a negative and not a productive principle, because it is not conceived as being suggested by any definite laws which could be applied in the explanation of phenomena, but only as an indefinite principle or substance which cannot be conceived or suggested by the mind, being with the Hindoos made synonymous with Annihilation. Instead of taking this One as a point of departure, therefore, Philosophy has always left this unknown something, or, this "unknown God," at the threshold of its speculations, and commenced its labors with a generalization of Phenomena under a spurious law of Unity, which is the natural law of Unity in Diversity. As every thing is one in its form, while it is discordant in its function or in its life, this natural law has been applied in the conception and classification of these phenomena from the point of unity, from the point of diversity, or from a point in which these seem to be combined, as occasion has required; and thus, from an external point of view, every thing has been individualized under the law of Tri-Unity, as internal, external, and medial, or as intellectual, affectional, and active: while, from an internal point of view, the manifestations of these have been separated as true and false, and as good and evil; the first being regarded as harmonious or homogeneous, as soul, body, and spirit; and the second being regarded, from an external point of view, as originating in the free self-determination of the individual, and from an internal point of view, as relatively and apparently opposite, but as really the same, either because they originate in the same Absolute Cause, or because it is perceived that they are governed by the same laws in their production. The most common philosophical position is, that "every thing is composed of opposites, so that the same is alike good and evil, living and dead, waking and sleeping, young and old;" as we have shown from the theories of the Eastern and Grecian philosophers, and also from the modern German school, who maintained that infinite and finite, unity and diversity, being and non-being, are one and the same; although this is a confounding of opposites that belongs more particularly to transcendental thought. In all its legitimate manifestations, Philosophy has recognized, on the one hand, a simple Infinite Substance as the cause of all things; and, on the other, a finite muliplicity in Creation, including a discordant dualistic opposition for which there was no means of accounting,—the idea of one perfect Infinite Cause being a direct contradiction to that of an imperfect Phenomenal World: and no ingenuity has been able to produce one from the other,—to account in any way for the existence of imperfection and evil upon any other ground than one that is fanciful and false,—or to account for and explain the phenomena of natural life, and the facts of the individual consciousness. Philosophy has always been obliged to recognize opposite ideas and laws which exclude each other, but which must be regarded as conditions of Existence; and to confess that the nature of these, and the manner in which they combine in production, cannot be discovered, although this discovery is essential to the very existence of Philosophy.

The question, therefore, is not, Why has not Philosophy before been realized as Absolute Science? The question now is, Have all the natural experiences of Philosophy been realized? and has the time therefore arrived when spiritual experiences have become possible for it? We think that those who have followed us in this description of the development of Philosophy in three entire spheres will confess that all natural expedients seem to have been completely exhausted, and that they have ended in a despair of the truth from any scientific point of view, except that of material science; and that, as a consequence of this failure, there is a growing disposition to fall back upon religious sentimentalism, as the only refuge from Scepticism and Atheism. Every thing, therefore, points to the present as the time when, if ever, we are to look for the construction of Philosophy upon an entirely new basis, and with entirely new results; and it is such a construction that we are now to commence. In order that we should be able to realize Philosophy upon a spiritual instead of a natural basis, or as a system of universal spiritual truth, we must, of course, first proceed to realize a conception, and obtain a statement, of the Universal Laws of Being, including the laws in which God exists, and through which he manifests himself; positing these as the ground for Philosophy, or as the foundation upon which its whole superstructure must rest. What, then, are these Universal Laws of Being? This question will be answered, and these laws will be stated, at the commencement of this work, as the foundation for a Universal system of Truth, which we denominate Philosophy as Absolute Science.

THE

UNIVERSAL LAWS OF BEING,

AND

THEIR OPERATION IN THE REALIZATION OF GOD AS A TRI-PERSONALITY

OF

HOLY GHOST, — FATHER, — SON,

IN THE RELATION OF

SPIRIT, — SOUL, — BODY.

"THERE ARE THREE THAT BEAR RECORD IN HEAVEN, — THE FATHER, THE WORD, AND THE HOLY GHOST: AND THESE THREE ARE ONE." — 1 John v. 7.

THE
UNIVERSAL LAWS OF BEING.

In the introduction to this work, and in the history of philosophical development which we have sketched as a preparation for the statement of Philosophy as Absolute Science, we have shown, that according to the nature of things, and also according to the most extensive philosophical recognitions, Philosophy must commence with conceptions of Absolute and Phenomenal Existence, and the relationship that exists between them; and we have also shown that the reason why no adequate conception of these has been obtained, and therefore why Philosophy has not been realized in the form of Absolute Science, is, that these primary facts have been conceived from a natural, unitarian, and pantheistic point of view, from which not a single phenomenon could be permanently and satisfactorily explained: so that the history of philosophy presents nothing but a succession of partial, contradictory, and discordant natural systems, which have been destructive to each other, and contain the elements of their own destruction. It must therefore be evident, that, to obtain an adequate foundation for Truth, we must realize a conception of the Universal Laws of Being which shall explain both Absolute and Phenomenal Existence; because we cannot conceive of any other rational foundation upon which either a conception of Being can be realized, or the phenomena of Creation explained. As a point of departure, or as the first step towards the realization of a conception of the Universal Laws which must constitute the ground of all Existence, we posit—

INFINITE LAW as a universal tri-personal sphere of INDEFINITE LIFE, subsisting Three in One as LIFE ITSELF. This tri-personal form of the Infinite we conceive to be individualized in three spheres, related as Spirit, Soul, and Body:—

ABSOLUTE LIFE, or the INFINITE LAWS OF SPIRIT.
ABSOLUTE SUBSTANCE, or the INFINITE LAWS OF SUBSTANCE.
PHENOMENAL SUBSTANCE, or the INFINITE LAWS OF MATTER.

This Infinite Law we conceive to be a threefold principle, constituted by the Laws of UNITY, UNIVERSALITY, and MARRIAGE, realized as ONE in the relation of Soul, Body, and Spirit, which are incarnated in an Absolute Sphere of Being, as WISDOM, LOVE, and POWER; and in a Phenomenal Sphere of Being, as TRUTH, GOOD, and BEAUTY. We thus conceive Infinite Life to subsist in three spheres, related as *Spirit*, *Soul*, and *Body*; each sphere including three laws, — an Intellective, an Affective, and an Active Principle, — combined and operating as One, in the relation of Internal, External, and Medial, as *Soul*, *Body*, and *Spirit*; by which these relationships are established as the normal and necessary condition of all Life. This INFINITE CAUSE we now posit as the First Person in the Godhead, who is the Holy Ghost, or the SPIRIT OF DEITY.

This Infinite Law is here stated as Indefinite, because it is conceivable only as Life without Form, and is therefore separated from Existence, which it is necessary to conceive as being constituted by forms of Definite Being; it not being possible to conceive Infinite Spiritual Cause except as an indefinite principle of Life. It will be seen that Existence cannot be conceived as resulting from the operation of these laws alone, because it must be supposed to include the operation of laws which are completely opposite to the Infinite Laws, not only as these have here been conceived, but as they have been recognized in all rational conceptions of the Infinite, as we have shown by the history of Philosophy; it being this fact that has made it impossible to realize any rational conception of Creation from a purely Infinite Principle or Substance. If we should conceive the Infinite to be the only Universal Law, we should exclude the possibility of conceiving any definite existence, either absolute or phenomenal; because we cannot, any more than could the Eleatic philosophers, pass from this Infinite Unity to a Finite Multiplicity: and this is necessary, not only to the conception of a phenomenal world, but also to the conception of Absolute Existence, or of a Personal God as Absolute Creating Cause. Existence is a definite Idea including divisibility, multiplicity, and diversity, and therefore demands a separating as well as a unifying and individualizing law; and must originally include the ideas of imperfection and evil, because these are necessarily introduced into it by this separating principle: but not one of these can be referred to the Infinite Life; and, if they do not subsist in it, they cannot proceed from it. Now, if Existence cannot be accounted for, even the existence of God as a self-conscious Personality, or as Absolute Creating Cause, because the ideas of diversity, partiality, and separation cannot be included in any conception of the Infinite, much less can Natural Life be accounted for; because we here find Falsehood, Hate, Imperfection, Death, manifested through propensities for Evil and for Destruction; and these cannot be referred to the Infinite Life as their source, but must be referred to some spiritual, self-subsisting cause opposite to the Infinite. Even if we should, like these Eleatic philosophers, refuse to recognize the existence of an external world, we should not avoid the necessity of recognizing some other than an Infinite Cause; not only because Existence cannot be accounted for upon this ground alone, but because the natural ideas here mentioned would still be facts of consciousness, which demand to be accounted for by the conception of some spiritual cause with which they correspond. It may therefore be seen, that in order to account for either absolute or phenomenal existence, or for any thing outside of the Infinite Life, — which cannot be conceived as including Existence or any form of Definite Being, — a Sphere of Universal Law opposite to the Infinite, and which we therefore call Finite, must be posited as a spiritual, self-subsisting Cause. Should we refuse to do this, and insist upon recognizing only One Universal Sphere of Being, we should not succeed in maintaining even this infinite ground, but should, like Spinoza, be obliged by a rational necessity virtually to deny its existence, by confounding or identifying this Infinite Cause with the phenomena of the Material Universe; so that natural phenomena, having their foundation in sensible experiences, would take the place of the spiritual causes which should be conceived as producing them, and we should be able to realize nothing but Materialism and Atheism. Now, in positing a second Universal Spiritual Cause, there is only one thing that we can do, and that is to conceive laws and substances opposite to those which constitute the Infinite, and therefore as being inversions of them; because a spiritual, self-subsisting cause must necessarily be conceived as universal; and we cannot, therefore, pass out of the limits of the Infinite without being obliged to posit another spiritual principle, also universal, which is a complete inversion of, and therefore a complete opposite to, the Infinite. We therefore posit —

FINITE LAW as a universal tri-personal sphere of INDEFINITE DEATH, subsisting Three in One as DEATH ITSELF, individualized in three spheres related as Spirit, Soul, and Body:—

ABSOLUTE DEATH, or the FINITE LAWS OF SPIRIT.
ABSOLUTE SUBSTANCE, or the FINITE LAWS OF SUBSTANCE.
PHENOMENAL SUBSTANCE, or the FINITE LAWS OF MATTER.

This Finite Law we conceive to be a threefold principle, constituted by the laws of DIVERSITY, PARTIALITY, and SEPARATION, realized as CHAOS in the relation of Soul, Body, and Spirit, which are incarnated in an Absolute Sphere of Being, as GUILE, HATE, and DESTRUCTION; and in a Phenomenal Sphere, as FALSEHOOD, EVIL, and DEFORMITY. We thus conceive Finite Law to subsist in three spheres, related as *Spirit, Soul,* and *Body;* each sphere including three Laws,—an intellective, an affective, and an active principle,—combined and operating as Chaos, in the relation of internal, external, and medial, as *Soul, Body,* and *Spirit;* by which these relationships are established as the normal and necessary condition of all Death.

The absolute necessity for this conception of a Finite Sphere opposite to the Infinite is so evident, and this sphere is so clearly a demand of the Reason, that we do not see how its subsistence, as a primary cause of Existence, can be disputed. Having realized a conception of Infinite Life as constituted by the laws of Unity, Universality, and Marriage, in which these three make One,— in view of Absolute Existence, and of a Phenomenal World, the conclusion inevitably follows, that as the condition of this Existence and of this Creation, and of realizing in the mind the conception of a Personal God as a Creating Cause, a Universal Sphere in every thing opposite to the Infinite, but including the capacity for becoming receptive and productive from the Infinite, must be recognized, before any thing outside of the Infinite Indefinite Life can rationally be conceived. Universal, indefinite laws and substances opposite to those constituting the Infinite must be recognized before Existence or Definite Being can be conceived, either in an absolute or in a phenomenal sphere. This is particularly evident with regard to the phenomenal world, because nothing can here be conceived that does not include both unity and diversity, and this law of diversity has always been excluded from the conception of Infinite Life; and because Creation presents to us a collection of phenomena produced by the combination of vital and destructive principles, the latter of which cannot be referred to the Infinite, because they are opposite to any rational conception of this principle, and correspond with the Finite Principle as here stated. To conceive Creation from the Infinite alone, we should have to suppose that the Infinite creates from itself the Opposite of itself; and although the ancient philosophers, in conceiving the origin of things from a strictly ontological and at the same time natural and unitarian point of view, were obliged to take this ground, it is one of the most irrational positions that can possibly be conceived, the tendency of which is to unsettle all our ideas of cause and effect, and also all our ideas of legitimate relationship. We are, therefore, fully justified in asserting that an opposite to the Infinite must be recognized before the first step can be taken in any legitimate conception of Definite Absolute Being as a Creating Cause, or in the explanation of the origin and nature of Creation or of a Phenomenal World. Some have supposed that the recognition of two universal spiritual causes would be the recognition of two Infinites, which is not admissible. But this arises in the mistake of conceiving the Infinite as the only universal, spiritual principle and substance, which excludes the possibility of recognizing any thing outside of this; a pantheistic idea which has been so extensively entertained as to prevent the realization of Philosophy in a rational form. We here recognize both the Infinite and the Finite as Universal Spiritual Principles and Causes: but we do not in this state a contradiction, because they constitute opposite spheres of subsistence which exclude each other, but the union of which is demanded as the condition of Existence; a universality that is shown in the fact, that the mind has never been able to conceive any definite form of being in which both infinite and finite laws, as they have here been stated, are not combined as the condition of its existence.

Having now shown that opposite self-subsisting, indefinite principles, substances, and causes must be recognized as constituting the opposite poles of Being, and having obtained a conception of these opposite Spiritual Causes, the question immediately arises, How can these opposite universal spheres, which exclude each other, and neither of which can be conscious of the other, become consciously united, and made to co-operate in production? Now, there is obviously but one way in which these things can be effected; and this is, that the opposite Laws included in these Infinite and Finite Principles should be combined in One

Individual, or in One Consciousness, so that the destructive may be made subject to the vital for the purpose of production, or for the incarnation of Life in Definite Forms; and it is evident that this can be effected only through an Individual begotten by the Infinite and born out of the Finite, because it is only in this way that any conscious communication between these opposite universal, spiritual causes can be effected, or that any definite consciousness can be realized in God. In stating this possibility, we do not recognize any immediate attraction between Infinite and Finite Laws, but have distinctly recognized the opposite fact, — that, being opposite, they exclude each other. The attraction by which these laws are brought together and united in production arises in the fact, that neither the Infinite nor the Finite Principle can obtain any definite manifestation without the aid of the other; and this creates an external attraction between them, — an attraction that is communicated through the substances through which Indefinite Absolute Spirit becomes manifested. We therefore recognize this external attraction, and also a capacity in the Finite for becoming receptive and productive from the Infinite; and that the necessary consequence resulting from this capacity is the realization of a Definite Absolute Individual, in whom these opposite Laws, incarnated and represented in definite forms, are brought together, and the possibility of their union is realized; an absolute process that is represented in all the works of Creation, where death is made to be productive from life, — evil from good, — and the natural, which is one with death and with evil, is made to be productive from the spiritual, not by its own development, but by a spiritual conception and birth. In stating the consequences which result from this birth from the Finite, we will first state our conception of the manner in which Absolute Life becomes incarnated and individualized as Definite Absolute Being, and as Absolute Creating Cause, in a tri-personality of Spirit, Soul, and Body. After this, we will state our conception of the manner in which infinite and finite phenomenal laws are combined by God in the production of the Material Universe, which in its natural condition represents, and in its spiritual condition becomes the medium for the phenomenal manifestation of, Absolute Causes.

The birth which resulted from this action of the Infinite upon the Finite — although containing that which, when fully developed, was to realize a perfect individualization of Absolute Being, and the Incarnation of the Infinite Life as Absolute

Creating Cause — could not have been realized at first in a perfect, spiritual, but only in an imperfect, natural condition, in which it could not have been consciously at-one either with the Infinite or with the Finite. The Individual so produced must have been constituted a dualistic substance, and have contained definite incarnations of Infinite and Finite; and therefore, although, as the condition of life and of consciousness, he must have included a tri-personal form of spirit, soul, and body, all these elements must have been constituted in dualistic forms as "life against death, and good against evil." Infinite and Finite laws could not have been united or made one in his substance and in his form, but only combined and manifested in a representative manner through a definite form of the Infinite, which must unconsciously have constituted the vital principle in him. This individual must, therefore, have realized a natural condition of Absolute Existence, in which he could not have been susceptible of an infinite, but only of a finite life, because the condition here described corresponds with finite, and not with infinite law; and by a natural condition we mean a discordant, dualistic, unreal condition, in which opposite absolute principles, of which the individual is unconscious, are represented by him, while his life corresponds with the Finite.

That this is the form and the condition in which every individual, both absolute and phenomenal, must necessarily commence his existence, may thus be shown: Existence, or definite consciousness, cannot commence as spiritual and real, because a spiritual condition is one and universal, and because spiritual life must be realized through the Marriage of Opposites in the Consciousness in view of the presentation of opposite Absolute Laws, and the choice, by the individual, of the Infinite as his life; and before these laws can be presented to his consciousness, in order that this choice may be made and this marriage consummated, they must be incarnated in definite forms. But, as no spiritual substance or form can be realized in the individual except through the spiritual marriage of opposites in him, this incarnation must be first realized as an unreal, representative appearance, governed by finite laws, in natural forms of consciousness and of life representing an experience of opposite spiritual laws and manifestations; which must precede a realization of these in the consciousness, and constitute a suggestive form in the conception and real experience of and union with Spiritual Law. These opposite natural forms must be developed successively and separately, as representing opposite states of existence, because these laws exclude each other, and cannot, therefore, be consciously combined in any consistent form; and because this natural condition is not a state of Being, but a state of Becoming, in which all phenomena must be realized under the finite laws of diversity and partiality, until all the forms of the individual have been successively developed from vital and from destructive points of view, as the representatives of the infinite upon the one hand, and of the finite upon the other, before he can be prepared for a birth into the spiritual, and for the realization of a permanent spiritual form. This being the mode in which Existence is necessarily realized, this Absolute Individual must have passed through a complete natural development of all the forms of his constitution as a preparation for his birth into a spiritual and real condition, in which he could become conscious of the Infinite Spirit, and become at-one with it by becoming a form for its definite manifestation; because the only way in which this Individual could become spiritual and real, and at the same time vital, was by becoming a conscious incarnation simply of the Infinite Life in a Divine Form, calculated for the definite manifestation of this life, and realized through the unification of infinite and finite laws with the subjection of the finite to the infinite. This could be effected only in the regeneration, by the operation of the Infinite, of the dualistic forms, representing the Infinite upon the one hand and the Finite upon the other, into forms harmonious with the Infinite Life; and, in order that this should be possible, it was necessary that Infinite Law should be offered to, accepted by, and substituted in this Individual, as his Life, instead of the Finite Law, which, in his dual natural condition, must unconsciously have constituted his life. We are, therefore, led to the following conception of the manner in which an Internal Sphere of Absolute Existence, or of Definite Absolute Being, became realized in God.

After the full natural development of all the forms of Absolute Existence had been completed in this Individual who constitutes the internal sphere of Absolute Being, he passed from a natural into a spiritual condition of consciousness, including a self-conscious personal experience of opposite universal and individual affinities which are receptive and productive powers, — the first corresponding with the laws of the Infinite, and the second with the laws of the Finite, with which they desire to become one, and from which they desire to become productive; these opposite

THE DIVINE SPHERE IN GOD.

laws being at the same time presented to his consciousness, that he might choose whether the Infinite or the Finite should become his Law, his Life, and the regenerator of his natural dualistic constitution, into one corresponding with itself as a medium for definite absolute manifestation. Now, as the Infinite — with which the universal affinity in this individual corresponds — is constituted by the laws of unity, universality, and marriage, united as one and constituting a sphere of Absolute Production, as Life Itself, while the Finite — with which the individual affinity corresponds — is constituted by the opposite laws of diversity, partiality, and separation, discordantly combined and constituting a sphere of Absolute Destruction, as Death Itself, — when these were presented to his consciousness, a conflict must immediately have taken place between these affinities, each demanding the destruction of the other; because two such loves or affinities could not be entertained, and therefore could not remain together in this individual, a moment, without this demand being made, any more than he could entertain both love and hate for the same object at the same time. This individual must, on the one hand, have desired the crucifixion of his individual affinity, — which was his personal life, — that he might become productive from the Infinite for universal, and not for personal ends, in the union of infinite and finite laws with the subjection of the finite to the infinite; while, upon the other, he must have desired the crucifixion of his universal, and the assertion of his individual affinity, that he might become productive from the Finite for personal, and not for universal ends, in the union of infinite and finite laws with the subjection of the infinite to the finite. Through the choice by this individual of Infinite Law as his Life, his affinity for finite law — this being the absolute love of Self, which would reject the Infinite Wisdom, expel the Infinite Love, and resist the Infinite Production — was crucified and born anew in his consciousness by the operation of Infinite Productiveness, — Marriage (or the union of opposites as one, with the subjection of the finite to the infinite, and of the individual to the universal, for the sake of an Infinite manifestation) was realized in him by the operation of Infinite Power, — the regeneration of his natural form into a medium for the definite manifestation of the Infinite Life was effected; and a DIVINE SPHERE OF LIFE, or a Divine Personality, as the internal sphere of Definite Absolute Being, was realized in God.

We have thus arrived at that point, in our investigation of

absolute causes, where originate the Christian ideas of Worship, Self-Renunciation, Sacrifice, Atonement, and Regeneration, through which is realized the union of opposites through voluntary sacrifice, and where we are made acquainted with the means through which the marriage or at-one-ment of man with God is effected. These means are — the realization by the soul of a spiritual consciousness, which includes a self-conscious personal experience of universal and individual spiritual affinities corresponding with Absolute Truth and Absolute Falsehood; this being accompanied by the presentation of these to the consciousness as the absolute laws, one of which must govern and constitute the life of the individual, and between which a choice must at once be made, — the choice of and submission to God, or to Absolute Truth, by which He becomes the only object of love, — the expulsion from the Consciousness of Absolute Falsehood, and the crucifixion and regeneration of the individual spiritual affinity corresponding with it, — and the regeneration of the natural form of the soul into a spiritual form suitable as a medium for the manifestation of Absolute Life in a phenomenal sphere of existence in the most external and diversified manner. We therefore ask particular attention to the statement of Absolute Phenomena that has here been made, because these are the great original facts, realized in an absolute sphere, of which Christianity is the phenomenal illustration, and furnish types of the universal laws which must govern the realization of spiritual life and salvation from the operation of finite law, which is spiritual death.

By reasoning from the ground of Infinite Life, we have now realized a conception of the internal sphere of Existence, as a Divine Sphere of Absolute Being constituting the second person in the Godhead as the Soul of Deity, and corresponding with the Father as recognized by the Church. It will be seen, however, that we have not yet realized Existence as Absolute Life and as Creating Cause, because, according to our original hypothesis, a Tri-personal form — as spirit, soul, and body — is the normal and necessary condition of life; and we have, as yet, only realized a conception of the spirit and soul of Deity. According to the terms of our original hypothesis, which is illustrated and sustained by the combined phenomena of the Universe, an external sphere as the Body of Deity is demanded as the condition of complete Individuality in God. This is the total amount of production that is possible in this Absolute Sphere of Being, and corresponds with the legitimate representation of this sphere contained in the

Scriptures, and in the Church which distinctly recognizes God the Father, God the Son as the only-begotten of the Father, and God the Holy Ghost who proceeds from the Father and the Son. And here we would remark, that, although we are obliged to describe a succession of events in forming our conception of tri-personality in God, — it being the process by which this tri-personality is realized that gives to this conception all its vitality, and its competency as a ground for Absolute Science, — it is not necessary that we should conceive them as happening in time, but only as the order of realization in God, which is to be regarded as an eternal or perpetual generative process. It is in this way that the ancient philosophers always regarded such descriptions; and even the world was not conceived by them as having been created in time, but as being "ingenerate or unmade." * Thus Proclus, in speaking of the generation of the gods, says, "We call it the generation of the gods; meaning thereby not any temporary production of them, but their ineffable procession from a superior first cause."

This external sphere of Absolute Existence must have been developed in a natural condition, or as a discordant dual representative of infinite and finite principles, as a preparation for the realization of a Spiritual Individuality, or the Son in God, in the same way that the internal sphere of Absolute Existence was developed as a preparation for the realization of a Divine Individuality, or the Father; and this individual must have been realized as a Sphere of Spiritual Life, or as a spiritual tri-unity of Wisdom, Love, and Power, as soul, body, and spirit, and have been made one with the Father and with the Infinite Life, by realizing the same kind of experiences, and therefore the same sacrifice of Individual Life and regeneration of the natural form, that was realized in the Father as the condition of Divine Life and union with the Infinite; because we have already shown that it is only through crucifixion, or self-renunciation, that Spiritual Life, or at-one-ment with the Infinite, can be realized. The Son is therefore spoken of in the Scriptures as "the Lamb slain from the foundation of the world;" for this language is not to be understood in a prospective sense, or as having reference to his subsequent incarnation and crucifixion, as it has been common to do; because it is obviously a literal statement that has reference to the formation of tri-personality in God, which alone made "the

---

* Aristotle.

foundation of the world" possible. It is therefore more definitely stated in the following words of St. Paul: "For it pleased the Father that in him should all fulness dwell; and, having made peace through the blood of his cross, by him to reconcile all things unto himself; by Him, I say, whether they be things in earth, or things in heaven." For although the reconciliation to God of "the things in earth" here relates to the subsequent formation of a divine-human sphere of life by the incarnation of the Son, which was consummated by a sacrifice of which his visible crucifixion was only a symbol or type, the reconciliation to God of the "things in heaven" by the blood of his cross evidently relates to the formation of that heavenly sphere which attended the consummation of tri-personality in God. When Jesus prayed to the Father, therefore, that he would glorify his name, "then came there a voice from heaven, saying, I have both glorified it, and will glorify it again." That these words relate, first, to a past glorification consequent upon the reconciliation to the Father of the things in heaven by the sacrifice of "the Lamb of God," and next to a promised glorification consequent upon the reconciliation to Him of "the things in earth" by the sacrifice of "the Son of Man," may be known, because Jesus afterwards says, "And now, O Father, glorify thou me with thine own self, with the glory which I had with thee before the world was."

That the account here given of the Son corresponds with the teaching of the Scriptures, may also be seen from the following words of St. Paul: "God, who at sundry times and in divers manners spake in times past unto the fathers by the prophets, hath in these last days spoken unto us by his Son, whom he hath appointed heir of all things; by whom also he made the worlds; who, being the brightness of his glory and the express image of his person, and upholding all things by the word of his power, when he had by himself purged our sins, sat down on the right hand of the Majesty on High; being made so much better than the angels, as he hath by inheritance obtained a more excellent name than they. For unto which of the angels said he at any time, Thou art my Son, this day have I begotten thee? Of the angels he saith, who maketh his angels spirits, and his ministers a flame of fire. But unto the Son he saith, Thy throne, O God, is for ever and ever: a sceptre of righteousness is the sceptre of thy kingdom."

We have now demonstrated the fact of tri-personality in God, by a legitimate course of reasoning from the conception of the Infinite as a Universal Sphere of Indefinite Life; all the conclusions to which we have here arrived being legitimate deductions from this single premise. It is true that this conception could not have been realized separate from the consciousness of an external world, because all production in the mind is from the union of opposites, as a representative of the absolute production here conceived; and Thought, which is a conception of Truth, results from the union of Inspiration and Sensation, which are the intuition of Law and the perception of Phenomena. It is in view of Existence as an absolute fact, and also of the phenomena of Creation as representative natural facts, combined with the intuition of Spiritual Law, that we arrive at the conception of Infinite Life; and it is in view of these that a second Universal Cause, which is a complete inversion of Infinite Life, is demanded. Tri-Personality, as here conceived, is not a trinity of *elements*, related as intellective, affective, and active, but is a trinity of *persons*, each one of which includes such a threefold form, and constitutes a separate Individuality and a different consciousness; and these three Persons constitute three several Spheres of Absolute Being, which are One in Essence, in the relation of spirit, soul, and body. The Father, as the Soul of Deity, therefore becomes conscious through a Divine Sphere of a definite form of the Infinite Life, which is the Spirit of Deity; while the Son, as the Body of Deity, becomes conscious through a Spiritual Sphere, which is related to the Divine as external to internal, of a more external form of the Infinite Life; it being therefore written, "In him dwelleth all the fulness of the Godhead Bodily:" so that, although distinctly Three, they are at the same time inseparably One. Neither is this Tri-Personality conceived as absorbing the Finite, but as being outside of and opposite to it; it being necessary that this universal sphere of Indefinite Death should forever remain as a means of realizing, through perpetual generation, a definite consciousness in God, — as the source of finite material in a perpetual Creation, — and as the cause and support of an Infernal Sphere of Existence opposite and antagonistic to God.

It will readily be seen, that from the point of view here established, instead of finding it difficult to conceive three distinct persons as constituting One God, we cannot rationally conceive God except as including Three Persons, because we see that all these three are necessary to constitute a definite individualization of Absolute Life as Creating Cause; an individualization of which Man is made the image or representative. As these three persons bear to each other the relation of spirit, soul, and body, a perfect unity or substantial individuality in God is conceived; while the character of each of these persons, their relationship to each other, and the kind of intercourse that must take place between them, are made perfectly comprehensible. They are made thus comprehensible because they correspond with the three spheres of the Universe, of which we can obtain a definite conception, — with the three spheres of the Mind, where the higher spheres become incarnated in, and definitely expressed and manifested through, the lower, — and with the three spheres of Universal Law, of which we may observe in Creation the greatest variety of illustrations. Each one of these spheres may be seen to possess an individuality and a consciousness that is peculiarly its own, while they are at the same time calculated to act together as one, in the relation of spirit, soul, and body; thus constituting a perfect representative of the three descending spheres of life which have here been described as constituting the tri-personal form in which God exists, and of which Man is the image. The Universal Science here constructed offers a familiar illustration of tri-personality in God; because its Ontological, Theological, and Psychological Systems, although belonging to three distinctly different spheres of thought, are here brought under the same governing laws, and realized as One Science in a perfect individuality of spirit, soul, and body. Having demonstrated the existence of God as a Tri-Personality, or his existence in three Spheres of Absolute Being made one, as spirit, soul, and body; and having shown the manner in which this tri-personality becomes realized, — this being the great fact which communicates to this conception all its vitality, and gives to us the principal foundation both for Philosophy and for Theology, — the next step pointed out to us is, that we should realize a conception of the laws of Phenomenal Being, and of the nature of the substances which furnish to God the Material for Creation, and describe the character of this creation; while the next is, that we draw from these conceptions of absolute and phenomenal being the Universal Laws which we apply in the construction of Philosophy as Absolute Science, and in the explanation of all the phenomena of natural and of spiritual life.

THE
LAWS OF PHENOMENAL BEING,

AND

THE NATURE OF PHENOMENAL SUBSTANCE

WHICH

FURNISHES TO GOD

THE MATERIAL FOR CREATION.

THE

LAWS OF PHENOMENAL BEING.

In our statement of God as a Tri-Personality, we have shown, that Infinite and Finite eternally subsist as opposite Universal Spheres of Indefinite Being, related as Male and Female, which together constitute the possibility of Existence, or of Definite Being, both Absolute and Phenomenal;—that the union of these resulted in a birth from the Finite of an Individual combining in a dualistic form definite incarnations and representations of Absolute Principles or Laws, and realizing a definite condition of Absolute Substance, which, after the sacrifice in this Individual of his finite life, became by its regeneration a Divine Substance, through which He became manifested as the Divine Principle of Life, which we call The Father, or the Soul of God;—that this incarnation necessitated the production from this Divine Principle of a more external Individual, for the reason that every thing must exist in a tri-personal form as spirit, soul, and body; in consequence of which the Son of God was realized as "the only-begotten of the Father," and a still more external condition of Absolute Substance was also realized, which, after the sacrifice of finite life in the Son, became by its regeneration a Spiritual Substance, through which He became manifested as the Spiritual Principle of Life, or as the Body of God;—and that by these processes an individualization of Absolute Life and Absolute Substance was realized as spirit, soul, and body, constituting Absolute Creating Cause. In doing this, we not only obtain a conception of God as a Tri-Personality of Holy Ghost, Father, and Son, as the Spirit, the Soul, and the Body of God, but also obtain a conception of the relationship between the Material Universe and God as its Creator, Preserver, and Governor; because, in the conception of this birth through the union of Infinite and Finite as the Universal Ground of things, we not only obtain an individualization of the Absolute as Creating Cause, but bring the material for creation within the limits of His Consciousness; this material being constituted by opposite indefinite phenomenal substances, or material laws, which by being combined in definite forms furnish mediums through which the Absolute may be represented in a natural, and manifested in a spiritual sphere; a conception of the capacity of this material being realized by each of these Absolute Persons, in correspondence with his sphere of life; so that a conception of Creation was realized by the Father as a Divine Idea, and by the Son as a threefold universal sphere of Definite Phenomenal Being; and, as Conception and Creation are with God the same, the realization of God as a tri-personal Creating Cause was necessarily attended by the realization of Creation as a Phenomenal Effect.

Two separate self-subsisting spheres of substance, which we designate Absolute and Phenomenal,—the first being adapted to the incarnation or definite realization of Absolute Causes, and the second being adapted to the representation and manifestation of these in the most external and diversified manner through a sphere of Definite Phenomenal Being,—were included in our posit of Infinite and Finite as the Universal Ground of Things; not only because without this recognition of phenomenal substance, and of its subsistence in this relation to Absolute Cause, the Existence of God would be incomplete, and the external manifestation and representation of His Infinite Perfections would be impossible, but because it is the only condition upon which the creation of a Material Universe, with Man as its head, can rationally be conceived: and, as a proof of this, we find that the failure to obtain this conception has compelled the rational mind to regard Creation as absolutely existing in God, or to regard the phenomena of the Universe as modes of manifestation in God as the Infinite Principle of Life; a pantheistic conception that is as inconsistent with true rationality as it is destructive to Christianity. These indefinite phenomenal substances, or these material laws, are not conceived as dead matter, but as self-subsisting substances and spiritual causes, susceptible of combination by the Creative Power in a definite natural substance in forms unconsciously representing Absolute Causes, and also susceptible of union in a spiritual substance in forms consciously manifesting in a phenomenal manner these Absolute Causes in the most external and diversified forms of Spiritual Life and of Spiritual Death: and, as a perfect correspondence exists between absolute and phenomenal substances in each sphere, we are able to use the same terms to designate the laws of absolute and the laws of phenomenal indefinite substance, although it will be necessary that we guard against confounding phenomenal with absolute conditions when these terms are used. It will, therefore, be understood that life is not communicated to these substances by an absolute power, because in this case all their manifestations would be absolute; but that a material life is inherent in them, and manifestations are therefore spontaneously produced upon their being combined in definite forms by an absolute power, the nature of these manifestations being dependent upon the particular form which they are made to take.

When God conceived or created the Universe, therefore, he created it from these indefinite material substances; and he creates it in his own image, that it may constitute a medium through which he can be represented and manifested in the most ultimate forms and in the most diversified manner. He therefore creates this Universe to become first Natural, and afterwards Spiritual: first, because nothing can become spiritual without first being developed as a natural dualistic representative form that is opposite to God in its life; next, because this is the order in which Definite Absolute Existence, or Tri-Personality in God, became realized; and, finally, because it would not otherwise be an image of Him, or constitute a medium through which He could manifest Himself in the most external and diversified manner, which must evidently have been the object contemplated by God in its creation. Man, as the head of this Material Universe, must therefore have been created with a capacity for obtaining reality for his life by the realization of a consciousness absolute in its form, which should represent and constitute a medium for the manifestation of One Absolute Principle, instead of being a representative of two which are opposite, which is the fact with regard to all natural existence; that is, he must have been created capable of realizing the most external forms and functions of spiritual existence, and thus of becoming a medium for the representation and manifestation either of Absolute Life or of Absolute Death. We may therefore state the fact of Creation in the following manner: By the combination of indefinite infinite and finite phenomenal substances by the Divine Activity, a definite condition of Matter was realized outside of the Personality of God, and therefore existing in a Phenomenal instead of an Absolute region, as an external medium through which God could become represented and manifested in the most ultimate or in the most external and diversified manner, in three spheres, which we call Spiritual, Ethereal, and Material, related as spirit, soul, and body; Human Substance constituting the spiritual region of definite phenomenal substance, and thus containing a threefold essence which is spiritual, ethereal, and material.

The soul, being created, cannot itself be an Absolute Cause; but it is made to include a capacity, through its relation with Infinite Substance and with God as its creator, for recognizing and becoming at-one with spiritual or divine-human forms of Absolute Law and of Absolute Phenomena, and for applying its knowledge of these in the realization of Absolute Science in that form which is termed in the Scriptures "the Wisdom of God." This is not realized from an absolute and creative, but from a phenomenal and receptive, point of view; neither can it be realized in a natural, but only in a spiritual, condition and sphere of consciousness, which are made possible to the soul by the assumption of a universal form of Human Nature by the Son of God, and by the realization in Himself and in Human Substance of a divine-human principle, by which a medium of communication is established between Man and his Maker.

As the Soul must be developed first as a dualistic natural, and afterwards as a tri-personal spiritual form, and as the natural must always be unconsciously sustained by the spiritual, it is created both dualistic and tri-personal. All its particular departments, therefore, contain natural dualistic forms representing Infinite and Finite; and also contain a supernatural form representing Spiritual Life through Marriage, or the union of opposites through voluntary sacrifice, which constitutes a medium through which the Divine Activity operates in the continuous creation, combination, and manifestation of these natural dualistic forms: while the general form of the Mind, and also of the Will, is constituted tri-personal by three spheres, related as Spiritual, Supernatural, and Natural; the first containing unconsciously, as the centre of life, spiritual forms representing the Universal Laws of Being, and the form of God as Creating Cause, and also a natural form representative of these by which they are connected with the natural consciousness; the second containing supernatural forms representing Spiritual Relationships corresponding with these laws, and also a natural form representing the manner in which these become realized; and the third containing laws and forms through which these can be incarnated in the most external and diversified manner. Besides this, every particular department of the mind, although internally dualistic, in its external form is individualized in three spheres as soul, body, and spirit, in which spirit is the manifesting principle, corresponding with the individualization of Infinite Life; while the Mind and the Will are individualized as spirit, soul, and body, in which the body is the manifesting principle, corresponding with the tri-personality of Holy Ghost, Father, and Son. This double form of the Soul, and its development first as Natural and afterwards as Spiritual, are necessary, first, because it is created as an Image of God, and this is the mode and this is the order in the realization of Absolute Existence, or of Definite Being, through which God becomes realized as tri-personal Creating Cause: next, because the infinite and finite substances from which it is created cannot in a natural sphere be united as one, but only be combined in a dual substance, for the reason that the union of opposites, which is by Marriage, can be realized only in the spiritual, after the natural development of all its forms has been completed, both in external and in internal spheres of individual consciousness; and, consequently, one of these spheres of phenomenal substance must act upon these natural forms as a vital and combining, and the other as a destructive and separating force; necessitating a continuous creative process, and the establishment, in the constitution of all natural things, of supernatural mediums through which the Divine can act in the construction, combination, and manifestation of the dualistic forms of life contained in them: and, finally, because it is through these mediums, in a regenerated form, that God must act as the governing and manifesting power of the soul in a spiritual sphere of existence, except when it becomes reprobate by union with Absolute Death. Man, as the head of the Material Universe, was constituted in this form a threefold indestructible Substance which is Spiritual, Ethereal, and Material, calculated to exist successively in three Atmospheres, in three Bodies, and in three Spheres of Consciousness, related as body, soul, and spirit, in the last of which he must become consciously united with one or the other of the Absolute Causes of Existence, and be regenerated into a form through which this Cause can be represented and manifested in a Phenomenal Sphere of Existence.

In realizing this threefold form of the Universe, of which Man is the head, we obtain a clear and definite perception of the relationship existing between this and the absolute causes of which it is the representative, and to which the Soul is calculated to minister, first as a natural representative, and afterwards as a medium of manifestation in the production of the most external and diversified forms of Spiritual Life. We see that the difference between God and Man is that between Absolute and Phenomenal Being. We see that Human Substance furnishes a medium through which Absolute Life and Absolute Death can become represented in natural forms, and also become manifested in an infinite diversity of spiritual forms in a self-conscious, comprehensible manner; but we see that it could not be Absolute, and could not become Divine, or become an independent Cause, but only a phenomenal medium for the manifestation of absolute causes: and we do not conceive this Substance as simple, but as containing in essence the sum of individual souls, which may be said to be created from the foundation of the world, and to become incarnated, or united to material bodies, in this atmosphere; it being from this Substance that all individuals derive their immediate support. As it is of the highest importance that we should obtain a clear idea of the nature as well as the origin of Human Substance, for the reason that our conception of the nature of the Soul and its relation to God must depend very much upon our conception of the nature of this Substance, we will endeavor to give a more comprehensive view of this subject, although it is not possible that any definite conception of infinite and finite material laws, or the manner in which they are combined in Human Substance, can be realized through the forms of the Understanding, but only a general impression that must be realized through intuitions of the Reason, these being sustained by the vitality which they communicate to the lower and more definite realizations of the mind.

In the statement that has here been made of Creation, we conceive that the Universe is created by God in his own image by the combination of the infinite and finite laws of Matter, which correspond with infinite and finite Absolute Substance and Spirit, as body to soul and spirit, and are therefore constituted by laws corresponding with the absolute laws, in a phenomenal sphere, as self-subsisting Material Causes; and that these are combined by Absolute Creating Cause in a definite dual substance, and constructed as an Image of God, containing dual natural forms representative of Infinite and Finite, and also tri-personal forms related as spiritual, supernatural, and natural, representing God as Absolute Creating Cause. We conceive that Human Substance, which as the vital principle of the Universe is in its essence a Microcosm or universal form, exists as a Universal Sphere of Phenomenal Life, separated or cut off from the sphere in which God exists as Absolute Cause, but related to Him as a medium for producing natural representations of opposite absolute things by gradual processes of growth and development, and for the spiritual incarnation and manifestation of Absolute Laws in a phenomenal sphere of existence in the most external and diversified forms. These natural representations are produced by the incarnation, through ethereal and material spheres, of individual souls; and this spiritual incarnation and manifestation are realized by their introduction into a spiritual sphere of consciousness, in which one of the absolute causes which have been represented shall constitute the law of their new spiritual existence, and become their regenerator into forms corresponding with it; the original infinite and finite spheres of Matter operating, in this incarnation, from within outwards through the successive spheres of the Universe, as phenomenal spiritual causes, the operations of these being combined by the divine creating power as already described. Now, as Human Substance, in its natural condition, is a combination, and not the union as one, of opposite spiritual substances, both of these must act upon this dual substance which has been constructed from them, and through this act upon the ethereal and material organizations corresponding with it, one as a combining and constructing, and the other as a separating and disorganizing force, making necessary the continuous constructive operation of the Divine Activity, by which Creation becomes a threefold continuous process. All the manifestations of this dual substance are necessarily governed internally by laws corresponding with finite phenomenal substance, which therefore constitute its natural life; because, until this dual substance has been made one through a spiritual marriage, the nature of which will be particularly described in the theological portion of our work, vital laws corresponding with infinite substance cannot govern it in any conscious manifestations, but only destructive laws which correspond with finite substance: and the reason for this is, that its substance is dual, its forms are discordant, and the phenomena produced by them are unreal and false, or the opposite of what they seem, and so correspond with the finite, and not with the infinite.

We cannot but recognize this original ground of Phenomenal Existence in infinite and finite spheres of Matter, because we cannot conceive any thing as existing except as this is a product from and a representative of something self-subsisting; and therefore the existence of a phenomenal world immediately suggests to the mind the necessity of recognizing some original self-subsistent ground from which it is produced: for the modern invention of conceiving the realization of a phenomenal universe from the simple exercise of the Infinite Will, although convenient as avoiding the consideration of a difficult subject, is not only more irrational, but is productive of more serious difficulties, than any other theory that has been conceived. We have seen that two modes were therefore adopted by the ontological philosophers to account for the existence of mundane things: the first being, that the seeds or germs of all things were contained in a fluid chaotic mass, which was the original Infinite Substance, and were developed from this by the separation from and the action upon this substance of a spiritual creating principle; and the second being, that all things have been produced by the transmutation of an ethereal or spiritual substance into definite forms through an inherent force or will; the ground being taken, that it was only by positing a simple substance as the origin of all things that the necessary relationship between God and the Universe could be obtained. We have seen, however, that both these theories are in the highest degree objectionable, as well as utterly impracticable: being objectionable, because they are thoroughly pantheistic, and thus destructive to every thing that is valuable to us as Christian men; and being impracticable, because the first, being exclusively materialistic, is obliged to realize life out of death; while the other, being exclusively spiritualistic, is obliged to realize death out of life. We may therefore see that no rational ground has yet been conceived for the realization of a material universe outside of the Personality of God, and still which is created by Him, opposite to Him, and capable of becoming at-one with Him. Such a ground has now been provided in the Universal Laws of Being here stated as the foundation of Absolute Science, because all the necessary materials are here furnished for the production of a phenomenal sphere outside of the absolute sphere of God, yet connected with and related to Him as its creator, preserver, educator, and governor; by which Pantheism is avoided, and consequences corresponding with causes are realized; so that all things can be explained, and it can be shown how it is that "the invisible things of Him from the creation of the world are clearly seen, being understood by the things which are made, — even his Eternal Power and Godhead." We have not only obtained a ground for the creation of a material universe with man as its head, and for the natural development of the soul as an unreal representative appearance, but we have obtained a ground for the immortality of the soul, for the creation of man as a spiritual form, and for the realization by him of free-will in a spiritual consciousness, in which God will become his Saviour and Regenerator.

It has here been shown that the soul is a Material Creation, and not an Absolute Cause; but the term "material" is used in a sense entirely different from that which is usually given to it, giving to the soul the highest and most truly spiritual position that can possibly be claimed for it, — that of a medium through which God will manifest Himself in a phenomenal sphere in realizing the most external image of his Divine Perfections. The Infinite and finite substances from which it is created are not conceived as "dead matter," but as the opposite spiritual poles of Living Phenomenal Substance. We do not conceive them as deriving their life from Absolute Spirit or Substance, but as self-subsisting, and as being constituted by phenomenal laws perfectly analogous to the Absolute Laws, which constitute the opposite poles of Absolute Being, as the condition of their becoming mediums through which the Absolute can finally become manifested: so that, while obtaining a universal medium for all external manifestations, we do not confuse the subject by confounding Spirit with Matter, or Absolute with Phenomenal Being; or attempt to produce Matter from Spirit, or the Phenomenal from the Absolute, by which spiritual pantheism would be realized. We show that Matter subsists in opposite phenomenal spheres, and must continually operate in the sustenance of all spiritual as well as of all natural forms of phenomenal life; and that, being constituted by laws corresponding with Infinite and Finite Absolute Spirit and Substance, when its opposite indefinite laws are combined in the production of definite forms, it furnishes, through the inherent vitality which it contains, a medium for the natural representation and the spiritual manifestation of Absolute Causes in phenomenal spheres of existence. We do this by realizing separate individualizations of Infinite and Finite as Universal Spheres of Indefinite Being, in each of which, laws of Spirit, of Substance, and of Matter, are conceived as constituting three separate universal spheres, related as spirit, soul, and body, from the union of which are realized an individualization of Spirit as Holy Ghost, Father, and Son, — an individualization of Substance as Infinite Substance, Divine Substance, and Spiritual Substance, — and an individualization of Matter as

Spiritual, Ethereal, and Material, which are represented in the spiritual, ethereal, and material forms of the Universe, of which Man is the head. We show that Man is created in the Image of God in a tri-personal form, containing spiritual, supernatural, and natural spheres; that he is created to exist and to become conscious successively in natural, supernatural, and spiritual atmospheres, bodies, and spheres of consciousness; in the last of which he becomes, through a free self-determination in view of a conscious presentation of opposite absolute laws, a specific medium for the manifestation in a phenomenal sphere of Spiritual Existence to one of the Absolute Causes of Being, by union with this Cause and the consequent regeneration of his form into a medium suitable for its conscious manifestation. It will therefore be seen that nothing is left to be desired as a ground for the realization either of absolute or of phenomenal existence, or for the explanation of the physical phenomena of the Universe, and of the relation of the Soul to Absolute Cause both from a natural and from a spiritual point of view.

It now remains that we should draw from the conceptions which have here been realized of Absolute Being as Creating Cause, and Phenomenal Being as a medium through which Absolute Causes are represented in the natural and manifested in the spiritual in the most external and diversified manner, the Laws or Formulas which we are to take as the external scientific ground upon which to construct Philosophy as Absolute Science in a tri-personal form, including Ontological, Theological, and Psychological systems, made one in the relation of spirit, soul, and body, and which we are to apply, in connection with the laws previously realized, in explaining all the phenomena of natural and of spiritual life. These we will now state as the laws of Unity, Duality, and Trinity, which, being related as body, soul, and spirit, constitute what we name THE LAW OF TRI-PERSONALITY.

THE LAW OF TRI-PERSONALITY.

UNITY,
THE LAW OF INDIVIDUALITY, AS BODY.

As the condition of Individuality, all things exist in the form of One; all particular forms being constituted by three principles related as internal, external, and medial, which are Soul, Body, and Spirit, manifested as one through the Spirit; and all universal forms being constituted by three Spheres related as Spiritual, Internal, and External, which are Spirit, Soul, and Body, manifested as one through the Body.

DUALITY,
THE LAW OF EXISTENCE, AS SOUL.

As the condition of Definite Being, all things exist from the union of two opposite principles related as Male and Female, which are vital and destructive spheres,—each of which is constituted by an internal and an external principle also related as vital and destructive; these opposites existing under a complex law of opposition and attraction, and this union being realized by an Absolute Power, through a supernatural sphere which is productive, in a manner representing Spiritual Life through Marriage, or the Union of Opposites through voluntary sacrifice.

TRINITY,
THE LAW OF LIFE, AS SPIRIT.

As the condition of Spiritual Life, the Individual must become at-one with Infinite Life by the marriage in him of spiritual opposites; this being realized through the consciousness of Infinite and Finite Law as a personal experience,—the voluntary sacrifice of Individual Life,—the realization in him of a spiritual substance as the centre of life,—and his regeneration into a spiritual form as a medium for the manifestation of Spiritual Truth, Good, and Beauty.

These formulas, which constitute the Law of Tri-Personality, are not assumed dogmatically, because they are legitimate deductions from a single premise, which is all that has really been assumed in this system as a hypothetical ground; and even this we hold to be a self-evident truth,—this being, that the Infinite constitutes the life of all things: and we wish here distinctly to state, that, if this one fact is conceded to us as a point of departure,—and to this none but the materialist or atheist can possibly object,—all the conclusions to which we have arrived must be conceded also. Those who are not able to see that the statement of tri-personality in God and in Man here made is a legitimate deduction from the simple recognition of Infinite Life, and can neither see that the Law of Tri-Personality—which has here been stated as the external ground of Absolute Science—is legitimately derived from this statement of tri-personality, will have to concede to us the right to take the tri-personal law here stated as our external point of departure. If we are able to show that all things exist in correspondence with this law, the demonstration of this science will be complete; because no more legitimate proof can be had of the truth of any science, than that all phenomena are found to correspond with what have been hypothetically assumed as the laws which should govern their production. Although the science here constructed has been developed in the mind of the writer from the single premise of Infinite Life, it is of little consequence, so far as intellectual demonstration is concerned, whether we start from this, or from the formulas now stated as constituting the Law of Tri-Personality. To those who are able to follow us from our first position, however, the demonstration will be more satisfactory, and much more important; because it will become to them an object of distinct vision or insight, and will therefore rest upon the sure foundation of Faith, instead of resting upon the superficial foundation of Individual Belief.

Before we proceed to apply the Law of Tri-Personality in the construction of Philosophy as Absolute Science, we will consider each of the elements composing it, for the purpose of separating from these laws the various natural theories which have been conceived as substitutes for them; and of showing, that while these laws as stated by us, being founded in a spiritual, trinitarian principle, are in the highest degree productive, these natural substitutes have been founded upon a natural, unitarian, and pantheistic principle which is destructive to Spiritual Truth.

THE LAW OF UNITY.

According to our statement of the law of Unity, "As the condition of Individuality, all things exist in the form of One; all particular forms being constituted by three principles related as internal, external, and medial, which are Soul, Body, and Spirit, manifested as one through the Spirit; and all universal forms being constituted by three Spheres related as Spiritual, Internal, and External, which are Spirit, Soul, and Body, manifested as one through the Body." Although this is a universal law, — which determines the external form of all existing things, both created and uncreated, both phenomenal and absolute, because it is founded in the nature of God as Absolute Creating Cause, — it cannot be applied in the explanation of the internal relationships of things, but only in the classification of their forms; and this applies especially to natural phenomena, for the reason that all natural things exist internally in a discordant dualistic condition, as representatives of opposite absolute principles, and are governed by laws corresponding with the Finite, which is Absolute Death; while this law, being a representative of Absolute Life, demands their recognition as harmonious and homogeneous, and their individualization as spirit, soul, and body. Being unable to posit a second universal cause, Philosophy has necessarily been confined to a natural and unitarian point of view, from which the law of Unity in Diversity — which is the natural substitute for the law of Unity here stated — is the only governing law. This law has therefore always constituted the destructive element in philosophy; for, although it has been obliged to recognize the opposition that exists in all natural things as the representatives of opposite absolute principles, it has also been obliged, in all its conceptions, to generalize these discordant natural phenomena under the law of Unity in Diversity, — by which opposites have been confounded, and regarded as one or as opposite, as the occasion has required, or as appearances may have suggested. From an external and intellectual point of view, things have been classified, under the law of Tri-Unity, as intellectual, affectional, and active, which are harmonious and homogeneous as internal, external, and medial, because this is the external form in which all particular forms must appear to exist; and all things have been classified, from an internal and individual point of view, as true and false, and as good and evil, because these correspond with the internal phenomena which are recognized by the individual consciousness: but as all these appearances are opposite to the real facts of which they are the representatives, and as truth and falsehood, and good and evil, are regarded from the point of the "Fancy," — which combines the opposite laws of "Contrast" and "Resemblance," — as relatively opposite, but as being produced by one cause, or by the free determination of a created phenomenon, all knowledge becomes fictitious, and thus false and deceptive. Even the Church, which is the great representative of the spiritual in a natural sphere of consciousness, has also been governed by the same destructive law, for the reason that she, too, has been confined to a natural and unitarian point of view, and therefore has never been able to recognize a second universal cause, but only to represent it; and so has never been able to recognize the fact of evil, except as a natural phenomenon, or as the product of some created existence: for, although the Church is the natural representative of the spiritual, — being herself natural, — it has not been possible that she should realize the spiritual either in her theory or in her practice, either in her belief or in her life.

We will now describe some of the destructive manifestations of this naturalistic substitute for the law of Unity, as it operates in Philosophy, in the Church, and in governing the private opinions and speculations of individuals. According to the account that has here been given of the history of philosophy from its commencement to the present time, the materials for which are furnished by the best authorities upon the subject, it has been divided between ontological, psychological, and eclectical systems. The pantheistic character of all ontological systems is the most palpably evident, because they set out with the purpose of accounting for the origin of all things from One Substance. By the Egyptians, by the Ionian Physiologists, and by the Pythagoreans, this substance was supposed to be a fluid, chaotic mass, in which what were relatively spiritual and material elements were confusedly mixed; but, becoming finally separated, the active principle was able to act upon the passive material in the production of the Universe. This was the first, and therefore the most material, of all the ontological theories of the Universe of which we have any knowledge; and although it may now seem to be absurd, because it does not recognize any principle sufficiently intellectual for the generation and preservation of the world, or show any relationship between these opposite elements by which one could be made to operate upon the other, it corresponds more closely than any other with the Mosaic account, which is the most perfect representation of the fact of Creation. It is the only ontological theory, which, while positing only one principle or substance, recognizes in this substance both material for creation and a creative power, distinctly separate; and it has, therefore, proved to be the most popular, as it has been the most practical, of all the theories of creation.

By the Ionian Dynamicists this one infinite substance was supposed to be a kind of fire, or fiery air, possessing an intelligent as well as a material character, and also the power of transmuting or transforming itself into an infinite variety of forms. They therefore concluded, that the universe consists of an eternal procession of phenomena, proceeding from, and returning again to, their source in this one infinite substance; and that imperfection, or evil, is occasioned and is regulated by the distance which separates these phenomena from the infinite perfection from which they spring. As this theory corresponds with the Persian doctrine of the emanation of all things from one infinite substance, and therefore does not recognize matter in its gross or atomistic form as originally subsisting, it is higher in its character than the theories of the Egyptian and Ionian Physiologists; but although representing creation from an infinite substance, as it does not recognize any thing higher than a material substance, however ethereal this may have been conceived to be, it is to be regarded as physiological in character. All these physiological theories, however, are representative of creation by a spiritual or absolute cause; it being reserved for the modern external psychological schools to construct a theory of pure Materialism, in which nothing higher than Sensation is recognized in thought, and nothing higher than Matter is recognized as the cause of the Universe.

The first theory possessing a decidedly spiritualistic character was realized by the Persians, who posited an infinite spiritual substance, in Light, as the origin and life of all things. They supposed that from this substance proceeded two opposite subordinate substances, — one of which corresponded with Light, and the other with Darkness; and that from the combined operation of these the world was created, in which these two opposite things are mixed. Now, the absurdity of this theory consisted in producing two opposite effects from the same cause, or in producing darkness from light; although, having posited an infinite spiritual substance, in light, there was no other way by which they could obtain a ground for the production of mundane things. The most purely spiritualistic of all ontological theories was that put forth by the Eleatic School; and was simply the positing of an infinite spiritual substance, excluding all finite multiplicity, and denying the existence of a phenomenal world. This theory was afterwards revived or re-asserted by the celebrated Bishop Berkeley, who demonstrated from this point of view the non-existence of a material universe. It is more purely rational than any other theory, because the premise upon which it is founded is the highest that can be conceived, and the conclusion drawn the only rational one possible, from the natural and unitarian point of view to which its originators were confined.

It will be seen that all these theories are strictly Pantheistic in character, and include some palpable absurditiy, which makes them both self-destructive and destructive to the truth. It was to obviate this difficulty, and to escape from the pantheistic condition which belongs to all ontological theories of the universe, that the Church put forth the theory, that God created the Universe from Nothing. The only argument, if it can be called an argument, that has been offered by them in support of this absurd doctrine is, that it is the only way of escape from Pantheism. Thus a late Catholic writer,[*] in answering the question, "Is not God all things,—the Universe Itself?" says, "*Mediante* the creative act, yes; otherwise, no: because conceived simply as real, necessary, and eternal Being, he is not conceived as productive; and no universe is or can be asserted. The difference between Philosophy and Pantheism lies precisely in the creative act of God. Pantheism asserts that real being is, and there stops; and, in doing so, asserts God as real and necessary being, and nothing else. Philosophy goes one step further, and asserts real

---

[*] "Brownson's Review," January, 1850.

being is Creator, and in doing so asserts the Universe; for existences are nothing but the creative act of God in its terminus, as is asserted in asserting creation out of nothing. To say that God *non-mediante* the creative act is the Universe, is not true; for then there is no Universe: to say that God *mediante* the creative act is all things, is the Universe, is true; for then the Universe is not only asserted, but asserted in its true relation to God, as being only from him, by him, and in him, through the creative act bringing it forth from potentiality into actuality. There is no possible bridge from God as real necessary Being to Existence, or from Existence to Him, but his creative act; and therefore we must either rest in Pantheism, or assert creation out of nothing."

Now, in the first place, the issue between Pantheism and what this writer calls philosophy is not correctly stated. It is not true that "Pantheism asserts that real being is, and there stops." With the exception of the Eleatic philosophers, all the ancient ontologists recognized either an active spiritual principle, or an active spiritual substance, that was creative, and creative in the same sense that is here asserted; that is, from itself; "bringing the Universe forth from potentiality into actuality:" so that the only difference between their theories and this modern device is, that theirs are legitimate and honest pantheistic statements, which are the best conceptions possible from a natural point of view; while this is an illegitimate statement that was made simply to conceal the fact of pantheism. In the next place, this theory is liable not only to all the objections which may be brought against these other theories of creation, but to others still greater. Creation from nothing is a palpable absurdity and a mathematical impossibility: but even were it possible for the Infinite God to create the Universe from nothing, if we allow him to be a God of Infinite wisdom, goodness, and power, we cannot conceive Him as *willing* all the imperfection and evil which we find existing in the world. All previous theories of Creation avoided this, by conceiving Evil to originate either in the material substance from which the Universe is created, in some form of created existence, or in distance from God in the process of emanation; but this theory, by being cut off from these evasions, and not being able to recognize any thing as intervening to thwart the designs of the Creator, or prevent the fulfilment of all his conceptions, must of course refer all imperfection and evil immediately to God. It will be seen, however, that all these ontological systems of philosophy are governed by the natural law of Unity, and are therefore substantially the same; that they are all equally pantheistic, and include an unqualified necessity that leads to fatalism, and thus to the destruction of all moral differences; and that all, except the Eleatic theory, include the gross absurdity of referring all natural imperfection to Absolute Perfection, and all natural evil to Absolute Good, as its Cause; which, if really admitted without any qualification, must destroy in us all hope of ever comprehending any thing, because it would destroy in our minds every boundary between truth and falsehood, as well as every distinction between good and evil.

As Psychology has heretofore been simply a generalization of the natural facts of the human consciousness, — for all supernatural or religious phenomena have been excluded in its construction, — as two classes of facts are here presented, one relating to truth and the other to good; and as all natural things come under the law of Duality, as "two and two, one against the other," — the establishment of the psychological method has always been followed by the realization, first of internal and external Moral schools, and next of internal and external Intellectual schools. As both these internal and external and these intellectual and moral elements are realized in discordant antagonism, and as these natural phenomena are confessedly the most diversified and discordant of all things, all psychological systems of philosophy necessarily become realized through the application of the law of Unity in Diversity in showing the nature of things, and of the law of Tri-Unity in individualizing and classifying phenomena; and this is necessary, because it is not possible that these discordant phenomena should, from a natural point of view, be individualized or brought into any scientific form under any other law. It will therefore be seen that psychology must always, in a natural sphere of consciousness, prove to be a destructive element in philosophy, and thus, in a particular manner, destructive to the truth, through the operation of these unitarian laws. The naturalistic and destructive character of psychology is made clearly evident, not only because its systems are realized in discordant antagonism, and the phenomena of which they are composed are realized in the greatest diversity and discord, but because it has always been productive of Sensualism upon the one hand, and Materialism upon the other, as the moral or as the intellectual element has prevailed; consequences which followed close upon its establishment by Socrates in ancient, and by Lord Bacon in modern times.

As psychology exists in so much diversity, and is so obviously governed by these destructive laws by which opposites are confounded and truth is destroyed, its particular forms need not here be enumerated.

In the eclectical systems of philosophy, the attempt has always been made to unite the conflicting elements which are contained in these ontological and psychological systems, but particularly to unite the opposite ideas and laws which it has always been necessary to recognize, but which have always appeared to exclude each other: these being recognized as Spirit and Matter, Infinite and Finite, Absolute and Phenomenal, Unity and Multiplicity, Subject and Object, &c. How they succeeded in this, we have already seen. We have seen that Emanuel Kant, the greatest of all the eclectical philosophers, after having exhausted all expedients in attempting to state and to produce the union of these opposites, abandoned the attempt, and came to the conclusion that nothing could be known of the supra-sensible; which, if true, would confine philosophy to the region of Sensation, and reduce it to a science of physical appearances, by which it would be destroyed; a result that has since been realized in the atheistic school founded by Comte under the name of "Positive Science." We have seen that the followers of Kant, not being able to believe that so little could be known, projected system after system, in the hope of effecting this separation and union; but that they all finally came to the conclusion, that there was no opposition to recognize,—that subject and object, being and non-being, were one and the same,—and that God first arrives at a definite self-consciousness in Man.

We see, then, that the history of Philosophy is simply the history of Unitarianism,—that this is founded, as its name denotes, upon the idea that every thing either emanates or is developed from One Substance or Cause,—and that it has therefore been obliged to affirm that there is really but one sphere of Existence; so that no separation could be made by it between Absolute and Phenomenal, between Spiritual and Natural, or between Divine and Infernal: for we see that this separation is first introduced by positing Opposite Universal Laws as the ground of Existence, which Philosophy has never been able to do; and as Creation represents in its forms and manifestations this universal opposition, when Philosophy comes with her Unitarian Formula to investigate phenomena, nothing can be explained by it, and so nothing can be understood.

In its most abstract or ideal condition, Unitarianism takes two opposite forms; one corresponding with Truth, and the other with Good. The first of these, which is ontological and relatively theoretical, we call Idealism, or Pantheism. This is again divided into internal and external forms; and we call these Spiritualism and Materialism, because in the first, Spirit, and in the second, Matter, constitutes the basis of all speculation; so that every ontological system is characterized by one or by the other. Both are therefore destructive in character, because, in proportion as Spirit is recognized as cause, Creation is dissipated, and no form of existence can be realized; while, in proportion as Matter is recognized as cause, Atheism is realized, and both spirituality and immortality are destroyed. It is true that these extreme results are not often distinctly produced in any philosophical system, because the human mind is not rational or one in its thought, but becomes conscious and is manifested in diversity and discord; and thus no single principle is often exclusively recognized and carried out into all the consequences to which it legitimately leads. Such, however, we can readily see to be the effects naturally resulting from these opposite applications of the natural law of Unity in the construction of ontological theories of the Universe. The second of these forms of Unitarianism, which is psychological and relatively practical, we call Realism, or Naturalism. This also is again divided into internal and external forms, which we call Intellectualism and Moralism. These psychological forms have already been described, and their naturalistic, external, and destructive character shown. But as the theories which have been realized by these two methods of psychological investigation appear in so much diversity and discord, and as they enter so largely into the practical affairs of life as well as into the intellectual theories of individuals and of the Church, we will here take a more particular notice of them as they appear in the forms of Transcendentalism and Moralism; although, as the latter has been generally recognized under the name of Unitarianism, we shall here designate it by that name.

Transcendentalism and Unitarianism are the internal and external exponents of the destructive laws of the Sentimental Nature, which are "Naturalism" in the religious, and "Sympathy" in the moral department. They are related as conscious and unconscious, and as consistent and inconsistent; for although, as related to Pantheism, the forms of thought peculiar to both these destructive principles are diversified and discordant, as related to each other they appear as consistent and inconsistent, as well as conscious and unconscious, for the reason that they belong to internal and external spheres of life, and the internal is always allied to consciousness, simplicity, and consistency, while the external is always allied to unconsciousness, duplicity, and inconsistency. It will therefore be found, that, although Transcendentalism and Unitarianism are both destructive principles, in many respects a perfect antagonism exists between them. Hence, while the former demands internal and real things, an internal realization of them, and an internal direction from them,—and thus, like John the Baptist, points in the direction of, and prepares the mind for, the spiritual birth,—the latter demands external and apparent things, an external realization of them, and an external direction from them that is as arbitrary as the laws of Moses, and thus becomes antagonized to this internal preparation of the individual; and, while the former demands actions which correspond with inclination, the latter demands actions which are contrary to inclination. It is true, that it is only for good that the transcendentalist demands consistency; and the reason for this is, that good is worshipped by him as the supreme principle: and as natural good exists in diversity and discord, so that he finds it impossible to produce harmony among its various forms, he comes to regard this diversity as a necessity of life, and to look upon theoretical or logical consistency as one of the greatest of absurdities; and this disposition is increased from the fact, that, in becoming rational instead of intellectual, he has repudiated logic and placed his reliance upon analogy, which relieves him from the necessity of admitting logical deductions, even from premises admitted by him to be true. It is also true that an external or apparent consistency is demanded by the unitarian; but the reason for this is that he demands an external conformity to an external standard, and applies the form of logic to realize conclusions drawn from this external arbitrary rule. It will be seen, therefore, that the consistency of Transcendentalism is real, while the consistency of Unitarianism is fictitious; so that, even in this, an opposition exists between them.

In the observation of phenomena, the same opposition exists. Relying upon internal recognition and direction, transcendentalists become observers of the phenomena of the consciousness, which include the motives or causes of action; while unitarians, relying upon external recognition and direction, become observers of the phenomena of life, which include the consequences of action.

Thus the first, although avoiding those metaphysical abstractions to which the pantheist is devoted as the laws of truth, become devoted to what they consider to be the laws of good; while the second, eschewing all internal laws or principles, devote themselves exclusively to the phenomena of good. The first, worshiping good as a supreme universal principle, and therefore believing that its realization is of the most vital importance, not only demand its realization in and for themselves, but insist that what appears to be good for them shall be enjoyed by all, and that what appears to be right to them shall be set up as the standard of right to all. By thus insisting upon the application of individual notions, which are unhealthy even in themselves, to all the unequal conditions and relationships of social life, without in the least regarding the consequences of such application, they run into all kinds of fanaticism, and produce all kinds of mischief; so that, in proportion as they are real, they become disorderly. The second, on the other hand, although they believe in the supremacy of good, and also believe in the capacity of the moral sense to perceive what is right, because they could not otherwise hold the individual, as they do, to the strictest accountability for his actions, and although they even believe that the moral sense is the spiritual principle in man, or the voice of God in the soul, at the same time distrust and repudiate all individual standards of right, and protest against all individual activity from such standards; setting up what public opinion and the laws have established as the rule of right, and demanding the obedience of all to this; so that, in proportion as they become orderly, they become unreal.

Again: the first deny that any tendency to evil exists in the nature of man, which they hold to be divine, maintaining that evil is only the imperfection of good; and assert that all the social abuses, which are called evil, result from a false organization of society and an unhealthy condition of the public sentiment; although, how public sentiment could become unhealthy, or society falsely organized, when the soul, of which these are only the manifestations, is divine, they do not attempt to explain. The second, on the other hand, admit that a tendency to evil as well as to good exists in the nature of man, and that these are produced by the exercise of a natural free-will inherent in him; and assert that the influence of social organization and the public sentiment, which are true and healthy, are necessary to check the one, and to encourage the performance of the other: and the reason for this difference is, that the first are too internal and rational, and therefore too consistent, to admit that evil can really exist in or be produced by a creature who either is formed exclusively by, or proceeds from, an infinitely perfect being in whom it never existed; while the second are too external and simply intellectual to seek for any thing beyond the merest external appearance. Of course, neither the transcendentalist nor the unitarian believes in the absolute nature of good and of evil, or in the absolute antagonism that exists between them. They believe in nothing but Nature, and therefore believe that no other than natural good and evil, which come within the sphere of Morality, have any existence except in the absurd dreams of churchmen. Neither believes, therefore, in Sin and Holiness, either as universal absolute facts, or as spiritual conditions of the soul, which are realized through a single act of the will; but only in those endless degrees of natural perfection and imperfection by which good and evil are represented to the natural consciousness. Unitarians believe that these degrees of condition are realized through the free self-determination of the individual, and that he is rewarded or punished for these determinations through the operation of certain moral laws which have, like those of society, been ordained for the encouragement of virtue and the punishment of vice; and that these laws are as unerring in their operation as those which govern the physical world, — a knowledge of one being quite as necessary to the moral and social, as that of the other is to the physical, safety of the individual; and an unconscious violation through ignorance quite as fatal as a conscious violation against knowledge. Transcendentalists, on the contrary, believe that the soul is subjected to no law but that of its own nature, and thus to nothing that is contrary to it; and that, as this nature is divine, the unrestrained gratification of every faculty and of every desire or tendency is necessary to its full development, and the realization of the greatest ultimate good to the individual. Such are the diversified and discordant manifestations which are produced by these internal and external exponents of Naturalism, under the operation of the law of Unity in Diversity.

So long as the individual is confined to an external sphere of consciousness, the tendency of Naturalism to self-worship and to self-destruction does not distinctly appear, either in his thought or in his life; because he is not only unconscious of the destructive laws which have commenced to operate upon him, but he is at this time more or less under subjection to society and to external moral rules, by which his external manifestations are regulated;

so that it is only from supernatural and spiritual points of view that the deceptive and destructive character of these experiences can be detected. But when he passes into an internal sphere of consciousness, where the individual himself becomes manifested, — when these destructive laws are conceived and applied as the governing laws of his life, — and when his own conceptions of truth and of good become to him "*the higher law*," which must supersede all other laws, and which he would make binding upon all, — when Personal Want, in the form of Good, is set up as the supreme principle, and the female personal affinity and laws of the mind, and even the female, obtain the supremacy, — then the impious and suicidal character of Naturalism becomes more apparent, and its tendency to produce the destruction of order and of life in all institutions, both natural and supernatural, and in all practical as well as in all rational thought, begins plainly to appear; because the individual now sets up his claim to an Infinite Personality, and to an infinite scope for his activity, unrestrained by any law but that of his own consciousness. But, although Naturalism is thus universally destructive, its full development, up to that final point which brings the individual into the most extreme natural opposition to God, and thus prepares for him a form representative of the Spiritual Temptation, is necessary for every individual as a preparation for his spiritual birth.

Nothing now remains to be noticed of the influence exerted by the natural law of Unity, but that which operates in the Church; and here it may be asked, How is it that the Church, which is founded upon conceptions of God as a Tri-Personality, and is the great exponent of the Supernatural, can be governed by a unitarian and naturalistic law? The reason is this: The Church is an institution established to superintend the development of the Sentimental Nature, which is the supernatural region of the mind by the means of which spiritual phenomena are represented to the consciousness, and the supernatural growth and development of the individual are effected, constituting his natural regeneration; this being symbolized in the Scriptures as the birth of water. Now, as this is a natural condition, which is realized while man is confined to a natural sphere of consciousness, in which he cannot, of course, be capable of spiritual knowledge, and so cannot be made to comprehend spiritual law, the consequence is, that this representation of spiritual things must be governed by a natural law as the condition of its reception by the natural man, and that, while the ideas which are committed to the Church by record and by tradition are supernatural, these have to be incarnated in an external natural order of thought and experience before they can be consciously appropriated in the construction of the life. It is in this way that the theological forms of the Church come to be governed by a unitarian and naturalistic law, and that these ideas come to be contradicted in being incarnated. It is true that the Church has no philosophical existence, but only a sentimental one, which is a life of feeling, and not of scientific thought; and that philosophy has always been to her a destructive principle, which she has been obliged to repudiate; but she has, at the same time, been obliged to resort to it for materials in constructing a form through which she could communicate her instructions; for as her religious ideas belong to a supernatural order, while her thought belongs to a natural order, she cannot give to her beliefs even a logical, much less a rational explanation; and every doctrine held by her is therefore held as a mystery, that cannot be comprehended, and consequently cannot be explained: and, although these beliefs include and are mainly founded upon her conception of God as a Tri-Personality, this is only a natural and most external representation of God, which, like all her other beliefs, she holds to be a profound mystery. But, although the Church is thus anti-philosophic in her beliefs in proportion as she is governed by a vital supernatural law and addresses herself to the religious sentiment, in proportion as she is governed by a naturalistic law and addresses herself to the natural understanding and the natural consciousness of the individual, so far she makes use, and is obliged to make use, of philosophy, which is unitarian and naturalistic. The Catholic Church is therefore more tolerant of philosophy than the Protestant, for the reason that she is a practical Institution calculated particularly for external direction, and is therefore more naturalistic in her thought; vital supernatural ideas being represented by her in external symbolic forms, the significance of which is apprehended through religious feeling, instead of being represented in the form of thought. She has therefore made extensive use of the various systems of Pagan philosophy in the support of her doctrines and precepts, selecting from each such portions as could be made available for this purpose. Indeed, the Epicurean, which is a purely material and atheistical philosophy, is the only system which did not meet with decided patrons among the fathers of the Church. The Platonic system — as it recognized an antagonism between the rational principle and the passions and appetites; which favored the asceticism of this Church, and harmonized with her natural conceptions of antagonism between the flesh and the spirit,—as it appeared also to furnish a rational statement of the idea of tri-personality in God—was at one time the most popular. Augustine, who was disposed to adopt something like Plato's idea of three divine hypostases as a rational interpretation of the doctrine of Tri-personality, contended that Plato was a Christian philosopher; and a union of Platonic and Christian doctrines was attempted by Justin Martyr, Athenagoras, and Clemens Alexandrinus. Subsequently the Stoic and Aristotelian became the favorite systems; and the latter of these, although it was, as we have seen, external and sensualistic in character, was very generally adopted by the scholastics who flourished from the eleventh to the sixteenth centuries. Indeed, Cousin informs us that there was "a project, which, for a moment promising success, finally miscarried, to *canonize* Aristotle as the philosopher *par excellence*."

We have now shown that the law of Unity in Diversity has always been the ruling law in Philosophy, in the Church, and in the private opinions and speculations of individuals. In Philosophy it has been shown to be not a productive, but a destructive principle; and the only reason why it has not been equally destructive in Theology is, that its influence has been overcome by the strength of the religious principle through which supernatural ideas, which constitute the life of theology, have been presented. As this religious principle loses its predominance in the manifestations of the mind, however, it will prove to be as destructive to theology as it has already been in philosophy and in individual opinion.

THE LAW OF DUALITY.

ACCORDING to our statement of the law of Duality, "as the condition of Definite Being, all things exist from the union of two opposite principles related as Male and Female, which are vital and destructive spheres, each of which is constituted by an internal and an external principle, also related as vital and destructive; these opposites existing under a complex law of opposition and attraction, and this union being realized by an Absolute Power, through a supernatural sphere which is productive, in a manner representing Spiritual Life through Marriage, or the union of opposites through voluntary sacrifice." This universal law will be fully illustrated, and thus completely demonstrated, by referring to the phenomena of Creation; because these will be found to exist, without an exception, in correspondence with this law. The fact that all natural phenomena exist in a dualistic and discordant condition has been one of the greatest sources of perplexity in all inquiries into the nature and origin of things. Not being able to posit a second universal sphere of Being, opposite to the Infinite Life, as one of the sources of Existence; and being obliged, therefore, to refer all things to one infinite substance as Cause, and to generalize all phenomena under the law of Unity in Diversity,—Philosophy, instead of being the interpreter of these phenomena, became their confounder: for although its exponents have been obliged, from the pressure of experience, to recognize this discordant dualistic condition, most of their efforts have been wasted in fruitless attempts to show how such discordant effects could be produced by a perfect Infinite Cause. In order that we may show that no law of duality has before been posited by which these phenomena could be explained, we will enumerate the various dualistic forms which have been recognized in Philosophy, in Theology, and in the Scriptures, as the representatives of this law.

A dualistic condition of mundane things, which included opposition or antagonism, has always been recognized both in Philosophy and in the Church; because it was only through such a recognition that the opposition existing between spiritual causes could be represented by the latter, although the fact itself has never been recognized by her; or that the former could be made to correspond with what is obviously the actual condition of all created things. It cannot but be acknowledged, however, that no dualistic theory has ever been posited in philosophy as a law by the means of which Existence could be accounted for, or the phenomena of Creation could be classified and explained by the discovery of their true relationships; because it has here been clearly and thoroughly demonstrated, that the law of Unity in Diversity, as a harmonious or homogeneous generalizing principle, has been universally applied as the governing law in philosophy. It is true that two opposite principles have been recognized by philosophy in Spirit and Matter, Good and Evil, Unity and Multiplicity, &c.; because matter, natural evil, and multiplicity are apparent facts which cannot be ignored; while a belief in spirit as an infinite invisible cause, which is one and universal, is derived from an intuitive recognition of the mind; and this it has therefore been necessary to recognize also, in order that materialism and atheism should be avoided, and the total destruction of every thing should not be conceived. Instead of furnishing any foundation for philosophy, however, the necessity of recognizing these opposite things has, as we have already seen, caused the greatest difficulty with which philosophy has had to contend; all the ingenuity of the philosophers not having been able to devise any method by which these opposite things could be united, or made to co-operate in the material and mental phenomena of the Universe.

The Egyptians recognized a duality of principles, related as internal and external, and representing what is commonly understood by Spirit and Matter; these being supposed by them to have been developed from out of an Infinite Chaos, in which all things originally were confusedly mixed; and the Ionian Physiologists, and also the Pythagoreans, posited a similar dual substance as the origin of things. These theories, however, were not only pantheistic but materialistic in character, and were not rationalistic, but simply representative or poetic. No absolute dualism was posited, but only a homogeneous compound consisting of internal and external principles related as soul and body, one being active and the other completely passive, which, by being separated, or separately developed, and afterwards united, became manifested in production. The Persians recognized a dualism of opposite causes, in Light and Darkness, from the combined operation of which all things were produced; but they also held that these were only secondary causes, which were emanations from "the One Unlimited All," or from one infinite spiritual substance; and the Ionian Dynamicists recognized a similar dualism in Fire and Earth, which they supposed to be emanations from or transformations of an infinite ethereal substance. Plato recognized an antagonistic dualism in Spirit and Matter; regarding spirit as the cause of all good, and matter as the cause of all evil: and some have supposed that Plato intended to recognize these as absolutely opposite principles or causes. But, if we examine his theory, we shall find nothing but a repetition of the Persian idea of two opposite secondary principles derived from one Supreme Numen, which is the only absolute substance, and the sole cause of all things which exist. This fact is distinctly shown in his partiality for and adoption of the dynamical theory of Heraclitus as the principal feature in his theory of the Universe, and in that strong bias for Eleatic opinions to which we have already alluded, and for which we have the authority of Ritter, the most cautious of all the historians of philosophy. The following description by Dr. Ogilvy of the theory of Plato also confirms the view that has here been taken, and is undoubtedly correct as to the main fact: "Although the author of all things was actuated in framing the universe by a general benevolence, whereby he was prompted to impart some portion of his own felicity to his creatures; yet, in creating matter, he formed something opposite to his own incorporated nature, and necessarily endowed it with contrary qualities. The influx of those qualities was at first repressed by the Maker, who was willing to render his creatures happy during the first ages, by an immediate and unremitted exertion of his own omnipotence. Nothing more is understood of the retirement of the Supreme Agent from government, than his permission, at a certain period, that things should proceed in their natural course, when the effect of matter upon the spirit with which it is united is forcibly represented by the agitation that prevailed universally, and by the immediate appearance of physical evil. Evil, therefore, is considered by Plato, as it was by his master, Pythagoras, not as a principle, but as an accident. It is a transient alienation from order and rectitude, occasioned partly by appetites, of which matter is the parent, and partly by weakness and human imperfection."

The dualistic theories of Zoroaster and of Plato were quite similar in character, although that of Plato was the most extreme of the two. Zoroaster regarded Darkness, and Plato regarded Matter, to be the cause of evil; and both regarded these as the unavoidable consequence of the determination of God to create the world, where light cannot exist without darkness, or good without being combined with evil. Both also regarded the soul of man to be an emanation from God, or a particle of divine substance; and his body to be suggestive and productive of evil in consequence of its relation to this material substance. The principal difference between them seems to have been, that Zoroaster supposed evil to have been produced by the remoteness of matter from the Light, or the divine life from which it emanated; while Plato supposed evil to originate in a blind refractory force which is an inherent attribute of matter: and this difference is a merely nominal one. Zoroaster writes, "Various orders of spiritual being, gods, or demons, have proceeded from the Deity, which are more or less perfect as they are at a greater or less distance in the course of emanation from the eternal fountain of intelligence; among which the Human Soul is a particle of divine light, which will return to its source, and partake of its immortality: and Matter is the last or most distant emanation from the first source of Being, which, on account of its distance from the fountain of Light, becomes opaque and inert, and, while it remains in this state, is the cause of evil; but, being gradually refined, it will at length return to the fountain from which it flowed."[*] Zoroaster thus taught that the body as well as the soul of man was finally to be united to or absorbed into its original fountain; while Plato taught that only the soul was to be re-united to God, and that the body, together with the passions and appetites belonging to it, was temporary or destructible, and to be got rid of as soon as possible,—a belief which looked towards the asceticism of the Stoic school, in which the philosophy of Plato was afterwards presented in a lower form.

Now, it will be perceived, that, in all these cases, this dualism is neither a positing of two opposite self-subsisting principles,

---

[*] See Brucker's "History of Philosophy."

substances, or causes, nor a legitimate deduction from any original premise, but only the result of a practical necessity. It was a necessary recognition by these philosophers, in order that their systems should in some measure correspond with what are the well-known phenomena of natural and physical existence, and seem to account for those opposite facts of the intellectual and moral consciousness, which are unity and diversity, and good and evil. This dualism was not therefore real, but only apparent; being either a nominal dualism of internal and external principles, related as soul and body, — which did not include any violent opposition, as in the theories of the Egyptians and Ionian Physiologists, — or a representative dualism which included all natural perfection or good on the one side, and all natural imperfection or evil upon the other; these opposite principles being conceived as emanations from One Infinite Substance, and representative, not of the infinite cause from which they emanated, but of the discordant phenomena of natural life.

Of this latter character is the dualism which was recognized by the Marcionites and the Manicheans in theories which grew out of the combination of Pagan ideas with the doctrines of the Christian Church. Marcion recognized "One infinitely perfect almighty and holy God, — the God who is Eternal Love; the Good, who alone is to be denominated God in the proper sense."[*] Besides this Infinite Being "existing from eternity," he recognized a dualism (corresponding with the Persian duality of Light and Darkness which has already been described) in " the Demiurge, a subordinate being of limited power holding a middle place between good and evil," and "Matter — with regard to which he appropriated to himself the common ideas — as the stuff furnished for the creative might of the Demiurge out of which proceeds Evil, — a wild, ungodlike impulse, which became concentrated in Satan."[*] As Neander says, however, "every thing had been seized by him on the practical rather than on the theoretical side;" and this dualism, like the others we have described, was adopted simply as a means of accounting for the phenomena of good and evil; and these principles were not posited either as absolute or as uncreated, but were recognized, as in the Pagan theories, as emanations from the Infinite. With regard to Mani, Neander says, "Mani adopted the Zoroastrian Dualism in all cases where he represented his ideas in images of

---

[*] Neander's "History of the Church."

sense; but he introduced into these symbols Buddhaist notions." If this was so, the dualism of Mani must have been a created dualism derived by emanation from the one infinite substance. Neander, however, believed this to have been an absolute dualism; for he says, "He supposed two principles absolutely opposed to each other, with their opposite creations: on the one side, God, the original good, from which nothing but good can proceed; from whom all destruction, punishment, corruption, is alien, — the primal light, from which pure light radiates: on the other side, original evil, which can work only by destroying, decomposing; whose essence is wild, self-conflicting uproar; matter, darkness, out of which flow powers of an altogether corresponding nature, — a world full of smoke and vapor, and at the same time full of fire that burns only, without shining." Should we accept this conclusion, it would make no difference in the result, because this could not have been a legitimate conception, but only a poetic representation, of Absolute Dualism; and no use could therefore be made of it from a philosophic point of view: we therefore find that Mani did not take up the metaphysical question of intellectual opposition, or the great problem of Unity and Multiplicity, but only the external and practical question of Good and Evil from a moral point of view; showing that this dualism was conceived simply for the purpose of seeming to account for the mixture of good and evil which are found to exist in the phenomena of human experience. Having made this posit of opposite dualistic principles, however, as the ground of his theory, it became necessary that Mani should make some attempt to show how it was that these opposite principles or spheres were combined in the production of mundane existence; or how it was that causes which must necessarily have been unconscious of each other could be conceived as co-operating in the creation of the world. He therefore undertook to do this; and nothing can exceed the absurdity of the method by which he conceived these things to have been effected; a process that has been thus described: "During an intestine war between the always discordant powers of darkness, the conquered party became aware of the hitherto concealed kingdom of light, and wished to despoil it. As, in the conflict for this spoil, a portion of the God-Light came in contact with Hyle or Matter; for the purpose of again restoring this, God, by means of the Mother of Life, or Soul of the World, took upon Himself form, and so ordered it, that the Sun-Spirit, Christ, and the ruler of the Ether, the Holy Ghost, should draw up the captured Light from the earth to themselves. In order that this might be prevented, the evil principle created the Man, whose nature sprung out of a mixture of this light with darkness, or with matter. According to his capability, the man yearned after the Light. Christ, the Son of the Everlasting Light, must therefore come into the world to free the Light-Soul, or to redeem it from its subjection to the material principle; this redemption being effected by the instructions which Christ began, and which the Comforter, (Mani!) from the discourses of Christ, and from the revelations which he himself received, proclaimed. The final consequences resulting from this were taught by Mani to be a universal conflagration of the world, the return of the lost souls to the kingdom of Light, and the fall of the Devil into powerlessness." *

Another poetical theory, devised for the purpose of accounting for the existence of evil in the world, was put forth by Plutarch. Dr. Cudworth, in his "History of the Universe," while showing that, although the heathen nations recognized a multiplicity of gods, they still regarded all things as the production of or as emanating from one infinite principle or substance, alludes to this and other similar theories thus: "We do, indeed, acknowledge that there have been some who have really asserted a duplicity of gods, — that is, of animalish or perceptive beings self-existent; one as the principle of good, and the other of evil. Now, it is evident that this opinion sprung from nothing else, but first a firm persuasion of the essential goodness of the Deity, together with a conceit that the evil that is in the world was altogether inconsistent and irreconcilable with the same; and that therefore, for the solving of this phenomenon, it was absolutely necessary to suppose another animalish principle self-existent, or an evil god; and it is plain, that, had it not been for this business of evil, they would never have asserted any more principles or gods than one. The chiefest and most eminent assertors of this ditheistic doctrine of two self-existent animalish principles in the Universe were the Marcionites and the Manicheans; but besides these, and before them too, some of the professed Pagans also entertained the same opinion; that famous moralist, Plutarchus Chæronesis, being an undoubted patron of it, which, in his book *De Iside et Osiridi*, he represents, with some little difference, after this manner: The generation and continuation

* See "Conversations-Lexicon."

of this world is mixed of contrary powers or principles, — the one good, the other evil, yet not so that they are both of equal force, but the better of them more prevalent; notwithstanding which, it is also absolutely impossible for the worser power or principle to be ever utterly destroyed, — much of it being always intermingled in the soul, and much in the body of the universe; these perpetually tugging against the better principle. In his *Timæan Psychogonia*, he does at large industriously maintain the same; there and elsewhere endeavoring to establish the doctrine upon rational foundations. As, first, that nothing can be made or produced without a cause; and therefore there must of necessity be some cause of evil also, and that a positive one too; he representing the opinion of those as very ridiculous who would make evil to be a natural appendix to the world, and all that evil which is in it to have come in only by the by, and by consequence, without any positive cause. Secondly, that God, being essentially Good, could not possibly be the cause of Evil. Thirdly, that as God could not, so could neither matter, in itself devoid of all form and quality, be the cause of evil, because it receives all its differences from the active principle that moves and forms it. Wherefore, evil must, of necessity, either come from nothing, or else it must come from the active moving principle, which is God. Now, from these premises, Plutarch concludes that the phenomena of evil could not otherwise possibly be solved than by supposing a substantial principle for it, and a certain maleficent soul or demon, unmade, and co-existent with God and matter from eternity, to have been the cause thereof. And accordingly he resolves, that as whatsoever is good in the soul and body of the universe, and likewise in the souls of men and demons, is to be ascribed to God as its only original; so whatsoever is evil, irregular, and disorderly in them ought to be imputed to this other substantial principle, — an irrational and maleficent soul or demon, — which, insinuating itself everywhere throughout the world, is all along intermingled with the better principle: so that neither the soul of the universe, nor the soul of men and demons, was wholly the workmanship of God; but the lower, brutish, and disorderly part of them, the effect of the evil principle."

It will be seen that the question raised by Plutarch, who was a poet and a moralist, but not a philosopher, was not an intellectual, but only a moral question, based upon the superficial and practical ground of natural appearance. It is true that even this natural appearance of evil cannot be accounted for, except upon the ground of evil in the spiritual cause, by which it must, of course, be produced; but, in the case of Plutarch, the phenomenon of evil only led him to infer the existence of an absolute cause as its origin, and did not lead him to posit any absolute principle, or to construct from such statement any theory by which imperfection or evil could rationally be accounted for. It was simply a recognition of the fact, that good and evil are to be referred to opposite spiritual principles or causes, — the sole object being to get rid of the absurdity of referring evil to God; but even the attempt was not made to explain the nature of these two principles, or to show how two opposite principles of any kind could possibly co-operate in the creation of the world, and thus how the opposite phenomena of good and evil could become mixed therein.

An apparently absolute dualism was recognized by the Hebrews, as we may see from the records of the Old Testament, because they were the legitimate representers of a supernatural order of thought; and absolute evil, as well as absolute good, must therefore have been represented, although it could not have been recognized, by them. But this dualism of the Hebrews was poetic, representative, and symbolic, and must have been so for the reason, that until humanity, and consequently philosophy, had been developed in three natural spheres, nothing but poetic representation was possible. Therefore, although this dualism was apparently an absolute one, from the manner of its realization it was made to contradict the dualism which it represented. In this process, the second term was forcibly transferred from the natural to the spiritual, where it could not possibly belong: so that, in point of fact, only one absolute principle was actually posited by the Hebrews. The manner in which they undertook to realize Evil as an absolute fact, or as an absolute personification, was through the apostasy of the angels. But the supposition that absolute evil could originate in the angels, who were not uncreated, but created, cannot be entertained for a moment from any rational point of view, but must be regarded as the poetic representation of an absolute fact that could not then be stated. Besides this apparent recognition of an absolute dualism in good and evil, the Hebrews also made a statement of dualism as a law of universal natural relationship. Thus we read in the book of Ecclesiasticus: "Good is set against Evil, and Life against Death. So is the godly against the sinner, and the sinner against the godly. So look upon all the works of the Most High, and there are two and two, one against the other." It must be seen, however, that this is only the representation of a law that could not be conceived, and so could not really be stated, because it is stated in terms which render it entirely useless for any practical purpose; and we therefore find that this formula, which is here given as a law of universal natural relationship, no one has ever thought of applying for the purpose of classifying and explaining these "works of the Most High."

A dualism similar to that of the Hebrews has been recognized in the Christian Church; where, in addition to a belief in the origin of Absolute Evil through the apostasy of the Angels, and its consequent personification in Satan and other infernal personages who were subordinate to him, Evil is conceived as originating a second time in the first man, Adam; by the apostasy or disobedience of whom, sin and death were introduced into this lower world, and the entire human race were brought under the dominion of Absolute Evil. As this theory of the Church, however, is also poetical and not rational, being only a natural representation of spiritual facts which could not at the time be stated; as the irrational and immoral character of all the theories of the Church, which are fast being abandoned and repudiated, must be obvious to the philosophic mind; and as all the questions which are involved in the theology of the Church will be fully considered and clearly explained in the theological portion of this science,—nothing more need now be said upon this subject.

A dualism has always been recognized in Philosophy, in Infinite and Finite, Spirit and Matter, Unity and Multiplicity, &c., which have been conceived as excluding each other, and still as being referable to one substance or cause; and in the modern eclectical school, founded by Emanuel Kant, this dualism was taken up, from the point of the Consciousness, as Subject and Object. As neither Kant nor any of his followers, however, were able to posit a second universal principle, for the reason that they were confined to a naturalistic point of view, the law of Unity in Diversity became their only governing principle; and the consequence of this was, that, separate from their recognition of the opposite elements in thought, which exclude each other, and still seem to be combined in every fact of consciousness, they were obliged to obtain their principles by generalizing phenomena, in which these elements are combined, and their conclusions by reasoning logically from these generalized appearances. Instead of separating, analyzing, and

THE LAW OF DUALITY. 133

explaining, therefore, they could do nothing but combine, and thus confound; and instead of being led to antagonize opposites, and to discover the law which realizes their union, it finally became their object to show that no opposition really existed between them. As these philosophers attempted to conceive opposite laws, the relationship between them, and the manner in which they become combined in production, before the laws of relationship and of production had been discovered, nothing but failure could have been expected; and we therefore find that nothing but failure was the result. Kant continued to recognize both subjective and objective, both the unconditioned and the conditioned, both the one and the multiple, but maintained that no conception of the subjective, the unconditioned, or the one, was possible to man, and consequently, that, separate from the knowledge derived from sensible experience, nothing can be known; while those of his followers who continued their speculations became lost in a variety of pantheistic, atheistic, and anthropomorphic delusions.

We have now shown that the dualistic theories which have been recognized in Philosophy and in the Church are simply the recognition of an apparent, representative dualism which is found to exist in the phenomena of natural life, having no substantial foundation, and not, therefore, being competent to furnish any law that can aid in the classification and comprehension of these phenomena. This is not the fact, however, with regard to the law of Duality that has here been stated as the universal law of Existence; because, as this law has been founded in a legitimate conception of the manner in which Absolute Existence is realized in the union of opposite Absolute Laws through the Law of Marriage,—and as every thing in the Natural exists as an image or representative of this opposition and of this union,—it is a law by the means of which, in connection with the law of Unity, all natural phenomena can be classified, analyzed, and explained; showing how it is that "the invisible things of God from the creation of the world are clearly seen, being understood by the things that are made, even his Eternal Power and Godhead."

THE LAW OF TRINITY.

According to our statement of the law of Trinity, "As the condition of Spiritual Life, the Individual must become at one with Infinite Life by the marriage in him of spiritual opposites; this being realized through the consciousness of Infinite and Finite Law as a personal experience, — the voluntary sacrifice of Individual Life, — the realization in him of a spiritual substance as the centre of life, — and his regeneration into a spiritual form as a medium for the manifestation of Spiritual Truth, Good, and Beauty."

This universal law of Life is founded in the process by which the union of Infinite and Finite Principles was effected, and Tri-Personality in God established. It may therefore be termed the Law of Marriage which realizes the union of opposites through the voluntary sacrifice of individual life, — a law that is represented in all the vital forms of Philosophy, of Society, and of the Church, and in all the legitimate forms of Art; but is represented in a particular manner in the ontological conceptions of philosophy, and in the theological conceptions, by the church, of Absolute Cause. As these are natural conceptions, however, they contradict the idea which they represent, and therefore cannot be applied by philosophy in the explanation of the origin and nature of phenomenal existence or the facts of the human consciousness, or by the church in the explanation of those theological forms by which the nature of God, of Man, and of Christ, and their relations to each other, are represented; for, as no posit of opposite universal causes as the ground of Existence has been made, no adequate idea of Marriage could, of course, have been realized either by Philosophy or by the Church. A threefold form of absolute substance has been recognized by philosophy, as the ground of her ontological speculations; but this was not because the nature of these forms or the manner in which creation is effected by them was comprehended, but because all natural things are found to exist in this threefold form, and it was inferred that the cause of these must also so exist. These conceptions of a threefold condition of one absolute substance represent the result of the operation of the law of Marriage in the realization of Tri-Personal Absolute Cause, related as spirit, soul, and body, and the activity of this cause in the creation of the Universe; while they contradict this law, because, instead of recognizing the law of Marriage, which realizes the union of opposites in God, and the law of Existence, through which opposites are combined and manifested by the divine providence of God in the production of Natural Life, nothing but the laws of Unity in Diversity and Tri-Unity have been applied in realizing conceptions of God, and of the phenomena of the Universe: and the consequence of this has been, that every thing belonging to a supernatural order of thought has been contradicted, and nothing could be understood; for we have already shown how destructive to philosophy these natural laws have been. A threefold form of Absolute Being has also been adopted by the Church as the foundation of her theology, for the reason that the Scriptures demand this threefold conception as a ground for the representation of Christianity: but in all cases the conception of this form has been suggested to her by some form of the human consciousness, and includes three divine persons whose manifestations in the salvation and regeneration of the soul are of a diversified and discordant character, corresponding with the moral manifestations of human nature in its most external natural condition, and do not suggest one spiritual idea to the mind; while, as we have shown, the realization of Tri-Personality in God is through the experience in an Absolute Sphere of those conditions which, in a phenomenal sphere, constitute the experience of Christianity. Although in theology the religious sentiment has assisted to give a tri-personal character to the conception of God, there has been a constant tendency in the Church to merge the idea of Tri-Personality in that of Tri-Unity, or simple individuality; a tendency of which the unitarians take advantage, to aid them not only to overthrow the idea of Tri-Personality, but to set up their destructive naturalistic forms of thought as the real Trinitarianism, perverting with unholy lips the sacred names of Father, Son, and Holy Ghost. As a preparation, therefore, for the application of the law of Trinity in connection with the laws of Duality and Unity, we will describe the various forms in which this law has been represented in Philosophy and in the Church.

A threefold form as applied to God, or to Absolute Cause, has been recognized from the earliest times in almost every religious and philosophical system. According to Jamblichus, even the Egyptians recognized a triple division of the godhead, in Eicthon, Cneph, and Phtha; representing the first, Eicthon, as an infinite indivisible unity,—the second, Cneph, Emeph, or Hemphta, as a perfect mind converting its intellections into itself,—and the third, which was designated Phtha, Ammon, or Osiris, according to the several powers ascribed to him, as the immediate principle of generation; and, if Jamblichus is correct, it is probable that Plato obtained his statement of three divine hypostases or persons from this source. According to Lücke, the Jewish theology, as recorded by Philo, asserts a similar threefold power or personality in God, as follows: "God, in his interior Essence, is inconceivable, occult, solitary, self-comprised, and without relations to any other existence. Although the absolute cause of all that is, God cannot, in his own Essence, and immediately, operate on the universe either in the way of creation, of preservation, or of government. Concealed in his absolute separation, God is manifest and an object of knowledge in the world, only through his Powers." These powers he terms Logoi, to one of which belongs internal conception, while to the other belongs external action, production, or creation; which makes this statement precisely the same in character as the one previously described.

The Persians recognized a threefold power, as the immediate cause of creation, in Fire, Earth, and Water, under the names of Zarva, Hormisda, and Satana; although, as we have seen, they also recognized a more internal trinity, in Oromasdes, Arimaneous, and Mithras, which represented the union of Light and Darkness in a third principle as the condition of production from them of the dualistic forms of the Universe. The Ionian Dynamicists also recognized this threefold form of Fire, Earth, and Water, making water to be the active or mediating principle through the means of which this fire and earth became united in physical forms. The form of trinity adopted or conceived by the Hindoos is similar to that of the Persians. It includes a supreme creating power, accompanied by a vital and a destructive principle corresponding with the phenomena of the universe; these being the mediums, or secondary causes, through which these phenomena are produced. This trinity is constituted by Brahma the Creator,

Vishnoo the Preserver, and Siva the Destroyer; these being incarnations of one infinite spirit which they denominate Brahm. That this was also a unitarian theory that recognized all things as emanating from one supreme infinite indefinite principle as absolute cause, may be seen from the following extract from the Laws of Menu, which are a part of the Hindoo Scriptures:—

"Let every Brahmin with fixed attention consider all nature, both visible and invisible, as existing in the Divine Spirit; for, when he contemplates the boundless universe existing in the Divine Spirit, he cannot give his heart to iniquity. The Divine Spirit is the whole assemblage of Gods; all worlds are seated in the Divine Spirit; and the Divine Spirit, no doubt, produces the connected series of acts performed by all embodied souls. But we must consider the Supreme Omnipresent Intelligence as the Sovereign Lord of them all; a Spirit which can only be conceived by a mind slumbering; but which he may imagine more subtile than the finest conceivable essence, and more bright than the purest gold. Him some adore as transcendentally present in elementary fire; others in Menu, lord of creatures; some as more distinctly present in Indra, regent of the clouds and the atmosphere; others in pure air; others as the Most High Eternal Spirit."

The trinity of Plato consisted of, first, the Psyche, or universal mundane soul, a self-moving principle and the immediate cause of all that motion which is in the world; next above this, an immovable and standing Nous or Intellect, which was properly the Demiurgus, or architectonic framer of the whole world; and lastly, above this multiform intellect, a higher hypostasis, one most simple and most absolutely perfect being; and this he calls the One in opposition to that multiplicity which speaks something of imperfection in it, and is Goodness Itself, as being above mind and understanding; the first intelligible, and an infinite fecundity together with an overflowing benignity. Macrobius made a similar statement, which is as follows: "God who is, and is called the first cause, is alone the fountain and original of all things that are or seem to be; he by his superabundant fecundity produced, from Himself, Mind; which mind, as it looks upwards towards its father, bears the perfect resemblance of its author, but, as it looks downward, produces Soul. And this soul again, as to its superior part, resembles that mind from whence it was begotten; but, working downwards, produces the corporeal fabric, and acteth upon body."

It is impossible to say whether this peculiar form of tri-unity originated with Plato, with the Hebrews, or with the Egyptians. The question of authorship, however, is a matter of no importance, because it is only the application to God of the common individualization of affection, intelligence, and will or activity, as spirit, soul, and body, and might therefore have originated with them all; being similar to, if not identical with, the Swedenborgian formula, which is, "The Divine Love, — the Divine Wisdom, — and the Divine Proceeding." They do not recognize three persons in God, but only three principles, and these statements neither contain nor suggest any spiritual idea; whereas, in a genuine statement of tri-personality in God, all these three elements of Love, Wisdom, and Power, must be recognized in each person, because he would not otherwise be a person; while these persons must be so conceived as to cover the whole ground of Christianity, and thus to constitute a foundation for Christian Theology; a fact that has been represented by the Church in the construction of its theological system. It is true, that, being metaphysical statements, the fact is recognized, that mind, or intelligence, must necessarily include the element of diversity, and that diversity includes an element of imperfection which cannot be referred to an infinitely perfect being; and it was for this reason that Love was assumed by them to be the supreme principle from which all must have emanated, and thus that mind, or intelligence, was referred to a secondary cause or inferior being: but, instead of representing a vital idea, this conception, on the contrary, represented an inversion of the truth; an inversion of order that will be found to characterize all the destructive manifestations of the mind. Not being able to conceive opposite Universal Causes, and therefore not being able to conceive how imperfection, which includes diversity and evil, could be introduced into the consciousness of God and the phenomena of the Universe, they were forced into the statement of the absurdity, that Imperfection was derived from Perfection; or that diversity was derived from unity, and evil from good. Even if it could be proved that in these statements the three descending spheres of Absolute Being, in which God exists as Spirit, Soul, and Body, had been correctly described, so far as they can be described from a natural point of view; that is, that a conception had here been obtained of an Infinite Personality which is separated from all thought or definite conception, — of a Divine Personality that includes the conception of Creation as a Divine Idea, — and of a Spiritual Personality through which this divine idea becomes realized in the production of a Phenomenal World (and this corresponds externally with the form of Tri-Personality that has here been conceived), — this could not help us to obtain the most distant conception of the Christian idea of God as a Tri-Personality, or be of the least use in the construction of a tri-personal law upon which Philosophy as Absolute Science, or even upon which any system of theology representative of Absolute Truth, could be founded. It is the fact, that our conception of Tri-Personality includes the recognition of opposite indefinite Absolute Principles, and a conception of the Law of Marriage through which these become united in realizing this threefold form, that gives to it all its spiritual and christian character, and makes it available as a foundation for Spiritual Truth; and neither this recognition nor this conception have before been possible, as we have already shown.

St. Augustine suggested a form of trinity; but it was much more imperfect than those already described, because it was simply a generalization of the natural manifestations of the individual, and does not contain any metaphysical idea. In his "Confessions" he says, "Which of us comprehendeth the Almighty Trinity? and yet which speaks not of it, if indeed it be it? Rare is the soul which, while it speaks of it, knows what it speaks of. Men contend and strive, yet without peace: no man sees that vision. I would that men would consider these three that are in themselves! These three are indeed far other than the Trinity: I do but tell where men may practise themselves, and prove and feel how far they are. Now the three I spake of are, To Be, to Know, and to Will. For I Am, and Know and Will: I am Knowing and Willing, and I know myself to Be and to Know." Now, it will be seen, that, in this statement, — which is a generalization of the understanding, and not a conception by religious sentiment, and therefore is not even a representative of any spiritual idea, — St. Augustine has committed the same mistake that we have shown to have been committed by M. Cousin, — that of taking the individual natural consciousness as a pattern of the Deity, or as a representation of Absolute Being, although this anthropomorphic idea is not here so boldly and unqualifiedly expressed. A threefold form of experience in God was conceived by the German Eclectics in the following manner: Infinite Substance is the one, original, self-subsisting cause of all that exists. Being one and universal in its nature, however, it became necessary that this infinite substance should pass out of itself, in order to realize itself, or become definitely conscious,—that in thus passing out from itself it became the opposite of itself, which is finite multiplicity, including imperfection or evil,—and that, in returning from this state of opposition to itself, it realized the union of opposites, established the law of unity in diversity, and constituted God a trinity of facts or of experiences, which were related as internal, external, and medial. It was in this way that the German philosophers after Kant undertook to explain Creation, or the existence of a phenomenal Universe,—to demonstrate that "Being and Nought" were one and the same,—and to show that it is through the forms of human nature that God first arrives at the condition of definite consciousness; although these pantheistic systems were made to include in discordant combination a variety of psychological, theological, and moral theories, which were suggested by the phenomena of human experience and by the theology of the Church. This threefold form of experience in God they undertook to illustrate and demonstrate by attempting the classification of all natural phenomena as internal, external, and medial; and, as the particular forms of things apparently correspond with this rule, they were able to some extent to carry out this classification with regard to external forms: but as the internal condition and relationships of things cannot be classified under this homogeneous form,—because they include an antagonistic dualism, and no law has been discovered through which they can be united,—their classification, instead of being productive, became destructive to the truth.

A variety of these threefold formulas has been conceived by the philosophers as convenient forms under which phenomena might be generalized: that of F. Schlegel was, "Life, Word, and Light;"—that of Amelius was, "Him that Is; him that Hath; and him that Beholds;"—that of Reinhold was, "The Thinker, the Thought, and the Act of Thinking;"—and there was one similar to this, "The Knower, the Known, and the Act of Knowing." But all the threefold forms which have here been enumerated, and indeed all that have ever been conceived by Philosophy, are generalizations of the consciousness from some partial point of view; some being generalizations of the functions of the Understanding, which are Intuition, Sensation, and Reflection; and some of the general functions of the Individual, which are Thought, Affection, and Will. It will therefore be seen that all these forms are realized by the application of the unitarian laws of Tri-Unity and Unity in Diversity to the most external natural forms of the consciousness, — laws which we have shown to be destructive to every thing to which they have been applied. Instead of representing, as they should, the modes of existence and manifestation in God, which must, as even these theorizers themselves allow, furnish the only legitimate foundation of Philosophy as well as of Theology, they only represent the most external natural modes of the human consciousness, which cannot suggest or even represent the spiritual. Having described the various forms which have been constructed by the Understanding in its attempt to describe or to represent the threefold form in which God, as well as all things created by Him, must exist; and having shown that they do not even represent any spiritual idea, but are antagonistic and destructive to the idea of the Spiritual, — we will proceed to describe conceptions which have been founded in intuitions from the sentimental region of the mind, and therefore are really representative of a spiritual order of experiences.

Separate from the form of Tri-personality realized by the Church from legitimate sentimental conceptions, illegitimate conceptions have been realized which are founded in destructive sentimental intuitions, by which a form of tri-unity is produced. Both Emanuel Swedenborg and Jakob Böhme appeared to recognize opposite absolute principles and spheres of being, which they termed Divine and Infernal. In his work entitled "Heaven and Hell," Swedenborg described, in the most particular manner, phenomena which he supposed to be incidental to these opposite spheres; and the following most extreme and monstrous statement, in which all Divine, Infernal, and Phenomenal manifestations are referred to God, was made by Böhme, whose religious conceptions, like those of Swedenborg, represented inversions of spiritual truth, but were more rational and intuitive: "The Holy Deity, being Triune in Nature and in Substance, has a Threefold Life, and manner of Working; whence the Divine Essence is manifested in Three distinct Principles, which cause and comprehend all possible Kinds, Degrees, and Powers of Being, Life, and Operation, and show forth themselves in the existence of, 1. The Dark World, or Hellish Nature; 2. The Light World, or Heavenly Nature; and 3. This Created Mixed World, or Temporal Nature." Notwithstanding all this, both Swedenborg and Böhme were pantheists of the extremest kind; recognizing "the Divine Wisdom, the Divine Love, and the Divine Proceeding," as the original source of all possible manifestations: and, although it seems incredible that such opposite effects as heavenly and hellish natures should ever be referred to the same absolute cause, it is an interesting example of the manner in which Falsehood, through an abuse or perversion of language and an inversion of legitimate ideas, makes that which is one appear as opposite and antagonistic, and then confounds these apparently opposite things, so that they cannot be distinguished; giving to the most complete intellectual insanity the appearance of the greatest profundity, and to a complete inversion of legitimate supernatural phenomena the appearance of a genuine Christian manifestation. Both Böhme and Swedenborg appeared to recognize opposite absolute spheres, in Heaven and Hell; but their statements in relation to these spheres were purely fictitious and deceptive, and calculated to confound the idea of such an opposition with that of natural good and evil: and this may be seen, because they in reality recognized only one absolute substance and cause, and failed to recognize any ground separate from this for a phenomenal universe. This confounding the Infinite with the Finite, and the Absolute with the Phenomenal, is clearly illustrated by the following statement, which was intended by Swedenborg to be an explanation of his theory of Being and of Creation: " From those things which are said in my works concerning the Creation, it is evident that God first made his Infinity Finite by substances emitted from Himself, from which exists his proximate encompassing Sphere, which makes the Sun of the Spiritual World; and that afterwards, by means of that Sun, He perfected other encompassing spheres, even to the last, which consists of things quiescent; and that thus, by means of degrees, He made the world finite more and more. These things are adduced in order that human reason may be satisfied, which does not rest unless it sees the Cause." *

The statement of Tri-personality, upon which the theology of the Church is founded, is necessarily unitarian and naturalistic in character; and it is therefore governed by the natural law of Unity, which is productive of diversity and discord, for the reason that it has not been possible for her to recognize opposite universal spiritual causes. The Church, however, does not, like the Pagan philosophers, conceive one original person or substance as the supreme cause of all things, and derive from this person, either by emanation or by creation as secondary causes, the second and third persons in her trinity. She posits at the commencement Three Persons, co-eternal, co-essential, and in every respect equal;

---

* " True Christian Religion."

by which she recognizes three distinct persons which cannot possibly be conceived as One God, and consequently recognizes three distinct Gods as the objects of her worship: so that the theology of Christianity becomes in the Church, but particularly in the Church of Rome, where to this is added the worship of Saints and of the Virgin Mary, as decidedly polytheistic as the mythologies of Paganism. This statement of Tri-Personality by the Church is a purely religious conception, constructed to meet the peculiar requirements which a representation of Christianity in the forms of religious dogmatism demanded, and for which the letter of the Scriptures furnished very inadequate materials. Being unable, from the natural position occupied by her, to realize a rational conception of God, of Man, and of Christ the Mediator, through the intuition of spiritual laws; and having realized, as natural substitutes for them, intuitions of supernatural phenomena representative of these laws, or of the spiritual phenomena which correspond with them, — she was obliged to incarnate these intuitions of phenomena, which are realized through the religious sentiments, in natural psychological phenomena and individual experiences, which, although representing these phenomena from an external, must have contradicted them from an internal, point of view, because the natural life is opposite and destructive to the ideas thus represented. This incarnation was necessary, because these phenomena had to be recognized by her as spiritual laws, and had to be connected with what was familiar to the individual consciousness in order that they should be comprehended and made the foundation of supernatural thought in forms that could be recognized and appropriated as laws of the individual life. In the construction of a system of theology by the Church from these religious intuitions, as interpreted by psychological and individual experiences which were external and natural in character, it was necessarily realized in correspondence with the common consciousness of the time; and as this was comparatively barbarous, — for the reason that a consciousness corresponding with supernatural thought was now in its infancy, — and was realized through a one-sided development of the Sentimental Nature in forms corresponding with universal laws as interpreted by external natural conceptions of justice which were rude and vindictive in character, the conception of tri-personality upon which the theology of the Church had to be founded partook of an irrational and comparatively barbarous character, — a character that has been defended only upon the ground that it is above all human comprehension, and is to be discerned only through a spiritual perception which is not subject to any intellectual criticism. As the theology of the Church was realized through the means of sentimental and not of rational intuitions, the statement of tri-personality by her did not partake of a metaphysical character, and therefore did not establish any specific relationship between the three persons constituting the Godhead, as had been done by the ontological philosophers, but only the relationship that exists between these several persons and the human soul, and the office which belongs to each in the creation, salvation, and regeneration of man. It is true that the nature of these persons became the subject of extensive discussion among the early fathers of the Church; but this was because it was found very difficult to show from a natural point of view how God could be three, and at the same time one; a fact that it was necessary for them to believe, and therefore necessary that they should explain: and besides this, in their time, religion and philosophy were very closely connected, and thus metaphysical and theological questions were more or less discussed together, notwithstanding there was no correspondence between them, but a perfect antagonism. Many of the early fathers of the Church, by whom Pagan philosophy and Christian theology were confusedly mixed, were in this way led to adopt in whole or in part the theory of Plato with regard to the three divine hypostases, because this was the best metaphysical statement with regard to God, or to Absolute Being, that could be found. In this case, however, their belief as philosophers had no connection whatever with their belief as churchmen; for, while the poetic statement of tri-personality by the Church furnished a suitable foundation for the construction of a system of theology harmonious with or truly representative of Christianity, this Pagan metaphysical statement was wholly unsuitable for any such purpose; because, being perfectly unitarian and naturalistic in character, it necessarily leads to a pantheistic fatalism that is destructive not only to Christianity, but to all natural morality. These Pagan tri-theistic statements were, therefore, as we are informed by Dr. Cudworth, opposed by the more sound and orthodox portions of the Church, as "including Arianism, Socinianism, or Deism, and thus favoring Atheism."

The poetic statement made by the Church of the doctrine of Tri-Personality, as the ground of their theology, included three persons, co-eternal, co-substantial, and in every respect equal, designated by the names of Father, Son, and Holy Ghost; and these Divine Persons were connected with the human consciousness by conceiving them as corresponding with the three elements of the moral nature, in which Good is produced by the combined operation of the principles of Justice and Sympathy, which are, in the natural, discordant: and the reason why the general form of the moral nature was taken as the foundation of this statement of Christianity by the Church is, that the religious and moral natures are related as internal and external, or as soul and body; and therefore, in a spontaneous incarnation of religious truth from internal recognition, the forms of the moral nature presented the only legitimate material. In this construction of a system of Christian theology by the incarnation of religious intuitions in the forms of the moral nature, therefore, the Father was conceived as the incarnation of Justice, and thus as a lawgiver to the human race; — the Son was conceived as the incarnation of Sympathy, or of Mercy, and thus as the Friend and Saviour of mankind; — while the Holy Ghost was conceived as a sanctifying influence proceeding from the Father and the Son, which becomes productive of Good in the soul: and the manner in which these conceptions were applied in the construction of a theological system is as follows: Taking the letter of the Scriptures as the ground of this theology, commencing with the Mosaic account of the creation, temptation, and fall of man, the following conception was produced: It was assumed that the first man, Adam, having violated the command of the Father in eating of the fruit of the tree of the knowledge of good and evil, and having thus committed an offence against an infinite being which demanded an eternal punishment, — although what this offence really was has never been explained, — the sentence of spiritual death, which is eternal damnation, was pronounced against him; and it was further assumed, that, in consequence of this sin by Adam, his whole nature became changed and corrupted, and that this corruption descended from him to his posterity, either by imputation or through natural generation, entailing upon them all the consequences of his apostasy, so that the doom of everlasting punishment in Hell was inherited by them from him.

Having applied her conception of the Father as the incarnation of Justice in accounting for the doom of spiritual death, which they supposed to be impending over the human race, the Church next applied her conception of the Son as the incarnation of Sympathy, or of Mercy, for the purpose of explaining the redemption of mankind from this doom and from the depravity inherited from Adam. She assumed that the Son became so much affected by his compassion for the miserable condition and prospects of the human race, that he offered to make satisfaction to the Father for the offence of Adam and his posterity by taking upon himself the human nature, and with it " the sins of the whole world," and suffering the penalty of death in their stead;—that, being an infinite person, he was capable of expiating an offence committed against the infinite, or of paying an infinite debt, which man, as a finite creature, could not do;—and that the Father, recognizing this competency in the Son, and considering his death to be equivalent to the death or damnation of the whole human race, accepted his Son as their substitute, who consequently became incarnated in a human form, and suffered death upon the cross, as related in the Scriptures;—and it was supposed by her, that, in consequence of this sacrifice by the Son, the human race was redeemed from the penalty of spiritual death incurred by the original sin of Adam: so that nothing was now left to be accounted for but the manner in which man was to be restored to the original condition of holiness before God in which he was created. To effect this, her conception of the Holy Ghost as the incarnation of Good, or as the Sanctifier, was introduced; and she further assumed, that, before the soul could really experience the benefit of Christ's sacrifice, a birth from the Holy Ghost was necessary, by which Christ should be born in the soul, and its regeneration effected. It was assumed, that, in consequence of the sacrifice of Christ, the Holy Ghost descended upon mankind; or that he came into the world for the purpose of regenerating it, and was continually present in each individual to whom the gospel had been preached, soliciting admission into his heart; but that, before this could take place, the fulfilment of certain conditions by the individual was necessary, which, being a free agent, he was able to fulfil or not, as he should choose. It was assumed, that if within the period of his natural life, which is limited to this atmosphere, he shall fulfil these conditions, he will be saved; but that if " he dies, and makes no sign," he is deprived of all benefit from this sacrifice of the Son, and must suffer the penalty of spiritual death originally incurred by all men through the sin of Adam. What constitutes the sign of grace and of deliverance, is, of course, the great subject of dispute: but this is always regarded as some particular form of belief or of practice, which is varied in each denomination and division of the Church; although it is held at the same time by the Protestant Church, that no one can experience a saving belief, or perform any service acceptable to God, except those whom He has chosen from the foundation of the world; all others having been ordained from that time to everlasting perdition.

It is difficult to make any statement of this dramatic parable upon which the Church has founded her system of theology, without seeming to make an unfair exaggeration. We neither desire nor intend, however, to throw any unnecessary odium upon that system which has for nineteen centuries served to keep alive a natural representation of the prominent ideas and facts of Christianity,—which has performed such incalculable service in the natural regeneration of the human constitution,—and which performs a still further use in furnishing external suggestive material in the incarnation of vital Spiritual Laws. We believe this to be a plain statement of the theory of the Church; a theory that could have originated only in a very immature condition of the human consciousness: and it must be at once seen that her statement of tri-personality in God was especially made as a foundation for her peculiar system of theology; that it is not suitable for any other purpose; and that, instead of being competent to furnish universal laws as a ground for Philosophy, it is a poetic statement that is in the highest degree irrational, and is regarded by the Church as a sublime mystery. When the religious sentiments which furnish support for these crude and imperfect representatives of the Supernatural become inoperative, and the mind descends from representations of the supernatural to conceptions of natural truth, and the individual demands a consistency and reality for his belief that is more congenial with self-conscious right and sympathetic feeling than with blind obedience to external direction and to crude conceptions of vindictive supernatural law, these doctrines become repudiated, and beliefs founded in internal and external natural appearances, which are the opposite of what they seem, take their place; and, when the individual enters into an internal or transcendental sphere of consciousness, he becomes conceptive of destructive supernatural laws through the operation of which the doctrines and symbolism of the Church are inverted, so that a representation of Absolute Falsehood, instead of Absolute Truth, beomes realized. When these, too, shall become exhausted, the individual must seek repose in the Spiritual Itself.

Having stated the laws of Unity, Duality, and Trinity, which together constitute the Law of Tri-Personality, according to which all things exist and become manifested; and having separated from these laws all the natural conceptions which have been substituted for them, — we will proceed to apply this threefold law in the explanation of phenomena, so that we may have both external and internal demonstration of its truth, and may show how it is to be applied in the multiplication of knowledge in all departments of thought. We shall first apply it in obtaining a statement, and demonstration by the most copious illustration, of the Laws of Representation or Correspondence according to which all things are constructed; next, in obtaining a statement, and demonstration by similar illustrations, of the Laws of Succession or Growth according to which all things become manifested; next, in realizing a complete System of Theology that shall describe the Nature of God, of Man, and of Christ the Mediator, from a spiritual point of view; and, finally, we shall apply this law in realizing a complete System of Psychology that shall include all the primitive forms of the Human Constitution. In this way we shall realize Philosophy in its only legitimate form, which is that of Absolute Science, in which Ontology, Theology, and Psychology are made completely one as Spirit, Soul, and Body.

THE
LAWS OF CORRESPONDENCE
OR OF
REPRESENTATION.

"FOR THE INVISIBLE THINGS OF HIM FROM THE CREATION OF THE WORLD ARE CLEARLY SEEN, BEING UNDERSTOOD BY THE THINGS THAT ARE MADE; EVEN HIS ETERNAL POWER AND GODHEAD." — Rom. i. 20.

"GOOD IS SET AGAINST EVIL, AND LIFE AGAINST DEATH: SO IS THE GODLY AGAINST THE SINNER, AND THE SINNER AGAINST THE GODLY. SO LOOK UPON ALL THE WORKS OF THE MOST HIGH; AND THERE ARE TWO AND TWO, ONE AGAINST THE OTHER." — Ecclus. xxxiii. 14, 15.

LAWS OF CORRESPONDENCE.

HAVING established by a strictly logical process the fact of Tri-Personality in God, by reasoning from the conception of Infinite Life as a point of departure, — having described the process by which Absolute Existence becomes realized as Creating Cause, and Infinite Life becomes the Living God, — having shown that the laws of Matter, and the susceptibility in them for realizing by combination a definite sphere of Phenomenal Being, are by this incarnation of the Infinite Life realized as an objective experience in the consciousness of God, and that this phenomenal sphere constitutes a medium through which Absolute Causes can be represented in a natural and manifested in a spiritual manner, in the most external and diversified forms, — and having constructed from these statements three formulas, as the Law of Tri-Personality, which we are to take as an external point of departure, and to apply in the construction of Philosophy as Absolute Science, — we will proceed to apply this law in the explanation of the Creation which necessarily resulted from this realization of God as Absolute Creating Cause, thus demonstrating the universality of this law. This is a strictly legitimate mode of proceeding, upon the ground that the phenomenal and absolute spheres of Indefinite Being are analogous, and that all phenomenal things must be constituted as representatives of facts which have been realized in an Absolute Sphere of Being; and this is shown to be a legitimate ground, because we not only demonstrate, but are taught in the Scriptures, that Man, who is the head of this Creation, is made "in the Image of God," and that "the invisible things of Him from the creation of the world are clearly seen, being understood by the things that are made, — even his Eternal Power and Godhead."

We see, therefore, that our subject now assumes an entirely different aspect, and demands an entirely different treatment; that, instead of continuing the application of a logical process, an analogical process must now be instituted, in order that we should be made to understand the nature of this creation, and particularly that we should understand the relationship that exists between the creature and the Creator. It is now demanded, that we apply the Law of Tri-Personality just realized; first, in obtaining a statement and illustration of the Universal Laws of Correspondence, according to which all things are created; and, next, in obtaining a statement and illustration of the Laws of Succession, or of Growth, according to which all natural changes are effected; because these laws must necessarily be contained in and suggested by this tri-personal law, and it is only by a statement of them, and also an illustration of them by reference to the phenomena of creation, that the nature of this law or the character of these phenomena can possibly be understood. The institution of the mode of demonstration by Analogy will probably be objected to by the logicians, who perhaps think that correspondences and analogies belong rather to poetry than to philosophy; although the use of these in the Scriptures and in the Church, as the medium for representing the highest truths, ought to make them suspicious of such an opinion: but they have yet to learn, that the Imagination, and not the logical faculty, is the true organ of Philosophy and incarnator of Truth; and that in the Reason, which is the highest power of the mind, originate Laws of Correspondence which are the life of Philosophy. The failure to obtain a conception of these laws as the foundation for Analogy, — which represents the relationships between internal and external, and between spiritual and natural things, — and the consequent neglect of analogy as a philosophical method or form, has prevented any advance in the philosophy either of the human mind or of the Universe, — has made the realization of philosophy in a scientific form impossible, — and has confined it almost exclusively to the sphere of psychology, which is a region of empiricism. This is a region of empiricism, because no conception of the opposite spiritual causes which all things are created to represent, or of the natural laws which constitute the life of human nature, can here be obtained; and because it is a region in which nothing but discordant and deceptive appearances can be known, in reasoning from which nothing but confusion and contradiction can result. Even the philosophers of the modern speculative school founded by Kant, who undertook the union of ontological laws with psychological phenomena, were led either to the conclusion, that the Absolute lies beyond the limits of human cognition, and that our knowledge is consequently confined within the limits of sensible experience; or to the still more destructive conclusion, that absolute and phenomenal — being and non-being — are the same, and therefore that the apparent is also the real. Before we proceed to state the Laws of Representation and of Succession which are suggested by our statement of the Law of Tri-Personality, we will consider the general subject of Correspondence, that we may be able to separate those correspondences which are fanciful, and therefore false and fictitious, from those which are truly representative; and that we may also be able to separate even these from the spiritual laws and forms of correspondence, upon which alone Philosophy can be founded.

Correspondence is the law of Incarnation by Representation, according to which all production is realized, and through which the Phenomenal becomes an image or external representative of the Absolute, the Natural of the Spiritual, and the External of the Internal; so that even "the invisible things of God from the creation of the world are clearly seen, being understood by the things that are made, — even His eternal power and Godhead." Physical representation thus becomes the ground of all consciousness, and of all expression through which the consciousness is communicated; Language being constructed to represent this relationship between internal or mental, and external or physical phenomena. We cannot therefore but perceive how indispensable to the discovery and comprehension of truth a knowledge of these relationships must be, but especially a knowledge of the laws which govern them, and through which we can therefore separate the true from the false and fictitious; and it is to the decline of this knowledge, which has resulted from the development of the mind from within outwards, so that little except that which is fanciful and false remains, that we are to ascribe the great depreciation that has taken place both in Art and in Philosophy. Now, although "the invisible things of God" are to be "clearly seen, being understood by the things that are made," we are not to suppose that natural phenomena can lead to a knowledge of spiritual things, but only that they will help us to incarnate the spiritual phenomena of which they are the representatives, when the Spiritual Itself shall be realized from the most internal point of the consciousness. Nothing can be more opposite than these natural and spiritual things, not only because the natural life of

Creation is opposite to the life of God, but because every natural phenomenon is the opposite of what it appears to be; and therefore, should we take these as a point of departure in the search after Absolute Truth, we should arrive at nothing but Falsehood. Natural Phenomena, whether these are derived from external observation or from internal observation in the consciousness, besides being false and deceptive, exist in the utmost diversity and discord; so that it is impossible to reason from them with any prospect of arriving at the truth, or even of realizing any consistent theory of life, either natural, supernatural, or spiritual. Even with regard to natural life, it has come to be a universally accepted rule, that we cannot reason from phenomena, but only from law; for even the most inveterate materialist or sensualist, who is simply a generalizer of phenomena, will allow that phenomena must be exhausted before the most universal generalization can be realized as the law through which he hopes to obtain an explanation of them. Those who reason from phenomena are therefore obliged to assume some phenomenon or generalization of phenomena to be a law, before any process of reasoning can be commenced. As Correspondence is a universal medium of representation, it is constructed in a tri-personal form, and is divided into three regions of experience corresponding with these three spheres; the relationship between which is that of body, soul, and spirit; the body being negative and destructive, the soul relative and representative, and the spirit vital and productive. The principles of the mind through which these forms of correspondence are realized are the Fancy, the Imagination, and the Reason; and we will therefore state the kind of correspondences which are produced by each of these, in order that we may learn how to separate the spiritual from the natural, and the true from the false and fictitious.

By means of the Fancy, we obtain, instinctively and spontaneously, a knowledge of those relationships between phenomena which arise in partial and superficial resemblances between their attributes, functions, and forms, and between these and the attributes, forms, and functions of the mind; its most important function being the power of instituting relationships between the mental states and the phenomena of material existence, in which it either incarnates these states by connecting them with visible forms and functions, or ideally invests physical phenomena with attributes of feeling and of thought. These forms of correspondence, which we call Metaphors or Similes, constitute one of the most external elements in language, and the most external mode of communicating a knowledge of the individual mental condition or state ; and is thus resorted to by those individuals, nations, and races who exist in an immature and external condition of the consciousness, and are obliged to depend upon a spontaneous feeling of relationship by which to illustrate what they are not able either to comprehend or to express. From the definition here given, which is one generally recognized, of the nature of the metaphor or simile as a form of correspondence, it will be seen, that although these poetic forms of the Fancy serve the purpose of illustration, give diversity and richness to language and to thought, and are necessary to constitute the body of correspondence, they can never furnish an appropriate medium for the expression of truth, for the reason that they present to us an appearance of relationship between things which have no real relationship; and they must, therefore, constitute a destructive element in every thing into which they are introduced. When separated from and thus not corrected by the higher powers of the mind, instead of furnishing a medium for the expression of truth, they will furnish a medium for the expression of falsehood. We accordingly find the Fancy to be the constructor of all the forms of Wit and of Humor; the foundation of which we shall hereafter demonstrate to be falsehood, because they are constituted by the combination of those things which appear to be like, while they are in reality the most unlike and opposite.

By means of the Imagination, which in a natural sphere of consciousness is simply apprehensive in character, and therefore confined to the perception of phenomena and their relations, we obtain spontaneously an apprehensive knowledge of those real relationships between phenomena which arise in the correspondence that has been ordained to exist between internal and external and between spiritual and natural things; and it possesses the power of recognizing those external things which symbolize the spiritual, as well as those which symbolize the internal natural conditions ; so that the knowledge furnished by the Imagination is as real as that furnished by the Fancy is fictitious. These conceptions of the Imagination, which give comprehensiveness and truth to language, and unity and rationality to thought, we denominate Analogies. As these are internal and intellectual in character, being contrasted with those of the Fancy which are external and affectional, they belong to knowledge or to truth, and are therefore useful for the purpose of demonstration or conviction as well as for illustration; and they constitute the soul of Correspondence, in a natural sphere of consciousness, the function of which is to incarnate the Supernatural in sensible images and in forms of thought. This constitutes the Imagination the highest incarnating power of the mind, because it becomes receptive of ideas from the Reason and from the Sentiment, which it incarnates in legitimate symbolic forms. Here originate, therefore, the highest forms of Philosophy, Theology, and Art; here originated those correspondences which constitute the letter of the Jewish Scriptures, and also that symbolism in which the history and teaching of Christ is embodied, which constitutes the letter or most external form of the New Testament. These correspondences do not of themselves communicate any supernatural truth to the mind, but only act upon the religious sentiment in producing an apprehensive recognition of it; and even this is realized only in the most external sphere of consciousness. They are supernatural forms which cannot be interpreted by the natural understanding except in a fanciful and fictitious manner, by which a meaning opposite to the real one is produced: and we therefore find that the history and teaching of Christ, which are entirely symbolic, have been used more than any other portion of the Bible to support naturalistic ideas, which are opposite and destructive to supernatural truth; while the correspondences of the Old Testament, which are more external and therefore still further removed from an apparent resemblance to the things represented, have been used to sustain the most destructive external manifestations. Although becoming thus destructive when interpreted by the understanding from a natural point of view, these supernatural correspondences and natural analogies of the Imagination are not only calculated to give a natural vitality to language and to thought, and to act upon the sentimental principles in an unconscious manner in the production of vital sentimental experiences, but they are also calculated to act as suggestive material in the conception by the Imagination, in a spiritual sphere of consciousness, of those spiritual forms of correspondence which are combined with the intuition of Absolute Law in the production of spiritual knowledge. Even these spiritual analogies of the Imagination do not, however, of themselves communicate any spiritual knowledge to the mind, because they are in relation to Spiritual Law external and representative, and are only calculated to combine with the conception of Universal Spiritual Laws in the realization by incarnation of Spiritual Truth.

Through the natural development of the Reason, which is the spiritual region of the mind, we obtain intuitions representative of the Universal Laws of Being and of the relationship existing between God and Creation from an ontological point of view; these being Supernatural Laws of Correspondence which unconsciously constitute the internal, vital, and productive powers in the realization of all Ontological forms of Philosophy, Religion, and Art. By means of the Reason in a spiritual sphere of consciousness, we obtain intuitions of the Universal Laws of Being which constitute the indefinite ground of Existence, and also of the laws through which these become united in the realization of Definite Being in Absolute and Phenomenal Spheres; and these constitute the ground from which we derive the Spiritual Laws of Correspondence, a conception of which must be realized as the condition of spiritual and real knowledge. By the conception of these laws, and their incarnation and application through the Spiritual Imagination, Truth becomes One and Universal, — the supernatural symbolic forms of the Imagination are invested with a higher life or significance, which brings them out of a poetic into a philosophic region of the consciousness, — the relationships of the natural, and those existing between the natural and the spiritual, are explained, — all hidden things are revealed, — and the records of Inspiration become harmonious and comprehensible. These spiritual laws of correspondence we have conceived and embodied in a statement of the Law of Tri-Personality, from which we obtain a conception of the Laws of Representation and of Succession, which govern the structure and manifestations of all created things.

Before we proceed to state and to apply these laws in the classification and analysis of these forms and manifestations, let us consider some of the difficulties which we shall have to encounter in carrying on this process; for, if we understand at the outset what obstacles we have to expect, we shall be better prepared for them, and better able to overcome them. If Absolute Truth could be recognized from a natural, unitarian point of view, our task would be an easy one; for then, all things being homogeneous, the external harmonious with the internal, the affectional with the intellectual, and the natural with the spiritual, the senses alone were sufficient as a guide to its discovery by tracing all effects in nature up to their spiritual cause. A science of Correspondence might then be constructed upon the basis of observation; and, by a generalization of the forms and the functions or apparent uses of things, we might obtain a knowledge of the laws which govern them, and the relations which bind them together. We have seen, however, that this process of classification by generalization under a naturalistic law has resulted in nothing but a succession of failures from the commencement of philosophy down to the present time, until every possible method has been exhausted without the advance of a single step: indeed, that, instead of advancing, philosophy has receded, and is now, so far as the truth is concerned, inconceivably far behind the position that was first occupied by it. It is this that has made the establishment of a new and opposite method necessary at the present time. It must be understood, however, that all these systems of philosophy have been constructed in harmony with the natural conditions of the human mind; and therefore, that, in establishing this new method, we establish something not harmonious with but antagonistic to the natural consciousness, or to what appears to the natural mind to be true. It calls upon us to deny all the natural perceptions of the mind, and to regard them, not merely as unreal, but as opposite to the real; and this can be done only by a faith in absolute truth that is strong enough to overcome the natural world.

It will be seen, then, that in constructing a system of philosophy upon the ground of universal spiritual truths, — although all natural things are to be explained by the application of these truths as the laws of absolute science, and cannot, as we may see, be explained in any other way, — the natural understanding, the natural affection, and the natural consciousness, must be brought into direct opposition to these laws, and consequently to most of the conclusions which are drawn from them: for the reason that "the natural man receiveth not the things of the Spirit of God, for they are foolishness unto him; neither can he know them, because they are spiritually discerned." This opposition between the natural and the spiritual is represented in the history of the Church and of the religious experiences of individuals, because the Church and the Religious Sentiments are the supernatural representatives of the Spiritual. The theological statements of the Church are therefore perfect contradictions to the natural understanding, to the natural affection, and to that which seems to the individual to be his real condition; and are only sustained by the predominating influence of those religious principles which are in harmony with a supernatural order of thought and of experience: so that, when these religious sentiments decline, and a natural order of thought obtains the ascendency, these beliefs of the Church come to be regarded as the most absurd and hateful of superstitions; while the religious individual, instead of being discouraged or alarmed at these contradictions, considers them as proofs of the genuineness of the doctrine; and thus the most glaring inconsistencies and improbabilities, instead of weakening, strengthen his belief.

The first obstacle that we meet in the investigation of phenomena is their division and antagonism, which arises in the fact, that all created things, and thus the human constitution, represent, both in their forms and in their manifestations, Opposite Universal Laws; for although they include supernatural forms, through which these opposites are combined and manifested, the manner in which this is effected cannot become a fact of consciousness; and these manifestations are, in the natural, realized in diversity and discord, for the reason that Marriage cannot here be realized, and all conscicus natural manifestations must be governed by the laws of diversity, partiality, and separation. In consequence of this, the individual cannot state any one general principle or law that is not contradicted by some other that is opposite, both of which it is necessary to recognize, because they are combined in manifestation; and we find in human nature principles relating to opposite orders of thought and of life which cannot become reconciled, so that the internal and supernatural aspirations and intuitions of the soul are constantly met and opposed by external and natural wants and beliefs; it being amid the conflict of these that the natural growth and development of the individual are secured. The most serious obstacle, however, that presents itself to the acquisition of spiritual knowledge, is the unreal and deceptive character of all appearances, or the fact that these are the opposite of what they seem. Many might very readily accept the statement, that the Spiritual is real, and the Natural is unreal, while they would deny the conclusion, that every natural appearance is false, or the opposite of what it seems; although the acceptance of one must demand that of the other. It is a belief which is, of all others, the most repugnant to the natural mind, because it has faith in appearances. Even with regard to physical things, which can be brought under the operation of chemical analysis, and thus subjected to the test of sensible experience, it is very difficult to convince the mind that this is true; but, when we come to those things which are the objects of internal consciousness, it is very much more difficult, because here no scientific test can be applied except that of

Absolute Science, which is now for the first time realized, and which demands of the individual the acknowledgment, that he does not and cannot know any one thing except what he derives from a knowledge of the Universal Laws of Being, and can connect by a legitimate chain of relationship with these laws. The unreal and deceptive character of the manifestations of human nature here mentioned arises in both an unconscious and a conscious deception, by which the subject becomes still more complicated. The natural mind is unconsciously deceptive: first, because it cannot know that the facts of its consciousness are necessarily false, but is obliged to believe in them as true; and, next, because both falsehood and unconsciousness are finite characteristics which must be represented in the manifestations of human nature. The external and the affectional principles of the mind, which as relatively female are the particular representatives of the finite principle, are therefore characterized by an unconscious spontaneity that is harmonious with the finite, presenting the appearance, and even communicating to the individual a consciousness, of truthfulness and simplicity in proportion as he is false and complex; and, although it is particularly difficult to recognize this as the most deceptive and destructive condition of the individual, it is necessary that we should do so. The natural mind is consciously deceptive, because the falsehood that inheres in these feminine principles of the mind is brought into the light as a fact of consciousness by its internal and intellectual or masculine principles; and, when these fail to gain the ascendency, they come into subjection to those which are below them; and the consequence is, that the individual aims to appear, and possesses the power of appearing, the opposite of what he is, even without the operation of any particular motive for so doing. This condition is, however, less dangerous than the first, not only because this calculated deception is made apparent, and we therefore guard against it, but because it is really less false, and therefore less destructive, although it is difficult so to regard it.

Another obstacle to the acquisition of spiritual knowledge arises in the manner in which the human constitution grows and becomes developed under the law of Contrariety, — presently to he stated and fully illustrated, — according to which the individual grows from below upwards, while his mind becomes developed from within outwards; because, by the operation of this law, the lowest and the highest things are brought together and are combined in manifestation, and the highest and most vital ideas are represented in the lowest and most destructive condition of the individual life; while, as the individual is developed, and becomes more simple, truthful, and vital, he is made to become conscious of, to incarnate, to appropriate, and to manifest as the laws of his life, the destructive laws of the mind which represent the finite: so that the experiences of human nature are brought into a state of complete contradiction, and the most vital things are represented to and by the individual in proportion as he is removed from the possibility of their realization. These difficulties are not mentioned to account for any imperfection in their explanation by this philosophy, but only to show some of the obstacles which the mind will have to encounter in its reception by the individual; because this science is so exact, so searching, and so universal, that all things are explained by its application.

The fact that Creation is not real, but is simply relative, and representative of opposite things which cannot be reconciled, while its life, of which the individual is not conscious, is constituted by laws representing the Finite, — is in all things the opposite of what it seems, — and exists in a state of perpetual change, so that, beyond the merest external form, things have neither consistency nor fixedness, — has made the study of human nature, from the natural point of view to which the mind has been confined, extremely difficult and unsatisfactory, and a knowledge of its real character utterly impossible. Being representative of opposite things which cannot be reconciled, its manifestations can be generalized only under the law of Unity in Diversity, by which they have been confounded; and, consequently, it has not been possible to recognize either the opposition that exists between the dualistic forms of the human constitution, or the changes which are continually taking place in its condition and relationships in consequence of its growth from below upwards, and its development, in a contrary direction, from within outwards. As the individual is confined to a belief in appearances, and therefore supposes what is simply representative to be real, these unreal appearances have taken the place, in the common belief, of realities which are opposite in character; and as these appearances are dualistic and contradictory, so that nothing can be affirmed that cannot also be contradicted, knowledge has been realized in a discordant and contentious form, and every opportunity has been given to the narrow-minded, the hypocrite, and the fanatic, for disputing the most vital of theoretical and productive forms, and for exercising the Fancy in confounding opposite things, so that neither can be understood, and every kind of interpretation can be given to them. These difficulties have been increased by the fact, that, in the structure of language, the same term is demanded to express or to represent a great variety of things which are similar, but have no real relationship; and that we are required to speak of things as they appear, although they are opposite to what they seem. With regard to physical phenomena, these false appearances can easily be detected and corrected by scientific experiment; but with regard to mental phenomena, or to the facts of the consciousness, no science has existed by which the false representative appearance could be separated from and antagonized to the real fact; and the consequence has been, that a superficial definition and use of langague based upon appearances, which are discordant, contradictory, and the opposite of what they seem, has almost universally taken the place of an exact and scientific definition and use.*

By the statement and application of the Universal Laws upon which our science is founded, all the difficulties to which we have here alluded will be overcome. We shall therefore find no difficulty in determining the true position, character, and relationship of every phenomenon, because, by the application of these laws, we obtain a perfect classification of all the forms of the Universe, including those of the human constitution; and also obtain a legitimate explanation of the manifestations of the soul in all the different spheres of its existence: and we are able to do this for the reason that we realize Philosophy as Universal Absolute Science, founded in a conception of Infinite and Finite Laws as opposite Universal Indefinite Causes, and of the manner in which God becomes individualized as tri-personal Creating Cause; because all things are created and are manifested as representatives of these spiritual facts. By applying the Law of Tri-Personality, which has been founded upon this conception, we shall be able to show that every thing in the natural is realized and becomes manifested through the supernatural combination of opposite elements representative of infinite and finite principles, — to describe the particular character of this opposition, — and to show the various and even opposite results which are produced by this combination and manifestation. We shall be able to show, that, although all Existence is necessarily dualistic, because it must contain elements corresponding with both Infinite and Finite, and therefore with

---

* Appendix I.

diversity and partiality as well as unity and universality, dualism does not necessarily include discord, — that, even in the natural, an individualization of these vital and destructive elements is effected by their supernatural combination and manifestation, by which a natural vitality becomes realized, — and that, although, upon coming into a spiritual sphere of consciousness, opposite absolute laws must be presented to the soul, and affinities for these realized as a personal experience, it is redeemed from this opposition and reconciled to God through the sacrifice of individual life. As the Law of Tri-Personality includes three fundamental laws which govern all the manifestations of Existence, — these being the laws of Opposition, Attraction, and Marriage, — before proceeding to apply this law in the conception, classification, and explanation of the forms, functions, and manifestations of natural and of spiritual life, by which it is to be verified, we will consider separately these three great laws, in order that their origin and the nature of their operation may be clearly understood. Having realized a conception of these laws, we will first apply them in the explanation of the forms and functions of Phenomenal Existence, describing these in a regular series from the most universal to the most particular, commencing with the Universe, and ending with the forms and manifestations of the Human Constitution, first in an external, and next in an internal, sphere of the natural consciousness. We shall next apply them in explaining the natural and supernatural phenomena of the human consciousness from a theological point of view, as contrasted with spiritual experiences; and, finally, we shall apply them in conceiving and explaining the spiritual phenomena which are incidental to the resurrection of the soul into a spiritual sphere of consciousness.

The LAW OF OPPOSITION, as a universal law of existence, may be referred to four principal causes: namely, that Infinite and Finite, as opposite spheres of Indefinite Being, constitute the opposite poles of Existence as vital and destructive powers; that, in the natural form of Absolute Existence, Infinite and Finite become incarnated and represented in opposite forms; that Creation, or Phenomenal Existence, is the result of a combination of infinite and finite phenomenal laws; and that the Material Universe, with Man as its head, is created to represent Absolute Existence. Every thing therefore comes into existence in a discordant dualistic form, constituted by vital and destructive elements, which are related as Male and Female, and Internal and External; the relationship between these being described in the

Scriptures as life against death, and good against evil; the godly against the sinner, and the sinner against the godly. As all these dualistic forms of Creation are externally representative of the opposite forms in Absolute Existence, in which Infinite and Finite become represented through opposite forms of Truth and Good, we will here state the origin, nature, and relationships of these universal forms of life, and show the manner in which they have been illustrated in the Scriptures, and in the Church.

We are to obtain a knowledge of the nature of Truth and Good, and of the relationship between these as male and female and internal and external, from a conception of the manner in which Infinite Wisdom and Infinite Love become incarnated in definite forms as Absolute Truth and Good, and these become represented in a phenomenal sphere of being. Now, in conceiving the incarnation of the Infinite, as Life Itself, in the definite forms of Existence, we have been obliged to conceive this incarnation as being produced through the means of an Opposite, which is the Finite, subsisting as Death Itself; that is, we have been obliged to conceive Existence as being produced by the Infinite through or out of the Finite, and therefore to conceive these infinite and finite principles, which constitute opposite spheres of Indefinite Being, as Male and Female: and the consequence of this is, that we are obliged to conceive this production as Dual, or as constituted by incarnations, upon the one hand, representative of the Infinite, as Male, as Internal, as Conscious, and as Vital, in forms of Truth; and, upon the other, of the Finite, as Female, as External, as Unconscious, and as Destructive, in forms of Good; these male and female spheres being also divided and antagonized as internal and external, which are vital and destructive, because both infinite and finite must be represented in each natural sphere: and we are also obliged to conceive these antagonistic principles as being combined and manifested through a mediating principle in forms representing Marriage, in which the destructive is made subject to the vital principle, in Use. These absolute relationships, through a conception of which we obtain a knowledge of the nature and relationships of truth and good, as natural productions, are represented in all the forms, functions, and manifestations of the Human Constitution. They are represented in the constitution of the Mind, first, in its supernatural and natural regions, — the first containing internal and external departments constituted by the Religious and Moral Sentiments, which are the exponents of supernatural truth and good, and are related as vital and destructive; and the second containing internal and external departments, constituted by the Understanding and the Instinct, which are the exponents of natural truth and good, and are related as vital and destructive. They are represented, next, as every department of the mind contains a male region which is relatively soul, and is perceptive and actively communicative, as a sphere of Law representing Truth, and a female region which is relatively body, and is receptive and passively productive, as a sphere of Phenomena representing Good; as each of these contains an internal and an external principle which are relatively intellectual and affectional, so that each department contains the laws of truth and good upon the one hand, and the phenomena of truth and good upon the other; and as all these dualistic forms are characterized as vital and destructive, requiring that the destructive should be made subject to the vital in order that any productive manifestation should be realized. These relationships are also represented by this, that it is only as the moral is sustained by the religious, and the affectional by the intellectual departments, that any productive manifestations can be realized; and only as the receptive is sustained by the perceptive region in each department, or becomes internally and unconsciously receptive from this region, that any consciousness of external phenomena can be experienced: and they are also represented by the fact, that it is only as the opposite perceptive laws have been combined in the opposite receptive forms, and the manifestations of both have been combined in the reflective or constructive principle, which constitutes the third region in each department, with the subjection of the lower to the higher for use, that any productive manifestations corresponding with truth, with good, or with beauty or use, can be realized by the mind. These relationships are also represented in the Personal Constitution, which includes Individuality or Will; this being founded in vital and destructive affinities for Truth, and vital and destructive affinities for Good, — the vital being relatively male, constituting the Not Me of the individual, corresponding with a universal principle, and representing the Infinite; while the destructive are relatively female, constitute the Me of the individual, correspond with a partial or personal principle, and represent the Finite; the appropriations made by these personifying principles from the productions of the Mind being combined and manifested through a threefold form of Individuality or Will in a supernatural manner, with the subjection of the personal to the universal in productive, and of the universal to the personal in destructive, manifestations. This representation may be seen in all the muscular motions, as well as in all the mental manifestations, because we cannot move a muscle without the simultaneous operation of Expansion and Contraction, or act upon a single external object without the compound perception of Force and Resistance, as we may know from the slightest reflection; and we cannot become conscious of any thing except through the union of Subjective and Objective, because this consciousness is realized through the concurrence of Intuition and Perception, — the first representing the law; and the second, the phenomenon. That the first in each of these dualistic combinations is a vital, and the second a destructive element, may readily be seen, because we know that expansion and force are active and vital characteristics which correspond with the Infinite, and that contraction and resistance are passive and destructive characteristics which correspond with the Finite; while the whole history of philosophy shows that Sensibility and Intuition, which are relatively subjective, constitute the vital, and that Sensation and Perception, which are relatively objective, constitute the destructive, elements in philosophy; it being this fact that led the pious Bishop Berkeley to construct that remarkable work which demonstrates, from the unitarian point of view to which philosophy has been confined, the non-existence of matter, or the impossibility of an external world.

In this statement, we show, that, in the natural, truth and good are related as male and female, internal and external, and vital and destructive; and that, although good, as the external principle, must furnish to truth material for its incarnation, it can become productive from it only by becoming subject to and unconsciously receptive from it; so that the manner in which these are united in production cannot become a fact of consciousness.* This separation of truth and good in the human consciousness arises, first, in the fact that truth is conscious, and good unconscious; and, next, in the fact that man is not a cause, but only a phenomenal consequence, — is not an absolute and creative principle, but only a phenomenal and receptive principle; being simply a medium through which Absolute Causes become represented in the Natural and manifested in the Spiritual, so that he becomes conscious only as he becomes receptive; because the

---

* Appendix II.

consequence of this is, that cause and effect, truth and good, and law and phenomena, are as much separated in his consciousness as the female is from the male, who can never become the same, but only harmoniously at-one in marriage. It is for this reason that production must necessarily be realized in every department of the human constitution by the union of truth and good in a supernatural manner, representing Spiritual Life through Marriage, or the union of opposites through voluntary sacrifice; because the only way in which good can become vitally productive from truth is by the sacrifice of its life through love, or by the simple recognition of it and subjection to it, surrendering its own will, and leaving truth to produce effects in its own way: and as this is a spiritual manifestation, that cannot be realized in a conscious and voluntary manner in any natural condition of the soul, something representative of this must be realized in a supernatural manner outside of the individual consciousness, as the condition of any natural productive manifestation. This separation in the consciousness of Truth and Good, as Law and Phenomenon, and as Internal and External, is not confined to the Natural, but extends into the Spiritual; and although absolute law and phenomena, as Absolute Truth and Good, will both be comprehended in a spiritual sphere of consciousness, neither the process of incarnation in which truth produces from good, nor the manner in which these are combined and manifested in spiritual beauty or use, can even then become facts of consciousness: for, although we shall then *know* God, we cannot *be* God, to whom alone such knowledge is possible; our knowledge being obtained by a conception of Universal Law, both Absolute and Phenomenal, and by tracing in phenomena their likeness through analogy to the laws in which they live. The separation of law and phenomenon has been fully recognized by philosophy, and it has therefore never claimed to comprehend Causation. Dr. Thomas Brown says, "A cause, in the fullest definition which it philosophically admits, may be said to be, that which immediately precedes a change. Priority in the sequence observed, and invariableness of antecedence in the past and future sequences supposed, are the elements, and the only elements, combined in the notion of a cause." Kant also, in his "Critic of Pure Reason," thus acknowledges the impossibility of this knowledge: "Now, seeing that all phenomena, whether considered as extensive or intensive, are continuous quantities, the proposition, 'All change is continuous,' might be proved here easily, and with mathematical evidence, were it not that the causality of a change lies entirely beyond the bounds of transcendental philosophy, and presupposes empirical principles. For of the possibility of a cause which changes the condition of things, that is, which determines them to the contrary of a given state, the understanding gives us *à priori* no knowledge; not merely because it has no insight into the possibility of it, but because the notion of change concerns only certain determinations of phenomena which experience alone can acquaint us with, while their cause lies in the unchangeable." This ignorance of causation may be seen in the fact, that although we can decompose all physical substances, and obtain a knowledge of the opposite elements which enter into their composition, we cannot recombine these elements in a reproduction of them. Thus we can separate water into the opposite gases which seem to constitute it, but which are in fact held in combination through a third invisible substance; but we cannot recombine these opposite gases in the production of water.

It is true, that, in the practical concerns of life, it is demanded that our actions correspond with some vital form of truth, in order that they should be considered and defended as good; because the fact that truth is the vital principle to good is a recognition of the Religious Sentiment as a representative of Spiritual Truth, and it therefore demands that a legitimate reason be given for our actions before they can be conscientiously sustained. But, although this recognition by the Sentiment may be good evidence that truth is the vital principle to good, it does not show how it is so: instead of this, it teaches that we are to live by faith in the truth alone; and that, separated from this truth as a divine productive power, we have no ability for the production of good, but only for the production of evil. Even the relationship between Truth and Good that has here been stated can apply only to the truth and good which belong to the same sphere or region of the consciousness, because these spheres and regions are divided and antagonized. Although truth and good are related as internal and external, and therefore good succeeds truth in the development of the mind from within outwards, natural good does not succeed, but precedes, spiritual truth; and external natural good does not succeed, but precedes, internal natural truth, which, instead of being the life of this external good, demands its sacrifice. When we come to consider the supernatural relationships of the soul, as interpreted by Religion and the Church, we find that the understanding is unable to trace even an apparent connection between the truths of Revelation and the good of Morality, but, on the contrary, perceives an opposition between them, — an opposition that was recognized in the most extreme manner by the founders of the Protestant Church; for as the good of the sentimental nature is realized in connection with a natural order of thought, while its truth is realized in connection with a supernatural order, which is opposite, good cannot here even be interpreted by truth, but must contradict it. This may readily be seen by referring to the doctrines of this church, which, from the natural ground of appearance, are the most destructive to good; because, upon this ground, if we are totally depraved, we cannot possibly have the power of doing any good, — if all our acts are necessitated or predestined, we cannot have the power of choosing between good and evil, — and, if we have already been saved by the merits or by the atonement of Christ, the performance of good upon our part cannot be necessary to our salvation. Besides these discouragements to the performance of good works, this church teaches, and is bound to teach, that a single attempt to do good as from ourselves, or as meritorious in ourselves, must insure our everlasting damnation. Now, in judging from a natural point of observation, we cannot but suppose that such beliefs must inevitably prevent, instead of leading to, the production of good works, because all natural motive for their production seems to have been destroyed. But the history of this church and of the religious experiences of mankind will abundantly show that this very belief is eminently productive of good works; and this alone would furnish a triumphant demonstration of the fact here stated, that truth and good are separated in the consciousness, and that production from the union of these is a supernatural operation; because it seems perfectly inexplicable, from any natural point of view, that such causes should become productive of such results.

We see, then, that, although Truth and Good are combined in all the manifestations of the Mind and of the Will, they become separated in the consciousness; and the relationship between them is here completely invisible from every point of view. We see, that, in a religious sphere, they become antagonized, — that it is only as religion declines that morality increases as a conscious internal experience, — that this "mammon of unrighteousness" becomes in its turn destructive of the truths by which Christianity is represented, — and that the worship of good is made to precede the reception of those truths of God which constitute "the true riches," and which demand of the soul an acknowledgment of total depravity. Even in a spiritual sphere of consciousness, there can be no perception of the relation of cause and consequence between truth and good, because, although here Faith must include the most perfect form of Rationality, and lead to a perfect union between the Understanding and the Reason, Good as an external manifestation must, as in the natural, be produced by the spontaneous operation of the moral and affectional principles of the mind; and the Understanding, even when spiritually enlightened, cannot, any more than in the natural, produce, but only interpret it. Although the spiritual character of these manifestations, the causes in spiritual life by which they have been produced, and the relationship between these spiritual causes and these phenomenal consequences, will be clearly comprehended as principal and representative, the manner of their production must always remain a mystery; and, the nearer we approach to an image of the divine-humanity of Christ, the more will our life become a life of faith, and the more shall we become spontaneously productive of Spiritual Truth, Good, and Beauty, which we shall refer to the divine operation of God.

The LAW OF ATTRACTION between opposites is founded in and represents the attraction that exists between Infinite and Finite Spheres, arising from the susceptibility inherent in the Finite for becoming productive from the Infinite, and also the attraction that exists between the intellective and affective principles both in the Infinite and in the Finite. The attraction between male and female spheres as forms of truth and good is founded in the attraction that exists between Infinite and Finite Spheres, arising in the necessity of their combination in order that any definite consciousness should be realized; this consciousness being made possible through the susceptibility in Diversity for becoming productive from Unity, — in Partiality, for becoming productive from Universality, — and in Death, for becoming productive from Life; by which an external attraction is combined with the internal opposition that must exist between these universal laws which exclude each other, but both of which are necessary to the realization of Existence or of Definite Being, making possible the union in production of these opposite universal causes. The attraction that exists between internal and external principles arises in the susceptibility for production alluded to above, and also in the attraction that exists between the laws of Unity and Universality in the Infinite, and between the laws of Diversity and Partiality in the Finite, the combination of which in definite forms is represented in all the internal and external principles of natural life, by which an internal attraction is combined with an external opposition; the internal attraction arising in the causes above mentioned, and the external opposition arising in the combination of these opposite laws by which the infinite is represented by all internal, and the finite is represented by all external principles. It may seem contradictory and false to say that any attraction can exist between things absolutely opposite which exclude each other; but, although nothing can be more opposite than unity and diversity, universality and partiality, or life and death, as neither can become incarnated or definitely manifested without the other, the most powerful external attraction must necessarily exist between them. We therefore find, that, in all created things, difference is a cause of attraction by which opposites are brought to unite in production, the motive power in each being the desire for a more perfect individualization and manifestation by union with something unlike itself, by which an extension of the individual is obtained; this object being, consequently, internally repulsive and externally attractive.

Three kinds of attraction are to be noticed, the relationship between which may be distinguished as that between body, soul, and spirit. The first is an external attraction that exists between those things which are calculated, by their physical constitution, to unite in external production; and therefore a spontaneous combination and manifestation of these take place whenever they are brought into contact. The second is an internal attraction that arises in the particular constitution of those principles which are calculated to combine in the production of truth, of good, or of use; so that, whenever these are brought into contact, they spontaneously combine in production: and that this is an attraction between opposites, may be seen, because the affectional are attracted towards the intellectual, the external towards the internal, and the female towards the male principles and spheres, in all the forms of the universe; and from the fact that an attraction exists between the extreme points in every department of the mental constitution, so that either the internal perceptive and the external receptive, or the external perceptive and the internal receptive, principles are combined together in its productions, as we shall have occasion to show. The third is an attraction that arises in the adaptation of supernatural ideas to promote the growth and development of the Individual Consciousness, and arises between the individual and those institutions in which these ideas are embodied, under the teaching and direction of which he must come in order that this growth and development should be secured; the motive power which operates to produce this subjection being the desire of happiness from the extension and manifestation, or from the growth and development, of the individual. This produces that attraction between the personal and the universal, or between the principles of good and truth, through which all improvement in the natural is effected; for although nothing can be more antagonistic than these opposites, and although truth is the crucifier of good, this subjection and this sacrifice are effected through the expectation that a greater good will finally be obtained by the individual. The principal institutions through which these supernatural ideas become operative are Philosophy, the Church, and the State, which include the subordinate institutions of Friendship, Fraternity, and Matrimony, because these are the great productive institutions of life. The attraction between the sexes is the strongest of all, for the reason that it is the most imperatively necessary, represents the attraction between Infinite and Finite, and includes a threefold bond of union, because they are related as male and female, intellectual and affectional, and internal and external; and this attraction is accompanied by an internal opposition that is equally strong, which produces, when not overcome by some internal or external attraction, a greater antipathy than is possible between those of the same sex, and is the principal cause of all domestic unhappiness and strife. The greatest opposition, however, is generally accompanied by the greatest attraction; and it is therefore common to see individuals binding themselves together for life, between whom, internally considered, there is not a single point of sympathetic contact. Many consider this to be the result of some strange infatuation that is opposed to all sound calculation, and look upon the passion of love, by which it is produced, as a kind of insanity; but it is, as we see, a legitimate natural phenomenon which results from the operation of a spontaneous instinctive force, founded in the law of attraction from opposition, that is stronger and more beneficial to the individual than any calculations of expediency that could be devised. But, as all these relations will be particularly described in other portions of our work, it is not necessary that we should dwell upon them here.

The LAW OF MARRIAGE, as the law of Spiritual Life, realizing the union of opposites through the voluntary sacrifice of individual life, has already been described as originating in an Absolute Sphere of Being, and as operating in the realization of God as a Tri-Personality, by the union of Infinite and Finite Laws, through the sacrifice of Finite or Individual Life, and the regeneration of the natural form; so that, instead of being a dualistic representative of Infinite and Finite, the Individual becomes at-one with the Infinite, and realizes an incarnation of the Infinite Life. Spiritual Marriage is again realized in a Divine-Human Sphere of Being, through the assumption by God of a Universal Form of Phenomenal Existence, the Crucifixion of Phenomenal Individual Life, and the Resurrection of the Phenomenal Form as Divine-Human; a marriage that will be particularly described in a statement of "the Incarnation of the Son of God," contained in our Theological System. Spiritual Marriage will also be realized in this divine-human sphere by all those who experience Salvation through the sacrifice of individual life, and the Resurrection through Regeneration of the natural form; or who become at-one with God through the Atonement of Christ, as this will hereafter be described. In all these cases, Marriage is realized through the act of God, consequent upon the sacrifice of individual life, which is constituted by finite laws, and includes a substitution at the centre of the consciousness of a new life from God, which is governed by the laws of Spiritual Life, and the production from this central spiritual life of spiritual forms of the mind and of the will, constituting mediums for the manifestation, not of individual want or will, but of the Will of God, in forms of spiritual truth, good, and beauty, or use.

The voluntary surrender of Individual Life, as antagonistic to God, that the individual may become productive from Him, for universal instead of personal ends, which is necessary in spiritual marriage, cannot, of course, be realized in a natural, but only in a spiritual sphere of consciousness, because the soul cannot until then become conscious of this life, and because its natural life is constituted by laws representing the Finite Spirit, which is manifested as Absolute Separation, or as an inversion of Absolute Marriage. Marriage must, however, be represented in the Natural, because all production must be here realized through a union of opposites which represents the spiritual union that is realized in Marriage; and, as this production cannot be realized through any natural process, it must be realized by a supernatural process, outside of the individual consciousness. The most perfect natural representations of this sacrifice of individual life, which is necessary to Marriage, are realized through the sentimental experiences of the individual. Through the operation of the religious sentiments in connection with the Catholic Church, individuals realize an experience in which they seem to have surrendered all desire for personal happiness, except that which is derived from the performance of religious duties, and in which the countenance acquires that heavenly expression which has been embodied by the early religious painters. Through the operation of the religious sentiments in connection with the Protestant Church, individuals have been led, under the influence of their religious belief, to make great sacrifices of personal inclination, which are also representative of this total individual sacrifice: although, as the individual has now become more self-conscious and more disorderly from the demand for Individual Liberty, the examples of self-sacrifice presented by this Church fall far short of those presented by the Catholic. In both these cases, however, there are two facts connected with them, which prove the natural and selfish character of these manifestations; and these are, first, that heaven, or a condition of future and everlasting happiness, is expected as a reward; and, next, that the individual endeavors in this way to work out his own salvation: for we shall clearly demonstrate in this work, that, although asceticism in the Church is a legitimate representative of this sacrifice of individual life, it is destructive to the very idea which it represents. When the Moral Sentiments become the governing sentimental powers, and "Sympathy" consequently becomes the governing sentimental law, a philanthropic manifestation, universal in character, is produced, under the influence of which the individual is led to make the greatest personal sacrifices for the sake of others. But this supremacy of good becomes realized under the influence of Feeling as a governing power, without any reference to Truth; and in fact originates in the supremacy of the law of "Sympathy," which is in itself one of the most destructive principles that the human constitution contains, because, in its essence, it demands universal individual gratification. We see, then, that it is not in the highest form of Natural Truth or of Natural Good, or even in that combination of these which we find in the sentimental experiences of the Catholic Church, that Marriage can be realized, although it is here represented; but only in the total sacrifice of individual life and motive-power, and the reception of a new spiritual love and life that is at-one with the Infinite; which can be realized only in a spiritual sphere of consciousness, and is the Charity that cometh from God. This fact is represented by St. Paul in the following words: "And now abideth faith, hope, charity, these three; but the greatest of these is Charity. Though I have the gift of prophecy, and understand all mysteries and all knowledge; and though I have all faith, so that I could remove mountains; and have not Charity, I am nothing. And though I bestow all my goods to feed the poor, and though I give my body to be burned, and have not Charity, it profiteth me nothing."

Marriage must be represented in the structure and manifestations of the Soul, as the condition both of natural and of spiritual life. With regard to the first, as the Human Constitution must present through its entire organization a discordant antagonism of vital and destructive principles, or of indefinite laws representing Infinite and Finite, of which the individual is unconscious, — as the condition of individual consciousness, or of natural life, this constitution must contain in every one of its departments a supernatural principle, constituting a medium through which the Divine Activity can operate in the combination of these laws in definite forms, or in the production of phenomena corresponding with them; and, as the condition of any productive manifestation, these laws and phenomena must be combined and manifested in a supernatural manner outside of the individual consciousness. With regard to the second, as nothing can be realized in the spiritual that has not been represented in the natural, — it being therefore written, "that is not first which is spiritual, but that which is natural, and afterwards that which is spiritual," — mediums through which Marriage is represented in natural forms must be developed in the human constitution as a preparation for their reconstruction as mediums for the manifestation of Spiritual Life; and religious experiences representing the marriage of the soul to God must be realized by the soul in a natural sphere of consciousness, in order that the consummation of this marriage should be possible when a spiritual consciousness shall be communicated to it. While all truth, good, and beauty, or use, may therefore be said to be the result of Marriage, because, even in the Natural, this is represented in their production, all these are, in the natural, produced from conflicting opposites; for, even with regard to the operation of those active principles representative of Marriage, through which natural uses are produced, we find that the conclusion or the action, as the case may be, results from a compromise between opposite facts and opposite motives, and not from the concurrence of all. Marriage is represented throughout the whole organization of the Mind, because, in every one of its departments, opposites are combined in manifestation through a productive principle representing the divine creative act, and constituting mediums through which the creative process is conducted, and God becomes the creator, preserver, and governor of the soul; and it is also represented in the Will, where the individual constructs a plan of life for himself by the combination of opposite intellectual, affectional, and sentimental experiences, in the endeavor to secure what seems to him good upon the whole, and through which at the same time the divine providence of God operates in producing for him what is really his greatest good. But we see that Marriage is not realized by the Mind, because all the conclusions of the individual are a compromise between opposite views of truth and of good which cannot be reconciled; and that it is not realized by the Will, because its development is partial and one-sided (what it gains in one region being lost in another), — because its ideal and actual states can never be made to agree, — and because even its determinations and its actions are always in discord with each other. Every individual entertains opinions which are mutually destructive, and is conscious of desires or wants which are perfectly antagonistic; and, although the Reason is continually demanding some law that shall give consistency and harmony to the soul, no such law has ever been realized by it. Division and discord are inseparable from natural life, because it is necessarily governed by the laws of diversity, partiality, and separation. Even Christianity, therefore, could not be proclaimed as One Gospel, but was divided and antagonized in the Gospels of Circumcision and Uncircumcision; although we are taught in the Scriptures, that "in Jesus Christ neither circumcision availeth any thing, nor uncircumcision, but faith which worketh by love;" and the letter of the Bible abounds with the most palpable contradictions, so that individuals and sects entertaining the most opposite beliefs build upon it, and quote its language with equal effect in the support of their peculiar opinions, while each one of these sects maintains doctrines which are as opposite as are these sects. It may therefore be said, that, while the lowest form of natural life is produced through marriage, even the highest must become realized in opposition and discord. This apparent contradiction will be best explained by considering the difference between the natural and the supernatural manifestations of the human constitution; between those for which an adequate motive may readily be assigned, and those which seem to be contrary to natural inclination: for although it has been customary to regard all the operations of human nature as simply natural, and clearly comprehensible under the relationship of cause and effect, this opinion cannot be maintained for a moment in view of the nature of existence, and of the facts which are disclosed to us by the application of the laws of our science in the development of a system of psychological truth. Though all the forms of the consciousness seem to be realized by the operation of natural causes, and though every personal manifestation seems to be produced by the individual will, and the strongest motive to determine the individual act, — yet all natural forms of truth, of good, and of use, must necessarily be produced by the divine providence of God, whose watchful care must be incessantly exercised in directing and counteracting the destructive tendency of that finite force which must continually operate upon all natural forms, and in combining and manifesting the discordant powers of the human constitution, so that the greatest amount of use may be produced by their operation, — because it is evident that these results could not be effected in any other way. Being constituted as a representative of both Infinite and Finite, the organization through which the soul obtains its natural consciousness is necessarily constructed in a dualistic form, as life against death, and good against evil; and consequently this natural form can become productively manifested only by the supernatural combination of its conflicting elements, with the subjection of the destructive to the vital power. In order that this subjection and this manifestation should be realized, and that man should be created in the image of God, and prepared by processes of natural growth and development for a resurrection into the spiritual, it is necessary that every department of his mind should contain an active and constructive principle, through which the Divine Activity can operate in the creation of these discordant natural powers, and their combination and manifestation outside of the individual consciousness in a supernatural manner, representing Marriage, or the union of opposites through voluntary sacrifice, and still that all these manifestations should appear to the individual to be made by himself; it being necessary that an appearance of reality should be communicated to his consciousness. This does not conflict with the fact, that the life of human nature is constituted by laws corresponding with the Finite, which are destructive to truth, to good, and to use, even as natural productions; because these constructive powers are not spiritual but supernatural forms, the life of which is natural; being perfectly analogous to the religious and moral sentiments which constitute the supernatural region of the mind, and which, while representing in their forms spiritual truth, good, and use, are governed in all their internal and in all their conscious external manifestations by these same destructive laws, so that nothing can be more completely separated and antagonized than the sentimental and the spiritual experiences of the soul.

These destructive natural laws must govern all the conscious manifestations of the supernatural principles, in which the natural motive powers are excited to act in the production of specific results and external manifestations contrary to these motives, as well as all the manifestations of the natural principles, for the reason that they are realized while the individual is confined to a natural sphere of consciousness; and we shall clearly demonstrate that these are the only laws which constitute the natural life of the soul, and govern all its relationships, all its internal manifestations, and all its conscious external manifestations. The operations of the dualistic natural principles of the mind do not therefore become united or made one, by being combined and manifested through these supernatural mediums, but are only combined through a compromise which appears to be made for the sake of individual knowledge or advantage; and therefore, when this advantage does not become apparent, the subjection of the destructive to the vital is effected outside of the consciousness in a manner not comprehensible to the individual. This subjection of the individual to the universal, through the sacrifice of personal want, is, as we shall show, the foundation of all truth, good, and use; and its representation in the natural is therefore provided for in a supernatural manner, because its realization is not there possible. We comprehend that this sacrifice of personal want can be made in the spiritual, because it is included in the realization of Christianity through an act of faith, as will be seen in our description of this fact. Such an experience is not possible, however, in a natural sphere of consciousness, but only a natural representation of this, because this consciousness is governed, under the law of necessity, by a purely selfish motive, which cannot really make any sacrifice; and the manifestations of these constructive principles cannot therefore be explained from a natural, but only from a supernatural, point of view. It is true that the selfish principle operates in a conscious natural manner in producing the sacrifice of the lesser for the sake of the greater want: but this mode of operation will not account for those sacrifices which cannot be traced to any selfish motive, and which are therefore made by the individual in an unconscious and spontaneous manner,— sacrifices which the individual is so continually regretting, as to lead to the theory, that the reproaches of conscience are nothing but the regrets of self-love for neglect in the gratification of individual desire; and also to suggest the opposite theory, that man is sometimes governed by unselfish or disinterested motives. There are several ways in which Divine Providence operates in the development of the human constitution, and prepares the soul for the spiritual. In the first place, the individual is placed under subjection to certain institutions which are connected with the Family, with the State, and with the Church, the origin of which is to be referred to a supernatural inspiration, and the subjection to which is accomplished by a supernatural operation through the productive powers of the mind and of the will. Through these powers, this inspiration operates in communicating to the mind, in a spontaneous and unconscious manner, vital and productive truths which cannot be comprehended by the natural mind, and in securing a recognition of and subjection to these truths, and to the institutions in which they are embodied, in the production of natural use; so that "the powers that be are ordained of God." Next, the individual is placed under bondage to physical conditions and natural circumstances calculated to restrain the manifestation of his predominant inclinations, that they may be restricted to a healthy exercise, and that he may become familiar with the fact of Sacrifice, which is essential to natural progress as well as to spiritual life. Next, as we have here shown, the mind is, through the active or constructive principles in its constitution, brought into a comparatively harmonious condition, in which the external and affectional are brought into subjection to the internal and intellectual powers, good is made subject to truth, and a compromise is effected between these antagonistic forms, by which natural truth, good, and use become realized. Finally, through the manifesting principles of the mind and of the will, the individual is led, by the expectation of advantage to himself which is never to be realized, to make sacrifices of personal want; and external manifestations are unconsciously and spontaneously produced, which are contrary to all natural motives, and are therefore to be regarded as supernatural manifestations. It is in this way that God becomes the governor of the World, and the creator, preserver, educator, and regenerator of the Soul in its natural condition.

The most perfect external representative of Marriage, in the Natural, is the institution of Matrimony. That there is a perfect analogy between the marriage of conjugal partners and the marriage of Christ with his Church, or of the Soul to God, is thus taught by St. Paul: "Wives, submit yourselves unto your own husbands, as unto the Lord. For the husband is the head of the wife, even as Christ is the head of the Church; and he is the Saviour of the body. Therefore, as the Church is subject unto Christ, so let the wives be to their own husbands in every thing. Husbands, love your wives; even as Christ also loved the Church, and gave himself for it; that he might sanctify and cleanse it with the washing of water by the Word; that he might present it to himself a glorious Church, not having spot or wrinkle, or any such thing; but that it should be holy and without blemish." The words here quoted from Paul's Epistle to the Ephesians were undoubtedly intended to be a symbolic illustration of the Universal Law of Marriage as it has here been stated, and not simply a direction for the government of individuals united in the conjugal relation. Matrimony is a legitimate natural representative of the relationship here described by St. Paul: and we are therefore led to conclude that the natural use of which it is productive, corresponds, in some degree, with that which is spiritual; and is intended to prepare the sexes for a spiritual marriage, precisely as the experiences of Religion are intended to prepare the soul for a marriage with God. It is only upon the ground that Matrimony is thus symbolic and useful, that the practice of solemnizing the marriage contract by religious observances can be defended; for, if it did not possess a particular supernatural significance, it would have been left to the superintendence of the civil magistrate, as pertaining to civil order, and not to religious faith. It is for this reason that the conjugal relation and its opposite have been so extensively used in the Scriptures, as symbolic forms representative of universal spiritual facts; that St. Paul has used it to illustrate the marriage of Christ with his Church, which is the marriage of the soul to God; and that it has been introduced into the great symbolic Church of Rome as a Sacrament, or sacred symbolic mystery. As Spiritual Marriage is realized by the union of infinite and finite laws, through the voluntary sacrifice of individual life, in which the lower is made subject to the higher for use, and the destructive are made subject to the vital principles in production,

— Natural Marriage, as a representative of this, must include the subjection of the external to the internal, of the affectional to the intellectual, of the natural to the supernatural, and of the female to the male principles, and therefore of good to truth, as the condition of any productive natural manifestation; and the institution of Matrimony must therefore include the subjection of the female to the male, through the voluntary sacrifice of the will of the female. The Domestic Principle, through which the most perfect natural marriage of the sexes becomes realized, is one of the most important of those constructive supernatural mediums which represent Spiritual Life through Marriage, or the union of opposites through voluntary sacrifice; and the manifestations which are realized through it furnish some of the best illustrations we have of the unifying power of Marriage: for the reason, that, being so important a medium of production, its supernatural manifestations are particularly predominant; and, being accompanied by the most powerful emotions which are realized by the individual consciousness, the matrimonial experiences of the individual constitute the most distinct and lasting of all his self-conscious realizations. Through the operation of this principle, we see individuals becoming harmoniously united, whose spheres of life are in the most violent opposition, because it represents that which exists between the Infinite and the Finite; but who become so united by the operation of this domestic principle, that truth and good, which in the natural constitute antagonistic spheres, as vital and destructive, become attractive and unconsciously unite together in production, with the subjection of the female to the male, through the sacrifice of the female will; a result that includes a faith in things opposite, unseen, and incomprehensible, which is perfectly analogous to the self-sacrificing devotedness of religious faith, and which cannot be traced to any natural causes, for the reason that self-love is the governing law of natural life. A particular description of the domestic institution, which includes this relationship between the sexes, will be given in the psychological portion of our work, and the domestic relationships will also be alluded to in illustrating both its ontological and theological portions: to these, therefore, the reader is referred for a more particular illustration of this subject.

In the statement of Marriage that has here been made, we have shown that Subjection is the great and indispensable law that must precede all production, because this production must be realized from the union of opposites; and that this law is particularly necessary in all natural production, for the reason that here every thing is dualistic, as male and female, and as internal and external, — that these female spheres and external principles are disorderly and destructive, — and that, consequently, the subjection of these to the male spheres and internal principles is imperatively demanded, in order that any truth, good, or use, should be produced; all falsehood, evil, and abuse being the result of the inversion of this relationship, in the combination and manifestation of these spheres and principles through the active or constructive mediating principles of the mind, and through the individualizing principles of the will. We thus show, that truth and good, and falsehood and evil, whether we use these terms in a spiritual and real, or only in a natural and representative sense, result solely from the use or abuse of the sexual relation; the first being produced through the female in subjection to the male, and the second being produced by the female when throwing off this subjection and becoming a ruling principle. It is for this reason that the Hebrew Scriptures are so filled with sexualisms, or with the uses and abuses of the sexual relation, that they cannot be translated literally and given to the people without subjecting them to a profane and destructive misunderstanding; for, in the external condition of the consciousness to which these Scriptures were addressed, these things had to be brought down into the region of sensation, and represented through historical and personal forms, according to supernatural laws of correspondence which cannot, in the natural, be comprehended by the understanding, but only apprehended through religious feeling. These Scriptures are more strictly confined to this external symbolic form than those of the New Testament, or even than the forms of the Catholic Church, which is the great symbolic Church representing Christianity in a supernatural sphere; because, until after the advent of Christ, Christianity could not even be represented in a supernatural or representative-spiritual form, but only symbolized in natural forms, which, separate from the life that is given to them by the revelation of Christ, do not suggest any supernatural truth to the mind.

We will now proceed to state and to illustrate the Laws of Correspondence, and the Laws of Succession, which have been derived from our statement of the Law of Tri-Personality; showing that the laws of Opposition, of Attraction, and of Marriage, as they have here been stated, govern all the forms, functions, and manifestations of Creation: and in classifying, analyzing, and explaining these, we shall show, first, that all particular forms are constituted by three principles related as internal, external, and medial, which are soul, body, and spirit, and exist as supernatural combinations of vital and destructive elements through productive manifesting principles. We shall show, next, that all these particular forms hold positions in some particular department, constituted by three regions, which are also internal, external, and medial, as soul, body, and spirit: first, a male region representing Truth, as the Soul of each department, which is perceptive, intuitive, and vital, as the region of Law, but containing intellective and affective principles, which are internal and external, and vital and destructive,—next, a female region representing Good, as the Body of each department, which is receptive, associative, and destructive, as the region of Phenomena, but containing intellectual and affectional principles, which are internal and external, and vital and destructive,—and, finally, a supernatural region representing Use, Marriage, or the union of opposites through voluntary sacrifice, as the Spirit of each department, which is reflective, constructive, and productive; being a mediating sphere through which these dualistic natural laws are combined in the production of phenomena corresponding with them, and these laws and phenomena are combined and manifested in natural forms, and also in supernatural forms not comprehensible by the natural mind, by the divine providence of God; these being forms of natural use, realizing the union of good with truth. We shall also show, that all general forms, which include all the particular forms belonging to any one sphere, are realized as a tri-personal individuality of Spirit, Soul, and Body,—the *spirit* constituting a vital sphere that is characterized as Real; the *soul* constituting a mediating sphere that is characterized as Representative; and the *body* constituting an incarnating and manifesting sphere that is characterized as internally destructive and externally productive: all these forms, and the manifestations referable to them, being governed by the laws of Opposition, Attraction, and Marriage. We will now proceed to show the manner in which these laws are represented in the structure of the Universe, in the formation of the Races of Mankind, in the structure and functions of the Human Constitution, and, finally, in the structure of Human Society.

THE

GENERAL FORMS OF THE UNIVERSE

WHICH ILLUSTRATE

THE LAWS OF CORRESPONDENCE.

In showing that the Universe is constructed in correspondence with the laws of Existence as they have here been stated, we will proceed first to realize a conception of the general form of the Universe by the application of these laws, and next to show how this conception corresponds with the theories of Philosophy. In accordance with these laws, the Universe is constituted by three several spheres of Phenomenal Existence, related as Spiritual, Ethereal, and Material, which are spirit, soul, and body; the material being the external incarnating sphere, and the spiritual being successively incarnated, through the ethereal and material spheres, in Individual Existence, which through successive births ascends to ethereal and spiritual spheres of conscious life; each of these spheres, as a particular form, includes opposite male and female spheres, antagonized as vital and destructive, each of which is divided into internal and external principles, also antagonized as vital and destructive; and these vital and destructive spheres and principles are combined and manifested through a third sphere, corresponding with the divine productive power; by which each sphere is made to constitute a threefold form of soul, body, and spirit, in which spirit is the manifesting principle and sphere. The form of the Material Universe we therefore conceive as follows; and, although this is nothing but an outline, it is necessary to complete the universal plan of Phenomenal Existence under which all the particular forms and manifestations of the Universe are to be classified and explained.

THE MATERIAL UNIVERSE.

THE SPIRITUAL SPHERE OF THE UNIVERSE.

This is conceived as constituting a Universal Sphere of Definite Phenomenal Substance, which includes in essence all human souls, each of these being constituted a tri-personal substance which is spiritual, ethereal, and material, and calculated to exist successively in Material, Ethereal, and Spiritual Atmospheres; and which also includes spiritual incarnating mediums, through which Spiritual Substance operates in realizing opposite Spiritual Atmospheres as opposite spheres for Spiritual Representation, and for Individual Spiritual Manifestation: for this reason, and because the Human Soul constitutes its internal and vital element, with which all other things must correspond as external representatives, we name this the sphere of HUMAN SUBSTANCE. The laws included in this sphere are suggested by the most universal forms of the human consciousness, and we name them —

RATIONALITY. — SENTIMENTALITY.
INTELLECTUALITY. — AFFECTIONALITY.
SPIRITUAL SUBSTANCE.

THE ETHEREAL SPHERE OF THE UNIVERSE.

This sphere is conceived as containing ethereal incarnating mediums in the Sun, Moon, and Stars, through which Ethereal Substance operates in realizing the internal condition of Gaseous, Liquid, and Solid Substance, in an Ethereal Atmosphere, as a sphere for Supernatural Representation, and for Individual Supernatural Manifestation. The opposite laws and the combining principle included in this sphere may be stated thus: —

REPULSION. — EXPANSION.
ATTRACTION. — CONTRACTION.
ETHEREAL SUBSTANCE.

THE MATERIAL SPHERE OF THE UNIVERSE.

This sphere is conceived as containing material incarnating mediums in the Mineral, Vegetable, and Animal Forms, through which Material Substance operates in realizing the external condition of Gaseous, Liquid, and Solid Substance, in a Material Atmosphere, as a sphere for Natural Representation, and for Individual Natural Manifestation. The opposite laws and combining principle included in this sphere may be stated thus: —

LIGHT. — HEAT.
AIR. — WATER.
MATERIAL SUBSTANCE.

We will now proceed to show the correspondence that exists between this statement, and what have been recognized in the theories of the philosophers as the general forms and laws of the Universe. With regard to the Material Sphere in this classification, we find that the elements here stated are precisely the same as those which have been recognized in Philosophy as the most external material forces of the Universe. The classification here made of them will be seen to agree with their obvious relationship, and also with the laws of our science, because Light and Heat plainly correspond with intellective and affective principles, and constitute a male sphere representing the Infinite; Air and Water correspond with intellectual and affectional principles, and constitute a female sphere representing the Finite; and Material Substance is an active, constructive sphere, through which these dualistic principles are combined and manifested in a manner representing Spiritual Life through Marriage: while the Mineral, Vegetable, and Animal Forms of Nature — which are the incarnating mediums in this substance, and the forms through which it operates — are related as soul, body, and spirit; the soul being vital, the body destructive, and the spirit productive. As a further illustration of the laws of our science, each one of these material principles is a threefold substance, in which the union of opposite elementary powers corresponding with Infinite and Finite is produced, and a perfect individuality of soul, body, and spirit, related as vital, destructive, and productive, is realized. Thus we find that Water appears to be composed of two imperceptible gases called Oxygen and Hydrogen, and that Air appears to be composed of Oxygen and Nitrogen; the first element in each being known to possess a vital, and the second a destructive character. We say that they appear to be so composed, because in their decomposition the vital principle, by which these opposite elements are united, disappears. It is true that the first element in each of these substances, when not accompanied by its opposite, produces a deleterious effect upon the forms of animal life; but this, instead of invalidating, tends to confirm our position, that all Existence is realized from the union of opposites, because it shows that the combination of these opposite elements in a productive material substance is necessary to the realization of a healthy material condition. Besides, the first of these elements has always been recognized as vital, and the second as destructive. With regard to Light, the following extract from "Field's Chromotography," which is one of the most celebrated works upon the subject of Colors, will show that the composition of Light is perfectly analogous to that of the other elements here mentioned: —

"Yet sensible light is not a simple substance, but an effect of the concurrence of two elementary powers, one of which is the active or vital principle of light, and the other passive or re-active, and to be regarded as the principle of shade or darkness; the first coincident, if not identical, with the oxygen of the chemist, and the other with the hydrogen: and however exceptionable this may be to those who have been accustomed to regard darkness as a mere privation of light, yet, as respects the artist, a principle of darkness, blackness, or shade, is as essential as the principle of light. Accordingly, the sunbeam, as it arrives to us, is a compound of the element of light and shade; and it may be analyzed, by refraction and in other ways, into oxidizing or whitening rays, and hydrogenizing or blackening rays, and at the same time into others that are variously compounded of these, and variously colored. Light hence appears, as before remarked, to be, in the sunbeam, the effect of the concurrence or conjunction of two ethereal, electrical, or elementary substances, or powers, — the one an agent, of which the Sun appears to be the fountain, or source; the other a re-agent, existing in planetary or atmospheric space, analogous to shade: if so, the sunlight is a species of oxidation or combustion, a sort of flame attended by a sensible or latent heat; and all light must be regarded as similarly constituted, and produced by the active uniting of an oxygenous or electrical principle with a phlogistic or thermal principle." This scientific analysis of Light shows not only that it is produced by the combination and manifestation of opposite elements through a productive principle, but that these opposite elements are connected with influences derived from the Sun, upon the one hand, and from the Moon, upon the other; because we cannot suppose this reaction to proceed from any other planetary influence.

With regard to the Ethereal Sphere in this classification, we find that the opposite laws included in this sphere have been recognized in Philosophy as the internal laws of Matter, though all have not been recognized by any one philosopher. By Boscovich and others, Gravitation, which includes the laws of Attraction and Repulsion, was supposed to constitute the most internal principle of Material Substance, or of "Matter as distinguishable from Body;" and by Descartes and others, Extension, which includes the laws of Expansion and Contraction, was supposed to constitute this most internal principle. As these laws have here been classified, they will be seen to illustrate the laws of our science, because Repulsion and Expansion plainly correspond with a universal and vital principle, representing the Infinite; Attraction and Contraction, with an opposite selfish and destructive principle, representing the Finite; and Ethereal Substance constitutes a unifying and productive sphere, through which these dualistic laws are combined and manifested in a manner representing Spiritual Life through Marriage: while Sun, Moon, and Stars, which are the incarnating mediums in this substance, and the forms through which it operates, are related as soul, body, and spirit, which are vital, destructive, and productive. We will now consider how these relationships have been represented in philosophy, and what have been the theories of the philosophers in relation to them.

By the ancient philosophers, the Sun was regarded as the vital principle of the Universe, and as the medium through which God operates in the creation of the world. By the Persians, who were the exponents of Creation by Emanation, or of the production of all things from an Infinite spiritual substance, the Sun was regarded as the vital principle of the Universe and as the highest representative of Deity, and consequently became to them an object of religious worship; while by the Egyptians—who represented a destructive instead of a vital principle, and were the exponents of Creation by Development, or of the production of all things from a Finite material substance — the Moon was regarded as the ruling power in the Universe and as the highest representative of Deity, and was therefore worshipped. The productive influence of the Stars as ruling powers of the Universe, which is to be inferred from the position that is occupied by them in this analysis, was also recognized by the ancient philosophers, but particularly by the Arabians, who worshipped them, and to whom, as the great Eclectical Race from which the Hebrews descended, the philosophy of the Stars belonged; and a Science of the Stars, under the name of Astrology, was at one time in great repute among all nations. But although, in these ancient times, the highest things were spontaneously and unconsciously represented in forms of Philosophy, of Religion, and of Art, these are no longer regarded as subjects of serious contemplation, for the reason that their significance and their influence have been entirely lost. We can therefore only refer to what has been the result of common observation with regard to these planetary bodies, and to the manner in which they have been used in the

Scriptures as representative forms, to illustrate the statement here made. We do not refer to the theories of modern astronomers, because they are entirely useless for the purpose of scientific illustration; and that they are so, we have the authority of Kant, that most acute of all the modern philosophers. He says, "The investigations and calculations of the astronomers have taught us much that is wonderful; but the most important lesson we have received from them is the discovery of the abyss of our ignorance in relation to the universe."

The Sun has been universally regarded as the source of light and heat, and as exercising a vitalizing influence upon this material sphere, so that its position in this analysis is fully sustained from the point of common observation. The Moon, however, has not been regarded as an opposite to the Sun, and therefore as the source of darkness and cold, — which we may see that she must be, — because no dualistic law of the Universe has been recognized, and this opposition in the causes of things was not therefore demanded. It has not been common even to allow that she exercises upon nature a destructive influence; and, in these days of naturalism, her influence has been almost entirely ignored, in the face of the most palpable facts of experience. At the same time, there are quite as many facts suggestive of the Moon's destructiveness as of the Sun's vitalitiveness: it is well known that she is productive of decay in vegetation; that all diseases acquire greater virulence at night, when the influence of the sun is partially withdrawn, and her influence is consequently increased; that she produces so great an aggravation of the symptoms of insanity, that this disease has been termed Lunacy; and that it is injurious to health, and in many climates even fatal, to sleep with the Moon shining upon the face, her destructive influence being increased by this passive condition of the individual. This destructive influence is generally counteracted by an opposite vital influence proceeding from the Sun, it being only when the Moon obtains an unusual predominance that any fatal result is produced; and it is therefore only in these extreme cases that the real character of her influence can be discovered. We see, then, that the conception of the Universe, here realized, is not without support, even from common observation, as well as from the ancient theories and traditions; although upon a subject like this, where so little can be known except from a spiritual ontological point of view, much support of this kind is not to be expected.

By the statement here made, — that the material universe exists in three spheres, which are spiritual, ethereal, and material, in the relation of spirit, soul, and body, while the incarnation, or the growth and development of the individual, must commence in this atmosphere; and that this incarnation of the spiritual soul is effected through ethereal and material substances as internal and external incarnating mediums, — an intimate relation is established between the ethereal mediums, which appear to us as Stars, and all the material forms produced in this atmosphere, but particularly those in which human souls become incarnated; because all lower forms must be vitalized by those which are above, and thus the ethereal must constitute the natural life of the material, and govern all its productions. From the statement here made, — that the Sun and Moon operate as vital and destructive powers, corresponding with infinite and finite laws, and that the Stars constitute productive mediums through which the opposite influences proceeding from these are combined and manifested by Absolute Creating Cause, — it follows, that, of the three substances which are combined in the productions of the ethereal and material spheres, the gaseous corresponds with the Sun, the liquid with the Moon, and the solid with the Stars; and as suns and moons are related, by universal consent, and also according to this analysis, as male and female, the combination and manifestation, through the Stars, of the influences proceeding from these spheres in the production of specific forms must appear as production by the male through the female, or by the action of Suns upon Moons; a production that we have shown to be represented by the ontological philosophers, first from a liquid substance, and next from a gaseous substance; and by the Hebrews from an eclectical and vital point of view, or as being realized by the spirit of God moving upon the face of the waters. The correspondence between the Sun and the element of Fire has been universally recognized; and the relation that exists between Water and the Moon is most conclusively shown by the influence which she exerts in producing the tides of the Ocean, or in upheaving and depressing its mighty waters. In the Mosaic account of the Creation, this threefold ethereal sphere is represented in the following manner: "And God made two great lights; the greater light to rule the Day, and the lesser light to rule the Night: he made the Stars also. And God set them in the firmament of the heaven to give light upon the Earth, and to rule over the day and over the night, and to divide the light from the darkness."

THE

GENERAL FORMS OF THE HUMAN RACE

WHICH ILLUSTRATE

THE LAWS OF CORRESPONDENCE.

In the five primitive races into which, according to the best authority, the Human Race is divided, we again recognize the universal fivefold form of all natural organizations; this being constituted by a double duality as "two and two, one against the other," combined with a fifth, which is an active and productive principle representative of Spiritual Life through Marriage: this "two and two" being constituted by male and female spheres, the first containing internal and external principles which are intellective and affective, these being masculine and feminine in an internal sphere; and the second containing internal and external principles which are intellectual and affectional, these being masculine and feminine in an external sphere; and this fifth principle constituting an active and supernatural sphere, that is universal and productive; these spheres being individualized as soul, body, and spirit. The five races here alluded to correspond in the most perfect manner with this form, and are as follows:—

MALAY. — MONGOLIAN.
INDIAN. — ETHIOPIAN.
CAUCASIAN.

According to this classification, the Malay and Mongolian races constitute internal and external elements in the Barbarous sphere, which, as relatively Soul, is vital and socially representative, — the Indian and Ethiopian races constitute internal and external elements in the Savage sphere, which, as relatively Body, is socially destructive, — and the Caucasian race constitutes the Universal and Supernatural sphere of the Human Race, which, as relatively Spirit, is socially productive. The first four races here enumerated, being but partially representative, are for this reason necessarily partial, imperfect, and comparatively unimprovable; a fact that is abundantly verified by history, as all writers describe them as stationary, or as entirely unchanged in their condition: while the Caucasian race constitutes a vital and real social sphere which is universally representative, and is capable of realizing the entire development of the Soul in natural and in spiritual spheres of consciousness; so that this is to be regarded as the only perfect and improvable race, and the only one to which a conscious representation and realization of the Spiritual is possible; facts which are also verified by history, as it is there shown to be the only race that is constantly progressive, and the only one that has ever accepted Christianity, and become subject to the Church. The question is not here raised, whether the distinction of race is or is not an external distinction that is confined to this atmosphere, because it is neither necessary nor possible that it should be settled. We may suppose that it is so; and that, internally considered, or with reference to an internal organization, all men belong to the universal race; and that, in leaving this atmosphere, the imperfect races come into the lowest position in this race, and commence from this a progressive development. There cannot be a doubt, however, that, with regard to this atmosphere, the distinction of race will always remain; not only because the imperfect races are stationary and unimprovable, but because this is a representative atmosphere, where all things must continue to represent the Universal Laws of Existence. In the account that we have given of the history of Philosophy, we have alluded to the general position and manifestations of the Hindoo and Chinese nations, who are the best representatives of the Malay and Mongolian races; and it will be seen that the character of these nations, as there described, corresponds with the position that is given to them in this classification. We will now illustrate and verify this classification by contrasting the Indian and Ethiopian races as these are represented by the Indians of North America and the African Negro, because they are the best specimens of these races, and because with them we are the most familiar; and our subject will receive the best illustration in contrasting these savage races, because, being the most imperfect and partial in their organization, we shall find a greater simplicity and uniformity in their characteristics and manifestations.

As these races are related as internal, intellectual, and masculine, and external, affectional, and feminine, in the most external sphere of human consciousness, in all the departments of the physical and mental constitution the internal and masculine element will be found to predominate in the Indian, and the external and feminine to predominate in the Negro; and we will therefore point out some of the contrasts to be found in the characteristics of these races, which grow out of this relationship between them. With regard to the physical constitution, the upper or superior element in each department is predominant in the Indian, while the lower or inferior element is predominant in the Negro; this being the exaggeration of a rule that is known to regulate the relative physical developments of the male and female. In the Negro, this exaggeration amounts to a ludicrous deformity, or inversion of symmetrical proportion, which has been celebrated in a great variety of mirthful productions. As these races belong to the lowest sphere in our classification of the races, and as this is relatively a female sphere, the muscular or sanguine, which is the female temperament, belongs to both, and therefore the muscles will be found to predominate over the bones in both; but, as the Indian is relatively internal and intellectual in this sphere, in him the bone and the muscle predominate, and in the Negro the marrow and fat, giving to him that peculiar oily appearance for which he is so remarkable. This may be seen to be a legitimate result from the relationship between them, as here stated, because, according to the Scriptures, where these are used as terms of symbolic correspondence, and also according to the theory of temperaments to be found in our psychological system, bone and muscle correspond with intellectual and masculine, and marrow and fat with affectional and feminine, principles in different spheres. In the Indian, the bones and the muscles are symmetrical, compact, and indicative of strength and of endurance, which are found to be characteristics belonging to him; while, in the Negro, this is reversed: in him the muscles are deficient in strength, by which he is made indolent, and unable to sustain, like the Indian, long and severe muscular exercise; and the bones in the body are deficient in quantity and quality, and curvilinear in form, which is indicative of weakness; while the cranial bones are extremely immature in their formation, the two plates being widely separated, and the space between them filled with a spongy, imperfectly formed substance, giving to the Negro head that great resistance to external force for which it is so remarkable.

With regard to the mental manifestations of these races, — the highest of which belong to the religious and moral sentiments, — we find, that, with the Indian, the idea of a future state of conscious individual existence, which is a vital religious manifestation, is one of the most vivid and operative of all his beliefs: while, according to Hegel, although the Negro has a belief in spirits, which we shall show to be a manifestation of the principle of "Naturalism," the destructive religious law, he has no belief in the immortality of the soul; all his religious experiences being of a physical and emotional character. As "Justice" and "Sympathy" are the vital and destructive laws of the moral nature, we find that the Indian manifests the sense of justice in its most external and vindictive form, exacting "an eye for an eye, and a tooth for a tooth," and is comparatively destitute of sympathy; while the Negro is profusely but externally sympathetic, and is unable to comprehend the nature of justice. The most remarkable of these contrasts, however, are those which arise in the intellectual manifestations of these races. As the representative region of the Understanding is the highest through which these races obtain their intellectual consciousness, — as the Fancy is the highest constructive principle in this region, — and as the vital manifestations of this principle are characterized as poetical and beautiful, while its destructive manifestations are inversions of these elements in the forms of the ludicrous, — the most external vital forms of the Fancy will be found to characterize the intellectual manifestations of the Indian; and the most external destructive forms to characterize those of the Negro, these being attended by laughter, as a prominent, spontaneous manifestation, because this is particularly excited by the lower forms of this destructive principle, which are deformity and obscenity. The first is therefore dignified, serious, and truthful, — expressing himself intellectually and symbolically, with concentration and poetic beauty; while the second is mirthful and deceitful, — expressing himself affectionally and musically, with superficial redundancy and jocose deformity. From the lower intellectual, which is the material region, the first is manifested in an internal and intellectual, and the second in an external and affectional manner: the first, therefore, manifests the quickest perception, without being in the least curious; while the second manifests the most abundant curiosity, without much intellectual comprehension. With regard to the individual manifestations, one is solitary, silent, and indwelling; while the other is sociable, loquacious, and external: one is brave, intent upon conquest, and cannot endure coercion of any sort, or exist in a state of servitude or of subjection, but will even pine and die if subjected to bodily restraint or to close confinement; while the other is cowardly, always ready to submit himself to control, and is fond of servile occupations and the performance of domestic uses; so that he selects and is selected for many kinds of service that are usually performed by females, and is never so happy as when provided with a good master. To conclude this comparison, while one is inordinately self-relying, and thus so unreceptive that he resists all education; the other is entirely dependent upon others, and is so receptive and imitative, that he represents without reproducing his model; and by attempting to copy his language and external deportment, without being able to realize a corresponding internal state, instead of a character, produces a caricature. These are only a few of the facts which might be mentioned as illustrating the representative character of these races, being those which most readily and at once present themselves. They are all in perfect correspondence with the fact, that the Indian is a representative of the internal, masculine, and intellectual principle in the lowest sphere of its manifestation; and that the Negro or Ethiopian is a representative of the external, feminine, and affectional principle in a corresponding sphere, as these principles have been and will continue to be stated and illustrated in this work. It is because the Negro is a representative of this principle alone that he is so deficient in internal intellectual and internal affectional capacity, and in that self-directing power which is the source of all systematic or calculated action; it being impossible that he should even realize a sufficient amount of intellectual vitality, either in the Instinct or in the Understanding, to serve as an imperfect substitute for the Will in spontaneity of action; a spontaneity that is to some extent realized by the Indian in his one-sided, intellectual condition. In consequence of this deficiency, no internal intellectual, affectional, or personal law can be realized by him; and he consequently becomes dependent entirely upon external direction. In his isolated, savage condition, therefore, he is degraded in the extreme; and when he comes in contact with other races, who can furnish an understanding to enlighten and a will to guide him, he always becomes subject as "a hewer of wood, and drawer of water." The same cause that makes him susceptible to external impressions, and of an external direction, by which he obtains the capacity for a merely verbal education, and becomes so useful as a servant, deprives him of the power of comprehending scientific principles, or laws of thought, and also of the power of self-direction; so that, when left entirely to his own resources, he becomes helpless, miserable, extinct. From witnessing this educational susceptibility in the Negro, and this capacity for and readiness in performing external uses, an opinion is apt to be engendered in an age like the present, in which the tendency is strong to regard most highly the most external things, — to worship good instead of truth, and to regard disagreeable sensations as among the greatest evils, — that the Negro is superior to the Indian, whose cruelty, contempt for learning, and aversion to the performance of external uses, shock the feminine partialities which now predominate. Indeed, so far has this worship of good and of the affectional principle been carried, that the Ethiopian has by some been regarded as the highest race. But it is certainly well known, that the most useful things, externally considered, are not the most valuable, and so are not held in the highest esteem; but, on the contrary, that those things are the most highly esteemed which do not seem to be of any use, while the most useful are esteemed the least.

The account here given of the Negro is a favorable one, because it describes him as he appears in an improved condition from contact with a superior race, by which he has been educated, and under the influence and control of which he lives. We know that there are some facts which seem to contradict this statement; but these can all be very readily accounted for, notwithstanding the deceptive character which particularly belongs to these most external individual manifestations. Individuals of the Ethiopian race, who have been brought under the influence of the white race, have not only been found capable of a certain kind of education to quite a considerable extent, but have seemed to realize a religious experience similar in character to that of the white race. There are causes, however, that will be found abundantly sufficient to account for these phenomena, and they can be shown to be nothing but deceptive appearances that have no conscious ground, law, or substantial principle, in the mind; being the product of those receptive, associative, and imitative powers which are excessively predominant in minds of this most external and affectional character. We therefore find, that, while the Negro is susceptible of a merely verbal education, he is entirely incapable of either mathematical, scientific, or philosophical knowledge; and that he reasons, not from principles, but from accidental associations, — a kind of reasoning that is fluent in proportion as it is superficial, and is found, together with this susceptibility for verbal education, in animals. We also find that his religious manifestations are not theological, but are emotional and physical, in character; having no ground either in the vital religious law, or in that vital condition of the religious sentiment upon which a recognition of the representations of Christianity in the Scriptures and in the Church depends. One cause of these religious manifestations of the Negro is the predominance of Hope in his mental constitution, which gives to him that excessive buoyancy and joyousness of disposition which is so remarkable in him, and which renders him one of the happiest of human beings. He is liable to be strongly excited upon religious subjects from this cause; because Hope is the motive power in Religion, and leads to all the emotional states connected with it, as we shall demonstrate in our analysis of the religious sentiments. Another cause is, that there is a strong disposition in the Negro to imitate every thing he sees done by the higher classes belonging to the white race, to which he looks instinctively for direction in all things. Besides this, there is a strong affinity for external forms of good in the races and nations, as well as in the individuals, who represent the affectional principle; remarkable instances of which we have seen in the Chinese and Egyptian nations: and thus, as far as Morality of a feminine kind — which is dependent upon sympathy — is connected with the forms representative of Christianity, so far will they be atractive to them; so that individuals belonging to imperfect races may be led to accept, as a substitute for their own rude theology, some of the more affectional forms of the Church, which correspond with natural instinct, and are harmonious with a pagan worship. Until, however, we can show that the Indians, the Chinese, and the Hindoos have become capable of accepting and of realizing Christianity, it would evidently be a great absurdity to suppose that the Negro could really be so; because, being of the black race, he is the furthest removed from the white or Caucasian, and is therefore the furthest removed from the possibility of such experiences.

That it may not be supposed that we have misrepresented the character of the Ethiopian race, or have even exaggerated the imperfections belonging to it, we will make an extract from Hegel's "Philosophy of History," where he presents the subject in an abstract and also in a practical way; and where the natural capacities and tendencies of the Negro are described, unmixed with the artificial and deceptive appearances that are contracted by contact with other races. The testimony of this sagacious philosopher, who has so graphically described the characteristics which belong to the Hindoo, the Chinese, and the Negro, is more reliable, as well as remarkable, in this case, because the German mind, being relatively naturalistic and transcendental, has an affinity for affectionalism as well as for sentimentalism, and he would therefore be more likely to be a partial than a severe judge of the negro character. M. Hegel says, —

"The peculiarity of African character is difficult to comprehend, for the very reason, that, in reference to it, we must quite give up the principle which naturally accompanies all *our* ideas, — the category of Universality. In Negro life, the characteristic point is the fact that consciousness has not yet attained to the realization of any substantial objective existence, — as, for example, God or Law, — in which the interest of man's volition is involved, and in which he realizes his own being. This distinction between himself as an individual, and the universality of his essential being, the African, in the uniform undeveloped oneness of his existence, has not yet attained: so that the knowledge of an absolute Being, an Other and a Higher than his individual self, is entirely wanting. The Negro exhibits the natural man in his completely wild and untamed state. We must lay aside all thought of reverence and morality, — all that we call feeling, — if we would rightly comprehend him: there is nothing harmonious with humanity to be found in this type of character. The copious and circumstantial accounts of missionaries completely confirm this; and Mahommedanism appears to be the only thing which in any way brings the Negroes within the range of culture. The Negroes indulge, therefore, that perfect contempt for humanity, which, in its bearing on Justice and Morality, is the fundamental characteristic of the race. They have, moreover, no knowledge of the immortality of the soul, although spectres are supposed to appear. The undervaluing of humanity among them reaches an incredible degree of intensity. Tyranny is regarded as no wrong, and cannibalism is looked upon as quite customary and proper; the devouring of human flesh being altogether consonant with the general principles of the African race. At the death of a king, hundreds are killed and eaten; prisoners are butchered, and their flesh sold in the markets: and the victor is accustomed to eat the heart of his slain foe. Another characteristic fact in reference to the Negroes is Slavery. Negroes are enslaved by Europeans, and sold to America. Bad as this may be, their lot in their own land is even worse, since there a slavery quite as absolute exists. Among the Negroes, moral sentiments are non-existent. Parents sell their children, and children their parents, as either has the opportunity. The polygamy of the Negroes has frequently for its object the having many children, to be sold, every one of them, into slavery. This is illustrated by the story of a Negro in London, who lamented that he was now quite a poor man because he had already sold all his relations.

"Turning our attention in the next place to the category of political constitution, we shall see that the entire nature of this race is such as to preclude the existence of any such arrangement. The stand-point of humanity, at this grade, is mere sensuous volition, since universal spiritual laws (for example, that of the morality of the Family) cannot be recognized here. Universality exists only as arbitrary subjective choice. The political bond can, therefore, not possess such a character as that free laws should unite the community. There is absolutely no bond, no restraint upon that arbitrary volition. Nothing but external force can hold the State together for a moment. A ruler stands at the head; for sensuous barbarism can only be restrained by despotic power. But, since the subjects are of equally violent temper with their master, they keep him, on the other hand, within limits. Accompanying the king, we constantly find the executioner, whose office is regarded as of the highest consideration, and by whose hands the king may himself suffer death, if the grandees desire it. Fanaticism, which, notwithstanding the yielding disposition of the Negro in other respects, can be excited, surpasses, when roused, all belief. An English traveller states, that, when a war is determined on in Ashantee, solemn ceremonies precede it: among other things, the bones of the king's mother are laved with human blood. As a prelude to the war, the king ordains an onslaught upon his own metropolis, to excite the due degree of frenzy. On such occasions, the king has all whom he suspects killed; and the deed then assumes the character of a sacred act. Every idea thrown into the mind of the Negro is caught up and realized with the whole energy of his will; but this realization involves a wholesale destruction. These people continue long at rest; but suddenly their passions ferment, and then they are quite beside themselves. The destruction, which is the consequence of their excitement, is caused by the fact, that it is no positive idea, no thought, which produces these commotions. In Dahomey, when the king dies, the bonds of society are loosed: in his palace begins indiscriminate havoc and disorganization. All the wives of the king (in Dahomey their number is exactly 3,333) are massacred; and, through the whole town, plunder and carnage run riot. The authorities have to hasten to proclaim the new governor, simply to put a stop to the massacre.

"From these various traits, it is manifest that want of self-control distinguishes the character of the Negroes. This condition is capable of no development or culture; and as we see them at this day, such have they always been. The only essential connection that has existed and continued between the Negroes and the Europeans is that of slavery. In this the Negroes see nothing unbecoming them; and the English, who have done most for abolishing the slave-trade and slavery, are treated by the Negroes themselves as enemies. The doctrine which we deduce from this condition of slavery among the Negroes is, that the 'Natural condition' itself is one of absolute and thorough injustice. Every intermediate grade between this and the realization of a rational State retains elements and aspects of injustice. But, thus existing in a State, slavery is itself a phase of advance from the merely isolated sensual existence, — a phase of education, — a mode of becoming participant in a higher morality, and the culture connected with it. Slavery is, in and for itself, injustice: for the essence of humanity is freedom; but, for this, man must be matured. The gradual abolition of slavery is therefore wiser and more equitable than its sudden removal."

Nothing could more completely sustain the account that has been given of the Ethiopian race in our analysis than this statement of Hegel. Not only are the statements made by us, showing that this race is the lowest and most external of all the races, and a representative of Affectionalism in its immature, primitive, and most concentrated form, fully confirmed, but the perfectly selfish and destructive character of this principle, as a representative of death or the finite, is described by him with the most appalling and overpowering effect. It is to the predominance in the Negro of this destructive affectional force, that has not been redeemed by the operation of any intellectual laws and converted into forms of intellectual and affectional life, that almost all the peculiar characteristics which have been alluded to by him are to be referred. From this supremacy of Affectionalism, and the consequent absence of all internal ties of relationship, the individual is led to convert the sexual and all the other necessary relationships of life into mere means of sensual gratification and profit, and brutal ferocity and force are introduced as the normal condition of society; by which are produced a state of universal slavery, and the exercise of unrestrained individual power, carried to the utmost extent that it is possible to carry them in any social combination. By this peculiar constitution of the Negro, "Sociability," "Sexuality," and "Destruction," which are the destructive laws of the Affectional Nature, are made to constitute the ruling affectional laws of his constitution; and as this law of Destruction, which is a love for destruction, has not in him been made subject to an opposite vital principle, which is a love of life, and as the department of the mind of which this constitutes the motive power is the executive department of the Affectional Nature, we may see why it is so difficult to restrain the manifestation of this principle in the Negro, when it has become excited, and why no regard for human life can be supposed to exist in him. Indifference to death, therefore, arises in the Negro simply in his *contempt for life*, while in the Indian it arises in the opposite, — *contempt for death;* and the Negro, in his natural state, has no belief in a future state of being, while in the Indian this belief is one of the most vivid and operative of all his ideas. How blind, then, are those individuals who would treat such subjects as if they were possessed of the same affections, capacities, sensibilities, and aspirations as themselves! and how wicked are they who would take advantage of white influence in exciting this unreclaimed and thus destructive affectional force of the Negro, when it can only bring destruction both upon their own heads and upon those under whose salutary control they live! If they in this err ignorantly, it is because the affectional principle has become predominant in themselves, and they, too, have unconsciously become destructive.

According to the classification of races that has here been realized in a scientific form, the Caucasian is the supernatural and productive race, which represents the realization of Spiritual Life through Marriage. This constitutes it the only perfect and improvable race, and thus the only one to which can belong a continuous progress, and, consequently, a history. In the natural condition of this race, it therefore becomes universally representative, instead of being partially representative like the other races, and is consequently subdivided into nations which represent, upon a higher plane, the same principles; it being necessary that the most general divisions of consciousness, or forms of human life, should be separately represented by the nations as well as by the races of mankind, and even by the individuals who compose them. For this reason, and because this race is improvable and continually progressive, diversity in individual growth and in mental development is necessarily incidental to it; and we consequently here find all the degrees of social culture, and all the varieties of character and capacity, that can be conceived as belonging to a civilized people. All the nations belonging to this race, however, include the element of progress; manifest a self-directing activity which aims at improvement by the increase of knowledge, of wealth, and of power; exhibit productions of philosophical and scientific thought, and also of genuine art; and, finally, are receptive of Christianity. These are the characteristics which distinguish this from the other races.

We may illustrate this fact of national representation by contrasting the French and English nations. It is well known that these nations are in every thing opposite, and naturally hostile; and this difference and this hostility arise in the fact, that they are the representatives of opposite individual and social principles, by which the French become relatively internal, intellectual, and democratic, and the English external, affectional, and aristocratic. Hence, although the form of government in France has always been highly aristocratic, as we shall show that it must be, in order that democratic results should be produced, its social institutions have always been democratic in character, while the tendencies of the people have been even excessively so; all their manners, customs, and modes of thought, being in direct opposition to externalism and formalism, and to all absolute rule not harmonious with the democratic principle, or with the principles of liberty, equality, and fraternity. It is this representative character that makes them so revolutionary, or so ready to overturn the government of the country when the accumulated evils which result from aristocracy have encroached too far upon the prosperity of the masses, — that leads them to regard the substance and to disregard the forms of things, which they seem to do from some intuitive perception of the natural opposition between them, — that leads them to prefer an aristocratic to a democratic form of government, because democratic results can be more readily secured to them through this form, — and that leads them to disregard many of the forms which usually regulate the intercourse between individuals, in order that the advantages which this intercourse is calculated to afford may be the more perfectly secured to them. It is this that makes them pre-eminently practical, prosperous, and happy, as a nation, and also eminently moral; and makes them superior to the English in Philosophy, in Science, and in Art.

With regard to England, although her government has always been comparatively popular or representative in its form, her institutions have been as decidedly aristocratic as those of France have been democratic; while the people are well known to be proud, arbitrary, and aristocratic, and, socially considered, to be as much devoted to persons and to the forms of things, as the French are to principles and to the substance of things. It is this that makes the people of England so averse to revolution, that they will suffer almost any amount of oppression, without being excited to revolt against their rulers. Revolutions in the government have therefore been produced either by religious changes, or from the conflicts of aristocratic leaders to obtain power. The consequence of this aristocratic condition of the institutions and the people of England has been, that there is no nation in the world where the higher and the lower classes are so extremely antagonized, or where the degradation of the lower classes is so great. The fact here alluded to, that democracy becomes manifested through an aristocratic, and aristocracy through a democratic form, is in perfect harmony with the law of "Contrariety," soon to be stated, under the operation of which the form and the substance of things become antagonized. This fact is readily apprehended by those who are really democratic, and is therefore recognized even by the common people of France; while by those who at the same time possess a knowledge of principles, and of the relation between causes and consequences, it is clearly understood. It was therefore said by M. Thiers, who belongs to this latter class, "An aristocratic element is more particularly suitable to republics;" and Louis Napoleon has added, "An aristocracy does not need a chief, while it is the nature of Democracy to personify itself in one man." It is this relation between Absolutism and Democracy which constitutes the ground of antagonism between the head of a nation and the Nobles, who constitute the Aristocracy; and is the cause of that contest for supremacy which has always been carried on between them, — a contest that is strikingly illustrated by the frequent conspiracies of the Nobles, and by the wars between the Nobles and the King, in France, where the power of the Aristocracy was at last overthrown by the great revolution, and is systematically kept in subjection under the Empire, which was established by the great Napoleon as the representative of Democracy.

It is not our intention, however, to carry out this comparison of national characteristics for the purpose of illustrating the position here assumed from an abstract point of view, — that the nations belonging to the Caucasian race represent the universal fivefold form of Existence; although the fact that individuals of every nation, as well as all nations, are to be classified under this general form, will be shown by the analysis of the principles of Democracy and Aristocracy in our statement of the "Structure of Society." To describe in an adequate manner the representative character of the congregated nations of the civilized world would require more time, space, and historical knowledge, than we could possibly command; and it will not therefore be attempted. We have been obliged to affirm this representation by these nations because it is demanded by our science; and we have referred to the French and English nations for illustration of this, because they offer the most striking and familiar examples, and are the most prominent national representatives of Democracy and Aristocracy, which constitute the internal and external elements of the State.

THE STRUCTURE

OF

THE HUMAN CONSTITUTION

WHICH ILLUSTRATES

THE LAWS OF CORRESPONDENCE.

Having shown that the races of mankind are constituted in conformity with the Laws of Correspondence here made known, we will proceed to consider the Constitution of Man as he is presented to our observation in the Caucasian Race, and show that he is created in the Image of God, and that this constitution is in every part an illustration of these laws. Thus far, we have depended upon legitimate logical and analogical deductions from premises originally assumed as self-evident facts, and upon illustrations drawn from external phenomena which belong to the region of material science and of common observation, which cannot well be disputed; but, in coming into the region of Psychology, the question arises, How can the laws of this science be illustrated by reference to the structure of the human constitution, when so much diversity of opinion exists as to what are the principles which constitute it? In resorting to Psychology for illustrations of these laws, we have taken the only possible course that was open to us. We could not make use of any of the existing theories of Human Nature, because they are simply psychological; that is, they are not founded in any ontological laws, but are only partial and promiscuous generalizations of the phenomena of the natural consciousness, which are thoroughly deceptive and discordant, and therefore are not only separated from all universal laws, which makes them unfit for the illustration of a universal science, but are destitute of any consistency either in themselves or with each other, and cannot therefore be classified under any scientific form whatever. We are therefore compelled to make use of the psychological system which forms one portion of this science, and which has been realized in its present form by the application of the ontological laws first stated to well-known philosophical facts derived from observation and from the consciousness, by which they have been systematized and explained. We are compelled to do this, because this system contains the only scientific and consistent statement of the principles of human nature, and therefore is the only one that can be used to illustrate absolute truth, or the laws of a universal science: and we have a right to take this course, because it is not the perfection of any logical process, or conformity with any received hypotheses, that gives to this science its claim to consideration, but the perfect universality and the perfect harmony, combined, that it presents; and also the use that it performs in accounting for and in explaining the phenomena of life, the facts of the Consciousness, the beliefs of the Church, the records of Inspiration, and the theories of Philosophy; all the principal forms of which have been conceived by us through the application of its laws, and their production demanded in the precise order in which we find them to have been realized. The mere fact that a scientific form can be constructed that shall embrace in harmonious combination so many spheres of thought, and such a variety of subjects, which had before been utterly discordant and hostile, and in which all partial and discordant systems and theories will be explained and accounted for, is of itself sufficient evidence of its truth: so that, unless some vital inconsistency can be detected, the system should be considered as demonstrated, so far as its general form and the laws which govern it are concerned, and therefore admissible for the purpose of illustration. This description will be made as general as is consistent with a distinct illustration of the Laws of Correspondence here stated; and the reader is therefore referred to the particular descriptions contained in other portions of this work for a more complete knowledge of the manner in which the laws of Absolute Science are illustrated by the structure and manifestations of the human constitution.

In making this statement of the primitive principles of the human constitution, we shall show that two forms of consciousness are necessary to man: a form of general consciousness, containing the principles of the Human Mind, which is developed from within outwards; and a form of personal consciousness, containing the principles of the Individual Soul, which is developed from below upwards, — that separate individualizations are demanded for these in threefold forms, as spirit, soul, and body; in which body is the manifesting principle, and in which the spirit is real, the soul is representative, and the body is externally productive, but internally destructive, — and that the manifestations of these are governed by the laws of opposition, attraction, and union in production. We will now state the most general form of the human constitution, showing the relation between its spheres and departments; and then describe each of these in order, from the highest to the lowest, and state the various principles by which they are constituted, — thus separating it into its constituent principles, and describing the general character that belongs to each department. In making a threefold individualization of the principles of the Human Mind, — which are the first in order, because they furnish the material for the incarnation of the Individual, or of the Soul, — we conceive this tri-personal form to represent the three descending spheres of Life in which God exists as a tri-personality of Spirit, Soul, and Body, and to be constituted by Spiritual, Supernatural, and Natural Spheres. The Spiritual sphere is constituted by the Reason, which is the medium through which the Universal Laws of Being are communicated to the consciousness. The Supernatural sphere is constituted by the Sentimental Nature, which includes the Religious and Moral Sentiments as opposite departments, — the first being internal and vital; and the second, external and destructive: these constitute an internal definite sphere of Truth and Good, and the mediums for the communication of phenomena which correspond with the laws of the Reason, and furnish materials in which they become definitely realized in forms that shall govern the development of the mind and of the individual consciousness. The Natural sphere is constituted by the Understanding and the Instinct as opposite departments, — the first being internal and vital; and the second, external and destructive: these constitute an external sphere of Truth and Good, and the medium for the realization of forms of thought and of affection which furnish materials in which all the higher forms of consciousness must become incarnated before they can be comprehended through definite conception, apprehended through external representation, or manifested in individual experience. This tri-personal form of human consciousness — the Human Mind — incarnates in definite forms two most universal and indefinite principles, named "Perfection" and "Imperfection," which are the opposite poles of this consciousness, and represent the Infinite and Finite, which are the opposite poles of Being.

FORM OF THE GENERAL CONSCIOUSNESS,

WHICH CONTAINS

The Principles of the Human Mind.

As the opposite poles of this Consciousness, and as the roots of the Mind, are two principles, representing Infinite and Finite, which we name —

PERFECTION. — IMPERFECTION.

These are incarnated and individualized by three Spheres, related as Spirit, Soul, and Body, which constitute the Human Mind, as follows: —

Spiritual Sphere, as Spirit.

THE REASON,
CONSTITUTED BY
TRUTH. — GOOD.
BEAUTY.

Supernatural Sphere, as Soul.

RELIGIOUS SENTIMENTS. — MORAL SENTIMENTS.

Natural Sphere, as Body.

UNDERSTANDING,	INSTINCT,
CONTAINING	CONTAINING
THE INTELLECTUAL FACULTIES.	THE AFFECTIONAL POWERS.

These most general divisions of the Human Mind we will now separate into the exact number of primitive principles which they contain, and show their correspondence with the laws of Absolute Science.

The principles of "Perfection" and "Imperfection," which constitute the opposite poles of the Mind, and are combined in all its forms and manifestations, are universal indefinite principles representing the Infinite and Finite. No particular description of them is therefore possible; and a knowledge of their character must be derived, through analogy, from our statement of the infinite and finite principles, and from our description and analysis of the vital and destructive forms and manifestations of the mind, which are their representatives. The first general division of the Mind is the Reason, or Rational Department: this contains the principles of Truth, Good, and Beauty, — as soul, body, and spirit, in which spirit is the manifesting principle, — constitutes the spiritual region of the mind, and is the medium through which Universal Spiritual Laws are communicated to the Consciousness. Being a medium for the communication of the Spiritual, the Reason does not, like the natural and supernatural departments of the mind, include a double duality of vital and destructive principles, representing the infinite and finite; but is harmoniously constituted as a perfect individuality of soul, body, and spirit. As the Spiritual, however, includes two opposite forms of Existence, one of which is Divine, and the other Infernal, the latter being an inversion of or total opposite to the former, — as these cannot be made known except as they are contrasted by the presentation of opposite laws, and of opposite external representations, — and as both must be included in any absolute presentation, for the reason that a choice between them must immediately be made, — each one of these principles is constituted by antagonistic forms as opposite spheres, so that the Reason shall be a sphere through which can be presented the laws of Spiritual Life, in Truth, Good, and Beauty; and the laws of Spiritual Death, in Falsehood, Evil, and Deformity. We therefore find, that in a natural sphere of consciousness, where these principles obtain a natural, representative development, a double manifestation is to be observed, which is productive of opposite orders of symbolic correspondences, representing these opposite spheres, and constituting the foundation of Art, which is the external representative of this department of the mind.

The next general division of the Mind is the Sentimental Region, or the Supernatural Sphere; and it is interesting to observe that this region of the mind — although it is calculated for the representation in the Natural, and the realization in the Spiritual, of Spiritual Phenomena, and thus to furnish materials in which spiritual ideas and laws can become incarnated — appears in a dualistic and discordant form, or as divided by two departments which are antagonistic to each other; and that these, like all the natural departments of the mind, represent the infinite and finite in dualistic forms, as " two and two, one against the other;" by which, diversity and discord are introduced, and also the necessity is realized that these should be combined and manifested in a supernatural manner, in order that any productive manifestation should be possible. This is necessary, first, for the reason that spiritual laws, for the incarnation and representation of which this region is calculated to furnish the materials, are both divine and infernal, and it must therefore be competent to realize forms corresponding with both Absolute Life and Absolute Death, in order that any conception of these laws should ever be realized in the consciousness, or any freedom of choice, consequent upon a spiritual condition of this consciousness, should be possible; and, next, because the incarnation of natural forms representing these phenomena in an unconscious symbolism, and in self-conscious forms corresponding with individual experiences, must be realized as a natural preparation for this great spiritual experience, — a natural preparation that must include both vital and destructive forms, realized by the successive development of these vital and destructive principles of the sentimental nature. This fact is particularly interesting, because it must settle conclusively the question of spirituality with regard to all sentimental manifestations, both religious and moral, without any reference to their psychological character; it not being possible either that spiritual life should be realized through a knowledge of phenomena separated from the laws with which they correspond and by which they are made comprehensible and vital, or that Spiritual Law, which is necessarily one, should be either communicated to, or manifested through, forms which have never realized any thing but dualistic and discordant conceptions of phenomena. Instead of being, like the Reason, threefold, the Sentimental Nature is divided into two opposite departments; one containing five principles appropriated to religious, and the other containing five principles appropriated to moral manifestations; these being arranged in the following order:—

Religious Sentiments.	*Moral Sentiments.*
SPIRITUALISM.—NATURALISM.	JUSTICE.—SYMPATHY.
INTUITION.—VENERATION.	SATISFACTION.—APPROBATION.
REVELATION.	OBLIGATION.

These will be found to correspond with and to illustrate the laws of our science: first, because these two departments constitute an internal region of truth and of good, including intellective and affective departments, which are antagonized as vital and destructive; and, next, because each of these departments contains a duality of male principles which are intuitive, perceptive, and vital, as a region of Law representing Truth, and related as intellective and affective, which are vital and destructive,—a duality of female principles which are receptive, associative, and destructive, as a region of Phenomena representing Good, and related as intellectual and affectional, which are vital and destructive,—and an active principle that is constructive and productive as the representative of Marriage, or the union of opposites through voluntary sacrifice; constituting three regions which are related as soul, body, and spirit, in which spirit is the manifesting principle; while all these are governed by the laws of opposition, attraction, and union in production. That the relationship between the moral and religious sentiments is governed, in the natural, by the law of opposition, may be known from the fact, that the Protestant Church, which was instituted as the exponent of those vital truths of Christianity which constitute the Gospel of Uncircumcision, not only recognized this fact, but separated good from truth as an antagonistic principle; this being one of the leading features which characterized the Protestant movement, as we shall presently have occasion to show. A prominent transcendental writer, in alluding to this opposition, has therefore said, "These two are so contrary, one to the other, as to fill the whole earth with the dust and noise of their contention." That the laws of attraction, and of union in production, are also illustrated in the manifestations of the sentimental region, may be clearly seen, because religious duties are always performed under a sense of personal obligation, which is a manifestation of the active principle of the moral department; because the Moral Sentiments have suggested to the Church suitable forms for the incarnation of her religious ideas; and because no religious institution can be found in which Morality is not included as an essential element. However strict a church may be in demanding a belief in salvation through faith alone, and in regarding a reliance upon good works as destructive, and even the performance of good works as hurtful to the soul, because endangering its salvation, good works are not the less insisted on; and we even find, that, the more rigid it is in enforcing the vital doctrine of salvation by faith alone, the more ascetic it becomes. That the principles in each department bear the relation to each other here ascribed to them will be shown in the descriptions of them that we shall have occasion to make in the theological and psychological portions of this science.

The next general division of the mind is the Natural Sphere. As the most external sphere which constitutes the Body of the Mind, it includes two elements which are intellectual and affectional, and internal and external. It contains all those definite and specific forms of the mind which are denominated Intellectual and Affectional, it being here that these become individualized as Understanding and Instinct, and constitute the incorporating powers of Human Nature; the Understanding constituting a theoretical and universal principle, that is relatively vital, in which all truth becomes incarnated in its most external or definite forms, or in the form of Thought, which has its ground in Sensation, or of which Sensation furnishes the body; and the Instinct constituting a practical, personal principle, that is relatively destructive, furnishing natural specific forms through which the individual motive power can become manifested in all the personal natural relationships of individual life. This region of the mind corresponds in its general form with the laws of our science; because it is dualistic in its form, while in its manifestations it illustrates the laws of opposition, attraction, and union in production. The internal attraction and external opposition that is referable to the relationship between internal and external principles will readily here be seen, because there is no portion of the mind where these are so essential to each other, and therefore where the attraction is so great; while, at the same time, Thought is to be recognized as the crucifier of Feeling, for the reason that the personal want and the intellectual law are realized in discord, requiring the subjection, through sacrifice, of the lower to the higher, in order that any use should be secured to the individual. Their union in production will be seen, first, because it is through the spontaneous productions of the Instinct that suggestive material is furnished for the incarnation of Thought in individual manifestations, — next, because it is only through the Understanding that any consciousness can be realized by the Instinct, — and, next, because it is only through the Understanding that the Instinct can obtain the knowledge, and thus the possession, of those objects for which it has an affinity. We will now describe these two great divisions of the mind, separate them into the exact number of their constituent principles, describe the relationship of these to each other, and show the correspondence between these and the laws of Absolute Science.

The Understanding is appropriated to the incarnation of ideas and laws in sensible images, and in forms of Thought founded in individual experiences, which must always, even in the Spiritual, constitute the body of Truth, in which all internal and spiritual ideas are incarnated, and through which definite knowledge is realized that is applicable to use; and we therefore find a perfect correspondence existing between the form of the Understanding and the entire form of the general consciousness, including the Reason, which is the Spiritual region of the Mind. The Understanding is thus calculated for the realization, through incarnation, of all the truth of which the mind can ever become cognizant, and so contains material for forms which cannot become developed in a natural sphere of consciousness; and the reason why the Understanding should be so competent is, that nothing can really be known that is not defined by thought, — that all thought must be embodied in language, — that all language is founded in sensation, — and that neither sensation, language, nor thought, is possible, separate from the Understanding. The nature of understanding, or the processes by which knowledge is realized, will be readily comprehended; because all production is governed by the same universal law, which is the union of opposites. Understanding is therefore realized through three processes, and requires for its manifestation three kinds of intellectual faculties, which are relatively internal, external, and medial, as soul, body, and spirit: these processes we denominate Intuition, Perception, and Reflection; and these faculties we denominate Perceptive, Receptive, and Constructive: the first make us acquainted with Law, — the second, with Phenomena, — and the third, with Conception, or Thought, which contains the relationship between these, which must necessarily be known before comprehension, or understanding, can be realized. This we may see from the point of the consciousness; for, as understanding is simply comprehending, and as comprehension is neither perception nor apprehension, but something that includes and combines both, this threefold process is demanded. These three elements of knowledge have generally been recognized by philosophers not of the sensualistic school; although Intuition has been referred by them exclusively to the Reason, when it should be referred to all the departments of the mind. This is a serious mistake;

for two reasons: first, because the Reason is not recognized as the source of Spiritual Law, which is entirely distinct from and opposite to the laws derived from physical and natural sources; and, next, because it makes the Understanding to be an imperfect or one-sided power, that requires the aid of the Reason before it can experience understanding; that is, before any thing can be understood or comprehended, even from a natural point of view. This defect has been corrected by this science, which produces a complete separation between the Reason and the Understanding; establishing the former in its full integrity as the only source of Universal Spiritual Laws; and establishing the latter, also, in its full integrity as the only source of Thought; and showing that these spiritual laws must be realized by intuitions from the Reason, and used as a foundation for Philosophy, through the union of the Understanding with the Reason, before consistency or harmony can be introduced into thought, and therefore before any thing either in the spiritual or in the natural can really be understood. We see, then, that, although nothing can be understood from a spiritual point of view before this union has taken place, the Understanding is of itself capable of comprehending all things that can be comprehended from a natural point of view, and must therefore include within itself all the laws which govern the construction of Thought, and be able to become conscious of these by intuition. We therefore find in the Understanding three orders of Intellectual Faculties, which we designate Perceptive, Receptive, and Reflective, or Constructive. By *perceptive* faculties, we mean powers of the mind from which we obtain intuitions of the intellective and affective laws which govern phenomena, and thus constitute their life; giving to the individual that comprehensiveness of mind, originating in the perception of Law, which we denominate genius. By *receptive* faculties, we mean two kinds of associating powers: one that is relatively internal and intellectual,— these being arranging or classifying powers which associate phenomena with reference to some recognized relationship, as cause and effect, or as premises and conclusion; and another that is relatively external and affectional,— these being impressible and retentive powers, which associate phenomena with reference to accidental and arbitrary relationships, or in the order in which they are presented to the mind through the external senses. By *reflective* faculties, we mean those active, conceptive, and constructive powers which possess the capacity of decomposing and recomposing all constructions referable to their own department, and of applying the laws which govern the phenomena belonging to it in the realization of new creations.

That a more definite conception may be obtained of the three kinds of intellectual power which belong to each one of the departments of the Understanding, we will illustrate these by a few extracts from the writings of Dugald Stewart, which describe manifestations in which some one of these predominates; although the receptive power which arranges thought with reference to cause and effect, and premises and conclusion, and constitutes the man of talent, is not separated with sufficient distinctness from that constructive power which applies intuitions of laws and principles in originating new combinations, and constitutes the productive genius. The external receptive and associating power here alluded to is thus described: "The species of memory which excites the greatest degree of admiration in the ordinary intercourse of society is a memory for detached and insulated facts; and it is certain that those men who are possessed of it are very seldom distinguished by the higher gifts of mind. Such a species of memory is unfavorable to philosophical arrangement; and, in general, I believe it may be laid down as a rule, that those who carry about with them a great amount of acquired information, which they have always at command, or who have rendered their own discoveries so familiar to them as always to be in a condition to explain them, are seldom possessed of much invention, or even of much quickness of apprehension."

The internal receptive and associating power, to which we have alluded, is thus described: "They who are really destined to extend the boundaries of knowledge, when they first enter on new pursuits, feel their attention distracted and their memory overloaded with facts, among which they can trace no relations, and are sometimes apt to despair entirely of their future progress. In due time, however, their superiority appears, and arises in part from that very dissatisfaction which they first experienced, and which does not cease to stimulate their inquiries, till they are enabled to trace, amidst a chaos of apparently unconnected materials, that simplicity and beauty which always characterize the operations of Nature. A person in whose mind casual associations of time and place make a lasting impression has not the same inducements to philosophize, with others who connect facts together chiefly by the relation of cause and effect, or of premises and conclusion. I have heard it observed, that these men who have risen to the greatest eminence in the profession of the law, have been, in general, such as had at first an aversion to the study. The reason probably is, that, to a mind fond of general principles, every study must be at first disgusting which presents to it a chaos of apparently unconnected facts. But this love of arrangement, if united with persevering industry, will at last conquer every difficulty, and reduce the dry and uninteresting detail of positive statutes into a system comparatively luminous and beautiful."

These internal and external associating powers are contrasted by him in the following manner: "There are, among men who are accustomed to the exercise of their intellectual powers, two classes, whose habits of thought are remarkably distinguished from each other: the one class comprehending what we call men of business, or, more properly speaking, men of detail; and the other, men of abstraction, or, in other words, Philosophers." "There are two extremes into which men are apt to fall in preparing themselves for the active duties of life. The one arises from habits of abstraction and generalization carried to excess; the other from a minute, an exclusive, and an unenlightened attention to objects and events which happen to fall under their actual experience. Although each of these defects has a tendency to limit the utility of the individuals in whom it is found to certain stations in society, no comparison can be made, in point of original value, between the intellectual capacities of the two classes of men to which they characteristically belong. The one is the defect of a vigorous, an ambitious, and a comprehensive genius, improperly directed; the other, of an understanding minute and circumstantial in its views, timid in its exertions, and formed for servile imitation."

With regard to men of genius, in whom the constructive power predominates, he says, "They who are possessed of much acuteness and originality enter with difficulty into the views of others; not from any defect in their power of apprehension, but because they cannot adopt opinions which they have not examined; and because their attention is often seduced by their own speculations. A man of original genius, who is fond of exercising his reasoning powers anew on every point as it occurs to him, and who cannot submit to rehearse the ideas of others, or even to repeat by rote the conclusions which he has deduced from previous reflection, often appears, to superficial observers, to fall below the level of ordinary understandings; while another, destitute both of quickness and invention, is admired for that promptitude in his decisions which arises from the inferiority of his intellectual abilities. The conversation, accordingly, of men of genius is sometimes extremely limited, and is interesting to the few alone who know the value and can distinguish the marks of originality. In consequence, too, of that partiality which every man feels for his own speculations, they are more in danger of being dogmatical and disputatious, than those who have no system which they are interested to defend. The conversation which pleases generally must unite the recommendations of quickness, of ease, and of variety; and, in all these respects, that of the philosopher is apt to be deficient. As the ideas which he associates together are commonly of the same class, or at least are referred to the same general principles, he is in danger of becoming tedious by indulging himself in long and systematic discourses; while another, possessed of the most inferior accomplishments, by laying his mind completely open to impressions from without, and by accommodating continually the course of his own ideas, not only to the ideas which are started by his companions, but to every trifling and unexpected accident that may occur to give them a new direction, is the life and soul of every society into which he enters. Nor is it the imputation of tediousness merely to which the systematic thinker must submit from common observers. It is but rarely possible to explain completely, in a promiscuous society, all the various parts of the most simple theory; and, as nothing appears weaker or more absurd than a theory which is partially stated, it frequently happens that men of ingenuity, by attempting it, sink, in the vulgar apprehension, below the level of ordinary understandings."

Having made this statement of the general functions of the Understanding which are demanded by the laws of our science, and shown that these have been imperfectly recognized by the philosophers from a more external and psychological point of view, but have been realized in a scientific form by the application of these laws, we will first divide the Understanding into the exact number of its constituent principles, and then describe in a general manner the manifestations which belong to its different regions, showing how these are made to illustrate the laws of Correspondence.

THE FORM OF THE HUMAN UNDERSTANDING.

The Material Region,
WHICH IS
THE BODY OF THE HUMAN UNDERSTANDING.

The Material Department, as Body.
SPACE. — SOLIDITY.
FIGURE. — NUMBER.
MOTION.

The Representative Department, as Soul.
PERCEPTION. — SENSIBILITY.
INDIVIDUALITY. — ASSOCIATION.
CONCEPTION.

The Constructive Department, as Spirit.
EXTENSION. — GRAVITATION.
PHYSICS. — CHEMISTRY.
CONSTRUCTION.

The Representative or Poetic Region,
WHICH IS
THE SOUL OF THE HUMAN UNDERSTANDING.

The Material Department, as Body.
REPRESENTATION. — ACTION.
PHYSIOGNOMY. — ACTIVITY.
HUMANITY.

The Representative Department, as Soul.
ARTICULATION. — INTONATION.
LANGUAGE. — MUSIC.
POETRY.

The Constructive Department, as Spirit.
CONTRAST. — RESEMBLANCE.
COMPARISON. — SIMILITUDE.
FANCY.

The Demonstrative or Philosophic Region,
WHICH IS
THE SPIRIT OF THE HUMAN UNDERSTANDING.

The Material Department, as Body.
CONSECUTION. — CAUSALITY.
RATIOCINATION. — PRACTICABILITY.
POLICY.

The Representative Department, as Soul.
INTELLECTUALITY. — AFFECTIONALITY.
DIDACTICS. — ETHICS.
PSYCHOLOGY.

The Constructive Department, as Spirit.
OPPOSITION. — CORRESPONDENCE.
METAPHYSICS. — ANALOGY.
IMAGINATION.

We see that the Understanding is divided into three regions, which correspond with the three regions of the general consciousness, and with the three spheres into which the Instinct is divided; all these being related as body, soul, and spirit: the body being negative and destructive, the soul relative and representative, and the spirit vital and productive. We also see that each one of these regions contains three departments, which have the same relation; and that each one of these departments contains five principles, constituting three regions which are related as soul, body, and spirit; the soul being vital, the body destructive, and the spirit productive. The first region contains a male duality of intellective and affective principles which constitute a perceptive region, from which are derived by intuition the laws which are combined in all the phenomena belonging to the particular department of knowledge to which it is appropriated, and also the moving or incentive power that leads to its pursuit as an object of science; it being the scientific character of this region that constitutes it vital. The second region contains a female duality of intellectual and affectional principles which constitute a receptive region, from which the power and inclination are derived of accumulating a knowledge of phenomena, which is simply a knowledge of appearances, and is sensualistic in character; the first associating ideas with reference to the relations of cause and effect, of premises and conclusion, and of recognized relationship; and the second associating phenomena with reference to accidental, casual, and arbitrary relationships. This region is relatively destructive, because the knowledge acquired by it presents the appearance without realizing the condition of real knowledge, and is thus deceptive in character; and because it leads the individual, through the desire for admiration, and for the possession of what seems to be knowledge, to neglect or to sacrifice the acquisition of true wisdom by reflection in the consciousness. The third region is constituted by an active and reflective principle which is conceptive and constructive, from which the power and inclination are realized of adapting means to ends, causes for the production of consequences, premises for the production of conclusions, and for tracing relationships between laws and phenomena in the particular department of knowledge to which it belongs; and which furnishes a medium through which the Divine Activity operates outside of the individual consciousness in the construction of supernatural forms, which represent a spiritual order of production and manifestation. It thus becomes vital and productive, and a representative of Spiritual Life through Marriage, in the subjection of the destructive to the vital for use. Nothing can be more decided, therefore, than the illustration presented by these three spheres of intelligence, or modes of intellectual operation, of the laws of opposition, attraction, and union in production, which, according to our science, must govern all the natural manifestations of the mind.

This general analysis of the Understanding, or enumeration and classification of the entire number of intellectual principles which enter into its composition, by the application of the laws of our science, presents a complete and systematic view of the intellectual nature of man, so far as it can be presented in the slight notice that we are able here to take of it, — a classification that is even more remarkable as showing the power of this science than the one obtained for Philosophy by the same means; for although that has been verified by the testimony of the best historians of Philosophy, and by the obvious character of the philosophical systems alluded to, this must be verified by the consciousness of all philosophic minds. This we shall see more clearly by reference to the theological and psychological volumes, where the particular principles and departments are analyzed and described; and the illustrations offered by these, of the universal laws upon which our science is founded, will be more satisfactory, because more definite, than those which are presented by this general statement.

The Instinct is appropriated to the most external and spontaneous manifestation of the individual through affectional forms, in which are realized all the relations of individual, domestic, and social life. We give the name of Instinct to these affectional powers, for the reason that they are characterized by unconscious spontaneity and a specific external activity, and thus correspond with the instinctive powers of animals; although they are as much more complicated, and as much more important, as the nature of man is superior to that of an animal. From the fact that these affectional powers are the most external manifesting principles of the mind, and correspond with Personal Want, their manifestations have sometimes been confounded with those of the Will; but these may be seen to be perfectly opposite in character, for the reason that the affection is unconscious and spontaneous in all its manifestations, while the great characteristics of the Will are self-consciousness and a calculated activity. Being designed for the manifestation of all the good of which the individual can ever become the medium, and thus for the incarnation and manifestation of all the good referable to the rational and sentimental spheres of the mind, the Affectional Nature is divided into three departments, which are three regions corresponding with the three regions of the Understanding, and constitute an individuality of spirit, soul, and body; each region containing the same five principles which must belong to all the departments in the natural and supernatural spheres of the mind. They are to be classified in the following order: —

Social Instincts, as Spirit.
SOCIALISM. — SOCIABILITY.
FRIENDSHIP. — FRATERNITY.
SOCIETY.

Domestic Instincts, as Soul.
CONJUGALITY. — SEXUALITY.
MATRIMONY. CONSANGUINITY.
FAMILY.

Individual Instincts, as Body.
VITALITY. — DESTRUCTION.
NUTRITION. — PROTECTION.
PRESERVATION.

These will be found to correspond with and to illustrate the laws of our Science, in the first place, because they constitute a perfect individuality of spirit, soul, and body; in which the body is negative and destructive, the soul relative and representative, and the spirit vital and productive. The individual department is negative and destructive, because it excludes all domestic and social relations and duties, and thus presents an aspect of unqualified selfishness and externalism which excludes all internal life; so that, while being externally productive, it is internally destructive. The domestic department is relative and representative, because it furnishes, in the relationships of the Family, symbolic representations of social and also of spiritual relationships, as we shall hereafter have occasion to show. The social department is relatively vital and productive, because it is only in society that man becomes vitally useful by the devotion of himself to objects of universal interest, in which the good of all is involved, instead of devoting himself to objects of personal or of domestic interest, for the exclusive good of himself or of his family. They will be found to correspond, in the next place, because each one of these departments is constituted as two and two, one against the other, with a fifth principle representing Marriage, or the union of opposites through voluntary sacrifice, — is individualized in three spheres, the first a male sphere representing truth, as the region of Law; the second a female sphere representing good, as the region of Phenomena; and the third a constructive sphere representing Use, which realizes the marriage of good with truth,—and is governed by the laws of opposition, attraction, and union in production.

To show that these laws are represented in the structure, in the forms, and in the manifestations, of this affectional region of the mind, we will describe the lowest department in this region, which constitutes the body of the Affectional Nature, and is therefore the manifesting affectional sphere; and this is the most satisfactory illustration that can be offered, because this is the most external department of the mind, and therefore presents the most definite representations of these laws. The internal principles in this department, which constitute the laws that are combined in all its external affectional forms, and are represented in all their manifestations, are here named "Vitality" and "Destruction," and have been recognized in all Phrenological Systems as the Love of Life, and the Love of Destruction; and, as these principles are the most definite representations of Absolute Life and Absolute Death which the human constitution contains, the law of Opposition is here represented in the most perfect manner. It is also represented in a manner that cannot be controverted, because the organs of these principles may be found lying side by side at the base of the brain, supporting the organs of the specific individual propensities; and the manifestations of the destructive principle, illustrating its function as a universal appetite for destruction, have been more extensively observed and thoroughly ascertained by the phrenologists than those of almost any other principle of the mind. Opposite absolute causes are represented in all the departments of the human constitution, but more internally, and therefore more obscurely, than in the principles of "Vitality" and "Destruction;" because, the more internal a principle is, the less conscious is the individual of its nature and of its operations. It is only because these principles represent absolute causes in the most external manner, and therefore in the most definite forms, that they seem to present a greater opposition than any other department of the mind. With regard to the instincts of "Nutrition" and "Protection," which, as internal and external principles, are relatively vital and destructive, this antagonism does not so readily appear, although it is in fact quite as decided, and even more interesting, as illustrating the laws of our science. "Nutrition" is obviously a vital power, because it not only suggests to the individual the proper nourishment for the body, but is the natural purveyor for all its physical necessities and appetites or wants. "Protection" may be seen to be a destructive power, because, although it leads the individual to anticipate danger, and to be watchful for it, in order that means may be provided for avoiding, escaping from, or overcoming it, it at the same time realizes the emotion of fear, which, when not overcome by the excitement of anger, or by the assurance of safety from its intellectual partner, becomes self-destructive; not only by paralyzing the mind, and thus preventing the desired aid, but by precipitating the individual into the very misfortunes from which this instinct, in its vital condition, would extricate him. The suicidal tendency of fear, which is so prominent a result from the inordinate excitement of this instinct that the phrenologists have supposed it to include nothing else, has always been recognized, and is a matter of common observation. Fear is not, however, the only emotion that arises in this affectional principle. All the sentimental and affectional powers include both an active and a passive condition, which are relatively vital and destructive; and while fear is the passive, anger is the active, condition of this instinct, which will be found to be still more destructive in its effects than its passive condition. The destructive tendency of anger may be distinctly seen, because it demands the immediate destruction of those things which are offensive to the individual, and because it paralyzes the judgment, and renders the individual incapable of any rational or useful exercise of his mind. This destructive tendency in the instinct of "Protection," which appears in the phrenological systems under the name of "Cautiousness," has been demonstrated in the fullest and most satisfactory manner by Dr. Gall, who has shown, by a great variety of observations, that when this instinct becomes a predominant or ruling power, either from morbid excitement or from an unhealthy external development, a tendency to suicide is the result.

The laws of Attraction, and of Union in production, are illustrated in a manner particularly striking in this department of the mind, for the reason that the opposition is here so extreme, and the combination of vital and destructive principles in all the manifestations referable to it is so clearly evident. The fact that death becomes productive from life is well known with regard to all animal and vegetable productions; it not being possible to conceive any physical organization that does not require for its support the destruction of some other form of animal or vegetable life: but the explanation of this fact can be obtained only from our science, which establishes the law of production from the union of opposites; and the illustration offered by the manifestations of this department is particularly remarkable, because we here see these vital and destructive principles palpably operating in the creation, protection, and preservation of the physical constitution of man. The combination and manifestation of these dualistic natural powers, in the preservation of the individual, is, of course, a supernatural operation that is referable to the active principle in this department, which is "Preservation;" it not being possible that such discordant elements should of themselves become productive of any thing but disorder and discord, which would be destructive to life. To suppose that they could, would be to affirm that Chaos contains in itself the power of producing order and life, or that "All nature's difference keeps all nature's peace," which none but the worshipper of nature can believe; although the fact that opposites do really become combined and manifested in an orderly manner in nature has given an apparent foundation for this absurd paradox. We give this as a specimen of the manner in which the laws of our science are illustrated by each one of the departments of the mind, without now proceeding any further in the description of these affectional powers; because all the principles of the mind will hereafter be described in a more particular manner than is possible here, and the correspondence between these and the laws of our science will be made more perfect and more apparent.

Through the threefold form of the Mind that has now been described, the individual becomes conscious of that particular or modified form of human nature which he was originally created to manifest. Through this form every kind of experience peculiar to human nature is realized by him, in the course of its development from within outwards, and still an experience that is in something different in its form from that of every other individual; furnishing the pattern according to which, and the materials out of which, his individual life is to be constructed. But it may readily be seen, that an individual department or sphere of consciousness is demanded, separate from this universal form of human nature, in order that any individuality, or any appearance of consistency, reality, freedom, or accountability, should be obtained for the soul. This necessity may be seen, because we have shown that this form of human nature is constituted dualistic and discordant as "life against death, and good against evil," so that all its productive manifestations have to be realized, through the operation of a spiritual power, in a supernatural manner outside of the individual consciousness; and, although productive and partially consistent manifestations are in this way obtained, they cannot be either self-conscious or calculated, and therefore cannot appear to the individual to be real or to be free. They cannot, as a whole, be even consistent, because, although the manifestations of any given department may present a comparatively harmonious appearance, as the different regions and departments of the mind are manifested in a dualistic and discordant manner, their manifestations present the most discordant combination of phenomena that can possibly be conceived, and there is no form in this consciousness in which they can be concentrated, individualized, and harmonized. It cannot be a self-conscious manifestation, and therefore cannot appear to be free, because it is obtained in either a spontaneous, an unconscious, or a supernatural manner not comprehensible; and although such a manifestation would be suitable for a creature, unreal, natural, and necessitated, it is not suitable for one who is destined to become real, spiritual, and free. In order that the individual should obtain any consistency or apparent reality for his life; in order that he should represent and be prepared for the spiritual condition which he is destined to realize, and be himself impressed with the idea of his own reality as a responsible free-agent, capable of a free self-determination by which the form of his being and the condition of his life is to be decided for eternity (and it is important, for many reasons, that all these ideas should be realized by him); and in order that he should become an individual, — it is necessary, that in addition to this general form of consciousness realized through the principles of the human mind, which are developed in each sphere from within outwards, or from the highest to the lowest principles of life, the individual should become developed from a personal ground, from below upwards, by successive growths, or from the lowest to the highest spheres of personal consciousness, in a self-conscious, comprehensible manner, as if he were a free and independent cause, engaged in the construction of his own destiny. This necessity is therefore provided for in a department or sphere of Personal Consciousness, which includes Individuality, or Will: through this the individual obtains a concentrated form of personal consciousness, which constitutes his individuality; becomes manifested as a Unit; and appears to construct his own life by a calculated, self-conscious, comprehensive activity; by which he obtains an appearance of consistency, and a consciousness of reality, freedom, and accountability. In this process he appropriates for personal use, from the materials furnished by the manifestations of the mind, such forms as correspond with the present wants of his personal constitution; and makes use of these appropriations, in the relation of cause and effect, as means for the production of ends in securing the greatest amount of good that is possible for him, or what is good for him upon the whole. Thus, instead of a dual and discordant consciousness spontaneously realized, the nature of which is incomprehensible to him, he seems to construct for himself a self-conscious, calculated, comprehensible individuality, which is consistent in character, and the composition and operations of which are thoroughly comprehended, because calculated and constructed by himself. We say that the individual *appears* in this way to construct his own life, — that this must so appear to him, in order that any apparent reality or freedom should be communicated to it, — and that it is absolutely necessary that he should believe in his reality, freedom, and accountability: but we do not mean to say that this is the fact; on the contrary, we affirm, that, not being an absolute cause, he cannot be a creator, and therefore cannot originate any thing, and that his natural life is an unreal appearance, that is the opposite of what it seems. While appearing to construct his own life, it is really constructed for him by the divine providence of God, who is the real governor of the World, and must either ordain or permit the production of every thing that takes place in the Universe; and therefore, although the individual determinations are governed by the stronges: motive, in his endeavor to procure the greatest amount of good for himself, these determinations are either counteracted or directed, so that what is really good for him upon the whole, instead of what he believes to be so, shall be provided for him. It is therefore written, "I am Jehovah, and none else; besides Me there is no God; forming Light, and creating Darkness, — making Peace, and creating Evil: I Jehovah am the Author of all these things." *

We will now describe this form of Personal Consciousness, and obtain a conception of the principles through which the Individual becomes incarnated as a Living Soul, and also of the manner in which this incarnation is effected. We have seen that the Human Soul is created with the capacity for being developed successively in three several spheres of consciousness, which are described in

---

* Lowth's "Isaiah."

the Scriptures as births of blood, of water, and of spirit; and which we have shown to be a development in an external-natural, an internal-natural, and a spiritual sphere of consciousness. We have also shown that the Human Constitution, in which this threefold consciousness becomes realized, is divided into two spheres, — a sphere already described as containing the principles of the mind, or of the general consciousness; and a personal sphere, now to be described, which includes three spheres of Individuality, or Will. The dualistic form of this personal consciousness, corresponding with the dualistic principles of the mind which is the form through which the individual obtains a definite consciousness and becomes specifically manifested, is constituted by two indefinite universal principles, which are affinities for Truth and Good, and constitute the most concentrated form of Individual Want; each principle containing Male and Female spheres, which are opposite Universal and Personal elements: these principles we name "Personality" and "Property." They are universal affinities, and also receptive and constructive or individualizing principles, which are related as internal and external, and correspond with truth and good; each of which is calculated for the unconscious appropriation and individualization of vital and also of destructive laws and phenomena, under the universal law of Contrariety, which governs all natural manifestations, and demands the combination of vital and destructive elements. These appropriations are therefore made by the personifying principles from the realizations of the mind, or of the general consciousness, the principles of which become developed in correspondence with the growth of these personifying powers, and therefore with the present want of the individual, under the operation of this law. The character of these appropriations in the external-natural and internal-natural spheres of consciousness, and the manner in which they become realized, will be described in illustrating this universal law of Contrariety. We there show, that, in an external sphere, the individual appropriates incarnations or representations of vital universal laws, combined with destructive partial and personal forms; while, in an internal sphere, he appropriates intuitions and conceptions of destructive universal laws, combined with vital partial and personal forms: the first being combined and manifested through the Will in a vital manner, or with the subjection of destructive partial and personal forms to vital laws incarnated in external forms and institutions; while the second are combined and manifested through the

Will in a destructive manner, or with the subjection of vital partial and personal forms to self-conscious conceptions of destructive universal laws corresponding with the natural life, which is representative of the finite principle. These combinations and manifestations are effected through the supernatural form of the individual soul, which is the incarnation of the individual as One in a Tri-personality of spirit, soul, and body, representing Existence, and constitutes Individuality or Will; the Spirit being conscious and vital, the Soul relative and representative, and the Body externally productive and internally destructive: and we conceive this tri-personality to be constituted by three principles, which are three spheres of life manifested as one, and we name them "Consciousness," "Relation," "Direction." Through this threefold sphere of manifestation, the individual realizes a form of life, or consciousness, representing Individuality, or Existence, and appears to construct his own life, in a natural manner, from a self-conscious determination of himself in view of opposite things, calculating means to ends in the production of what appears to him to be his greatest good; while in reality his life is constructed in a supernatural manner by the divine providence of God, in the production of what is in reality the greatest good for the individual. The form of this sphere of personal consciousness is therefore to be stated as follows: —

FORM OF THE PERSONAL CONSCIOUSNESS,

WHICH CONTAINS

THE PRINCIPLES OF THE HUMAN SOUL.

The dualistic form of the Soul is constituted by two indefinite universal principles, which are the most concentrated form of Individual Want: —

PERSONALITY. — PROPERTY.

These are combined, incarnated, and individualized by three principles, in three spheres of manifestation, related as spirit, soul, and body; which constitute a definite, self-conscious, tri-personal individual principle, which we call Will, or Individuality: —

CONSCIOUSNESS.
RELATION.
DIRECTION.

We shall be assisted to make this conception of the personal region of the human constitution more definite by referring to the forms of the mind which have already been described, and to the universal laws which govern the construction of all forms of existence. We have shown, both from the ground of Absolute Science and from the Scriptures, that every thing is created as a dualistic form, constituted as "two and two, one against the other;" we have shown how every thing does so exist; and that, in the constitution of the human mind, this two and two are constituted, both in the general form of the mind and also in each one of its departments, by male and female spheres, each one of which is constituted by male and female elements, through the supernatural combination of which, incarnation and multiplication are effected; these being spheres of Truth and of Good, each of which contains an internal element corresponding with a universal and vital, and an external element corresponding with a partial, or personal, and destructive principle, and representing infinite and finite laws. We have shown that these male and female spheres and elements are related as vital and destructive, the opposition between them being characterized in the Scriptures as "life against death, good against evil, the godly against the sinner, and the sinner against the godly;" the male demanding the subjection of the female, that production may be effected through the establishment of universal laws for universal ends, thus representing the Infinite; and the female demanding the subjection of the male, that production may be effected through the establishment of universal laws for personal ends, thus representing the Finite: these male spheres and elements constituting the Not Me of the Individual, and these female spheres and elements constituting the Me of the Individual. This relationship is represented in a great variety of external forms in the Hebrew Scriptures, and in a more internal manner in the Epistles of St. Paul: while in the writings of Philo Judæus, who was a Hebrew, and a cotemporary of Paul, we find the following most explicit statement of it: "Of the ideas which are brought forth by the mind, some are male and some female, as in the case of animals. Now, the female offspring of the soul are wickedness and passion, by which we are made effeminate in every one of our pursuits; but a healthy state of the passions, and of virtue, is male, by which we are excited and invigorated. Now, of these, whatever belongs to the fellowship of men must be attributed to God, and every thing that relates to the similarity of women must be imputed to one's self."

We have also shown, that besides these dualistic principles, which are susceptible of a vital or of a destructive manifestation, as the universal or as the partial and personal becomes the governing power, each department contains an active, productive, and constructive principle or sphere, through which the operations of these discordant dualistic principles are combined and manifested by a spiritual power in a supernatural manner outside of the individual consciousness, or in a manner not comprehensible by him, and also in ways which he seems to comprehend, in the production of natural truth, good, and use; this being the only way in which any productive manifestation of these dualistic powers can be effected: so that, although all things seem to be produced by the individual himself in a natural manner, all things are really produced in a supernatural manner by the divine providence of God. These dualistic principles correspond with the dualistic personifying powers, and this supernatural sphere corresponds with the supernatural individualizing and constructing power which we denominate Individuality, or Will.

With regard to "Personality" and "Property," we conceive the office of these principles to be the appropriation of, or making one with the individual as property, by processes of abstraction, generalization, and individualization, such laws and partial or personal forms realized by the mind as are adapted to the present want of the individual; because, as these realizations of the mind are laws and forms universally applicable and not exclusively adapted to the present want of any one individual, unless a selection from these were made by the individual of such as are adapted to his present want, and these were individualized in systematic forms calculated for practical use, no personal use whatever could be made of them. This being the office to be performed by these principles, the laws which must govern and the functions which must characterize these personifying principles are clearly pointed out to be Appropriation and Construction. These personifying principles have been recognized in Phrenology, and also by Swedenborg, and manifestations referable to them have been described in most philosophical systems. Although the Phrenologists do not regard the Will as belonging to, or as constituting any particular department of, the human constitution, but take either the Swedenborgian view, which is, that Will is synonymous with Affection, or an opposite view, that it is "constituted by the Intellectual Faculties,"* they have

---

* Combe's "System of Phrenology."

discovered the organs through which these personifying principles are manifested, and have made a variety of observations with reference to them, under the names of "Firmness," "Self-Esteem," "Secretiveness," and "Acquisitiveness:" the first being described as giving consistency of character, and as being "mistaken for the Will;" the second, as the source of "pride and self-complacency," and as "the love of ruling over others;" the third, as manifesting falsehood and cunning, the desire to conceal and to defraud, and the power of controlling and directing the individual manifestations; and the fourth, as the sense of property, which covets, and desires to appropriate for personal use, and also to hoard up, whatever is desirable to the individual. Swedenborg recognized two of the functions belonging to these principles as constituting what he named "the proprium" of man, and describes them as follows: "Man from inheritance wishes to become great, and also wishes to become rich; and, so far as these loves are not bridled, he wishes to become greater and richer, and at length the greatest and the richest; and he would not then be at rest, but would wish to become greater than God Himself, and to possess Heaven Itself. This hankering lies hid in man's life and his life's nature." Swedenborg, however, has here not only given a one-sided view of these personal principles, but has confounded natural with spiritual things, in making them infernal in character; and this is the more remarkable from the fact that his position was a pantheistic one, which claimed that all things were produced from the Divine Love, by the Divine Wisdom, and that the divine providence constantly operates to draw the soul from Hell, in which its "proprium" is founded, into Heaven. We do not know which is the most absurd, — the idea of an infernal production from a Divine Substance, or the idea that this infernal production is gradually brought back to the divine: a notion that seems to be a version of an old Pagan idea, revived by the German Eclectics, that the Infinite, in going out from itself, produces the opposite of itself; and, in returning back to itself, produces the union of opposites. The theory of Swedenborg, however, is even more absurd than this, because it connects with this pantheistic idea the notion of individual freedom; so that this return to the Divine is made to depend, not only upon the individual consent, but upon the continuous free self-determination of the individual. It is true, as we have seen, that the life of human nature is constituted by laws corresponding with the Finite, which is the source of infernal life; but this was not the idea which Swedenborg intended to convey, because this life belongs to all natural things, and some of these he supposed to be Divine, and some are representative of divine things. It is also true, that the personal element included in each personifying principle is the most concentrated form of self-love and representative of the Finite which the human constitution contains, and therefore appears to be especially infernal in character. But these personifying principles must in each individual be constituted to appropriate material for all the natural forms of life, both vital and destructive, for the manifestation of which he was originally designed to be the medium; and must also contain affinities for opposite spiritual laws and forms, of which the individual becomes conscious in his resurrection into the spiritual. This sphere of the human constitution represents in a particular manner the Infinite as well as the Finite, because it is the supernatural sphere of the Soul; and it contains affinities for universal and vital as well as for partial and destructive laws and forms, not only because it is created to represent both Infinite and Finite, but because its substance corresponds with both, and is not, as Swedenborg supposed, simply Finite, and opposite to the Infinite. Even the demand that is here made for actual knowledge and susceptibilities for use, which is so literal, and destructive to supernatural ideas, communicates a consistency, reality, and efficiency to the life, that could not be given by any spontaneous and unconscious manifestations; and although this department manifests the desire to become great, or to rule over others, and also the desire to become rich, or to accumulate property, it also manifests the desire for Self-Government, and an affinity for Universal Law, which is the crucifier of the Individual. As the personifying principles are so remote, concentrated, and indefinite, and include opposite forms and modes of manifestation, it has been extremely difficult to obtain any adequate conception of them by the ordinary, unitarian methods of investigation; and it is probably for this reason that the personal department or sphere of the human constitution has been less understood than any other. This difficulty may be inferred from the fact, that, after such a multitude of observations by the Phrenologists, with the advantage of having discovered the organs of these principles, the results are so meagre and superficial.

It now remains for us to consider the nature of the Will, as the supernatural manifesting principle of the Individual. From what has already been said upon this subject, it will be seen that the

Will is not a concentration and individualization of the facts of the general consciousness, because we have seen that only what corresponds with the present want of the individual is appropriated by him for personal use, and also that these manifestations of the mind are spontaneously produced, and include supernatural manifestations which are realized in a manner incomprehensible to the individual; while the Will must appear to construct a plan of life in a self-conscious, comprehensible manner, founded upon causes and consequences known to the individual, so that it is contrasted with the manifestations of the Mind, as self-conscious and calculated, against unconscious and spontaneous. It will also be seen that a double function necessarily belongs to the Will, as both a self-conscious and a supernatural principle; and that, while, externally and apparently, the individual seems here to calculate all his manifestations upon the ground of cause and effect in endeavoring to secure what is good for him upon the whole, internally and really, all the manifestations of the Will are directed in their production by the divine providence of God in the realization of what is really the greatest good for the individual. We have said that the Will is realized in three spheres of personal consciousness, or as a tri-personal form of spirit, soul, and body; the spirit being self-conscious, vital, and real, the soul relative and representative, and the body externally productive and internally destructive. This threefold form, which is constituted by the principles of "Consciousness," "Relation," and "Direction," we will now describe.

The external principle, which constitutes the Body of the Will, and which we name "Direction," is the manifesting principle of the Individual. It therefore presides over all his physical relationships, and controls all his external manifestations, calculating means to ends in the relation of cause and effect for the production of what, upon the whole, or in view of all his knowledge and experience, he believes to be his greatest possible good, as this is seen from the most external point of view. It thus realizes the most external, affectional, feminine, and receptive condition of the individual, for the reason that it is developed while he exists in his most external and unreal condition; and becomes inactive, as he advances and becomes internal and real. It is therefore principally confined to an external recognition and individualization of those duties and most external relationships imposed upon the individual by the Church and by the State, and therefore realizes that development of the Will which is coincident with what is termed "the birth of the soul by blood." As it is the body of Will, or Individuality, and therefore its manifesting principle, all the internal appropriations of the individual, which are realized in the development of the higher principles of the Will, here become manifested in the production of their most external results; it being through this principle that the individual constructs a plan of life for himself in which all his internal recognitions, conceptions, and determinations become incarnated, and from this that they become manifested in the most ultimate form through the body, in a calculated system of muscular movements; although in the natural, where development and growth are partial or one-sided, and all things must become manifested in diversity and discord, only a partial realization of this threefold function becomes possible. It is relatively the destructive element in Individuality, for the same reason that the Catholic Church, by which the development or growth of this principle is superintended, is the destructive element in the Church; and that is because, as body, it is confined to what is external, and thus contradicts and prevents the realization of what is internal: and it is relatively the productive element in Individuality, not only because it is the manifesting principle of the Will, but because it is through this principle that the divine providence operates in the external direction of the individual in production, and thus in counteracting and in directing the individual determinations, so that his real wants may be provided for, and what is really good for him, upon the whole, secured.

The internal principle, which constitutes the Soul of Individuality, or of Will, and which we name "Relation," is the reconstructing principle, and presides over all the internal and personal relationships of the Individual, calculating means to ends for actualizing those relationships which have been adopted by the personifying principles as laws of the individual life, establishing internal forms of personal manifestation in the combination of these, and thus demanding a reconstruction of the principle of "Direction," in order that these may be included in the external plan and manifestations of the individual life. It therefore corresponds both with the internal or sentimental sphere, which constitutes the soul of the mind, and with the internal sphere of the consciousness, in which internal conceptions of relationship are realized by the individual; and it is through this principle, therefore, that opposite moral and religious obligations are combined and manifested in a supernatural manner. It is upon this principle that the Sentimental Nature operates in that natural regeneration of the individual which is designated, in the Scriptures, baptism and birth by water; its baptism or partial regeneration being effected in an external, and its birth or total regeneration being effected in an internal, sphere of the natural consciousness. It is so designated, because water is an externally purifying and an externally or physically elevating substance, the effects of which are most perfectly representative of this external-natural regenerating process, and is thus connected with the sentimental nature, and with its regenerating influence through the principle of " Relation," as a supernatural correspondence ; and this nature is therefore made to constitute the element of water, in the threefold form of " blood, water, and spirit," into which human nature is to be regenerated. These processes of baptism and of birth, by which the partial and the total purification and elevation of the soul are effected, constituting its natural regeneration, are therefore symbolized by the Church in the Sacrament of Baptism; the first by the partial use of water in sprinkling, and the second by the entire submersion of the individual. Now, as the sentimental nature contains two opposite departments, we shall find that two opposite classes of manifestations are to be referred to this principle, one corresponding with its moral, and the other with its religious experiences, in each sphere of the consciousness. In an external sphere of consciousness, it is calculated, in the first place, for obtaining conceptions of the external forms of individual relationship corresponding with the external directions of the Moral Sentiments, and of establishing these as governing laws of the Will. It thus connects the individual with others, in all the various relations of life, from an external point of view; these relationships being used by the individual, in a systematic manner, as means for the production of ends; and establishes forms of manifestation, with regard to them, which are the best calculated to secure the realization of the ends proposed in these conceptions. In the next place, it is calculated for obtaining conceptions of the external forms of individual relationship corresponding with the external directions of the Religious Sentiments, and of establishing these as governing laws of the Will. It thus connects the individual with a supernatural order of thought, secures the performance of the religious duties connected with it, and becomes receptive of immediate supernatural influences, as well as of those which are communicated through the religious sentiments; and thus religious ideas and obligations, and supernatural impressions, are introduced into the Will, and become governing laws of the individual life. In an internal sphere of the natural consciousness, it is calculated, in the first place, for obtaining conceptions of the internal forms of individual relationship corresponding with the internal directions of the Moral Sentiments, and of establishing these as governing laws of the Will. It thus connects the individual with others, in the various relations of life, from an internal point of view, or from the point of internal instead of external use, and establishes forms of manifestation calculated to secure the realization of the ends proposed in these conceptions. In the next place, it is calculated for obtaining conceptions of the internal forms of individual relationship corresponding with the internal directions of the Religious Sentiments, and of establishing these as governing laws of the Will. It thus connects the individual with supernatural ideas which represent an inversion of the laws of spiritual life, and establishes these as governing laws of the individual life; for these internal religious, as well as these internal moral, experiences are realized from the destructive side of the sentimental nature, which corresponds with the Finite, and are therefore antagonistic and destructive to those which are realized in an external sphere of the consciousness.

The spiritual principle, which constitutes the Spirit of Will, or Individuality, and which we name "Consciousness," is the introspective, unifying, vitalizing, and self-determining principle, and presides over the entire sum of individual recognitions and relationships, and determines him in view of all the materials which enter into his consciousness. It is therefore the principle through which he obtains a knowledge of his entire individual position in view of all his light and all his love, — of all that he has, and all that he has not, made one with himself by individual appropriation; or in view of all that he is, and all that he hopes to be; demanding an absolute law by the operation of which all his experiences shall become one, or harmonious, as a perfect individuality of body, soul, and spirit. Now, although this principle is particularly appropriate to the spiritual sphere of the consciousness, it obtains a natural development, and realizes manifestations of a natural character, which are of the utmost importance in preparing the individual for the Spiritual Birth; for it must be obvious that he must obtain the most full and precise information with regard to his natural condition from an internal-natural point of view, before he can be placed in that self-conscious spiritual position which includes a free self-determination, and which must therefore include a perfect knowledge of his own condition, from both a natural and a spiritual point of view.

Although these principles of the Will correspond with, and are thus appropriate to, the three several spheres of consciousness into which the soul successively comes, and become developed successively, as it grows from below upwards and is born of blood, of water, and of spirit,—it will be understood that the entire Will, as well as the entire Mind, is an original creation, but that the individual becomes conscious of himself as he becomes developed through individual appropriation and construction, and through supernatural communication and direction. As a tri-personal form is the necessary condition of life, all these principles of the Will must, of course, be in some degree united in manifestation. In natural spheres of consciousness, however, this union is comparatively an unconscious one, for the reason that the development of the Mind and the growth of the individual are necessarily partial, and the spheres of the Will are also discordant, so that they cannot become consciously developed together. The most external principle is influenced by those which are higher, in proportion as the individual becomes internal: but this internal growth is accompanied by a decline of power in the external manifesting principle; and although all its self-conscious manifestations are constructed as means for the production of use to the individual from a natural point of view, in his endeavors to realize what is good for him upon the whole, all its internal presentations and conceptions, and all its external manifestations, are realized under the direction of Divine Providence, by which the individual is provided with what is really the most useful to him; and this, of course, will be very far from what he proposes to himself, from the natural and false point of view to which he is confined.

There is no subject that seems to be less understood than the Will, and none about which there has been so much dispute; and the principal reason for this is, that, from the nature of its constitution, it seems in a particular manner to be the opposite of what it really is, while the necessities of the individual demand that he should believe it to be what it appears: for, being the personal and self-conscious department of the human constitution, upon which the individual must rely for information with regard to every thing that is presented to him from within as an individual experience, it is extremely difficult for him to recognize the fact that every one of these internal experiences, as well as every thing that is presented to him through the external senses, is an unreal and deceptive appearance that is the opposite of what it seems. The Will has been regarded in Philosophy, not as a complex department of the human constitution, whose laws, functions, and phenomena were to be separately investigated and described, but as a simple, independent power of the soul which acts as a sovereign, and determines the individual to this or that decision or act; and therefore the principal if not the only question in regard to it has been, "What is it that 'determines the Will?" Some have taken the ground, that it is determined by motives, or by the particular wants of the individual constitution, and is thus necessitated; and some have taken the opposite ground, that it determines itself without reference to these motives or wants, and is therefore free. Some have assumed, with Locke, that the Will is determined by "the present and most pressing want or uneasiness;" and some have taken the more rational position, that it is determined by a calculation of "what is good for the individual upon the whole;" while the phrenologists teach, according to Mr. Combe, "that the knowing and reflecting faculties constitute the Will." Although the phrenologists have not discovered the organs through which the Will is manifested, and do not recognize it as a separate principle or power of the mind, they have discovered the organs of the personifying principles, and have described some of their most external manifestations under the forms of "Firmness," "Self-Esteem," "Acquisitiveness," and "Secretiveness." They have also observed some of the lower manifestations of the Will, but refer them to sources in the mind with which they have no relation. Thus M. Broussais, in treating of the organ of "Cautiousness," has described, in the following manner, manifestations which are referable to the lowest principle or region of the Will: "Dupuytren was the celebrated surgeon of the Hôtel Dieu; a man of great talents and decision of character. He calculated all his actions and all his words. He never used an expression or executed a gesture of which the effect was not foreseen. He practised one manner with the student,— another with the patient of the lower orders,— another with the patient of a higher class,— another was reserved for princes,— another differently graduated was exhibited towards his professional brethren, and to them alone, — and, finally, still another for the public in his gratuitous consultations. Cuvier also was a man who calculated all his actions. He spoke exactly what he wished to express in regard to events, and never manifested a sentiment or project which he had not specifically designed to communicate. This is the power which enables its possessor to restrain the manifestation of all his faculties, and to allow them to act only on proper occasions." We have now described this department of the human constitution in a particular manner, and have shown that the principles of the Mind furnish the means through which the Will becomes developed, and also the forms through which the individual becomes specifically manifested. We have shown that the principles of "Personality" and "Property" constitute the most concentrated form of the Individual as Male and Female, whose office it is to appropriate and to construct or individualize those intellectual and affectional experiences of the mind, or those laws and forms of truth and of good, which are congenial to their constitution, and suited to the present want of the individual, into systematic forms, in which the lower is made subject to the higher, by which they are adapted to the immediate use of the individual, both from universal and ideal, and from personal and practical, points of view; and that in this way the individual obtains an orderly arrangement of, and thus a systematic command over, all his intellectual and affectional acquisitions and wants, which prepares them for combination in the Will for the purpose of realizing an individual plan of life, by which he can be directed in the most systematic and profitable manner in realizing what is good for him upon the whole. This combination and individualization are effected by means of the three principles of the Will here enumerated, which constitute a tri-personal individual form that becomes developed from the lowest to the highest in the growth of the individual from below upwards as body, soul, and spirit, and becomes manifested from the highest to the lowest as spirit, soul, and body; the spirit being self-conscious, vital, and real, the soul relative and representative, and the body internally negative and destructive, while it is at the same time externally productive as the manifesting principle. These three principles correspond with the spiritual, the supernatural, and the natural regions of the mind, or of the general consciousness: their full development, as accompanied by a corresponding development of the mind, is alluded to in the Scriptures as births of blood, of water, and of spirit; and they will represent in their spiritual condition and regenerated form the Spirit, Water, and Blood which constitute the divine-humanity of Christ.

We have now given a general analysis of the Human Constitution, enumerated all the primitive principles which it contains, and shown the precise relationships which exist between them; and this will therefore be found to include, not only a comprehensible ground for every individual manifestation that can possibly be conceived, but also to include the ground for a knowledge of those relationships between the various departments of thought and of life which are necessary to the comprehension of their true nature, as a substitute for those empirical and fictitious individual opinions, founded in appearances, which have heretofore been entertained upon these subjects. We would call particular attention to this statement of the forms of the human constitution, and the relationships between its spheres, departments, and principles, which are established by the application of the laws of Absolute Science, because the conception of these here realized reveals the character of every principle and form of life: so that, even from the very general description that we are able now to give of them, more light is thrown upon the nature, and the relative dignity and importance, of the various forms of human manifestation, than can be obtained from all other sources; while this will, of course, be greatly increased by the more particular statements that will be made in the succeeding volumes. By this conception and classification, under the Universal Laws of Existence, we do not simply offer an addition to knowledge already acquired, but we realize a universal and permanent form that cannot admit of any addition, subtraction, or change. The number of these primitive principles, which is eighty, or "fourscore," will therefore be found to be the same as that named in the Scriptures, in which all natural, supernatural, and spiritual forms and relationships are represented. We there read: "The days of our years are threescore years and ten; and if by reason of strength they be fourscore years, yet is their strength labor and sorrow." That this description is not to be understood literally, but refers to the fundamental principles of human nature by which its mental states are produced, or to the permanent forms of life and the states of life produced through these forms, may be inferred from the definitions of these words given by Swedenborg, who says, "Day signifies what is perpetual and eternal; and by Years are signified states in the manifestation of the Soul." These primitive principles we will now enumerate and classify under one general form.

THE HUMAN CONSTITUTION.

FORM OF THE GENERAL CONSCIOUSNESS,

WHICH CONTAINS

THE PRINCIPLES OF THE HUMAN MIND.

As the opposite poles of this consciousness, and as the roots of the mind, there are two principles, representing Infinite and Finite, which we name —

PERFECTION. — IMPERFECTION.

These are incarnated and individualized by three spheres related as Spirit, Soul, and Body, which constitute the Human Mind: —

Spiritual Sphere, as Spirit.

THE REASON, OR THE RATIONAL DEPARTMENT,

CONSTITUTED BY

TRUTH. — GOOD.
BEAUTY.

Supernatural Sphere, as Soul,

CONTAINING

THE RELIGIOUS SENTIMENTS,	THE MORAL SENTIMENTS,
WHICH ARE	WHICH ARE
SPIRITUALISM. — NATURALISM.	JUSTICE. — SYMPATHY.
INTUITION. — VENERATION.	SATISFACTION. — APPROBATION.
REVELATION.	OBLIGATION.

Natural Sphere, as Body,

CONTAINING

THE UNDERSTANDING,	THE INSTINCT,
CONSTITUTED BY	CONSTITUTED BY
THE INTELLECTUAL FACULTIES.	THE AFFECTIONAL POWERS.

THE HUMAN UNDERSTANDING,

WHICH INCLUDES

𝕿𝖍𝖊 𝕯𝖊𝖒𝖔𝖓𝖘𝖙𝖗𝖆𝖙𝖎𝖛𝖊 𝖔𝖗 𝕻𝖍𝖎𝖑𝖔𝖘𝖔𝖕𝖍𝖎𝖈 𝕽𝖊𝖌𝖎𝖔𝖓,

WHICH IS

THE SPIRIT OF THE HUMAN UNDERSTANDING.

The Material Department, as Body.
CONSTRUCTION. — CAUSALITY.
RATIOCINATION. — PRACTICABILITY.
POLICY.

The Representative Department, as Soul.
INTELLECTUALITY. — AFFECTIONALITY.
DIDACTICS. — ETHICS.
PSYCHOLOGY

The Constructive Department, as Spirit.
OPPOSITION. — CORRESPONDENCE
METAPHYSICS. — ANALOGY.
IMAGINATION.

𝕿𝖍𝖊 𝕽𝖊𝖕𝖗𝖊𝖘𝖊𝖓𝖙𝖆𝖙𝖎𝖛𝖊 𝖔𝖗 𝕻𝖔𝖊𝖙𝖎𝖈 𝕽𝖊𝖌𝖎𝖔𝖓,

WHICH IS

THE SOUL OF THE HUMAN UNDERSTANDING.

The Material Department, as Body.
REPRESENTATION. — ACTION.
PHYSIOGNOMY. — ACTIVITY.
HUMANITY.

The Representative Department, as Soul.
ARTICULATION. — INTONATION.
LANGUAGE. — MUSIC.
POETRY.

The Constructive Department, as Spirit.
CONTRAST. — RESEMBLANCE.
COMPARISON. — SIMILITUDE.
FANCY.

𝕿𝖍𝖊 𝕸𝖆𝖙𝖊𝖗𝖎𝖆𝖑 𝕽𝖊𝖌𝖎𝖔𝖓,

WHICH IS

THE BODY OF THE HUMAN UNDERSTANDING.

The Material Department, as Body.
SPACE. — SOLIDITY.
FIGURE. — NUMBER.
MOTION.

The Representative Department, as Soul.
PERCEPTION. — SENSIBILITY.
INDIVIDUALITY. — ASSOCIATION.
CONCEPTION.

The Constructive Department, as Spirit.
EXTENSION. — GRAVITATION.
PHYSICS. — CHEMISTRY
CONSTRUCTION.

THE HUMAN INSTINCT,

WHICH INCLUDES

The Social Region, as Spirit.
SOCIALISM. — SOCIABILITY.
FRIENDSHIP. — FRATERNITY.
SOCIETY.

The Domestic Region, as Soul.
CONJUGALITY. — SEXUALITY.
MATRIMONY. — CONSANGUINITY.
FAMILY.

The Individual Region, as Body.
VITALITY. — DESTRUCTION.
NUTRITION. — PROTECTION.
PRESERVATION.

FORM OF THE PERSONAL CONSCIOUSNESS,

WHICH CONTAINS

THE PRINCIPLES OF THE HUMAN SOUL.

The dualistic form of this Consciousness is constituted by two indefinite universal principles, which are affinities for Truth and Good, and constitute the most concentrated form of Individual Want; each principle containing Male and Female spheres, which are opposite Universal and Personal elements: these principles we name —

PERSONALITY. — PROPERTY.

These are combined, incarnated, and individualized by three principles, in three spheres of manifestation, related as Spirit, Soul, and Body, —

WHICH CONSTITUTE

SELF-CONSCIOUSNESS, INDIVIDUALITY, OR WILL.

CONSCIOUSNESS.
RELATION.
DIRECTION.

Now, although this is a new classification of the most general forms of the Human Constitution, and although, in being realized by the application of universal laws, they here appear in new relationships, and with a new life and significance, most of these forms have been recognized at different times in different philosophical and phrenological systems. The religious and moral sentiments have not only been recognized, but regarded as constituting an internal sphere of truth and of good; while the intellectual and affectional powers have been recognized as constituting an external sphere of truth and of good: and this is the position held by them in this classification. The rational department, which appears in our Science as the Reason, has not only been recognized by many philosophers as a spiritual power of the mind, but has been divided into the elements of Truth, Good, and Beauty, in which it has here been individualized,—or, we should say, the natural substitutes for these; and the Will has been generally recognized by them as constituting the individual manifesting principle. We see, then, that this general classification harmonizes with theories which have been extensively received; showing, that, although realized from an internal point of observation through the application of universal laws, they are supported by the experiences and observations of philosophic minds, realized from a more external point of view. In all the important statements that we make, we shall show how far they have been represented in Philosophy, in the Scriptures, and in the Church; and this will be done, not for the purpose of supporting these statements,—because we rely solely upon internal evidence, and show the universal ground in which they have their life,—but for the purpose of explaining, and thus giving vitality to, these representations of the truth; and also for the purpose of illustrating and making more definite the new and abstract statements of Absolute Science, by referring to what has already been made familiar. In this illustration, we shall take every convenient opportunity, not only in the theological but also in the ontological portions of this work, to make quotations from the Bible; because this is not simply a theological and moral, but a philosophical work, that is universal in character, and of supernatural origin. These will sometimes be made without any comment: but, for the most part, we shall interpret the symbolic language in which this sacred volume is written; and we shall do this for the double purpose of illustrating the statements here made, and of showing the manner in which the Scriptures are to be explained from the point of Absolute Science. In doing this, we shall show, that all our statements are perfectly harmonious with the representative forms of the Scriptures; that, from the spiritual position here established, a new vitality is imparted to them; and that the large portion of their contents, to which little or no significance has heretofore been attached, is filled with representations of the most profound philosophic truth. The Bible has never been regarded as having any reference whatever to Philosophy, but has been supposed to be simply historical, poetic, and religious in character. We shall show, however, that the form of the Scriptures is constructed, according to legitimate correspondences founded in the real and permanent relations of things, to represent universal conditions and relationships, which are ontological, theological, and psychological in character.*

As we have alluded to three spheres of the Mind, as spheres of the general consciousness; and to three spheres of the Will, as spheres of personal consciousness,—the first being developed from within, outwards; and the second being developed from below, upwards,—and have also alluded to three spheres of Consciousness, entirely distinct from these, into which the soul successively comes,—it may be well here to make an explanation with regard to these, in order that confusion may be avoided, and that these three kinds of consciousness into which the soul successively comes, which have never before been recognized or distinctly separated, may be accurately defined; because a comprehension of the difference between these spheres is of the utmost importance. By the three spheres of the general consciousness, we mean the three regions of the Mind, related as spirit, soul, and body, into which its primitive principles are divided, without any reference to the quality of their manifestations; the first being constituted by the Reason,—the second, by the Religious and Moral Sentiments,—and the third, by the Understanding and Instinct: all these being developed successively, from the highest to the lowest, in each sphere of the consciousness into which the soul successively comes; and also growing, or becoming developed, from below upwards, as the individual becomes more and more internal and self-conscious. By the three spheres of personal consciousness, we mean the three regions of the Will, also related as spirit, soul, and body, corresponding with the three regions of the Mind; these being the

---

* Appendix III.

principles of "Consciousness," "Relation," and "Direction," which become developed from below upwards, and also from within outwards in each sphere, commencing in the lowest sphere of consciousness; so that the highest things become represented in the lowest condition of the Individual. Being the universal individual manifesting principle, all these spheres of the Will become manifested in the most external sphere of consciousness, although in different degrees and in a different manner; the principle of "Relation" being manifested partially in a conscious but external manner, or through a consciousness of external forms of relationship; and even the highest principle being slightly manifested in a spontaneous and unconscious manner, by which the manifestations of the lower principles become elevated in character.

The three spheres of Consciousness, related as body, soul, and spirit, and as external, internal, and spiritual, into which the soul successively comes, — which are also developed from the lowest to the highest, and which correspond with the three regions in the mind and in the will, — have reference to, and are appropriate to, three corresponding Atmospheres, which we have described as material, ethereal, and spiritual; although all must to some extent be realized in this, in order that vitality should be communicated to the most external things. They constitute three distinct kinds of life and of consciousness, which are so distinctly separated and antagonized, that their realization by the individual is represented in the Scriptures by BIRTHS of Blood, of Water, and of Spirit; these being realized by successive crucifixions, resurrections, and regenerations. What makes the separation of these spheres of consciousness more difficult is the fact, that both the internal and the spiritual are represented in this atmosphere, which is a universal sphere of representation in which all forms of truth, of good, and of use, both natural and spiritual, must be represented in forms that can be connected with the individual consciousness; the spiritual being here represented by both vital and destructive religious conceptions and manifestations, which are supposed to be really spiritual, when the individual is the farthest removed from any vital spiritual realization, — the externalist being the farthest removed from vital spiritual experiences, and the internalist from vital spiritual thought. Even transcendentalists, who have entered into an internal sphere of consciousness, have not been able to conceive this to be a different kind of life, which is entirely shut out from an external sphere, but suppose it to be the same kind of internalism that has in all ages been realized in opposition to externalism; although these, too, are the farthest removed from each other, inasmuch as the internal things realized in an external sphere are vital, while those realized in an internal sphere are destructive. As a general description of the difference between these external and internal spheres of consciousness, we may say, that, in an external sphere, the individual is governed by the vital laws of the mind, incarnated in external forms and institutions, unto which he is made subject through Society and the Church ; while, in an internal sphere, the individual is governed by the destructive laws of the mind, of which he becomes intuitive and consciously conceptive, and is made subject to these laws through what he recognizes as "the higher law," or the law of Consciousness, which has become to him a higher conscience. In an external sphere, therefore, the individual is governed by influences external to himself; by the recognition of relationships with regard to their external form and use; and by the recognition of truths, as laws of the Will, which have reference to the external direction of himself, and to his personal position and condition from an external point of view : while, in an internal sphere, the individual is governed by influences from within ; by conceptions of relationship which have reference to their internal form and use; and by the recognition of truths, as laws of the Will, which have reference to the internal direction of himself, and to his personal position and condition from an internal point of view. In an external sphere, the individual life is dual; including, on the one hand, a life of personal inclination, and of plans for its realization, which are concealed, but which constitute his real life; and, on the other hand, a life of duty, and of compliance with external forms and requirements, which is an external, unreal appearance, that is contrary to, and in discord with, his internal and real position. In an internal sphere, the individual life is comparatively simple, in which it is his principal aim to make this life consistent, and perfectly harmonious with his highest ideas of truth and of good. While in the first, therefore, he aims to appear what he is not, in the second he aims to appear what he really is; although, as duplicity and insincerity govern in this atmosphere, it is seldom that this simplicity of life is here understood, or is believed to exist.

THE STRUCTURE OF SOCIETY

WHICH ILLUSTRATES

THE LAWS OF CORRESPONDENCE.

It will be readily seen, that, in all nations, the operations of social life are included in two great facts, which are Teaching and Governing. This we find to be recognized by Mr. Carlyle in his "Past and Present." He there says, "Aristocracy and Priesthood, a Governing Class and a Teaching Class; these two, sometimes separate, and endeavoring to harmonize themselves, sometimes conjoined as one, and the king a Pontiff-king: then did no society exist without these two vital elements, then will none exist. It lies in the very nature of man. You will visit no remotest village in the most republican country of the world, where, virtually or actually, you do not find these two powers at work. Man, little as he may suppose it, is necessitated to obey superiors. He is a social being in virtue of this necessity; nay, he could not be gregarious otherwise. He obeys those whom he esteems better than himself, wiser, braver; and will for ever obey such, and even be ready and delighted to do it. The Wiser, Braver, these a Virtual Aristocracy everywhere and everywhen, do, in all societies that reach any articulate shape, develop themselves into a ruling class, an Actual Aristocracy, with settled modes of operating what are called laws, and even private-laws or privileges, and so forth: very notable to look upon in this world. Sorrowful, phantasmal, as this same Double Aristocracy of Teachers and Governors now looks, it is worth all men's while to know that the purport of it is and remains noble and most real. Dryasdust, looking merely at the surface, is greatly in error as to those ancient kings. William Conqueror, William Rufus, or Redbeard, Stephen Curthose himself, much more Henry Beauclerk, and our brave Plantagenet Henry,— the life of these men was not a vulturous Fighting: it was a valorous Governing, to which occasionally fighting did, and always must yet, though far seldomer now, superadd itself as an accident, a distressing impedimental adjunct. The fighting, too, was indispensable for ascertaining who had the might over whom, — the right over whom. By much hard fighting, as we once said, 'the unrealities, beaten into dust, flew gradually off, and left the plain reality and fact, "thou stronger than I; thou wiser than I; thou king, and subject I," in a somewhat clearer condition.'"

Now, although it is true that Teaching and Governing are the two great facts which Society includes, it is no less true that each of these is divided into two elements, which are related as internal and external, — the internal constituting the vital element in each combination; and Mr. Carlyle has omitted, in his estimate of social influences, these internal and vital powers, and has confined himself to the external powers which are exercised by Aristocracy and the Church; showing that "Dryasdust" is not the only one who looks "merely at the surface." The foundations of Society lie much deeper than Mr. Carlyle supposes; and, although he has stated important facts in relation to these, he does not seem to understand the nature of them, because he does not understand the relation which they bear to others more important. He has recognized the fact, that valorous fighting and valorous governing are united in the same individuals; and he has in this way got might and right confounded in his mind, without understanding either, or why they should be thus combined. Mr. Carlyle recognizes only those who are born to be rulers, upon the one hand, and those who are born to be ruled, upon the other, without comprehending upon what either this ability to rule, or this desire to be ruled, are founded, and therefore not comprehending the nature of the relationship between these parties, which is the chain that binds them together. It is true, as he says, that man, as a social being, is necessitated to obey superiors, although there is a sad inversion of these things in the natural, where it is the superior who obeys: but it is also true, that man, as a social being, is necessitated to obey himself; arbitrary rule and self-government being the polar extremes of social life, which must in some way be united in order that Society should exist. As the great object of social combination is the realization of the greatest amount of good to the individuals who form it, Society is the result of the combined energy of the masses directed towards a common end by those to whom its construction and administration are intrusted; this being the gratification of the want of each individual, so far as it can be gratified, without infringing upon the wants of others: and in this individual want is, of course, included an affinity for Law that is antagonistic to personal inclination, as well as the desire for self-gratification. We may see that society is governed externally by this collective individual want, even in that rudest form of society which exists among the Negro tribes; for although nothing can be more despotic than the rule of the African King, should this not harmonize or be consistent with the collective want or will of the people, this king is at once turned over to the women to be strangled, and a new one takes his place.*

We see, then, that the power that governs is only the exponent of the want and of the power which reside in those who are governed; that is, that the aristocratic power only constitutes the body of the State, through which an internal or democratic power must be incarnated as the condition of a vital social manifestation: and we may also see that the Church is only the exponent of that amount of religious and moral truth which exists unexpressed in the minds of the people, and which, therefore, they have an affinity for, and a capacity for apprehending and recognizing as true. We therefore find, that, as soon as any particular form of the Church ceases to be a true exponent of this individual want, its authority is at once overthrown, so far as the non-concurring individual is concerned, who separates himself from it, and gives his allegiance to some new form that is a better expression of his want, and of his idea of the truth. It therefore becomes perfectly plain, that no society can exist without two jointly governing powers, related as internal and external, which are Democracy and Aristocracy; and two jointly teaching powers, related as internal and external, which are Philosophy and the Church; and also that these separate elements must necessarily be represented by separate exponents; so that no civilized society can exist without these four principles, distinctly embodied in and manifested through opposite governing and teaching classes. Indeed, the rule of Democracy and the teaching of Philosophy have sometimes entirely superseded those of Aristocracy and the Church; a fact that is illustrated by the great French Revolution, of which Mr. Carlyle has written the history, and which might have suggested to him these elements of Society.

We find, then, that there are two elements in Knowledge, and

---

* Hegel's "Philosophy of History."

two modes of teaching corresponding with these: the first being internal, and conducted by Philosophy through comprehension in the consciousness; and the second being external, and conducted by the Church through apprehensive sentimental recognition. We also find that there are two elements in Government, or in the State, which we name Democracy and Aristocracy; and two modes of governing corresponding with these, the exponents of which are the democratic and aristocratic classes. The first, being internal and universal in character, demands self-government through internal universal law, and provides for the aggregate want of the community, or for what is the greatest good of all; subordinating the individual to the Universal, as embodied in the State, in order that this may be realized. The second, being external and partial or personal in character, denies and repudiates the principle of self-government through internal universal law, and sets up the principle of arbitrary rule by means of external law originating in individual will: instead of providing for the aggregate want, or for the greatest good of the community, therefore, it provides for the greatest good of those who are the representatives of learning, wealth, and power; subordinating the Universal to the individual, by making the people subject to this aristocratic class, that this result may be accomplished; and by thus asserting, instead of restraining, individual power, it identifies might with right, and subordinates the State to the Individual, indeed substitutes the Individual for the State. The form of Society is therefore to be stated thus:—

PHILOSOPHY. — CHURCH.
DEMOCRACY. — ARISTOCRACY.
SOCIETY.

Here, then, we find the demand of our science most perfectly responded to: Philosophy and the Church are intellective and affective principles, related as internal and external, which constitute a region of Social Law; and Democracy and Aristocracy are intellectual and affectional principles, related as internal and external, which constitute a region of Social Phenomena; while these are combined and manifested through one productive form, which is Society. The laws of Opposition, Attraction, and Union in Production, are illustrated in the relationships between these principles: the law of Opposition by the fact, that Philosophy and the Church, and also Democracy and Aristocracy, exist in the most palpable antagonism, as may be seen from the history of Philosophy, of the Church, and of the State; and the laws of Attraction and Union are illustrated by the fact, that these opposite principles cannot be manifested separately and antagonistically, but must be and are combined and manifested in all social productions.

As Philosophy and the Church are so fully stated in other portions of this work, and are besides so well understood as to their general features and relationship, we will not give any description of them here, but will pass to an analysis and description of Democracy and Aristocracy,—the internal and external principles that constitute the Female Sphere which furnishes, under the form of the State, the form or body to Society, through which all external social results must be produced. Although the nature of Philosophy and the Church is well understood, the nature of Democracy and Aristocracy is one of the most difficult subjects that can possibly be named, and is one upon which the most superficial opinions are now entertained. In considering this subject, the two great questions to be answered are these: What is the abstract nature of these opposite principles which we denominate Democracy and Aristocracy? and, How do these become manifested through the democratic and aristocratic classes in the State? The terms "democracy" and "aristocracy" are almost entirely used to designate certain forms of government: the first being used to designate the rule of the people, or of those chosen by the people; and the second, to designate the arbitrary rule of a privileged hereditary class. These particular forms of government, however, are only the most external manifestation of causes which have their foundation in the vital and destructive elements of the human constitution; and, besides this, the form and the substance of government are opposite, and become destructive to each other, so that this definition only serves to mislead. If democracy and aristocracy referred only to the form of government, it would have to be inferred, that in this country, where the Constitution does not recognize the existence of any privileged class, or of any hereditary governing class, and where the principle of universal suffrage in the choice of rulers is fully carried into practice, aristocracy could not exist; when the fact is, that not only is it quite as prolific in this as in any other country, but the very democratic form that here so extensively prevails becomes its fosterer, and furnishes a medium through which it can be the most extensively manifested: and although this may seem to be a paradox, and may be an unpalatable doctrine to those aristocratic persons who would appear to be democratic, we shall show that this must be the fact.

Aristocracy is by some thought to consist in the possession of wealth and of learning; and although this definition is almost as external as the other, and is equally imperfect, because it substitutes the external condition of the individual, instead of the external form of the government under which he lives, for an internal principle and social element which originates in the particular construction of the human constitution, it is an improvement upon the more common definition, for two reasons: first, because the form and the substance of government are necessarily antagonized, so that an aristocratic form becomes necessary to the production of democratic results, while a democratic form becomes productive of those which are aristocratic,—a fact that makes this first definition an inversion of the truth; and, next, because, although it is not possible that poverty and ignorance can constitute democracy, or that wealth and learning can constitute aristocracy, so that the poor or the ignorant man, upon becoming rich or learned, necessarily passes from one to the other, there is a legitimate relationship between aristocracy and wealth and learning, as objects which it especially desires to possess, and has the capacity to accumulate. It is true that this association of aristocracy with wealth and learning arises simply in the observation of a fact, and is not attended by any knowledge of the real cause of this phenomenon; for all knowledge with regard to Society has been realized from the observation and generalization of social phenomena, without reference to the real causes of these in the human constitution. As these definitions do not convey to us any information with regard to the real nature of these social principles, we will proceed to state their causes in the human constitution, and show how these are connected with the various social manifestations.

Society is constituted by the individualization of masses of individuals between whom a certain correspondence exists which makes practicable their harmonious co-operation in the production of legitimate social results; and therefore, in every healthy and productive form of Society, all discordant elements are either entirely excluded, or made subject upon a principle different from the one that governs its own association. Society must therefore correspond in its organization with the nature of the human constitution, and even with the aggregate condition of the particular individuals who compose it, and who must be combined under laws of relationship which are productive. It must therefore become developed, not only in correspondence with the development of the human constitution, but in correspondence, and simultaneously, with these individuals; and the reason why so much ignorance prevails upon the subject of Society is, that the nature of the human constitution—of which it is the most external individualization and aggregate manifestation from some partial point of view—has not been comprehended, but has been misapprehended, because studied from a natural and unitarian point of view, from which no spiritual law could be obtained by the application of which its forms could be conceived, and its discordant dualistic manifestations could be separated, classified, analyzed, and combined in the production of legitimate psychological truth. In order that we should understand the nature of Society, we must understand the nature of Man scientifically; that is, not only psychologically, or from the point of the individual consciousness, but also ontologically, or from the point of Universal Law. Having obtained this knowledge of the principles of the human constitution, and of the various modes in which they are combined and manifested, we are able to obtain a conception of Society that will explain the various phenomena resulting from the operation of the antagonistic principles of which it is composed.

We have already shown that the internal sphere of Society is constituted by Philosophy and the Church, as the Teachers, and the external sphere, by Democracy and Aristocracy, as the Governors of Society. Now, as Society is a universal sphere that includes all the manifestations of the human constitution as a final result,—as Democracy and Aristocracy constitute the external sphere of Society, the first being characterized as internal and intellectual, and the second as external and affectional, by which they become the most external exponents of these manifestations,—and as the first is representative of the male and internal elements of the human constitution, which are universal and vital, while the second is representative of the female and external elements, which are personal and destructive,—we are here presented with the whole ground of Democracy and Aristocracy, and are directed to the sources from which we are to realize a conception of democratic and aristocratic principles and forms of manifestation. The most general conclusions to be derived from these premises are,—that Democracy is characterized as masculine, internal, intellectual, and universal, and Aristocracy as feminine, external, affectional, and personal,—that the internal spheres and principles of the mind, which correspond with Truth, will predominate in democratic, and the external spheres and principles of the mind, which correspond with Good, will predominate in aristocratic manifestations,—that the male element in the Personifying Principles will predominate in the former in the appropriation of laws and forms of truth and of good corresponding with the Universal, and the female element in these principles will predominate in the latter in the appropriation of laws and forms corresponding with the Partial and Personal,— and that, in the manifestations of the Will, the principle of "Relation" will predominate in the former, under the direction of the sentiments of "Intuition" and "Satisfaction;" while the principle of "Direction" will predominate in the latter, under the direction of the sentiments of "Veneration" and "Approbation;" and, consequently, that democratic individuals will be led to rely for direction upon internal authority, and to regard the realization of internal law as necessary to the vitality of all individual manifestations and conclusions, and of all external phenomena; while aristocratic individuals will be led to rely for direction upon external authority, to regard a conformity with external law as necessary to the vitality of all individual manifestations, and a recognition of the highest individual authority as necessary to the vitality of all personal conclusions.

There are several things, however, to be kept in view in pursuing this inquiry into the nature of Democracy and Aristocracy. First, Society is a universal sphere, where the individual becomes totally incarnated in his most external form, which is the point of individual manifestation; and it is therefore made to include a diversified and discordant combination of phenomena, which it is difficult to analyze and classify under these general forms, for the reason that these principles are inconsistently and deceitfully combined in individuals, and are manifested in the greatest possible diversity. Next, the form and the substance of things are, in the natural, divided and antagonized; and therefore, although democracy and aristocracy are related as vital and destructive, the democratic and aristocratic forms of government are related as destructive and vital; while the democratic, as the progressive class, seems to be socially destructive, and the aristocratic, as the conservative class, seems to be socially productive. Next, the legitimate manifestations of the democratic and aristocratic classes are confined to an unconscious, external sphere;

while the phenomena which are now presented to our observation are realized in a self-conscious sphere, upon entrance into which the disorganization of Society commences; when the aristocratic class, being conservative, and the exponent of external law, necessarily becomes vital; while the democratic class, as the party of progress, and as the exponent of internal law, necessarily becomes destructive, because the destructive laws of the mind have become supreme. The first must therefore retard, while the second must accelerate, the destruction of the State. Finally, these classes are separated, from a constructive point of view, into those who ideally conceive laws and principles of government, and those who practically construct forms of government; and, from a productive point of view, into those who recognize these laws and principles, when stated, as just, and those who submit blindly to arbitrary forms: and there is also the greatest diversity in the mental and personal constitution of these, by which democratic and aristocratic elements are differently proportioned, so that the manifestations become indefinitely diversified. This great diversity, together with the deceptive appearances which have here been alluded to, makes the subject of Society extremely complicated, and impossible to comprehend from any external or apparent point of view. In obtaining a conception of democracy and aristocracy, it is therefore necessary that we should first obtain a statement of the opposite elements in the human constitution which constitute the ground of these principles,— next, conceive these as individualized in personal forms, from an ideal point of view, in order that they may appear in definite forms corresponding with our experience,— and, finally, obtain a conception of the democratic and aristocratic classes, as they actually co-operate in the realization of those external productive forms of Society which constitute the State. A thorough development of the subject, according to this plan, would require a volume; but we will consider each of these topics in a manner sufficiently definite to give a general idea of the nature of democracy and aristocracy from the several points of view here mentioned.

We say that the source of Democracy is in the male and internal, and the source of Aristocracy is in the female and external, elements of the human constitution: and this applies to spheres as well as principles; it being understood, as we have already explained, that all the internal principles and spheres are relatively vital, represent the Infinite, and have an affinity for Law, and for all that corresponds with the Universal; while all the external principles and spheres are relatively destructive, represent the Finite, and have an affinity for Phenomena, and for all that corresponds with the Partial and Personal. It is not necessary that we should here describe these, because they have already been so accurately enumerated and classified, that they may readily be separated, and their character comprehended; and because they will be more fully described and illustrated in the course of this work. We will therefore proceed to individualize the predominant operation of these vital elements in democratic, and of these destructive elements in aristocratic, manifestations.

As a representative of the Finite, Aristocracy is a contracting, and also a separating, power; and as the representative and exponent of the external, affectional, and female elements in the human constitution, it is internally destructive, and externally productive. It is upon this ground that Aristocracy becomes both the constructer and the worshipper of forms, and is calculated to be the external directing or executive power to both the individual and the State. As the most prominent objects corresponding with Aristocracy are Learning, Wealth, and Power, — as the aristocratic organization is favorable to their acquisition, — and as this acquisition is the principal end of all aristocratic endeavor, — we will consider these separately, and show their relation with the aristocratic principle.

It will be readily seen, that, according to the definition of Aristocracy here given, Learning must be an aristocratic attribute. If Aristocracy does, as we say, originate in the predominance of the female and of the external elements of the human constitution, this must be so; because these include the receptive powers of the Understanding, and particularly the most external principles, to which belong the accumulation of facts, or of the most external combinations of phenomena, in all the departments of knowledge. It is therefore that the aristocracy are always admirers of learning and of the learned, and the advocates of Education as the only means of preparing the individual for society. The kind of knowledge which the aristocratic individual accumulates, will be, in some measure, regulated by the influence of his predominating powers; but, as a general rule, works on Morality will take precedence of those on Theology, the productions of the Fancy will be preferred to those of the Imagination, and historical collections to philosophical speculations. He will be attracted towards those forms of thought which are affectional and fictitious, such as we find in works of fiction both poetical and narrative, especially those which are dramatic; and he will also be attracted towards those which are external, material, and practical, such as we find in the biographies of distinguished individuals, in the accounts of travellers, in natural and political history, in works of political economy, and in the more external forms of psychology which are moral and practical. These tendencies are usually accompanied by a predominance of the Fancy, and consequently by a command of and fondness for language and the learning of languages, and a partiality for florid expression abounding in similitudes and antitheses, and in wit and humor, as we find in the works of Shakspeare. Unless literature is made a profession, however, by aristocratic persons, their attention is apt to be directed towards more active occupations for the accumulation of wealth and the exercise of power; and their leisure to be occupied by physical exercises, or by amusements in which games of calculation and chance, combined, form a conspicuous part.

The appetite for Wealth, or for the accumulation of property, is eminently an aristocratic attribute, because it is founded in the finite function of Absorption, and in the affectional and feminine function of Reception, and is referable to the personal element in the personifying principles, and to those principles of the mind and of the will which correspond with personal individual want; to all of which, aristocracy is intimately related as the external manifesting principle. The aristocratic individual succeeds in the accumulation of property, because, in addition to this appetite for wealth, he possesses the kind of information and of practical ability necessary to this accumulation. In the first place, he possesses the power of external direction, and the ability to construct a consistent plan of life from the most external point of view, together with the power of restraining the manifestation of all tendencies inconsistent with the realization of this plan; these being derived from the principle of "Direction," which is the most external power of the Will, and consequently predominates in the aristocratic organization. In the next place, he possesses that accumulation of practical information out of which this plan of life is to be constructed by adapting means to ends in procuring the greatest amount of good for himself, and also possesses that logical power which is the external instrument used in the construction of this plan; although it will be understood that this logical power, and this ability to construct systematic plans for the accumulation of property and for the exercise of power, belong only to those who are internal and intellectual in the aristocratic class. In those who are external and affectional, this love of accumulation appears in a love for those external and physical things which minister to the affectional, sensational, and emotional states of the consciousness; or for those things which can be used for the immediate indulgence of the lower propensities, rather than for those which can be profitably used in systematic plans for the personal benefit of the individual, and of those connected with him; and they therefore become dependent upon the more intellectual and constructive class. The literary taste of this external and affectional class is a disorderly one, which inclines them towards what is exciting to the feelings, and is fictitious, frivolous, and obscene. The desire for accumulation is equally disorderly in them; and a disposition is manifested to obtain property by fraud, deception, or violence, and to use it with prodigality, and without calculation, from the impulse of the moment, under the influence of morbid sympathetic and affectional, as well as of more obviously selfish motives. Thus, individuals in whom this lower side of aristocracy predominates cannot construct any systematic plan of life, or control the manifestation of their inclinations for a remote end, notwithstanding that the control over the muscular system, and a consistent physical direction, are in them the most complete. As this external form of Aristocracy is the most concentrated representation of the Finite that human nature presents, many extremely external and destructive characteristics will be found manifested by this class, producing a disorderly, deceptive, selfish, and destructive condition of the individual; while, at the same time, he will appear to be the most genial, joyous, generous, and well-disposed; hiding a selfish heart under a smiling face, and being the most polite when he means to be the most cruel. Some of the characteristics here mentioned, however, are not peculiar to the lowest, but may be observed, in various degrees, in the manifestations of the higher class.

The love of Power is an aristocratic attribute; because the personal principle, with which aristocracy corresponds, prompts the assertion of the Individual in opposition to the Universal. Aristocratic law therefore sets up, in the State, individual against social right; which is setting up the right of the strongest, and is the worship of Individual Power. This worship of individual power as a principle, or as an abstraction, therefore becomes a prominent aristocratic attribute; and the individual worships this power, whether it is possessed by himself or by other individuals; although we must be careful not to confound this manifestation with that recognition of individual supremacy in the State which arises in the opposite, democratic recognition of Universal Law, or of the subjection of the Individual to the Universal, which is the foundation of all social order. In this love of power, there is a twofold manifestation; one that is internal and relates to the individual, and one that is external and relates to others. Although the aristocratic individual will always desire to elevate himself to the greatest possible height, and to command all who are below him, he at the same time desires to become subject to and to be controlled by all who are above him in the possession of the aristocratic attributes; the former characteristic predominating in proportion as the individual is internal and intellectual, and the latter in proportion as he is external and affectional. When not possessing the power or capacity for ruling, the individual submits to the rule of those who possess this power, and becomes their most devoted worshipper; and he submits to this rule both from his inherent love of power and of the powerful, and that he may obtain the right to domineer and tyrannize over others. We accordingly find it to be established as a well-known and generally recognized fact, that those who are the most servile in their obedience to superiors in station are the most arbitrary and despotic in their treatment of inferiors, or of those over whom they may have obtained control. Aristocracy is adapted to the exercise of power over others, or to the control of the external manifestations of others, for the reason that the capacity for external direction, which is the function of the most external principle of the Will, is especially an aristocratic attribute. It is particularly well adapted to perform this service for the State, in the external sphere of consciousness to which it is confined, because the individual is in this sphere necessarily dependent upon external direction from sources which represent vital spiritual laws; and the tendency of Aristocracy is to become subject to these, while at the same time it possesses the power of external direction in the greatest perfection. This adaptation of Aristocracy to the uses of the State, however, is attended by influences of an opposite character, which lead to a great variety of social abuses; for, when not controlled by predominant social tendencies and made subject to the Church, it must lead to the destruction of that, which, under this supervision, it has been the means of constructing. By its tendency to establish individual power, it becomes the advocate of the law of might, or the right of the strongest, which, if not restrained, produces the destruction of the State; and this is the more deceptive and dangerous, because it appears under the disguise of individual liberty. There are other aristocratic manifestations, however, which do not wear so attractive a disguise. Possessing, as he does, the greatest facility in combining external phenomena in the relation of cause and effect with the subjection of the lower to the higher for use; and being at the same time animated by a love for external accumulation, including a tendency to deception and fraud in its acquisition, and by a desire to appropriate every thing to personal use, — the aristocratic individual is able to disguise all his real designs, and to regulate himself in the most exact manner to conform externally with all the requirements of State and Church; while at the same time, and under the same disguise, his plans for the realization of all his personal aims are followed with the most untiring industry and perseverance, and with the most abundant prospect of success, because he is able to suppress or to control every thing in his own consciousness not consistent with the success of his plans, and because these are concealed from observation, and forwarded by means of the most rigid calculation. He is thus punctiliously observant of all the proprieties of life, so far as these are presented to the observation of the world; and the task of playing a part, or assuming a false appearance, is undertaken by him, not only because it is easy, and necessary as a matter of calculation, but because it is a pleasant and desirable manifestation of his power. He may therefore present an appearance of politeness and good-will towards all who happen to hold a recognized position in society, which is no indication of his real feelings and intentions towards them; while to all others he is either patronizing, contemptuously exclusive, or actively hostile. Although the capacity for external direction in the realization of plans of life both for himself and for others is now secured to him, — a capacity which is indispensable to those who have the direction either of public or of private affairs, — this is accompanied by a tendency which leads him to make use of this power for the gratification of his personal ends by the sacrifice of every opposing influence. Therefore, although Aristocracy must furnish a form to the State, and provide for the administration of its government, its tendency is always towards the abuse of power and the subversion of all true government; for the object of this is the greatest good of all those who are governed. Being external and feminine, a superficial and affectional character is communicated to the individual, which is deceptive in relation to himself, and destructive in relation to others, producing an excellence of form at the expense of excellence in the substance. It not only bestows upon him stores of verbal and practical knowledge, with the ability to use them for practical purposes, by which external possessions are multiplied and a great diversity of uses performed, but it communicates to him a great variety of showy and attractive qualities related to the beautiful, the good, and the true, externally considered, which are well calculated to deceive those who cannot penetrate this attractive exterior, and discover what is concealed behind all these fair appearances. These give to it a charm, the influence of which it is difficult to resist, the value of which it is almost impossible fairly to estimate, and the deceptive and destructive character of which it is almost impossible either to recognize or to allow.

Aristocracy leads the individual to covet all the external advantages which have here been enumerated, and to estimate himself and others according to the possession of these, whether inherited, or acquired by individual effort; and to look down upon and desire to control arbitrarily all whose possessions are less, while he venerates those who are superior to him in any of these respects. It leads the individual to trust in expedients, and to distrust principles, — to be practical instead of theoretical, — to regard the authority of the most distinguished individuals, as the highest rule of truth and of right, and what society has established, as the greatest good, — to regard the forms rather than the substance of things, — and to delight in learned formalities, and in shows and ceremonies of all kinds which dazzle the mind, excite the feelings, and give the impression of external elevation from learning, from wealth, or from power. It makes the individual conservative, and leads him to desire imitation instead of originality, and thus to reproduce the thoughts and institutions of the past; so that, although the friend of learning and of talent, it is the foe of genius, which demands progress and improvement. Being individual and affectional, as the representative of the female side of the human constitution, Aristocracy desires the supremacy of those families in which is concentrated the greatest amount of learning, of wealth, and of power, or practical ability; and we therefore find, that, when the domestic region of affection becomes a ruling motive power, the reign of Aristocracy commences. It is therefore that Aristocracy always pays particular attention to the institution of the Family and to the elevation of the Female, so far as these are estimated from an external and aristocratic point of view, — to the accumulation, preservation, and transmission of family possessions, so that the family power shall be perpetuated, — and to the elevation to power of the most distinguished families. From this tendency to elevate the Family above the State, Aristocracy is as much disposed to limit the supreme power in the State, which should be the exponent of the democratic principle, as it is to limit the action of the people, — aims to secure to each individual who has passed the Aristocratic ordeal the liberty of exercising all his natural and acquired advantages exclusively for his own benefit, and thus to establish the right of the strongest, — lavishes rewards upon external ability, dexterity, and skill, in both the theoretical and practical departments of knowledge and of life, — and is continually multiplying facilities, in the form of monopolies and exclusive privileges both individual and corporate, by which learning and talent may be fostered and rewarded, and a concentration of wealth, learning, and power, under and according to aristocratic rule, may be consummated.

This description has been made from an abstract point of view upon the ground of the predominance of the Female side of the Human Constitution, the external and receptive principles of the Mind, the external element in the personifying principles, and the external principle of the Will, which are all relatively destructive. Both in Aristocracy and Democracy, however, vital and destructive elements are to be recognized, but particularly from a practical point of view. Both commence their operation as vital principles, because they concur in the support of the vital institutions of Society which are constructed by the Church through the influence of a supernatural power; although it is true that this is done from opposite points of view and from opposite motives, one being relatively universal, and the other personal; and both become socially destructive in proportion as these institutions, which are founded in the subjection of the individual to universal law, are repudiated or perverted for the purpose of obtaining the exclusive gratification of personal individual want. At the same time, it must be conceded that there is a constant tendency in the aristocratic class, to whom, in a great measure, the administration of the laws is intrusted, to exercise the power conferred upon them, as an individual attribute, in an arbitrary or despotic manner, for personal gratification and advantage, and not for the good of others, or for individual instead of universal benefit; a tendency which can be modified or controlled only by the influence of opposite, democratic tendencies in the mind of the individual, or by his subjection to the Church, and the sacrifice, under its direction, of the individual inclination.

As a representative of the Infinite, and the exponent of the masculine, intellectual, internal, and universal elements of the human constitution, Democracy becomes internally productive, and therefore constitutes the natural life of the State, and the cause of all its productive power from the internal realization and application of Social Law. By recognizing Social Law from a universal point, it demands the State as a Unit, and the rule of the People through one recognized head, who shall protect the masses from the power of the aristocracy, which is built upon learning and wealth, and the tendency of which is to make the rich richer and more powerful, and the poor poorer and more imbecile and degraded. It thus includes faith in one supreme ruler of the State, who shall be the supervisor and regulator of all the subordinate departments of the social fabric in providing for the greatest good of the whole people, and in restraining all individual manifestations which are inconsistent with this great end of the social institution. It repudiates the aristocratic doctrine of personal liberty, or individual right, as being the right of the strongest in disguise; and demands social or universal right, which is protection from the individual: that is, it demands the equal right of all individuals; and this cannot be obtained without the restraint of individual power, from whatever source this power may be obtained. Now, it may not at once be apparent, that the freedom of the individual, or the liberty of the individual to exercise his own natural powers exclusively for his own benefit, is not a democratic but an aristocratic manifestation, or is an exercise of the law of might that is in direct opposition to the law of right, from a social point of view. If we call to mind, however, that, if this liberty of the individual was not restrained by legal enactments to protect the institution of the family, no healthy domestic institution could be realized, we may comprehend how much more necessary it is that this liberty should be restricted with reference to society at large; because, as the social affections are much weaker than the domestic, it is clearly evident, that, without a corresponding protection, the social institution could not in any measure be sustained, and preserved from the encroachments of individual selfishness. Some have been so far misled by the word "Liberty" as to mistake individual for social right, and to suppose that the former is recognized and demanded by the democratic principle. This is a strange mistake, because Individualism is the very essence of Aristocracy, and is, in the spiritual, an infernal principle, as we shall clearly show. It is true that democracy demands liberty for the individual; but it does not demand either license or monopoly: on the contrary, it denies them as aristocratic, and would as soon allow physical as mental strength and dexterity an unrestrained and unlimited liberty of action. It demands that true liberty which is founded in the subjection of personal to universal objects and ends; a subjection that is the only safeguard to liberty for the masses. It resists subjection to individuals; but it does this that it may realize a true subjection to universal law, instead of a subjection to arbitrary rule or individual caprice: and hence it regards independence to be, not the negation of dependence, but dependence upon an internal and universal, instead of an external and individual, power. Therefore, while Democracy demands Liberty, it demands at the same time Equality and Fraternity; because it demands that no individual in the community shall be injured, either immediately or remotely, by the action of another; and also that all shall contribute in some way towards the realization of the great object of the social institution, which is the greatest good of all its members. Liberty cannot be conceived separate from Equality and Fraternity, without destroying its vitality, and establishing the right of the strong to defraud, domineer over, and oppress the weak: indeed, the right of all that is external, false, and evil, to oppress and destroy all that is internal, true, and good. It will be understood, however, that, when democracy demands equality and fraternity, it does not demand the destruction of that social order which separates the various classes in a community, and establishes the rank, the station, and the consideration that belong to each; for this would be to establish the form upon the ruins of the substance. As social liberty includes individual subjection, so does social equality include degrees of individual condition, and social fraternity include an intercourse that is based upon this inequality; and these are therefore always recognized and submitted to by the democratic principle.

Under the influence of Democracy, the individual desires internal rather than external gifts and acquisitions, and estimates himself and others according to these. Regarding, thus, the substance rather than the form, he has little confidence in education, and little respect for any authority, either in theory or in practice, that has not received the sanction of his own judgment; while he desires to originate rather than to imitate, and is the enemy of all mere forms and ceremonies, and the display of external advantages. Instead of wishing to control others in an arbitrary manner, he desires that they should be governed by internal recognitions of truth and of good, and the true relationships of things; and instead of using all his efforts for the elevation of himself, or for external accumulations either of knowledge, of wealth, or of power, his time and thoughts are readily bestowed upon objects which belong to social use rather than to personal advantage, and to abstract truth rather than to immediate practical use; and thus, although he does not readily accumulate external facts, or possess the faculty of arranging them in new and entertaining forms, he succeeds in multiplying the knowledge of those internal principles and relationships which give vitality to thought and to the life.

The manifestations here described are the vital manifestations and recognitions of the democratic principle, which are the most perfectly realized in the most immature condition of the individual, while he is under the influence of the vital laws of the mind, and under subjection to the Church, which is the representative and exponent of those laws as they are incarnated in vital institutions and forms of thought. After the individual has completed his development under the influence of these vital laws, he commences a development under the operation of the destructive laws of the mind; and democracy becomes developed from within outwards, descending from the substance into the form, which is opposite. In this development, it not only becomes productive of some of the destructive external results of aristocracy, by the gradual extension of the principle of personal liberty, without realizing any of those vital effects which spring from its adherence to vital external forms; but it realizes conceptions of destructive supernatural laws, which it insists upon applying as universal laws of thought and of life. In this development, spurious democratic forms take the place of genuine democratic recognitions; and the supernatural forms of Society are gradually ignored and repudiated, until they are destroyed by the complete establishment of "Naturalism" and "Sympathy" as the ruling laws. It is true that the individual endeavors to establish realities for forms, so that provision for individual want, instead of com-

pliance with arbitrary external direction, may be obtained; and to establish the internal recognition of truth and of right, in the place of orthodox canons of faith and of practice, so that a reality may be communicated to his life. Liberty of conscience, and freedom from all restraint in thought, in speech, and in action, are therefore now established as fundamental doctrines of the democratic creed, by which the development of the individual from a self-conscious point of view is provided for. Instead of a government either of Individuals or of Institutions, democracy now demands a government of Principles, and the reign of Ideas; and takes for its motto, "Principles, not men." The individual therefore gains a reality, truthfulness, and sincerity of character, which is kinder than it seems; and acts towards others according to what he believes to be their intrinsic merit, and their real relationship to himself, and not according to their artificial, external, recognized position. But this improvement of the individual is gained at the expense of both his intellectual and his social position and condition, because in this development of the individual from a self-conscious point of view, by the application of conceptions of the destructive supernatural laws, the manifestations of the mind and of the will become more and more naturalistic, until the principles of "Naturalism" and "Sympathy" become fully developed as representatives of Absolute Falsehood and Evil. In this way, Democracy becomes the agent of these destructive sentimental laws in producing the gradual destruction of the Church and of the State.

We have here shown, that democracy originates in the vital, and that aristocracy originates in the destructive, elements of the human constitution, and that these vital and destructive elements are combined in the constitution of every individual; so that it is the predominance of one or of the other which constitutes him democratic or aristocratic. A still further division exists, however, in both the democratic and the aristocratic classes, the ground of which is to be found in the predominance of "Personality" or of "Property" in the Personal Constitution, by which they are separated into internal and external portions; the first being characterized by a predominance of the internal receptive principles of the mind, and the second by a predominance of its external receptive principles, in consequence of which the knowledge of one becomes real and practical, and that of the other becomes superficial and verbal: and these are all the general divisions or social distinctions that it is possible to recognize from this point of view. As human nature, however, exists in the greatest diversity that is consistent with life, so that no two individuals are precisely the same either in their structure or in their manifestations, it is important that we should recognize another difference existing between the members which compose a State, which originates in a difference of Substance that is fundamental and perpetual. We have seen that Human Substance was created to be a medium for the representation in the Natural, and the manifestation in the Spiritual, of opposite Absolute Causes in the most external and diversified forms, and consequently that this substance contains in essence an infinite diversity of individual souls, which were calculated for the realization of this diversified representation and manifestation. Now, in the Natural, where the manifestations now being described as democratic and aristocratic are realized, this diversity has not been brought into a perfect harmony through the recognition and application of absolute laws and the realization of spiritual life; so that production is here effected through the conflict of opposites, instead of their harmonious co-operation, and therefore this difference of quality is particularly conspicuous. This difference has often been mistaken for that which exists between democracy and aristocracy; and, among the more external minds both in external and internal spheres, an inversion of the true relationship between aristocracy and democracy has been produced by drawing an imaginary line, separating those who are noble and refined in their tastes and in their habits from those who are ignoble and vulgar. It will therefore be necessary to bear in mind that these two extremes in the quality of individuals belong equally to the democratic and aristocratic classes, this difference between them being the foundation of all the subdivisions under which individuals become associated in the various occupations and amusements of social life; so that the democratic and the aristocratic combine together in every department of individual, of domestic, and of social life, in realizing the development of the individual in all these departments.

From the description of democracy and aristocracy that has here been given, it will be seen, that, in the external sphere of consciousness, Democracy originates in the predominance of the vital elements of the human constitution, and Aristocracy in the predominance of its destructive elements; and that, as the union of these opposite elements is necessary in order that any intellectual, sentimental, or affectional production, or any individual manifestation, should be realized, the union of democratic and aristocratic elements is necessary in the formation of the State, and the union of democratic and aristocratic classes is indispensable to its welfare, and ever to its existence: for although it has been necessary here to describe these opposite principles in a somewhat extreme manner, in order that their true character may be known, we must not lose sight of the fact, that opposition, attraction, and union in production, are all here to be recognized. As democracy and aristocracy are related as internal and external, the latter must furnish the medium through which the former becomes manifested, so that both are necessary in order that the State should be constituted, and no separation of them can take place without its destruction; and although they are related as vital and destructive, as the form and the substance are antagonistic, the establishment of a democratic form must always end in the rule of aristocracy and the destruction of the State, this being effected in an internal sphere of consciousness through the operation of the destructive laws of the Sentimental Nature.

Enough has now been said to show that the laws of our science are fully illustrated in the forms and functions of Society, because we have shown that it contains a dualistic form of " two and two, one against the other," and that these antagonistic elements are combined and manifested through a productive sphere in a manner representing Spiritual Life through Marriage; the union of these opposites in production being accomplished through a subjection of the personal to the universal, and of the lower to the higher, for use. This statement will hardly be disputed, because it is well understood, and will be generally conceded, that Philosophy and the Church are antagonistic powers which constitute the internal, and that Democracy and Aristocracy are antagonistic powers which constitute the external, principles which are combined in Society; and also that the latter are individualized in the State, which is manifested through a Constitution, either as a Republic, a Monarchy, or an Empire; this being administered either by a temporary Delegation, a permanent Aristocracy, or an absolute Ruler; so that the laws of Opposition, of Attraction, and of Marriage, are here completely illustrated. In describing the *structure* of Society under the Laws of Correspondence, we have pointed out the sources in which democracy and aristocracy originate, the tendencies which belong to them, and the kind of manifestation of which they become productive, so that their character and relation to each other as vital and destructive principles might be distinctly shown from the most universal or abstract point of view; and we have also shown how these opposite principles become manifested through the democratic and aristocratic classes. In describing the *development* of the State under the Laws of Succession, we shall show the manner in which these principles become successively developed, and the State passes through the periods of infancy, maturity, and decay; and, in describing the *formation* of the State in our psychological analysis of the instinct of "Society," we shall state the process of its construction, and show why its form must be aristocratic, and at the same time constitute a medium through which the democratic principle is manifested. This completes the enumeration of all the fundamental natural forms and functions of the Universe, all of which are found to illustrate in the most perfect manner the Laws of Correspondence which have here been established; it having been shown that all these exist in dualistic forms as "two and two, one against the other," and that these are combined and manifested through an active and constructive principle in a supernatural manner representing Spiritual Life through Marriage, or the union of opposites through voluntary sacrifice, in which the lower are made subject to the higher, and the destructive to the vital principles, for the purpose of production; and it having also been shown that all these illustrate the laws of Opposition, of Attraction, and of Marriage. We will therefore pass to the statement and illustration of the Laws of Succession, or of Natural Growth and Development.

THE

LAWS OF SUCCESSION,

OR

NATURAL GROWTH AND DEVELOPMENT.

"THE THING THAT HATH BEEN, IT IS THAT WHICH SHALL BE; AND THAT WHICH IS DONE IS THAT WHICH SHALL BE DONE: AND THERE IS NO NEW THING UNDER THE SUN. IS THERE ANY THING WHEREOF IT MAY BE SAID, SEE, THIS IS NEW? IT HATH BEEN ALREADY OF OLD TIME WHICH WAS BEFORE US. THERE IS NO REMEMBRANCE OF FORMER THINGS; NEITHER SHALL THERE BE ANY REMEMBRANCE OF THINGS THAT ARE TO COME WITH THOSE THAT SHALL COME AFTER." — Eccles. i 9-11.

LAWS OF SUCCESSION.

THE ground for a succession of Natural Phenomena is to be found in the nature of Creation, and in the character of the Laws which must govern all its natural manifestations and constitute its natural life. In the account that has already been given of the Universe, we have shown that it was created from infinite and finite phenomenal substances, or material laws, as a Dual Substance, containing in every department opposite laws and forms, representing Infinite and Finite, and also a supernatural medium, through which the Divine Activity operates in the continuous creation, combination, and manifestation of these dualistic laws and forms, outside of the individual consciousness, in a manner representing Spiritual Life through Marriage, or the union of opposites through voluntary sacrifice. We have shown that the necessity for this continuous creation of all natural things arises in the fact, that this Definite Substance is not realized by the union as one of these opposite phenomenal substances or material laws, for the reason that this union can be produced only through the realization of a spiritual consciousness by the soul, and the consummation in it of a spiritual marriage; it being only through this that a spiritual condition of substance and of life can be realized. Until this has taken place, human nature, and all the external things representative of it, must exist in a dual natural condition, in which infinite and finite phenomenal laws have been combined, but not united; and, in consequence of this, both infinite and finite material forces must continually operate upon all phenomenal natural forms, one as a vital and the other as a destructive power, in their decomposition and recomposition, under the control of a divine creating Power, who makes use of these vital and destructive forces in the production of a series of natural representative manifestations, by which the soul is supplied with every possible variety of experience for its natural instruction and development.

All natural things must be realized as a continuous series of phenomena, instead of being realized in a permanent form, because the natural life is constituted by finite laws of diversity, partiality, and separation; and these are opposite to the infinite laws of unity, universality, and marriage, through which alone any universal, permanent form, and therefore any complete individuality, can be realized. We have shown that the Universe is created from infinite and finite phenomenal substances, as a Dual Substance, in dualistic forms, and in a natural condition, in which its manifestations are necessarily partial, unreal, dualistic, discordant, and chaotic; requiring that its discordant elements and its natural laws, which exclude each other as the representatives of infinite and finite, should be combined and manifested in a supernatural manner, outside of the individual consciousness, in forms representative of spiritual marriage, in order that any productive condition should be realized in it; that, consequently, neither the infinite material laws, which demand unity, universality, and marriage, nor the laws of spiritual life, which demand the union of opposites through the voluntary sacrifice of individual life, and are represented in its supernatural manifestations, can operate through it, or become the laws which constitute its life; and hence that this life must be constituted by finite laws of diversity, partiality, and separation, because these are the only laws which correspond with its condition, and are therefore the only laws which could flow into, animate, and govern it. This life is derived from Human Substance, which is the universal sphere of Definite Phenomenal Being, from which all particular forms are sustained; and this life is constituted by the internal manifestation of this Substance in definite Laws of Diversity, Partiality, and Separation; because, as we have already shown, the life of Human Substance is constituted by the laws of Finite Phenomenal Substance, and its internal manifestations must therefore correspond with these laws. In this way, laws which are in themselves destructive operate through all natural forms, which produce manifestations representing both infinite and finite, — both divine and infernal life, — and therefore represent truth and good, as well as the falsehood and evil with which they correspond; and they are even made to operate through the supernatural principles of the human constitution, which produce manifestations representing Spiritual Life, or the union of opposites through voluntary self-sacrifice. Now, it will be seen that these laws must necessarily demand the greatest diversity, partiality, and separation consistent with the representative character of all natural forms; and that they must necessitate the realization of all natural substances, forms, and manifestations, under a law of perpetual change, so that the phenomena belonging to every natural sphere must be realized in a perpetual revolution or succession of circles. We therefore give to this law the name of "Circularity." The particular mode in which this succession of phenomena is produced is regulated by the law of "Contrariety;" this being founded in the law of Duality, which is the law of Existence in the threefold law of Tri-Personality, which demands and regulates production from the union of opposites. This law of Contrariety, as conceived by us, demands that all natural production shall result from the combination of opposite principles and processes; that all changes of substance shall be governed by a law of growth from below upwards; and that all changes of form shall be governed by a law of development from within outwards: this law must therefore apply to every form of existence, as well as to every collection of forms, and thus to every principle of the human constitution, as well as to the opposite spheres which constitute it. We will now proceed to state and explain these laws, and to illustrate them by reference to the most important forms of life and of the consciousness.

THE

LAW OF CONTRARIETY.

In our description of the structure of the Human Constitution, we have shown that it includes two opposite spheres which are combined together in production,—a personal sphere which constitutes what is relatively Substance in the Human Constitution, because it includes the indefinite forms or personal affinities of the individual, which are universal appropriating powers, and also includes Self-Consciousness, Individuality, or Will, which becomes developed through the means of these appropriations; and a general sphere which constitutes what is relatively Form in the Human Constitution, because it includes the principles of the human mind, which furnishes all the definite forms through which the individual obtains his consciousness, and becomes specifically manifested. Now, as the law of Contrariety demands that all changes of Substance shall be governed by a law of growth from below upwards, and that all changes of Form shall be governed by a law of development from within outwards, it consequently demands that the individual shall grow from below upwards, and that his mind shall be developed from within outwards; that, as the manifestations of his mind became degraded by being produced through lower forms, they should also become elevated by a more internal or self-conscious life; and that, as the manifestations of the individual became elevated by being produced through higher and more internal regions of Individuality or Will, and also by a more internal and self-conscious life, they should become degraded by the realization of an affinity for the lower or more external productions of the mind, and by the consequent appropriation and application of these as laws of the individual life. As the Personal Constitution, and also each department of the Mind, contains vital and destructive laws, representing Infinite and

Finite, which must be developed successively, — in the personal constitution from below upwards, or from destructive to vital; and in the mind from within outwards, or from vital to destructive, — the destructive personal laws must first be incarnated and manifested in combination with forms corresponding with the vital laws of the Mind, which are representatives of Spiritual Life; and the vital personal laws must be incarnated and manifested in combination with conceptions of the destructive laws of the Mind, which are representatives of Spiritual Death. With regard to the quality of his life, therefore, the individual is constantly ascending; while, with regard to the forms of his life, he is continually descending: and the consequence of this is, that the lowest and the highest things are brought together, and are made to combine in production, — the points of elevation and degradation are reversed and confounded, so that things are the opposite of what they seem, — and all forms which are vital as the representatives of spiritual truth, good, and beauty, or use, have to be repudiated and destroyed, while forms which are opposite to these are substituted in their place as the governing laws of the individual belief and life, before spiritual realities, of which these are the natural representatives, can be presented to the consciousness, and realized in the life.

The necessity for this may be shown from a more external point of the consciousness in the following manner. As the incarnation of the soul is commenced in this external and material atmosphere, it must, of course, take its departure from the lowest and most external point of the individual consciousness, and ascend by gradual processes of natural growth and development in a manner analogous to that by which the lower forms of life, which are its material representatives, are produced; and, as this development and growth of the individual are obviously produced by the subjection of his personal want to laws which are communicated to him through the principles of his mind, he must, of course, commence with the appropriation of laws corresponding with spiritual life, which must be communicated to him in the most external forms, corresponding with his individual position, as the condition of his subjection to them, and of their use to him in his growth and development; and these laws must be realized by him in a more internal, conscious, and comprehensible manner as he becomes elevated, in his growth from below upwards. But as the human constitution is, in every one of its departments, representative of both Infinite and Finite Principles,

— as the Soul is destined to become at-one with one or the other of these in a spiritual sphere of consciousness, — as, in realizing this consciousness, there must be presented to it laws and forms of spiritual life, upon the one hand, and of spiritual death, upon the other, that the individual may choose which of these shall constitute the life of his new, Spiritual Existence, — and as natural forms representative of these must have been conceived, and applied as the laws of the individual life, as a preparation for this spiritual presentation, — the laws appropriated by the individual must include those which are destructive as well as those which are vital and productive; and as only one of these can be appropriated at any one period, owing to the violent antagonism between them, in the conception and application of these laws, it is necessary that those which are vital, as the representatives of Spiritual Life, should be applied in the development of the individual while he is confined to an external condition and sphere of consciousness, and that those which are destructive, as the representatives of Spiritual Death, should be applied in the development of the individual when he has become elevated in his condition, and internal in his consciousness. It is necessary that vital and not destructive laws should operate in the external sphere, not only because the highest and most internal forms are then demanded under the law of Contrariety, but because, if the destructive laws should be applied, not only would the development of the individual be prevented, but he would be destroyed; because, in this external sphere, every thing is brought down into the region of Sensation, and carried out into external manifestation in the life: so that, separate from the law of production here stated, we may see the necessity that the destructive laws of the mind should be applied as laws of the individual life in an internal, and not in an external, sphere of consciousness. In this internal sphere, they can be applied without the same disastrous consequences, because, although they are destructive to all the productive forms and institutions which have been established as the representatives of the laws of spiritual life, the individual, in becoming internal and self-conscious, loses the power of external manifestation, and is principally confined to impracticable theories, which cannot be carried out in the life, and the object of which is the production of laws and forms of thought representative of Absolute Falsehood, as a preparation for his entrance into a spiritual sphere of consciousness. These conceptions of destructive laws and forms are also useful in producing the destruction of theories and institutions, which, although externally representative of spiritual life, are destructive to the ideas which they represent; because they are governed by a natural law, correspond with natural thought and the natural life which are opposite to these ideas, and retard the progress of the individual, or the realization in him of self-conscious, independent experiences, and must therefore be removed from the belief and from the life, as a preparation for the reception of those which are spiritual and real. We see, then, that the law of Contrariety is sustained, both from a theoretical and from a practical point of view, as one of the laws which regulate the phenomena of natural life, or the changes which take place in the growth and development of the human constitution. We will now illustrate this law by showing its operation in the State, in Philosophy, in the Church, and in the manifestations of the Sentimental Nature, through which supernatural laws are communicated, and forms corresponding with these are established, through the operation of which the development of the Individual Consciousness is produced; and, in doing this, we are to show, that, in each of these, the most opposite things are combined in production, — that each one of these is addressed to, and is associated in production with, individuals who are in a sphere the most opposite to that which is represented by it, — and that, as it becomes internal and self-conscious, and therefore elevated as to its substance, it becomes external and naturalistic, and is thus degraded in its form.

THE STATE may be seen to illustrate the law of Contrariety, because it is realized at the commencement of every social development in its most perfect natural form, while the people who become subject to it, and are associated with it in production, are confined to the rudest or most barbarous condition of the individual consciousness. The State performs, at its commencement, a service that is perfectly analogous to that performed by the Church, with which it is at this time closely united, and to which it is subordinate, in establishing the highest forms of social organization, and in subjecting the people to their productive influences. A directing power is thus furnished by the State for the guidance of the individual at a time when his consciousness is not sufficiently elevated for the purpose of self-government, and a dependent condition of the people is realized that is represented in an extreme and external manner by the complicated machinery of Chinese society, in which the most minute directions regulating the performance of all the duties of life are furnished by the State, and emanate from the supreme head of the Nation. This may be seen to illustrate the law of Contrariety, because it is evident that a true social condition is not here realized, but only represented, and, in being represented, is contradicted; and because, in proportion as the individual becomes fitted to fulfil his duties to the State from an internal, real, and self-conscious point of view by the elevation of the individual condition, all legitimate social forms are repudiated and destroyed by him. Although Society as originally constituted, including the subjection of the individual to the State and of the State to the Church, is the legitimate representative of that spiritual form which is founded in the laws of spiritual life, it is the furthest removed from a true social organization, for the reason, that, instead of promoting, it prevents the growth and development of the individual from an internal, real, and self-conscious point of view. The individual is here completely subordinated and made subject to the State, as he must indeed be in order that any real social organization should exist; but, in being thus subordinated, he becomes annihilated, and nothing but an external appearance representing a true social condition is produced. In order that a true social condition should be realized, instead of being represented, it is necessary that the individuals who compose the State should have been prepared by a complete development of all their powers and capacities from an internal, self-conscious, and individual point of view, through a course of independent individual experiences, as well as from an external, unconscious, social point of view; and this cannot, of course, be accomplished while the individual remains in bondage to the State, and also to the Church, under which the individual is necessarily crushed: for although this bondage is self-imposed, and this sacrifice of the individual is willingly submitted to by him, he is, for these very reasons, the more completely annihilated. It will thus be seen that the form and the substance of social life are not identical, but are, on the contrary, the farthest removed from each other in the order of production, because they belong to opposite spheres of life, — that between these two extremes must intervene the development of Individualism and Naturalism, which, instead of leading the individual to subject personal want to universal law through vital social forms, lead him to substitute the Individual for the Universal, or to establish personal want from a universal point of view through destructive social forms, — and that, in passing from the form to the substance of Social Life, all those ideas and institutions which have represented a true social condition, and have been productive of social use, must be repudiated and destroyed, and even inversions of these realized, in order that the individual may be prepared for the Spiritual State.

PHILOSOPHY may be seen to illustrate the law of Contrariety, first, because it is composed of the most antagonistic elements that can possibly be conceived. This antagonism may be seen from various points of view: first, in the principal ideas which it includes, such as unity and diversity, spirit and matter, subject and object, substance and phenomena, perfect and imperfect, infinite and finite, — ideas which have excluded each other, but both of which must be conceived and combined in order that any legitimate philosophical form should be realized; next, from the fact, that, while it is thus Dualistic, it is at the same time Unitarian, for the reason that it recognizes one Absolute Cause as the origin of all things, so that it has been obliged to produce diversity from unity, matter from spirit, the finite from the infinite, the imperfect from the perfect, and therefore death from life, and evil from good; and, finally, from the fact that it includes ontological and psychological elements which are antagonistic, — that, as Ontology, it contains opposite systems which are relatively spiritual and material, — and that, as Psychology, it contains intellectual and moral systems of the most conflicting character, the first of which is divided into ideal and sensual, and the second into disinterested and selfish systems, which are equally at variance with each other. It may be seen to illustrate this law, next, because, while Philosophy is at its commencement realized in its most perfect natural form, it is separated from any individual self-conscious realization, and confined to an unconscious poetic representation; being realized in the most external and unconscious individual condition, which is the farthest removed from a true philosophic capacity, or from the realization of any legitimate conception of Absolute Law. We therefore find that the ontological development of philosophy, which is its highest natural form, commenced in the East, where the individual consciousness was in the most external, natural, and dependent condition that can be experienced by any nation of the Caucasian race, to which alone a philosophical development is possible; and the systems there constructed are found to combine Spirit and Matter in the greatest antagonism, and to the greatest possible extent. Finally, it may be seen, because, while Philosophy commenced with the highest position that it has ever occupied, which was that of a representative of universal, absolute science, every subsequent development has, as we have already shown, resulted in a degradation of its form, while this has been accompanied by its elevation as a self-conscious realization. We may therefore see, that as Philosophy must be developed from its highest to its lowest forms, by the last of which it must be destroyed, — a fact that has already been demonstrated by reference to history, — its highest natural representation must be the farthest removed from its spiritual realization as Absolute Science, these being produced at the opposite poles of the human consciousness; and therefore, that, in passing from one to the other, all the symbolic forms by which the nature of God as Absolute Cause, and the nature of Creation as Phenomenal Consequence, have been represented to the mind, must be repudiated, in order that Spiritual Truth, or Philosophy as Absolute Science, should finally be realized as a self-conscious, comprehensible, individual experience.

THE CHURCH may be seen to illustrate the law of Contrariety, first, because it exists in a discordant dualistic condition as the exponent of two opposite Gospels, — one, "the Gospel of Circumcision;" and the other, "the Gospel of Uncircumcision," — and has been developed in opposite forms; these being individualized, and most violently antagonized, in the Catholic and Protestant Churches. It may be seen, next, because each of these Churches contains theological forms which contradict each other, so that they become realized in the utmost diversity and discord; and also contains opposite elements, the antagonism between which is the most extreme that has been realized in the whole history of human thought, because it is an opposition between the Natural and Supernatural. And, finally, it may be seen because the most violent antagonism existed between the supernatural truths represented by the Church at the time of her establishment, and the actual condition of the individuals who united with her in production; and between the discipline which she enjoined, and the personal inclinations of those who became subject to her.

That the Church was really established in this discordant dualistic condition, as the exponent of the opposite Gospels of Circumcision and Uncircumcision, — the opposition between which will hereafter be explained, and is suggested by the terms used to designate them, — we learn from St. Paul, who states that the first was committed by the Lord to Peter, and the second to himself; we also learn this from the antagonistic doctrines taught by these apostles, and the disputes which are recorded as having taken place between them,—from the Peterine and Pauline elements which were discordantly combined in the Church from its commencement, for which fact we have the authority of the best historians of the Church,—and from the fact that the first of these elements became incarnated in the Catholic Church, which is therefore said to have been founded by St. Peter,—this being the only evidence that it was so founded; while the second was subsequently incarnated in the Protestant Church, which, obviously, is entirely founded upon the teaching of St. Paul; because these Churches exclude each other, and are antagonized in the most violent manner that it is possible for two institutions to be,—an antagonism that has led to more individual persecution than any other in the records of history.

This discordant dualistic condition of the Church is shown, not only by this division and antagonism, but also by the discord that exists in each one of these divisions; because nothing can exceed the violence of the antagonism between the forms of these Churches, as will be particularly shown in the theological portion of this work. This discord was especially conspicuous in the early periods of the Church, before the individual consciousness had been developed, from a supernatural point of view, by the infusion of supernatural ideas into the forms of individual thought and life; because, besides the antagonism between its own legitimate elements, another element of discord was introduced, by the fact that it was, at its commencement, combined with the forms of Pagan philosophy, upon which it was necessarily dependent for materials in which to incarnate the supernatural ideas of Christianity realized through intuition or religious inspiration; and these were diametrically opposite, both in the ideas in which they were founded, and in the sphere of consciousness to which they belonged. All this discord in the Church arises in the opposition between Natural and Supernatural ideas and forms of thought, which must be discordantly combined in every natural form representative of Christianity; it being the first of these that characterizes the Gospel of Circumcision, and also the Catholic Church; and the second of these that characterizes the Gospel of Uncircumcision, and also the Protestant Church, which is its exponent. These opposite ideas and forms must be so combined, for two reasons. The first reason is, that, in Christianity, supernatural ideas representative of spiritual life must be incarnated in forms which are connected with individual experiences; and that the greatest antagonism exists between these may be known, not only because the natural motive power is opposite to this life, and these individual experiences are deceptive, unreal appearances, but because it was these partial and personal forms which Christianity came to crucify, and to make subject to forms of universal law. The second reason is, that both Religion and Morality must be included in the construction of every Church, and be combined, not only in its discipline, but in its theology; and as these are antagonized as the representatives of truth and good, of the universal and the personal, of the spiritual and natural, and of the infinite and finite, separate incarnations of religious and moral ideas, as supernatural and natural, have to be conceived and discordantly combined in all its teachings. The same cause, therefore, which necessitated the establishment of two opposite Gospels, and of two opposite Churches, as their exponents, necessitates the same antagonism in these, and in all the portions into which they become divided.

The antagonism that existed between the Church at its commencement, and the individuals who were made subject to and co-operated with her in production, may be seen, because this was the condition of her usefulness, and the cause of her establishment. Instead of being gradually developed, therefore, from the lowest to the highest point, in correspondence with the growth of the individual from below upwards, she appeared at her commencement in the greatest perfection, power, and splendor, and in the most violent opposition to the individual desire, which was more destructive at this time than at any subsequent period, as the crucifier of the individual; all the forms of his thought and of his life, and all the institutions through which he became subject to these forms, were established in a supernatural manner through her: so that no greater division and antagonism can possibly be conceived than that between the Church, and the individuals connected with her at the period of her establishment; the Church being realized in its most perfect form as the universal representative of Spiritual Life, and the individual being realized in his most imperfect condition, and being the farthest removed from the realization of this life. This antagonism, subjection, and co-operation are obviously demanded by the law of Contrariety, and are necessary both to the development and the preservation of the soul; because it is clearly evident, that, in the external and destructive condition in which the consciousness of the individual must first have been realized in his growth from below upwards, the only way in which he could be preserved from destruction, and manifested in a productive manner, was by his subjection to external forms and institutions representative of spiritual life from a universal point of view, and therefore most violently antagonized to the condition of the individual. These were also demanded because this was the only period of the soul's progress in which a vital ground of universal supernatural representation could be established in the consciousness from the most external and unconscious point of view; and this was necessary, first, because external forms representative of spiritual life must be provided as the governing laws of the thought and of the life, so that all the manifestations of the individual may be made to correspond with these as the condition of order and of use, and that his natural regeneration may be effected from the most external supernatural point of view, — next, because these external forms were required as a ground for the realization of internal, self-conscious supernatural experiences and forms of thought, through which the destructive personal inclinations of the individual could be crucified, and his natural regeneration effected from a more internal point of view, — and, finally, because these external and internal experiences are necessary, as furnishing suggestive material in the incarnation of the Spiritual Itself, when this is presented to the consciousness from within.

It will therefore be seen, that the Natural and the Spiritual Church are realized at the opposite extremes of the consciousness, and that between these the worship of Naturalism intervenes. As the individual becomes developed from an internal and self-conscious ground, he repudiates all the external representatives of spiritual life, substitutes forms corresponding with a natural order of thought and experience, and is driven from the Church; being first obliged to continue his development under the direction of natural conceptions founded upon external appearances, and susceptibilities for natural use; and being finally led, through the development of his personality, and of his mind from within outwards, in an internal-natural sphere of consciousness, to the conception and appropriation, as governing laws of his consciousness, of supernatural laws representing Spiritual Death, instead of external representations of the laws of Spiritual Life; a realization that must precede the spiritual birth of the soul. In passing from the representation to the realization of Christianity, therefore, it becomes necessary that those religious forms and symbols which are the representatives of spiritual ideas, and are therefore mistaken for them from a vital supernatural point of view, should be sacrificed and repudiated, and even those which are opposite substituted in their place, in order that the progress of the soul may be secured, and the Spiritual Itself be finally reached and realized.

The Law of Contrariety is illustrated in the most particular manner by the manifestations of the Sentimental Nature and the development of the Individual Consciousness. The general illustrations of this law are, first, that the internal and vital sentimental laws are represented and become physically incarnated through the external and destructive sentimental principles in the most external and destructive condition of the individual consciousness, while the external and destructive sentimental laws are realized and become intellectually incarnated through the internal and vital sentimental principles in the most internal and vital condition of this consciousness; next, that, in an external sphere, the individual appropriates these incarnations and representations of vital laws in combination with destructive partial and personal forms, while, in an internal sphere, he appropriates these intuitions and conceptions of destructive laws in combination with vital partial and personal forms, these being combined and manifested through the Will, in the first case productively, and in the second destructively, in relation to supernatural truth and good. This law is also illustrated by these particular manifestations, which are individualized under four forms, developed successively and antagonistically; these being Catholicism, Protestantism, Unitarianism, and Transcendentalism; each one of which is developed under the operation of this law. We will therefore describe these forms in the order of their production, and state the opposite sentimental principles and the opposite individual forms which operate in their production and experience by the individual.

Catholicism, as the lowest and most external form of vital sentimental experience, was produced through the unconscious operation of the principles of "Spiritualism" and "Veneration" in the Religious, and of "Justice" and "Approbation" in the Moral department, as the governing sentimental principles; the first, in both cases, being the vital male, or perceptive principle, and the second the destructive female, or receptive principle. These vital laws were incarnated in the Catholic Church, according to laws of correspondence, in a supernatural, incomprehensible manner, in physical forms and spontaneous external manifestations, by which Spiritual Truth, Good, and Beauty were represented, and natural and supernatural uses became realized by the individual through the unconscious, spontaneous apprehensive recognition of these forms. This recognition was entirely disconnected from any comprehension of that which was represented by them, and also from any connection or comparison with internal individual experiences; and was productive in the individual simply of emotional states of the consciousness and of external physical manifestations representative of spiritual life. These forms were established as the governing laws of the individual life, by the subjection of the individual to this Church, through the sentiments of "Veneration" and "Approbation," in their most external condition, by which he became receptive entirely from her, in the development of the principle of "Direction" in the Will, — a principle through which the individual obtains a consistent and calculated external manifestation and direction of himself, under the highest external influence that can operate upon him. Externally considered, this is the most perfect form of Individuality that can be realized in a natural condition of the soul, because it is constructed after a vital supernatural form or pattern provided by the Church; while, internally considered, it is the most imperfect, because it is completely artificial and unreal, even from a natural point of view; the individual not having yet commenced his development from an internal, self-conscious position, and his real personal condition being, in its growth from below upwards, the most imperfect and destructive, — this not having been changed, but only concealed from observation. It will therefore be seen, that no two things can, in the natural, be more antagonistic than the form and the substance of the individual at this period of his growth and development.

Protestantism, as the highest and most internal form of vital sentimental experience, was produced through the conscious operation of "Spiritualism" and "Justice," which are the vital sentimental laws, — through the external development of "Intuition" and "Satisfaction," which are the vital receptive sentimental principles through which these laws must become incarnated, and through which the incarnations of these laws must be recognized, — through a personal affinity for these forms of vital law, as incarnated in forms of thought, and connected with the individual consciousness, — and through a consciousness of destructive personal forms, or of forms of individual manifestation that correspond with the personal want, which is destructive, because opposite to the universal; these being recognized, not from an external point of view, as in Catholicism, but from a point of self-conscious experience. In consequence of this change from an external and unconscious to an internal and self-conscious condition, and the consequent demand for manifestation from within, instead of manifestation in subjection to external forms, the individual comes into a discordant dualistic condition of the consciousness. Conceptions of vital supernatural phenomena are realized upon the one hand, and a consciousness of destructive personal forms is realized upon the other; and these have to be combined in the individual manifestations with the subjection of the personal to the sentimental element; because these sentimental conceptions, which are religious and moral forms, are necessarily appropriated by him as the laws of his belief and life. This antagonism of universal and personal in the consciousness not only characterizes the religious and moral conceptions of the Church, but is the foundation of many of the peculiarities of Protestant experience; and it may be seen both in the violence of its voluntary asceticism, and in the conflict that is continually going on between these two opposing forces in the individual, giving to his character a contradictory appearance that may be termed picturesque, and is often unjustly stigmatized as hypocritical.

In consequence of this demand that every thing should be realized from the point of the individual consciousness, the vital sentimental laws, instead of being incarnated and represented from a universal point of view, as we find them to be in the Catholic Church, became incarnated simply from the point of individual self-consciousness, by which the forms representing them were realized as limited and one-sided. They were one-sided, because the mind becomes so developed from a self-conscious point of view, as we shall have occasion to demonstrate; and they were limited, because they were confined to forms which can be incarnated by self-conscious individual experiences, and consequently excluded all forms of symbolic correspondence, which constitute the principal foundation of the representations of Christianity by the Catholic Church, and of Art as a representative of the Spiritual. Instead of an unconscious recognition of supernatural symbolism, through which vital supernatural ideas were incarnated in physical forms, ceremonial observances, and social institutions, these ideas became consciously incarnated by the Understanding in forms of thought founded in individual experiences, by which they were made to constitute a conscious internal power in the production of self-conscious, instead of an external force productive of unconscious, individual manifestations. In this incarnation, Moral Good, as a representative of personal want, which is destructive and a representative of the Finite, was made subject to Religious Truth, as the supernatural representative of the Universal, which is vital, productive, and a representative of the Infinite. The individual became subject to these religious and moral conceptions through the sentiments of "Intuition" and "Satisfaction," which now became developed from an external point of view, and operated in the external development of the principle of "Relation" in the Will, — a principle through which the individual obtains knowledge from a self-conscious position of the external form of all his relationships, both natural and supernatural, and obtains both an internal and an external direction of himself in conformity with them. In this way, monstrous conceptions of religious truth became realized upon the one hand, and practical conceptions of individual duty were realized upon the other; and, although these moral manifestations were excessively ascetical and pharisaical, they were necessary to restrain the unruly and destructive propensities which are incidental to an immature condition of the individual newly released from subjection to the Catholic Church. The highest religious and moral ideas were thus brought down into forms which could be comprehended and manifested by the individual in his lowest self-conscious condition; and the religious truths contained in the Scriptures were made to operate upon him in an internal, instead of an external manner. At the same time, in consequence of the demand now made, that every thing should be realized from a self-conscious point of view, as the condition of its vitality, all the external objects of veneration in religion and in art were at once repudiated and destroyed, as the objects of an idolatrous worship; and the Protestant became violently antagonized to the Catholic Church, notwithstanding that the supernatural ideas represented by them were the same. By this conscious experience of supernatural ideas, and this demand for their incarnation in individual experiences in connection with the most external moral conceptions in which a vindictive conception of Justice is predominant, the most opposite things were brought together and combined in production; pretensions to saintship were violently contrasted with the actual condition of the individual, and with a consciousness of destructive personal affinities; and the acknowledgment, that the individual is totally depraved, and cannot be good or become so through his own effort, was violently contrasted with the most ascetical and pharisaical manifestations. No two things, therefore, can, in the natural, be more antagonistic than the beliefs of the individual, and also his beliefs and condition, at this period of his growth and development.

Unitarianism, as the lowest and most external form of destructive sentimental experience, was produced through the unconscious operation of "Naturalism" and "Sympathy," which are the destructive sentimental laws, — and the internal development of "Veneration" and "Approbation," which are the destructive receptive sentimental principles, — combined with a consciousness of vital personal forms, or forms of individual manifestation, which corresponded externally with a universal instead of a personal principle, while they corresponded internally with the destructive sentimental laws. In consequence of this change from vital to destructive sentimental laws, and from destructive to vital personal forms, a total change was produced in all the individual manifestations, and in all the sentimental experiences; the Scriptures were interpreted from a destructive moral and natural, instead of a vital religious and supernatural, point of view; and Religious Truth was regarded as natural and destructive, and was made subject to Moral Good which was conceived as spiritual and productive. Unitarianism thus became realized as Natural, in opposition to Supernatural; natural ideas based upon a conception of the dignity of human nature, — upon independent individual power, — and upon a capacity in the individual for becoming perfect, or indefinitely wise and good, through his own effort, — took the place of a belief in the total depravity of human nature, and the dependence of the individual upon God for preservation, for direction, and for salvation; and a belief in unreal, natural appearances took the place of a belief in supernatural forms and manifestations which represent the spiritual and real. In this incarnation, religious forms belonging to a supernatural order, as the representatives of vital supernatural phenomena, were either repudiated, or perverted and made subject to moral ideas belonging to an external natural order of thought and experience, as the representatives of destructive spiritual phenomena. Conceptions of religious and moral truth perfectly antagonistic to those of the Protestant Church were thus realized by the individual, and were appropriated by him as laws of his belief and life. In the development of the mind from within outwards, and the growth of the individual from below upwards, these Unitarian experiences become incarnated from time to time in forms more and more naturalistic, external, affectional, and destructive, and are combined with personal forms more and more internal, self-conscious, simple, vital, and real, in producing a complete external development of the principle of "Relation" in the Will from affectional and moral, instead of intellectual and religious, points of view. As Unitarianism is characterized as external, natural, and practical, from its belief in individual freedom, power, and capacity for increasing knowledge and goodness, and from its belief in natural appearances exclusively, — this being the only form of sentimental experience in which the supernatural is excluded, — there is less antagonism between the phenomena of which it becomes productive than in the other forms here described; but, as the spheres of general and of personal consciousness which are combined in this production are as violently antagonized, the law of Contrariety is quite as well illustrated.

Transcendentalism, as the most internal form of destructive sentimental experience, is produced through the conscious operation of the principles of "Naturalism" and "Intuition" in the religious, and of "Sympathy" and "Satisfaction" in the moral department, as the governing sentimental principles, — the first, in both cases, being the destructive male, or perceptive principle, and the second the vital female, or receptive principle, — and through a consciousness by the individual of an affinity for vital personal forms, or for those forms of individual manifestation which correspond with universal, in opposition to personal, want. For although it is now necessary that the destructive sentimental laws should be consciously developed as governing powers, and that the individual should realize an affinity and demand for the universal manifestation of Personal Want, — which is a manifestation of himself as God, — he becomes vitally conscious as to his personal condition, and demands a true manifestation of himself for universal ends. These destructive laws are incarnated in internal conceptions which represent inversions of spiritual truth, good, and beauty, or use; and these conceptions are established as the governing laws of the individual belief and life, by the subjection of the individual to his own internal conceptions and impulses, and become productive, first, of internal conclusions and external manifestations destructive to all the forms and institutions representing spiritual life, which have been established by supernatural means through the Catholic and Protestant Churches;

and, next, of self-conscious manifestations in the internal development of the principle of "Relation," and the external and natural development of the principle of "Consciousness," in the Will. In this way, the individual realizes, on the one hand, the most violent opposition to all vital forms, functions, relationships, and institutions: and, on the other, a vital personal condition, in which vital personal forms, corresponding with universal, and therefore destructive to personal, want, are recognized; and he becomes internally self-conscious, demands a perfect simplicity and truthfulness for his life, and realizes a total individualization of himself from the most internal natural point of view; this being the highest and most real natural condition of the individual which prepares him for the Spiritual Birth: so that no two things can be more antagonistic than the form and the substance of the individual at this period of his growth and development.

THE

LAW OF CIRCULARITY.

A LAW of Circularity as applied to mundane things was universally recognized by the ancients; although, owing to the pantheistic position to which all nations, excepting the Hebrew, were necessarily confined, the law conceived by them provided for the return of all created things to their original fountain or source in God, from whom they again emanated or proceeded. Brucker says, "It is an opinion still found among the Indians, and probably of very ancient date, that there is in Nature a periodical restitution of all things; when, after a return of all derived beings to their source, they again set forth, and the whole course of things is renewed. The Egyptians conceived that the Universe undergoes a periodical conflagration, after which all things are restored to their original forms, to pass again through a similar succession of changes. Plato believed that men had gradually degenerated from the primeval state of innocence and equality, and that the whole world would be ultimately destroyed, and renewed after the lapse of vast astronomical cycles. In common with many of the Grecian sects, the Stoics believed in the old Hindoo, Chaldean, and Egyptian calculations concerning the destruction of the world by water and by fire. This universal devastation was to take place at stated intervals, with vast astronomical cycles between. All was to be restored to a state of order, innocence, and beauty; the old tendency to degeneracy would end in a similar destruction, to be again renovated; and so on alternately for ever. Seneca says, 'A time will come, when the world, ripe for renovation, will be wrapped in flames; when the opposite powers in conflict will mutually destroy each other. The world being melted and re-entered into the bosom of Jupiter, this God will continue some time centred in himself, immersed in the contemplation of his own ideas. Afterwards a new world will spring.'" This peculiar view of Creation originated in the fact, that these ancient pagan philosophers were obliged to conceive all things as produced from Infinite Substance by the activity inherent in it: so that Creation was with them simply a mode of manifestation in the Infinite; and therefore a return of Creation to its original condition was necessarily regarded by them as an absorption of all things into the Infinite Substance. A law of Circularity is taught in the Jewish Scriptures, and is also symbolized by them in the destruction of the world by Water and by Fire: but with them this was not an entire destruction, but only a change in its condition, and represented the termination of those external and internal circles of growth and development which will be described in this work as births of the soul by blood and by water, the last of which is succeeded by a birth into the spiritual. A law of Circularity is also referred to in the Book of Ecclesiastes, in the following words: "That which has been is now, and that which is to be hath already been; and God requireth that which is past. The thing that hath been, it is that which shall be; and that which is done is that which shall be done: and there is no new thing under the sun. Is there any thing whereof it may be said, See, this is new? It hath already been of old time which was before us. There is no remembrance of former things; neither shall there be any remembrance of things that are to come with those which shall come after." Notwithstanding that Succession as the law of Creation was in this way truly represented, the significance of this representation is now entirely lost; and it is commonly supposed that the world was created perfect and entire from the beginning, and has continued so to exist, subject only to the changes in form produced by the action and re-action of material substances and laws upon each other, and to those which are produced in them by man; and that all the changes in him are produced through the free determination of himself towards good or towards evil, and by the constant accumulation of knowledge, by which every generation is made wiser and better than the last; so that instead of that deterioration or retrogression of Society which was recognized by the ancients, and has been noticed by modern philosophical historians, nothing but progress is now recognized: indeed, it has become common to suppose that the Universe exists entirely separated from its Creator, and from the causes which constantly operate upon it. Now, even Pantheism is a more rational belief than this, because it represents the fact that Creation cannot be separated either from the causes in which it originated and from which it is supported, or from the constant operation of an Absolute Power by which its forms are perpetually produced; but, in obtaining a conception of the universal laws which constitute the ground of things both in absolute and phenomenal spheres, we have been able to rise above the pantheistic representative forms of philosophy, and to realize a conception of Creation that is harmonious with Rationality and with Christianity. In our description of the creation of the Universe with man as its head, we have shown, that although it is created from infinite and finite substances or material laws which correspond with infinite and finite absolute causes, as these belong to a phenomenal and not to an absolute sphere, the Universe is realized outside of the sphere in which God exists as Absolute Cause, and still is connected with the Absolute as a medium for its natural representation and spiritual manifestation in a phenomenal sphere of being; and that, being created from opposite indefinite, self-subsisting substances as a representative of opposite absolute things, while confined to its natural representative condition, all the manifestations of the soul must be produced by the influx of these opposite material forces into forms created as representatives of infinite and finite principles, and by the combination of these vital and destructive forces by the Divine Activity in the production of specific phenomena which externally represent both infinite and finite, while they are governed internally by finite laws which constitute its natural life; so that, instead of being an Absolute Cause, as the common belief in human free-agency supposes, the human soul is simply a phenomenal form that is entirely dependent upon God for the continuation of its existence, and even for the manifestation of its life. Not being an absolute cause, but only a phenomenal consequence, the soul must always be confined to a phenomenal sphere of being, and remain simply a medium for production; for although it is destined to become at-one with the Absolute in a spiritual sphere of consciousness through a free determination of the individual in view of opposite Absolute Laws of which he must then become conscious, and one of which must be chosen by him as his life, it is even then only a medium for the phenomenal manifestation of the Absolute; and this does not change the character, but only the quality, of his life, so that he will be able to become cognizant of spiritual forms of Absolute Law and of Absolute Phenomena as a self-conscious, comprehensible experience, and to witness the combination and manifestation of these by the Divine Activity in forms of spiritual truth, good, and beauty; by which he becomes a medium for the manifestation of Absolute Cause in the most external and diversified manner. We have shown, however, that Creation in its natural condition is an unreal phenomenon that is the opposite of what it seems, being constituted in every part by dualistic forms representing opposite absolute principles, and therefore productive of manifestations representing spiritual life upon the one hand, and spiritual death upon the other, while its life is constituted by definite forms of the laws of finite phenomenal substance; and that, being a dual substance created from infinite and finite substances which are only combined, and have not been united as one, both infinite and finite material forces must continually operate upon all natural forms, one as a vital and the other as a destructive power, in their decomposition and recomposition under the control of a divine creating power, who makes use of this continuous destruction and reproduction in the realization of a series of natural manifestations which furnish to the soul every possible variety of experience for its natural instruction and development, — a variety of manifestation that must include the greatest diversity, partiality, and separation that is consistent with life; because, as these are the laws which constitute the natural life, they must govern the production as well as the manifestation of all natural things. The continuous destruction and reproduction in the natural, that has here been shown to be necessitated by the substance, constitution, and condition of Creation, does not rest entirely upon this internal evidence, but is represented in well-known physiological facts, of which this gives the only possible explanation, for the reason that life and death, or production and destruction, must necessarily be referred to opposite spiritual causes, in order that any rational explanation of them should be given. As the soul is subjected to the operation of these opposite influences, one vital, producing growth, and the other destructive, producing decay, and as the production of all its forms and manifestations must be governed by the laws of diversity, partiality, and separation, the law of Circularity is demanded; because, under these finite governing laws, there can be no such thing as aggregation or indefinite multiplication, but only successive unfoldings and births, by which all the forms and functions of natural life are successively produced and destroyed, so that only a partial manifestation of the Soul can at any time be realized in the Natural; the successive unfolding of its forms constituting its development, and the successive births of its substance, by which it becomes elevated in its consciousness, constituting its growth. The Natural is not therefore a state of Being, but only a state of Becoming, in which nothing remains for a moment the same, and in which the Soul is not only in a state of continual change, but is also in a state of partial development, in which every thing is gained at the expense of something that is lost, so that Change becomes a permanent characteristic of Natural Life. These changes are regulated by the law of Circularity now being described; and, in illustrating this law, we shall show in what these changes consist, and the order in which they appear.

Besides this law of Change, however, which the destructive influence of finite law imposes upon Creation, there is a law of Permanence by which also it is governed. This is seen, first, in the fact that it is a medium for representation, in which the natural is representative of the spiritual, and the external of the internal, so that the forms of all things remain the same, however much the substance may have been changed; and it is seen, next, in the fact, that, in every change in the consciousness and in the condition of the soul, a permanent advance has been made towards the Spiritual. This gives to Creation a condition of permanence, and converts the whole Universe into a representative of absolute causes and of spiritual conditions and relationships, as we have already shown in our statement of the Laws of Correspondence. This law of representation is not so distinctly illustrated in the Caucasian race as it is in the imperfect races, for the reason that it is only in this race that a full development of those natural experiences can be realized which must be obtained by the individual before the spiritual can be presented to his consciousness; and growth and development are therefore in this race so rapid, that quite a material change is often perceived in the course of a single life, separate from those changes which the individual experiences in passing from infancy to old age: although, even in this race, this law of permanence operates in giving a comparative stability to the forms of truth, of good, and of use, but particularly in giving to each nation of this race a certain type of character which is permanent; much of the diversity that is here observed being occasioned by the departure of individuals from different points in the great circle of human development, and by that infinite diversity in the forms of the soul that is demanded by the laws of creation. In the imperfect races, however, which are more particularly representative races, every thing is permanently representative; and, as there is here no development, character remains stationary and uniform in the members of each race.

In describing the phenomena which are realized in the natural growth and development of the human constitution under the law of Circularity, several things are to be considered; namely, that there are three Atmospheres into which the soul successively comes, a Material, an Ethereal, and a Spiritual atmosphere, the last of which is either Heaven or Hell,—that there are three Bodies into which the soul successively comes, or rather in which it becomes conscious, a material, an ethereal, and a spiritual body (and by body we mean the whole organization through which the soul becomes conscious, and is manifested both mentally and corporeally),—that there are three Spheres of Consciousness, or kinds of Life, into which the soul successively comes, an external-natural, an internal-natural, and a spiritual consciousness,—and that these atmospheres, bodies, and spheres of consciousness have a certain adaptedness to each other in the corresponding spheres, but not out of them, so that only those phenomena which belong to an external sphere of consciousness are appropriate to this external atmosphere. It cannot therefore be supposed, that all the conditions of the consciousness which are here to be described, and which include the entire natural development of the individual in an internal as well as in an external sphere of consciousness, are to be witnessed in this atmosphere, except in a limited number of individuals; although, were there not here some manifestations belonging to internal-natural and even to spiritual life to constitute "the salt of the earth," the race would become brutalized, and, instead of progress, we should find nothing but decay; as the Scriptures would become buried in the letter, and thus totally obscured for ever, were there not portions which obviously represent the spiritual and furnish the direct teaching from which the doctrines of the Church are derived. In illustrating the law of Circularity, therefore, we shall first describe and illustrate the phenomena which belong to an external sphere of the natural consciousness, and which are therefore appropriate to this atmosphere; and then describe those which belong to an internal sphere of the natural consciousness, and are appropriate to an ethereal atmosphere, but are, to some extent, realized in this. In doing this, we shall confine ourselves to those manifestations of the white or Caucasian race, to which alone belongs development, and therefore a history, which are to be found in the history of the development of the Individual through the operation of the Sentimental Nature, — in the history of the State, — and in the history of Art, including Philosophy as its highest element. There is one illustration of this universal law, however, of a purely physical character, which has been furnished by recent geological discoveries from an examination of the rock formations anterior to the creation of man, and which is so remarkable that we cannot refrain from noticing it here: this is, that, in the succession of plants and of animals, a degradation of the old always preceded the introduction of a new species; showing that their development had been from within outwards, or from higher to lower forms. This is alluded to in the following manner by Dr. Bushnell in his work entitled "Nature and the Supernatural:" "Thus, in respect to misshapen monsters and deformed growths, it is a remarkable fact, that as the layers of Geology rise, and creatures are produced that stand higher in the scale of organic perfection, the number of deformities and retrograde shapes is multiplied. This fact has been strikingly exhibited by Hugh Miller in refutation of the development theory. It is also shown by Miller, that the fishes lost ground, or grew deformed in organization, as the human era drew nigh."

ILLUSTRATIONS OF THE LAW OF CIRCULARITY

IN THE DEVELOPMENT OF THE INDIVIDUAL THROUGH THE OPERATION OF

THE SENTIMENTAL NATURE,

UNDER THE DIRECTION OF

CATHOLICISM, PROTESTANTISM, UNITARIANISM,

AND

TRANSCENDENTALISM.

WE have already shown, in illustrating the law of Contrariety, that the Individual Consciousness is developed by the operation of the Sentimental Nature, through which the individual becomes subject to certain institutions, ideas, and forms of thought, which furnish the laws of the individual life, and which he unconsciously or consciously submits to according to the progress he has made in growth, which is the cause of his becoming internal and self-conscious, — that the supernatural forms which become realized and individualized in the supernatural sphere of human development through the constructive sentimental principles, and furnish those laws of faith and of practice to which the individual submits, are the Catholic and Protestant Churches upon the one hand, and Unitarianism and Transcendentalism upon the other, — that these Churches are the unconscious and the conscious representatives of "Spiritualism" and "Justice," which are the vital laws of the Sentimental Nature, and that Unitarianism and Transcendentalism are the unconscious and the conscious representatives of "Naturalism" and "Sympathy," which are the destructive laws of the Sentimental Nature, — and that the vital sentimental laws must be first, and the destructive laws last, in the order of realization and application in the development of the Individual Consciousness. As growth is from below upwards, however, it is not the internal and conscious, but the external and unconscious, element in the Church, and in its opposite, that first becomes realized; and thus Catholicism and Protestantism become realized and succeed each other as external and internal representations of the vital, and Unitarianism and Transcendentalism become realized and succeed each other as the external and internal representatives of the destructive, sentimental laws. In illustrating the law of Circularity, we therefore take our departure from the Catholic Church, or the Church of Rome, because this constitutes the body or most external form of the Christian Church, and is therefore necessarily commissioned to superintend the most external development of the individual consciousness through the operation of the Sentimental Nature in the universal birth of Water. That the Catholic is the most external natural form which constitutes the body of the Christian Church, may be known, because it is, like the Hebrew, a representative Church, in which ideas belonging to a supernatural order, and constituting the life of all productive natural forms, are brought down into the region of Sensation, and represented to the mind through physical symbolic forms, which are either images or ceremonial observances; and because she exercises a general supervision over all the manifestations of individual, of domestic, and of social life. We do not mean to say that the Catholic is the representative *principle* in the Church, because, in all spheres or departments, the internal principle, or the soul, is always the representative principle. The body is representative, because in it all internal things are symbolized in external or physical forms and functions; a fact that is particularly obvious in the constitution of the human body, both in its internal and in its external forms and functions. As it is not the body, however, but the soul, as it is not the physical but the mental constitution, that is the particular representative or image of God; so, in the Church, it is not the Body of the Church, which is the Catholic, but the Soul of the Church, which is the Protestant, that is the internal, and therefore the highest, representative of Christianity. While in the Catholic Church, therefore, the vital truths of Christianity, or the great truths of Salvation, are represented by physical symbols, which produce their effects in an unconscious and spontaneous manner; in the Protestant Church, these are represented by doctrines, or by forms of thought which are connected with states of the individual consciousness,— doctrines that are repudiated by the Catholic Church as being antagonistic to Christianity. We have seen that three separate periods in the development of the soul are recognized in the Scriptures, as births by blood, by water, and by spirit. Now, these are successive regenerations of the individual, and have reference to his development in the three spheres of consciousness into which he successively comes; these being natural, supernatural, and spiritual. The vital supernatural element in these natural and supernatural developments or regenerations, which are represented in the Scriptures as births of Blood and of Water, has been superintended by the Churches of Judaism and Christianity; the constitution of the first being contained in the Scriptures of the Old Testament, and that of the second in the Scriptures of the New Testament. As the birth of Blood is realized through the subjection of the Individual to the Universal from the most external and unconscious point of view, in which vital supernatural laws incarnated in external forms are established in a supernatural manner outside of the individual consciousness as the laws of the individual belief and of the individual life, the Jewish Church was a Theocracy, in which Church and State constituted one corporation; and all forms of truth and of good, and all forms of Art, as the most external representatives of these laws, even the pattern according to which the Tabernacle was constructed, were supposed to be communicated immediately from God. Now, although the Christian Church was established as a Supernatural Institution, in which vital supernatural laws were to be represented and connected with the individual consciousness by being incarnated in natural thought and self-conscious individual experiences, and this Church therefore necessarily commenced with the intuition of supernatural ideas corresponding with Christianity; as the Natural must always exist in a discordant dualistic condition; and as, in every sphere of personal experience, the Individual grows from below upwards, realizing in this growth, first an external and unconscious, and next an internal and self-conscious, order of experiences, — Christianity became represented through two opposite forms of Revelation, which are designated in the Scriptures the Gospels of Circumcision and Uncircumcision: and consequently, in its development, or in the realization of its permanent form, the Church necessarily became divided and antagonized in opposite Churches as the exponents of these opposite Gospels. The first, therefore, became developed as an external Church corresponding with the Jewish, and representing the theocratic condition of this Church as a Universal Power having jurisdiction over both sacred and secular things. This Church was therefore called Catholic or Universal, and was realized as the exponent of the Gospel of Circumcision, which was committed by the Lord to Peter, who is recognized as the founder of this Church; and was also realized as the superintendent of what is relatively the birth of Blood in this supernatural development of the human constitution, which is the most external condition of the consciousness, in which the Individual recognizes all individual, domestic, social, intellectual, moral, and religious forms from the most external point of view. The necessity for this individual subjection to the Church as the medium through which supernatural truth is represented in external symbolic forms is to be explained in the following manner: When the individual passed from a natural to a supernatural sphere of consciousness, through the recognition of supernatural ideas and of corresponding external forms representative of Christianity, however internal and self-conscious he might have been from a natural point of view, he entered into this new supernatural condition as a child; all his natural acquisitions, which were only obstructions to his supernatural education, were at once surrendered as "mammon of unrighteousness;" and he necessarily commenced his supernatural development from the point of external representation. This was necessary, because, in the natural, all consciousness is realized through the union of opposites, or of internal with corresponding external recognitions; Sensation being the ground of Perception, and Perception the ground of Thought: so that all knowledge of Being, of Life, or of Individual Condition and Relationships, must have its foundation in external individual experiences, and Truth must be lived before it can be conceived. From this it follows, that supernatural personal experiences must have been realized before supernatural thought could be conceived, as these must constitute the external material in the incarnation of supernatural ideas; and that these could not be realized until the individual had been regenerated from an external point of view (constituting his birth by blood), and unconscious, spontaneous, supernatural manifestations had been produced to constitute the external suggestive material in the realization of supernatural thought. This is one of the reasons why the Individual should grow from below upwards, and commence every sphere of his development in his most immature external form and condition, when no internal individual consciousness can be realized, and he must consequently be guided and governed in an external, and not in an internal, manner.

It is true, that, although the growth of the Individual is from below upwards, the development of his Mind is from within outwards, and therefore that impressions of supernatural ideas representative of Christianity were realized as an internal sentimental experience, constituting the supernatural seed of the Church; but, as nothing existed in thought or in individual experience corresponding with these, they necessarily became mixed up with natural or pagan philosophic forms, and interpreted from this pagan point of view. Even St. Augustine, the most prominent of all the fathers of the Catholic Church, commenced, so late as the fourth century, his labors in the service of Christianity from this pagan point of view; and it was not until he realized, in his own personal consciousness, experiences in which these supernatural impressions could be incarnated, that he really became a convert to Christianity, was able to free himself from the trammels of Platonism, and attain to the conception of genuine supernatural thought. "It thus became with him a fundamental idea, that divine things must be incorporated with the life and the affections, before we can be capable of an intellectual knowledge of them."* Being specially prepared for this purpose, he was able, through the realization of supernatural intuitions and personal experiences combined, to incarnate these ideas in internal and external religious symbolic forms; it being through supernatural means that an external Church was gradually formed to superintend the supernatural development of the human constitution from the most external point of view. We are not, however, to confound the experiences of those through whom this Church was constructed with those of the individuals who were to be brought under subjection to this Church for the purpose of supernatural regeneration. These individuals could not have been internally self-conscious, and therefore could not have been internally conceptive; first, because internal supernatural illumination is confined to those through whom the Church is to be constructed; and, next, because no organization had been prepared, by growth from below upwards, for the spontaneous production of supernatural phenomena; it being for this reason that centuries elapsed before even this most external Church could be fully developed. It was therefore necessary that incarnations of vital supernatural ideas should be presented to them from without, and presented to them not only externally, but supernaturally, in practical forms, or in combinations which are adapted to practical individual use. Patterns of all the relationships of the soul, both supernatural and natural, were therefore communicated through this most external Church, who must superintend the most external

---

* Neander's "History of the Church."

supernatural development of the Human Constitution; and these are preserved by her, through both record and tradition, and individuals are made subject to her, and become receptive from her of these external forms, that they may make application of what she teaches, as the laws of their belief and of their life.

The first office performed by this Church is the development of the Sentimental Nature in the most external sphere of its activity, when it is dependent for this activity upon emotional states, excited by the presentation of physical symbolic forms which represent the phenomena that are incidental to the realization of spiritual life. It is not, therefore, by teaching either theological dogmas, or theories of social relationships, which must necessarily be connected with an internal and self-conscious condition of the mind and of the will, in order that any effect should be produced by them, but by presenting physical symbols and ethical rules representative of spiritual truth and good, and by enjoining physical observances which are representative of spiritual use, that this Church operates in the external development of the Sentimental Nature, and produces a practical effect upon the life; so that vital supernatural laws are legitimately represented, and a substitute for legitimate moral manifestations is provided. The next office performed by the Church is the development of the intellectual and affectional powers of the mind from the most external point of view. That the mind is dependent upon this Church for its external intellectual development may be known from the fact, that Philosophy, in each sphere of its development, takes its departure from the most external Church, as we have clearly shown in our account of the history of Philosophy; and from the fact, that the Catholic Church originally superintended both the production and the use of every kind of intellectual construction. That it is also dependent upon this Church for its most external affectional development, may be known from the fact, that all individual, domestic, and social duties, as well as all religious and moral obligations, are established by her through external symbolism and dogmatical teaching. Christian society, in the most external sphere of its experience, must become receptive from this Church of all these external forms, and come under entire subjection to her in all secular as well as in all sacred things, in order that an external ground for the conscious production of all forms of truth and of good may be established in the Mind, and become consciously operative through the Will. Constituting, as she does, however, the body of the Church, she becomes destructive to the vital ideas which represent Christianity. This may be seen, because she is the exponent of the Gospel of Circumcision committed to Peter, which constitutes the natural and destructive side of the Gospel, and teaches the partial crucifixion of the natural from selfish motives, or the salvation of the soul by Works; and thus is destructive to the Gospel of Uncircumcision committed to Paul, which constitutes the supernatural and vital side of the Gospel, and teaches resurrection into the spiritual, and the justification of the soul from Faith: for, although this vital truth is unconsciously represented by the Catholic Church in symbols and ceremonial observances, it is contradicted in her dogmatical teaching. This Church may also be seen to be destructive, because she denies all internal or independent individual action, and would confine every one to an external reception of all things from her, by which all development of the mind, and all growth of the individual consciousness, would be prevented. Independent individual effort is the condition of all real knowledge, and thus of all mental development and of all individual growth. This may readily be seen, with regard to the realization of truth, because it is only as the laws which govern phenomena, and communicate to them all their vitality, are conceived by the mind, or realized in the consciousness, —which must, of course, be through independent individual effort,—that these phenomena can be understood, or made to be productive: and it may be seen with regard to the realization of good, because this cannot be regarded as a real individual manifestation so long as it is the result of external arbitrary direction separate from the individual desire, or so long as the conscience of the individual is supplied by the Church instead of his own consciousness; and thus no development of the moral nature can be realized, and no individual experience of good can be cultivated, except as he is allowed to indulge in the spontaneous manifestations of his own affectional and sentimental powers, guided by his own conceptions of the laws of moral obligation. But as this Church forbids all belief and all action, except under her direction, she would prevent all progress, both in theory and in practice, and thus all reality, both in knowledge and in the life; and, as she would exclude all independent action of the mind upon the subject of Christianity, she would prevent its actual realization, because it must come to us by inspiration from within, and the mind must pass through a long preparation of internal experiences, and the individual through a long series of personal experiments in his growth from below upwards, before he can be prepared for this, his highest experience.

The Church of Rome, however, only superintends the formation of the body of the Consciousness, or the birth of the soul by Blood, in a supernatural sphere, which is the most external form of its supernatural growth and development: for although this contains a recognition of forms representing all the relationships of natural and of spiritual life, and thus produces an external development of the moral and religious as well as the intellectual and affectional powers; and although an emotional experience is thus realized, far surpassing all subsequent experiences, because the emotions are powerful in proportion as the mental manifestations are external, — this constitutes a representative, and not a real, condition of the soul. The service performed by this Church is of the highest importance, because the forms thus secured must furnish a ground of personal manifestation which shall act as suggestive material in the conception of supernatural thought; but, after this ground has been fully prepared, the influence of this Church becomes destructive, and must therefore be thrown off, because it would keep the individual confined to an external, artificial, unconscious condition, and prevent the realization in him of an internal, real, and self-conscious state. After the individual has realized these external materials for development under the superintendence of this Church, and obtained an external direction of himself under the government of those laws of relationship which she has established, he commences a course of development from within outwards of the principles of his mind, and a growth from below upwards of the principles of his will, from a self-conscious, internal, instead of an apprehensive, external, point of view; by which individual conceptions of truth and of good are to be realized in the place of unconscious reception of these from the Catholic Church. Now, as the Sentimental Nature constitutes the supernatural region of the mind, from which are derived the laws that govern the individual life, it is the development of this nature from a self-conscious point of view, and the application of its laws in the development of the individual consciousness from the same point, that must succeed the dominion of the Catholic Church; and as this nature is founded in opposite, vital and destructive, laws, — those which are vital having been unconsciously but fully represented by the Catholic Church, — it follows that the conscious conception of these vital laws, and their application in the reconstruction of the individual life, must be first in the order of realization,—that an unconscious representation of these destructive laws must be next developed as the external principle which must always precede the internal in any sphere of production, and be applied in the reconstruction of the individual life,—and that a conscious conception of these destructive laws must be finally realized and applied in the reconstruction of the individual life. The development of the Sentimental Nature from a self-conscious point of view, as it has here been described, being distinctly presented to us in the phenomena of Protestantism, Unitarianism, and Transcendentalism, which are seen to have succeeded each other in the order here named, it remains for us to show that each one of these has been developed from within outwards; and, as religious and moral elements are combined in the realization of all these systems,—and as these are related as internal and external, as may be seen by reference to our classification of the sentimental principles of the mind,—it is only necessary for us to show that each of these commenced with a religious, and ended with a moral development; or that Truth predominated at its commencement, and Good at its close. What, then, does the history of these movements disclose to us with regard to this fact? We find, that, in the Protestant Church, it was not good, but truth, not moral but religious sentiment, that was first developed; and that its progress has been a descent from ideas belonging to a supernatural into those belonging to a natural order, as the history of this Church shows in the most unequivocal manner: for it shows that she commenced with the entire separation of moral good from religious truth, as naturalistic and destructive, and by the establishment of the doctrine of Salvation by Faith as the foundation of Christian Theology; and that she has ended by the recognition of Morality as the most important element in the Christian life. The repudiation of good by this Church, by which it was regarded as a natural phenomenon, that was, in the forcible language of Luther, to be separated from Christianity "as far as the heavens are from the earth, and even farther if possible," and which, although necessary for the sake of social order, "might be the means of precipitating us into the very abyss of Hell," was one of the most remarkable phenomena that attended the establishment of this Church, and would alone be sufficient to decide this question; because the separating and antagonizing religion and morality, or Faith and Works, in this extreme manner, show most conclusively the purely internal and strictly religious position which she then occupied. From this point, the Protestant Church has gradually descended into the region of natural experience, both with regard to truth and to good: its estimation of the importance of religious doctrines, and its belief in them as revealing the only means of Salvation, have steadily declined, and given place to a recognition of the importance of moral manifestations, and a belief in them as the only evidence of Grace and of acceptance with God; and even these doctrines have been gradually perverted by naturalistic interpretations, so that little vitality remains in the theology of the Church; while most of those who minister in her churches, and are the most popular with the people, are heretics in religion, and are even fanatical with regard to the destructive social and moral theories of the day; showing that the people, as well as the pastors, have "departed from the faith once delivered to the saints," and have passed from a representative spiritual to a natural order of thought and of experience, — and that the internal life which vitalized these representative forms has departed, and been succeeded by an open scepticism or by a lifeless formalism. It may be seen, however, that the law of growth is also illustrated in these manifestations; and that in the place of a belief in the legitimate doctrines of the Church, and a willingness to comply with its ascetical requisitions, individuals obtain a more internal and self-conscious life, greater breadth, simplicity, and sincerity of character, and more universal and philanthropic views; by which they become elevated in substance, as they become degraded in form.

Unitarianism was a production simultaneous with Protestantism, and, like that, originated in an internal excitement of the Sentimental Nature, which, for reasons already explained, became consciously active, in the latter from a vital, and in the former from a destructive, point. As these were realized through self-conscious experiences, an internal ground for belief was established as a substitute for the external ground of authority established by the Catholic Church; and the Bible was established as a divinely inspired external rule of faith and of practice that was calculated to act as a suggestive principle in the realization of these internal individual conceptions; so that each individual was constituted an interpreter of this divine record. This was, therefore, interpreted unconsciously from opposite points of view; by the Protestant, from the point of "Spiritualism" in the religious, and of "Justice" in the moral, department of the mind, these being the vital laws in these departments: and by the

Unitarian, from the point of "Naturalism" in the religious, and of "Sympathy" in the moral, these being the destructive laws in these departments. As the superintendent of a vital internal development of the Sentimental Nature, Protestantism became the exponent of Religious Truth and of a Supernatural order of thought; while, as the superintendent of a destructive external development of this nature, Unitarianism became the exponent of Moral Truth and of a Natural order of thought based upon appearances. In its origin, however, which we take as the point of departure in its development from within outwards, Unitarianism contained an element of religious truth which claimed to belong to a true spiritual order of thought; although this, by being realized through the interpretation of the Scriptures from the point of "Naturalism," was violently antagonized to, and destructive of, the doctrines of Protestantism, and, indeed, contained perversions of these doctrines, by which all vitality was destroyed in the representations of spiritual life there contained. From the fact that Unitarianism was instituted as the exponent of Moral Truth, and as a representative of Naturalism, the degradation that it has experienced, in its development from within outwards, is not, of course, to be compared with that in the Protestant Church, where the change is from a supernatural to a natural order, which is opposite: but those who are familiar with the history of Unitarianism will readily acknowledge, that, at its commencement, it was in its form comparatively "Orthodox" in religion, and that from this point it has gradually receded, until even its form has become exclusively moral and purely naturalistic, so that Christianity, according to its highest conception, is simply "being good and doing good;" and a regard for the Scriptures, as divinely inspired, has degenerated into a belief that it is the production of barbarous periods of civilization, is human in character, poetical in form, partly spurious and partly fictitious, and is now valuable only for the moral teaching which it contains; so that the change of form is as great as could be expected where so little change was possible. The change that has been produced in Unitarianism from growth is more remarkable than that produced by its development. As it becomes internal, the influence of the destructive law of "Sympathy," of which it is the particular representative and exponent, becomes more and more apparent; so that, from being externally moral, and therefore conservative, it becomes internally moral, and therefore fanatical, through naturalistic conceptions of Good corresponding with personal individual want, by which the most extravagant notions of personal liberty are set up, which are even more destructive than the internal conceptions of Transcendentalism, for the reason that the experiences of Unitarianism are the most external and affectional or feminine that are ever realized by the soul, and it is therefore the most demonstrative and externally destructive. Even those who are now leaving the Protestant Church do not come into a primitive Unitarian condition, but into this more internal and fanatical phase of it: so that the strange and somewhat confusing phenomenon is now presented to us, of Protestantism, Unitarianism, and Transcendentalism joining in one common crusade against all the legitimate ideas which belong to a supernatural order of thought, and all the productive institutions which have been founded upon them; demanding the destruction of Ecclesiasticism, which is stigmatized as "the despotism of Babylon," and universal individual freedom for all the nations and races of mankind.

As a system of Belief, Transcendentalism is realized by the incarnation, in conscious internal conceptions, of intuitions from the destructive laws of the Reason, which are the inversions of those ideas relating to universal causes, or to the nature of Being and of Existence, which are realized in its legitimate natural development; by internal conceptions of the destructive laws of the Sentimental Nature, which demand universal individual self-assertion and self-gratification; and by the application of these laws in producing theories of belief and of life. Its religious element was conceived and applied in realizing conceptions of God, of the Soul, and their relations, by Jacob Böhme, a German theosophist, or mystic, of the sixteenth century. Its moral element was specifically developed, a century later, by Emanuel Swedenborg, a German naturalist, who, after devoting the greater part of his life to the investigation of physical substance, in the hope of discovering in this way the nature of the Soul, became a somnambulist, or clairvoyant, as it is now called, and in this externally unconscious condition became receptive of supernatural impressions, mostly of an external character, in the form of visions; in which he supposed himself to receive immediate communications, through glorified spirits, of divine truths, which he systematized and proclaimed as "The New Christian Religion." These works of Böhme and Swedenborg constitute the Transcendental Scriptures, or Sacred Books, and are freely and variously interpreted and received by individuals through the unconscious operation of the same destructive powers of the mind through which they became realized. From the extremely internal and abstract character of the religious system of Böhme, and from the fact, that, in the inversion of Truth by him, opposite conditions of being are so stated that only an apparent opposition exists between them, and these are again so confounded that it is difficult to separate them, they have been extremely difficult to investigate, and consequently slow in gaining attention. The writings of Swedenborg, although, on the contrary, extremely external and practical, are so completely dogmatic and contradictory, and are so pervaded by irrationality, that they are almost as difficult to comprehend as those of Böhme, and the interpretations of them are therefore of the most extreme and diversified character; but that he is regarded by the Transcendentalists as, before all others, the great moral teacher, is shown in the following extract from Mr. Emerson's lecture on Swedenborg: "The moral insight of Swedenborg, the correction of popular errors, the annunciation of ethical laws, take him out of comparison with any other modern writer, and entitle him to a place vacant for some ages among the lawgivers of mankind. Plato is a gownsman: his garment, though purple and almost sky-woven, is an academic robe, and hinders action with its voluminous folds. But this mystic is awful to Cæsar. Lycurgus himself would bow." As Transcendentalism does not correspond with this, but with another atmosphere, it cannot here be carried out into all its consequences; so that all the changes which it is calculated to produce in the theories of individuals, and in the condition of society, cannot here be known, except as we can anticipate the consequences of such causes. The fact of development from within outwards, however, is here more striking than in the phenomena of Unitarianism, for the reason that it has a positive religious development, which that has not; and its religious and moral developments are therefore seen to succeed each other in the most unmistakable manner in the writings of its founders; while its growth from below upwards may be seen in the more internal and destructive character of its manifestations through the individuals who are affected by it. The peaceful, beneficent, and conservative position of Swedenborg presents a marked contrast to the palpably fanatical and destructive manifestations which are now being realized in this country from the increased activity of the destructive sentimental laws, and which, if not stayed by Him who hath "measured the waters in the hollow of his hand,"

and saith, "Hitherto shalt thou come, but no further, and here shall thy proud waves be stayed," must end in its destruction. We have now shown that the three systems of belief which have been realized through the development of the Sentimental Nature from a self-conscious, comprehensible point of view, have been developed from within outwards, and have, at the same time, obtained a growth from below upwards, according to the universal law of Succession that has here been stated; and that in each one has been realized a form destructive to Christianity.*

* Appendix IV.

ILLUSTRATIONS OF THE LAW OF CIRCULARITY

IN THE

HISTORY OF THE STATE,

AND THE

MANIFESTATIONS OF THE SOCIAL INSTINCT.

THE two manifesting principles in the State, which stand in the relation of internal and external, are Democracy and Aristocracy; these being, as we have already seen, Internalism and Externalism, or Universalism and Individualism, in social life: the first, the representative and exponent of Social Right; and the second, of Individual Right, which we have shown to be the right of the strongest, and to identify might and right. As we have already, in our analysis of Society, shown these principles to be antagonistic, and related as vital and destructive; and as we have also shown that Democracy is in harmony both with a vital socialistic law, and with the Church, as the vital element in Society,—it only remains for us to show that something like a true social condition, in which Democracy, as the exponent of this vital law, was a governing principle, has at some time existed; in which the individual was not considered or recognized, except as a member of the State; and in which the sacrifice of individual for the sake of the general good was not a rare but an ordinary occurrence among the people, as well as a social demand provided for by the laws. We say, it only remains for us to show that such a state has actually existed, and has been succeeded by a state of civilization, in which — instead of an all-pervading sentiment of patriotism, a desire for public instead of private good, and the recognition of social instead of individual right as the animating principle to individual activity — we find a passion for individual and family aggrandizement, and a jealous guardianship of individual rights. What, then, is the information which history communicates upon this subject?

Such a disposition and such customs as we have now described as belonging to a true social condition, we find to have existed among the Spartans, and subsequently among the Romans; and such laws we find to have been instituted, and most cordially responded to by the members of the Spartan and Roman Commonwealths, as any one may learn by referring to Plutarch, who is a reliable and recognized authority. Of the Spartans, he says, "Like bees, they acted with one impulse for the public good, and always assembled about their prince. They were inflamed with a thirst for honor, an enthusiasm bordering upon insanity, and had not a wish but for their country." It will be seen, even from this short extract, that these social results were not the production of arbitrary laws, enacted contrary to the will of the people, as some, who cannot conceive of such, or of any true social condition, have been led to suppose; but were produced from the popular heart, of which these laws were only the exponent. The vital social ideas embodied in these laws were spontaneously recognized by the masses, and not only willingly submitted to, but demanded as the most pressing want of the individual, because a vital social principle must at this time have constituted the governing affectional law of the individual in his development from within outwards. It is true, that, as the growth of the individual is from below upwards, the social principle must be manifested at the commencement of society in the rudest possible manner, although this rude manifestation is the highest social form that is possible in a natural sphere of consciousness. We are not, therefore, to expect to find in the history of these early Commonwealths the highest results of social combination, but only the most external representation of the highest social form.

The form of society in these ancient Commonwealths was Aristocratic; and this was necessary, because, as we have already shown, the aristocratic principle must furnish the form through which the democratic principle becomes manifested, and this form is therefore demanded by it: but the laws by which they were governed may be seen to be democratic in their character, because they provided for the good of the State, or of the whole people, and made the good of every individual subordinate to this, as the only means by which the greatest good of all could be obtained. The necessity for the manifestation of democracy through an aristocratic form, as well as the fact of opposition between the form and the substance, may be well illustrated by reference to the two governments of Sparta and of Athens. The form of the first was aristocratic, while the form of the second was democratic; and they who look only upon the surface suppose this to have been really the relationship between them. That the opposite of this was the real fact, however, may very easily be shown, because the Spartan Commonwealth commenced by an equal division of all property, and the enactment of laws which should prevent its excessive accumulation by individuals; while the Athenian Commonwealth, on the contrary, commenced by a classification of the people upon the basis of property, and the enactment of laws which encouraged its accumulation by individuals, while power and influence were monopolized by the wealthy and the learned; and, although this is only one fact among many others of a similar character, this alone would be sufficient to determine the question, and prove that the first was a democratic, and the second an aristocratic, institution.

We may see these same facts illustrated with equal force by reference to the character and institutions of the French people. Although this is confessedly the most democratic people in the world, being constituted as a representative of the democratic principle, they have always lived under a highly despotic form; and even now, although urged on by a large intellectual and fanatical class, who have become desirous of realizing association under a popular or democratic form, are still inclined to prefer the absolute rule of some one man who shall faithfully represent the mass of the people, or personify the public will.* We see, then, that the question of Democracy is not to be decided by the form of a government, but by the spirit of its Laws. Democracy being the law of universality, as applied to social life,—by which the social elements become individualized, and all partial objects are subordinated, and made to minister to the one grand object, which is the greatest good of the community,—that government is of course the most democratic which provides the most effectually for this result, whatever the form may be. Tried by this rule, which cannot be objected to, whatever objections may be made to the application of abstract principles, we shall see that the early Commonwealths to which we have referred are as perfect illustrations of a true social condition, in which the democratic principle becomes the ruling law, as it is possible to

---

* This was written at the time of the revolution of 1848. Soon after that, the Empire was happily re-established under the rule of Napoleon III.

realize in the external natural condition to which the race is confined in this atmosphere, where the highest principles must be manifested in combination with the lowest sphere of life.

Having shown that a true social condition in all its essential characteristics has really existed in the past, our position is established; for so far has the Instinct of Society deteriorated, and so far has society at the present day been removed from such a condition, that it is difficult to conceive that it has ever existed, the possibility of its realization is scouted as the wildest of dreams, and its existence regarded as the greatest of calamities. That a state of socialism has been succeeded by a state of civilization, in which the protection of individual rights is the principal object of legislation, and is considered to be the principal object of social compact, will not probably be disputed in this age of copy-rights and letters-patent, or in a country where gold, as well as the golden calf, is so much worshipped. By this protection of individual right, and this growth of individualism, might and right become gradually identified; a concentration of learning, of wealth, and of power, on the one hand, and of ignorance, poverty, and imbecility, upon the other, ensues; and from these two extremes of social condition results that amount of degradation, in both extremes, which leads to decomposition, or social death; a result that is necessary, both for a return to first principles, or to a primitive order of things, and for ascension into a higher sphere of social consciousness, both of which must be provided for in this atmosphere.

This periodical revolution of society in this atmosphere has not only been represented in the Scriptures, but has also been recognized as an historical phenomenon; and philosophers have attempted to construct a science of history simply by generalizing the historical facts which have been observed always to succeed each other; although no satisfactory explanation of these facts could, of course, be obtained in this way, because neither the causes which produce nor the laws which govern them could be discovered. Professor Hedge, alluding, in a lecture before the Lowell Institute, to the theory of Vico upon this subject, says, according to a report of this lecture for the press, " From an examination of the languages, laws, and religions of different peoples, and a survey of the courses of events among the different nations of the earth, Vico arrived at these conclusions: 1st, That human society is based upon three fundamental conditions, — worship, or belief in Providence; marriage, or restraint of the passions; and sepulchral rites, or belief in immortality. 2d, That society has three great periods,—the theocratic, the heroic, and the civilized. 3d, That the civil and political life of nations, so long as they preserve their independence, assumes successively four consecutive forms of government. The theocratic age produces domestic patriotism; the heroic age produces aristocracy, limiting the abuse of power; then comes democracy, or popular government, founded in the idea of natural equality; and, lastly, monarchy, or imperial rule, establishes itself upon the ruins of democracy. 4th, When a nation or society has passed through these stages, and is irreclaimed by the revolutions it has experienced, it still continues to decline and corrupt, and passes at last into a second state of barbarism. Faith expires, religion languishes, men grow brutal, cities decay, society lies supine, until regenerated by some providential impulse from within. Then the cycle of history begins anew, and society repeats with new aspects its appointed trust."

Although this is a confused and imperfect account, the facts to which it alludes will be found to illustrate and confirm the laws of growth and development demanded by our science, and may be stated in the following manner: In its development, Society realizes three great periods, and appears successively in three forms; the first being a Theocratic, the second an Aristocratic or heroic, and the third a Democratic or popular form. The theocratic form of society is that in which the Church and the State constitute one corporation, under the rule of the Church; and a supreme devotion to the State governs all individuals in the subjection of individual to social right, or the good of the individual to that of the whole people. The aristocratic form of society is that in which the State becomes separated from the Church, under the rule of a privileged hereditary class, presided over by one of their number as King, or under the rule of the King and the Nobles, upon the ground of arbitrary individual rule; and a supreme devotion to the Family, instead of the State, governs the manifestations of individuals. The democratic form of society is that in which the rulers of the State are elected by the people, who in this way attempt to take the government into their own hands; the results of which are a chaotic condition of the State, or of the political institutions of society, which consequently becomes disorganized or decomposed, and a gradual degradation of individual condition tending to a state of barbarism.

This corresponds better with the description of Vico's theory by M. Cousin, which is as follows: "According to Vico, the existence of a people forms a circle, every part of which he has determined with precision. In every people there are always, and there are necessarily, three degrees, three epochs,—the first, the epoch of development, improperly called barbarism, in which religion governs; in which the actors and the legislators, thus to speak, are Gods,—that is, Priests: it is the divine age of each people. The second is the substitution of the heroic principle for the theological principle: the divine is still there, but there is also something human; and the hero is, thus to speak, in history, as in the first mythology, the medium between heaven and earth. Finally, in the third age, man proceeds from the hero, as the hero proceeds from the God, and civil society arrives at its independent form. That done, man, after being completely developed, wastes away; the nation ends; a new nation commences with the same nature, and runs through the same circle."

We will now describe the external causes by which, and the particular manner in which, these social effects are produced, and the several states of Society are made to succeed each other in the order and manner which have here been described. We have already shown that the intellectual and affectional principles of human nature, which are individualized as Understanding and Instinct, constitute the Body of the Mind, where all ideas and laws must be incarnated in order that they should become productive; and where the individual becomes specifically manifested through intellectual and affectional forms, which are relatively internal and external, and universal and individual. We may therefore see that the instinctive or affectional principles of the mind must furnish the immediate individual motive powers in all forms of external manifestation; and so generally has this function of the affectional nature been recognized, that it is common to regard the Affection as synonymous with the Will. We have also shown that this affectional department of the mind is divided into three regions, related as spirit, soul, and body; the first being appropriated to the spontaneous realization of Social, the second of Domestic, and the third of Individual relationships and duties; these being related as vital, as representative, and as destructive, with regard to the forms and uses of Society. Now, as, according to the laws of Succession, of which we are now furnishing the illustrations, the mind becomes developed from within outwards, and therefore commences in the highest and ends in the lowest regions of the consciousness, in each of its most general divisions, it follows that the region of Affection which is socially productive must be the first; that which is socially representative, the second; and that which is socially destructive, the last in the order of development and manifestation: and that the three social periods which have been recognized by the philosophers, and here described, must be produced by this development of the mind from within outwards; these three regions of Affection furnishing the most external motive power in their production. We will therefore give a general description of the phenomena which naturally result from the successive development of these three regions, and their manifestation as ruling powers in the individual life from an external point of view.

Under the operation of the Social Instincts, which are first in the order of development, the State becomes constituted in its Theocratic form, and the individual not only becomes merged in the State, not having, and not desiring to have, any thing incompatible with the good of the whole community, but is also able to apprehend, when stated, all that belongs to a true social order, and is conducive to social right and to social prosperity in the greatest good of the whole people. He therefore demands that concentration shall be prevented, and diffusion encouraged, so that extremes of social condition may be avoided; and thus Property, instead of being worshipped as the greatest good, is distrusted as the greatest evil. Obstructions to its accumulation are therefore devised, and the greatest simplicity of life is encouraged. Individuals pull down their houses when thought to be too costly or luxurious, — readily sacrifice their lives when required for the public good, — and hold all things as trusts, to be surrendered either temporarily or entirely when any benefit to the State can be made to accrue thereby. As we have before said, this is not an imaginary condition of society, but one of which we have the most authentic historical records; and although becoming realized, as our science demands that it should, in a comparatively barbarous period of human development, it presents the highest form of the State that we know, because it illustrates more perfectly than any other period the true principles of social combination, and represents that spiritual state or kingdom in which Priest and King are united " after the order of Melchisedek." It will therefore be seen that this is the true democratic period; for though the form of the State is aristocratic, and the concentration of power in its head is the most extreme, the laws and the government are more truly socialistic and democratic than at any subsequent period. We have already alluded to this opposition between the form and the substance, and shown that, although the democratic principle is the life of the State, the democratic form is destructive to this life; and that, when the form of democracy becomes the most completely developed, the aristocratic principle becomes the ruling power. This antagonism between the form and the substance is demanded by the law of Contrariety, which governs all natural production; by the operation of which, growth and development, and thus substance and form, become divided and antagonized.

As the Social Instincts decline, the Domestic, which constitute the region below them, become developed and manifested as the ruling affectional powers. Under the operation of these, the State becomes divorced from the Church, and constituted in its aristocratic or heroic form. This includes the assertion of the Individual in opposition to the Universal from a social point of view; by which individual right is set up in opposition to social right, individual power is set up in opposition to the greatest good of the whole people, and the arbitrary rule of the strongest is not only established, but is perpetuated in the family as an hereditary right. As a desire for individual subjection, and the sexual instinct, are included in this department of the affectional nature, many of the prominent manifestations of this period may be traced to these sources. Hence the origin of chivalry, — the elevation of, and the increased devotion to, the female, — and hence the troubadour, or warrior minstrel, who combined the combative, the amorous, the poetic, and the musical qualities, which become developed simultaneously at this period; for it will be seen, by referring to our analysis of the mind, that the poetic and the musical departments of the Understanding are in a region corresponding with the domestic region of the Instinct. As the female element in the personifying principles, from which are the love of property and the love of ruling others, now becomes developed from a self-conscious point of view, these will be found to be leading characteristics in the aristocratic manifestations of this period, producing the concentration of wealth and of power in the most aristocratic families, by which they become permanent institutions, and the ruling powers, of the land. The individual power that is brought into action by this transition from an internal masculine to an external feminine and consequently productive state, with all its accompanying incidents of glory, of luxury, of splendor, and of power, is imposing in the extreme, and would lead the superficial mind to suppose that this was really a higher form of society than the former. But the great inequalities of condition which grow out of it, the prevalence of might over right, the oppression of the lower by the higher classes, and the administration of the government for the glory and aggrandizement of the privileged few, while the real wants of the people are neglected, show most distinctly that a principle has been introduced which is destructive to the life of the State.

As the Domestic Instincts decline, the Individual, which constitute the lowest region, become developed and manifested as the ruling affectional powers. Under the operation of these, the State becomes constituted in its democratic or popular form, the object of which is to obtain a government of the people by the people, or self-government from a universal point of view. In this form of government, all hereditary power, and even a long continuance of power in any individual, is prohibited, — all distinctions of rank, and all exclusive privileges, are ignored as aristocratic, unequal, and oppressive, — all political honors, emoluments, and advantages, of every kind, are opened to all who will compete for them, — and education is provided for all, at the public expense; so that merit is ostensibly the only passport to station, to influence, and to power in the State, and every thing seems to be placed upon a footing of the most complete equality. This is certainly a perfect form of Democracy; and did we not know that the form and the substance are necessarily antagonized, and that things are therefore the opposite of what they seem, it would be difficult to credit the fact that this form is the cover and producer of more aristocracy than any that has preceded it, and must lead to the complete destruction of the State. Such, however, is the result demanded by our science; and such seems to be the fact, according to the observations and decisions of the philosophers; and, if the causes which lead to the adoption of this form have here been correctly stated, such a result is the only one to be expected.

Many obvious causes may be mentioned which render a just government of the people by the people impossible; a government that is never demanded where the people are truly democratic, or have been made completely one with the State by the vital operation of the social instinct. As democracy demands the greatest good of all who constitute the State, it must demand, as the condition of realizing this greatest good, the restraint of individual liberty, or the subjection of the individual to the State;

that is, to laws which have been constructed upon the principle of universality for the greatest diffusion of social advantages; because this is the condition of liberty to the whole people, or the realization by them of social right. This subjection of the individual is demanded, because the want of the people is not harmonious, but diversified and discordant, and a great disparity exists between individuals with regard to the natural gifts which are the sources of their power; and because the strongest and most productive individuals are the most aristocratic, and therefore the most destructive from a social point of view. A power above the people that is completely separated from all private influence and motive must therefore be exercised to secure to the whole people the greatest good that is possible for them, by providing opportunities for the exercise of individual ability, and for the improvement, and even amusement, of the masses, which otherwise could be enjoyed only by the more fortunate or more productive individuals; and this power must especially be exercised in protecting the ungifted majority against the power exercised by the gifted minority, the tendency of which is always to monopolize, or concentrate in itself, the elements of learning, wealth, and power. It therefore becomes necessary that laws calculated for the good of the State, or of the whole people, should originate in a source remote from the people; because, not being affected by private interests, it will be more likely to act for the public good. Legislation is not therefore democratic in proportion as it originates in the popular branch of a government, but the reverse, because this is the most likely to be affected by these interests; first, because it is the legitimate channel through which the most external, and therefore the most destructive, aristocratic influence operates in securing, through special legislation, individual advantages inconsistent with the public good; and, next, because these "representatives of the people" are the most likely to sell the interests of the people, or to act in some other way equally destructive to the interests of the State. Here do congregate the political demagogues, who, although claiming to be democratic, and clamorous for the rights of the people, are the most external and destructive portion of the aristocratic class, and the most mischievous portion of the community. It is also through this branch of the government that radicalism, or the spirit of unreason in the people, is sure to operate in producing the destruction of that which is established and is therefore most likely to be conducive to the public good, because the tendency of popular legislation is always to deteriorate the existing law. It is therefore that checks upon this power were instituted in this country, both in the smaller and more conservative branch of the government, and in the executive veto; a power that has been pertinaciously defended, and preserved inviolate, by the real democracy of the country.

The destructive tendency of popular legislation may thus be accounted for. Upon the general ground that democracy is internalism and universalism, and aristocracy is externalism and individualism, in social life, democrats, although they may understand the true principles of government, and therefore may be good statesmen, are not good politicians; because they are not gifted with that power of external direction, or with that instinctive knowledge of character, and that feminine tact in the government of others, which are necessary to the conducting of political affairs: and it is also upon this ground that they do not desire political power and rule, although they may be willing to exercise it for the public good at the sacrifice of private inclination. This necessarily throws the active duties of political management into the hands of the aristocratic portion of their own party, or into the hands of their opponents, which is still worse. These, being fluent, specious, abounding in the knowledge of forms and precedents, and of the statistics of political life, quick in taking advantage of circumstances, and anxious for personal power and social elevation, readily succeed in getting themselves appointed to offices of political trust and influence; so that, aside from certain leading measures to which parties are particularly pledged, the character of legislation is very nearly the same under the rule of either party. In the more internal and socialistic periods, this is well understood; and the evils arising in the exercise of power by this class are avoided by seeking out rulers from among those who are disconnected from political life, and who have no desire to rule. But, as the mind grows external in its modes of thought, the people are deceived by appearances, — mistake the form for the substance, which is opposite to it, — and confer power either upon men of fancy who are practically imbecile and actively destructive, or upon those who desire to possess power over others, and are therefore sure to abuse it.

These general facts would not be sufficient to produce the effects which we are now considering, without being combined with the changes in the mental constitution that we have here described. Even these are only the most external and immediate cause of these phenomena, being only the most external of those changes which take place in the development of the mind from within outwards. These include the change from an unconscious manifestation of the vital laws of the mind to a conscious manifestation of its destructive laws; and a change in the personifying principles, by which the individual first comes unconsciously under the destructive laws of the sentimental nature, and finally conceives and appropriates them as the ruling laws of the individual thought and life, in the manner already described. Through the operation of the causes which have here been enumerated, a radical form of democracy is produced, which is in reality a form of Individualism, and the very essence of Aristocracy deprived of all the corrective influences which make it a practical and efficient social power. Aristocracy now appears divested of all reverence for superiors, — of all regard for truth and justice, — of all the salutary influences which flow from religion, — and of all that appreciation of order which is obtained by the subjection of the lower to the higher, and must accompany any true social organization; and, in consequence of this, each individual claims to understand the wants of the State, and demands an administration of the laws, and such changes in the laws, as shall accord with his particular conception of social right. Selfishness now appears in its most destructive form, because it takes the form of personal liberty, instead of personal subjection, and demands gratification for the individual from a universal point of view, which is the destruction of all social order; while, as a decreasing respect for truth and for justice is combined with an increasing demand for individual good, and a consequent thirst for gold, by which this good is to be obtained, the individual becomes more and more regardless of the means by which he acquires wealth. Justice is sold in the halls of legislation, and can rarely be obtained without the payment of an equivalent, while injustice may be purchased to any extent; so that legislation is, for the most part, exercised for the benefit of the rich, the unscrupulous, the designing, and the fanatical. Truth having passed into neglect, and fiction having taken its place, the most palpable falsehoods are asserted, and the grossest inconsistencies are manifested, even by public men, with the most unblushing effrontery. "Sympathy" having taken the place of "Justice," as the ruling law in all moral manifestations, the principle of Duty, under its operation, becomes fanatical and mischievous; and, while the individual is not himself willing to make sacrifices, he makes war upon all who will not sacrifice under his direction. He thus becomes unjust and cruel, under the pretence of being humane; and under the excitement of fictitious woe, and of imaginary evil, causes the greatest of evils, and sufferings which are the most real.

The contrast between this false appearance of democracy and that which is genuine may readily be seen, because it sets up the individual in the place of, and in opposition to, the State, and would concentrate that which should be diffused through the whole people. Instead of being willing to sacrifice himself for the State, the individual would sacrifice the State, because it does not conform to his opinion, or harmonize with his morbid, fanatical feeling. Instead of the simplicity of life which always characterizes a really democratic condition of society, we have the most ruinous luxury, sensuousness, and sensuality; and instead of a distrust of wealth, and the institution of checks to its concentration, and of facilities for its diffusion, the acquisition of wealth becomes the great object of life, and all possible facilities for individual accumulation by traffic and monopoly are demanded, and obtained by the expansion of credit, the adulteration of the currency, exclusive privileges, and other like expedients. Consumers are multiplied, and producers are diminished, by the excessive competition that is in this way created in all kinds of business which promise the speedy accumulation of wealth; and this leads to all kinds of fraud, and to the adulteration of all the necessaries as well as all the luxuries of life.

These are some of the social evils that are produced by the changes in the manifestations of the human constitution, by its development from within outwards, which have been here described. The description is, of course, somewhat extreme, because we have been obliged to describe the manifestations of the most external and destructive classes, without making allowance for that personal elevation which results from the growth of the individual from below upwards, but which is not sufficient to prevent these destructive results. It is a necessary experience, and an important period in the development of the soul, because the utmost limit of individual capacity in the masses is brought into activity, the most external forms of human experience are secured, and the evils of Individualism are exposed. But it is not possible that the great diversity of personal want, which now springs up in the masses and struggles for gratification, can end except in disappointment, because, where all would become rich, the result must be poverty to all; and where all would govern, and none are willing to obey, the State must come to an end. This descent from a social into an individual region of experience may be seen to be necessary, first, upon the ground that the mind must become developed from within outwards, and, next, upon the ground that the destructive side of the human constitution must be developed and manifested from an external point of view, in order that its quality may be made to appear, and that the tree may be known by its fruits; for it is evident, that, so long as the individual is conscious and becomes manifested through the legitimate forms of the mind, this destructive manifestation cannot take place, and that full natural development of the individual, which is necessary as a preparation for his birth into the Spiritual, cannot be realized. In order that a complete natural development of the human consciousness may be obtained, it is necessary that the Personal Principle should be asserted in opposition to the Universal, and should become incarnated and manifested as the "Man of Sin, who opposeth and exalteth himself above all that is called God, or that is worshipped; so that he, as God, sitteth in the temple of God, showing himself that he is God." In realizing this incarnation, however, all the legitimate institutions of Society, which are founded in the supremacy of the Universal, must be sacrificed, and a return to Chaos from a social point of view must result. Although this seems like a simple retrogression, it is in fact, with regard to the individual, an advance, because it secures to him experiences which are indispensable as a preparation for the realization by him of a spiritual consciousness. This destruction of the State is perfectly analogous to the destruction of the Church, and the same reason exists for both; it being only the natural representative form that is destroyed, and this is done that the spiritual reality may finally be reached and realized.

ILLUSTRATIONS OF THE LAW OF CIRCULARITY

IN THE

HISTORY OF ART.

It is perhaps difficult to recognize the fact, that the wonderful creations of Art, which have come down to us so replete with material perfection, and so truly representative of spiritual life, are to be classed with the religions, the philosophies, and the societies of the ancient times, and are finally to be replaced by productions which are real and spiritual; and it is more difficult to do this, for the reason that Art, in the natural, is to a great extent representative of things which cannot be conceived by the mind in the form of thought, and must therefore be realized in an unconscious and spontaneous manner. Even Art, however, is subject to the universal law of natural development from within outwards; and the internal correspondences, the vital supernatural symbolism, and the unity of design so truly artistic, which were realized by it at its commencement, must be succeeded by the discordant diversities, the crude experiments, and the external imperfections, of a simply natural experience, which includes a worship of Nature, and a literal representation of her phenomena; and finally, this natural experience must be succeeded by a false or inverted supernatural symbolism, which, though externally more perfect and internally more ideal, is representative of spiritual death. This development is not, however, simply destructive, because this degradation is accompanied by an elevation, arising in a more internal and self-conscious life, which compensates, in some measure, for its loss of character; for although a great degradation in the form of Art must be acknowledged, extending to the Sublime, to Beauty, and to the Beautiful, new characteristics are developed, which, although they belong either to externalism, to affectionalism, to naturalism, or to an inverted supernaturalism, are necessary to the full natural development of Art, as a preparation for its resurrection into the spiritual. Although, in this process, the very idea of Art becomes lost, — its ideal being supposed to be derived from Nature, and the perfect imitation of Nature to be its only true vocation, — a variety in the illustration of natural condition, position, and relationship, incidental to the self-conscious development of the soul, is obtained, that will be useful as suggestive material in its spiritual incarnation, and without which, Art would be confined to the illustration of a simply religious condition of the soul. The true artist of our time, therefore, does not attempt a reproduction of the forms of ancient art, which can be nothing but an absurd and lifeless imitation, but aims to develop Modern Art, because he believes this also to be real; and he believes this, because the true artist works from the highest point of his own consciousness, in illustrating the internal by means of the external, which is the legitimate province of Art. We see, then, that the condition of Art must keep pace with the condition of the human consciousness, and that, as the forms of this become developed from within outwards, passing from vital supernatural to natural, and from these to destructive supernatural forms, Art must represent these changes, and become antagonized to the forms of ancient art; and this is necessary, not only because these cannot now be appreciated, reproduced, understood, or even felt to be true, but because an opposite ideal has been conceived as the life of Art. It is this change in the human consciousness — which includes a change in the incarnating power through which the conceptions of Art become realized — that constitutes the difference between ancient and modern art. At its commencement, Art was the unconscious, spontaneous production of the Imagination; because this is the highest intellectual incarnating power of the mind, and must therefore become the agent in the development of Art from within outwards; and its productions corresponded with the highest forms and recognitions of the consciousness, from vital rational and supernatural points of view: and although the Imagination must always make use of the Fancy, as a subordinate agent which must construct the body of Art, this lower incarnating power, as well as the Imagination, was then governed by its vital law, and manifested under the influence of the vital laws of the Reason and of the Sentiment; so that the harmonious relations of contrast, which constitute the true picturesque in Art, were realized through the Fancy as the most external element in all its constructions. In the Fine Arts, to which our attention will be particularly directed, because they offer the best illustrations of the changes of consciousness to which we have referred, the natural element in Art, which is the Beautiful, was realized in its legitimate form in subjection to its spiritual element, which is the Sublime; and the legitimate correspondences which represent the relationships between internal and external, and between spiritual and natural things, were combined in ideal forms of truth, of good, and of beauty. With regard to its external form, it obtained a perfection that cannot be realized at any other time; because the physical was then in its greatest external perfection, and the artist therefore possessed an intuitive knowledge of physical substance, and of his own physical structure and functions, or muscular states, combined with the greatest power of physical perception and conception, and also with the greatest perfection of muscular development, and power of external manifestation. These causes gave to him that astonishing rapidity and precision of manipulation,—that intimate knowledge of forms, substances, and colors,—and that facility in combining them,—for which he was so celebrated; a knowledge of physical life that cannot be supplied by the greatest amount of external observation, to which modern artists are confined; and a power of the hand that cannot be acquired by any amount of study and practice, upon which modern artists must rely. With regard to its Ideal, it had two distinct ideals, which were antagonized as external and internal, and as natural and supernatural,—one that was peculiar to Grecian, and the other to Roman Art. These were both legitimate, because they were derived from the Imagination as representatives of the vital religious law, and both the Sublime and the Beautiful were combined by them in legitimate representations of truth, good, and beauty; but as Greek Art became realized before the supernatural birth of the soul, while Roman Art was realized through the experience of Christianity, the Grecian ideal was obtained by the Imagination from those analogies which represent the Spiritual from a natural point of view, while the Roman ideal was obtained by the Imagination from those analogies which represent the Spiritual from a supernatural point of view; and thus, while Greek Art demanded natural perfection, and the Incarnation of the Divine in the Human, Roman Art demanded the repudiation of the natural as a preparation for resurrection into spiritual life, and represented Divine-Humanity, which produces the union of the human with the divine through voluntary sacrifice.

When, however, the development of human nature from a self-conscious point of view commenced by the establishment of Protestantism, and it was demanded that every thing of a supernatural character should be connected with self-conscious individual experiences, the apparent, or what seemed to be real, was set up as a substitute for the ideal, and all the symbolic correspondences by which Christianity had been represented from an external and physical point of view were consequently repudiated and warred against as idolatrous; or were, as Mr. Ruskin says, "trampled under foot at once by every believing and advancing Christian;" and preparation was thus made for the construction of Art upon an opposite ground, and with opposite ideals, as the representative of Anti-Christianity, and as the exponent of "Naturalism," and "Sympathy," which are the destructive sentimental laws. Now, as these laws are incarnated from external and from internal points of view by Unitarianism and Transcendentalism, which succeed each other, Modern Art comes to include two separate ideals, which are successively realized: the first being simply Natural, as the production of the Fancy under the influence of its destructive law, and therefore confined to physical and natural phenomena realized through external intellectual and affectional states of the consciousness; and the second being Supernatural, as the production of the Imagination under the influence of its destructive law, and therefore aiming to illustrate the supernatural ideas, and conceptions of supernatural law, which have been realized through intuition from the principles of "Naturalism" and "Sympathy." These schools, therefore, produce a complete inversion of Ancient Art, and are characterized by diversity instead of unity, by action instead of repose, by affectionalism instead of intellectualism, and by sensualism and individualism instead of idealism and universalism; the picturesque and poetical aspects of physical and natural life being conceived, combined, and represented by these schools from a superficial and disorderly point of view, so far as a limited knowledge of form and of color and a diminished power of manipulation will allow. It is true, that in the Fine Arts, but especially in Painting, modern artists excel in the imitation of physical phenomena, and can use these in a fanciful manner, or according to the deceptive similitudes of the Fancy, in illustrating an external-natural, and even an internal-natural, order of experiences; and, as the Natural is the great domain of Unitarian Art, a vast amount of individual character can be represented under the greatest variety of circumstances, and natural life can be represented in all the variety of its physical, intellectual, and affectional aspects and relationships. But as the Fancy is, in this school, the only incarnating power, a superficial, fictitious, and untruthful character is given to Art; and it becomes, on the one hand, simply a poor imitator of natural life, — this being opposite to its legitimate function, which is to represent spiritual life; and, on the other, a falsifier of Nature, which is still more objectionable, because it weakens the power of legitimate natural perception in the mind, and either confuses or inverts all true physical and natural relationships; for, although the Fancy cannot realize any conception of the destructive laws of the mind, it is at this time unconsciously governed by them in the production of illegitimate effects which must partake, more or less, of the nature of caricature, varying from the slightest deviation from true proportion and relationship to those palpable deformities and false contrasts which are elements in the Comic. Even when the Imagination comes in aid of the Fancy, — as it does in the internal development of modern art, — being now governed by its destructive law, it is unable to realize any of those legitimate correspondences between supernatural and natural, and between internal and external things, which characterize and constitute the inspiration of ancient art; or any of that instinctive knowledge of relationship between ideas and physical forms, colors, and substances, which is the primary basis of Art as a representative medium. Instead of this, it realizes inverted forms of these correspondences and relationships, by which an inversion of ancient art is produced.

The effects which have here been described are realized as a consequence of the development of the destructive laws of the mind, and their incarnation in the forms of Art by the Fancy and the Imagination while governed by the destructive, instead of the vital, law of their constitution. In accordance with a law already stated and illustrated, this destructive development of Art commences in its lowest form and condition, which is characterized as natural, unconscious, external, and affectional; and this we designate Unitarian Art. This is constructed exclusively by the Fancy, as the exponent of the Natural, from the most superficial point of view; and therefore appearances, and partial resemblances, are, in its constructions, confounded with realities and real relationships, which are opposite to them. The Fancy is the only constructor of Art at this period of its development, because it is realized in an external sphere of the consciousness, and confined to its lowest region. It is only when the mind comes into an internal sphere of consciousness that the Imagination can again become the constructor of Art; and then it comes under the influence of its destructive law, and realizes inversions of legitimate religious symbolism, and of the legitimate relationships between internal and external, and between supernatural and natural things; and this we designate Transcendental Art. In order that we should show the degradation in Art, therefore, we are to show, first, that the Imagination ceased to be the constructor of Art, and that the Fancy became its constructor under the government of its destructive law, and under the influence of the destructive laws of the mind; and, next, that the Imagination has become the constructor of Art under the government of its destructive law, and as the exponent of the destructive laws of the mind which have been incarnated in conscious conceptions; and that its productions consequently include inversions of legitimate religious symbolism, and of all those vital laws and relationships which were represented by ancient art. It will be necessary, therefore, that we first show the kinds of manifestation referable to the Fancy and the Imagination, and also show what are the vital laws and relationships represented by ancient art.

All that can properly be termed Art is founded in Laws of Representation, which are, in the natural, realized unconsciously and spontaneously through the Fancy, the Imagination, and the Reason: the Fancy being the exponent of natural relationships, which are destructive; the Imagination, the exponent of supernatural relationships, which are representative; and the Reason, the exponent of Universal Laws, which are vital and productive. In all legitimate Art, therefore, these three elements are individualized, and harmoniously combined as body, soul, and spirit; the body and the spirit, as representing the Human and the Divine, being united through the soul, as the representative of Divine Humanity: the Fancy realizing forms of natural perfection, which constitute the Beautiful; the Reason realizing forms representative of the Divine Perfections, which constitute the Sublime; and the Imagination realizing forms of Beauty, which represent Divine Humanity, — Spiritual Life through Marriage, — or the union of opposites through voluntary sacrifice. But as the Reason includes opposite forms, — a vital form representing "Perfection," and a destructive form representing "Imperfection," — and as every department of the mind includes vital and destructive laws, which must be combined in all its manifestations, but one of which must govern them; so that these are divided into vital and destructive manifestations, — opposite forms of Art become realized, and are made one with the individual consciousness. In the development of the mind from within outwards, Art becomes realized as simply destructive, or as representing conscious conceptions of these destructive laws of the mind; and the Fancy and Imagination become constructive of forms of Art which are founded in an inversion of the legitimate idealism of ancient art. These are realized, not as harmonious individualizations of body, soul, and spirit, but as dualistic and discordant representations of Chaos; and Naturalism and Affectionalism are set up in opposition to Idealism and Intellectualism. Thus, instead of representing Spiritual Perfection by the Sublime, which is the highest element in Art, the sublime is ignored, as idealistic, while a representation of Spiritual Imperfection by the Ludicrous is substituted, — instead of recognizing External Nature and the Beautiful as the lowest and as the destructive elements in Art, they are regarded as vital, and as the highest, — and instead of recognizing Man as a representative of Beauty, through the realization of a supernatural life, it degrades him by making him representative of imperfection, or evil, and dependent for his vitality upon the influence of external nature; while animal life, and the landscape, become the most prominent elements in Art.

Let us explain: The vital and destructive perceptive laws, included in the department of which the "Fancy" is the constructive power, are "Contrast" and "Resemblance;" the first of these being the law which regulates the combination of opposites for the purpose of making the higher conspicuous through contrast with the lower, and the second being the law which establishes external and partial resemblances in form and in function between things which are internally and really opposite. The vital phenomena in this department, which are realized through the combination of these opposite laws by the Fancy, with the subjection of the destructive to the vital, in the production of definite forms, are harmonious relations of contrast between physical opposites as mediums for the representation of natural and affectional states of the individual consciousness, including forms, upon the one hand, and colors upon the other, as intellectual and affectional elements which, in relation to Art, are vital and destructive; and it will be understood that these harmonious relations of opposites are perfectly distinct from the perception of geometrical proportions and of harmonies of color, which is realized by the lower perceptive faculties of the mind. This perception is entirely separated from any relationship between physical properties and internal, individual experiences, the perception of which first appears in the "Fancy," and gives to its manifestations their representative character. The destructive phenomena in this department, which are realized through the combination of these opposite laws by the "Fancy," with the subjection of the vital to the destructive, are superficial resemblances between physical objects, and also between the external characteristics of these and the affectional states and indefinite conditions of the individual consciousness; being external, partial, and fictitious relationships, which are useful in representing in a superficial manner that which cannot be definitely expressed, and also in giving breadth and color to the mental manifestations and the individual communications: but which become destructive when assumed to be real, or to be truly representative of the real conditions and relationships of things. It will therefore be seen that these forms of the "Fancy" can never constitute a medium either for the expression or the representation of Truth, because they institute harmonious relationships between things which are really opposite; and that, when the Fancy comes under the government of its destructive law, and harmonious relations of contrast can no longer be conceived, while fictitious similitudes and contrasts of opposites are its only materials for representation, it must become a medium for the construction of the Comic, because this is founded in the most violent contrasts, combined with the most external resemblances. This destructive manifestation of the Fancy, by which opposites are confounded so that nothing can be truly known, appears in the forms of false Art, known as Wit and Humor; which we shall carefully analyze and illustrate in our psychological system: showing that the tendency of the first is to degrade what is high, what corresponds with the Rational and Supernatural, and therefore with the Imagination; and that the tendency of the second is to elevate what is low, what corresponds with the Affectional and Natural, and therefore with the Fancy; and that both of these forms are constituted by the combination of things which are not naturally connected, or which have no real natural relationship, and also of things which appear to be, or are superficially, like, while they are really the most unlike and opposite.

The vital and destructive perceptive laws which are included in the department of which "Imagination" is the constructive power, are "Opposition" and "Correspondence;" the first of these being the law which separates those things which appear to be like but are opposite, and thus antagonizes the individual to the universal, the natural to the supernatural, and the external to the internal; and the second being the law which perceives, or directs the mind towards, those things which are really related; but, being unconscious of the laws of relationship, sees as one what are opposite, and identifies the symbol with that which it represents. The vital phenomena in this department, which are realized by the supernatural combination of these opposite laws in vital symbolic forms of which "Imagination" becomes conceptive, are representations of the relationships which have been established between the forms and functions of the Universe, and the laws and conditions of Absolute Existence, in the image of which it is created: they therefore represent the opposition that exists between the Individual and the Universal, and the means by which they become reconciled and united, through the Sacrifice of Personal Life, and the Regeneration of the natural form, by which the Human becomes Divine-Human; these being in harmony with the vital form of the Reason from which the Universal Laws of Correspondence are to be derived, and in correspondence with all the vital forms and institutions, both supernatural and natural, which have been established by supernatural means through the Church. The destructive phenomena in this department, which are realized by the supernatural combination of these opposite laws in destructive symbolic forms of which "Imagination" becomes conceptive, represent inversions of the relationships and manifestations which are symbolized in the vital forms here described.

From the statement here made, it will be seen that the Imagination and the Fancy are related as Supernatural and Natural, — the first being the exponent of the internal, the rational, the sentimental, the sublime, and the perfect; and the second, of the external, the affectional, the beautiful, and the imperfect; but that both become manifested in a vital or in a destructive manner, as the vital or the destructive incarnating laws, — as the vital or the destructive elements of these laws, — and as the vital or the destructive elements in the principles which here become incarnated, predominate and rule. Even the Sublime — which is the vital element in Art, because it symbolizes the attributes of God — contains a destructive element, which is known as the material sublime, and is a prominent element in external natural productions; and this is not, therefore, found to be conspicuous in the productions of vital supernatural art, except in its decline, but is found in those which represent the Natural,—as in the Egyptian and other corresponding developments. In the more vital forms of Art it is excluded, as natural, and as interfering with that higher, internal sublimity presented by the religious experiences of the soul, and by the more internal symbolic forms. In transcendental art, therefore, where the deification of Nature is consummated, the material sublime is contrasted and combined with the beautiful, and the beautiful is combined with deformity, in the production of False Art, which is representative of Spiritual Death. Vital and destructive phenomena are, however, realized in both the unconscious vital and the conscious destructive conditions of these incarnating and manifesting intellectual powers. In the vital and external condition of the individual, these opposite rational, supernatural, and natural phenomena are combined in the unconscious, spontaneous production of artistic forms, with the subjection of the destructive to the vital elements and of the destructive to the vital incarnating law. In the destructive and internal condition of the individual, he becomes consciously conceptive of Laws of Correspondence realized through the destructive form of the Reason, which, instead of being unconscious and poetic, are conscious, rational, and metaphysical, forms; and he also becomes consciously conceptive of the destructive sentimental laws and of inverted sentimental phenomena, which are combined in the productions of false art.

In showing the degradation in Art that is produced by the Fancy while under the control of destructive laws (which is the first period in the development of modern art), we are to show that, while ancient art was religious, this modern art is profane,— that the first was internal, rational, and ideal; making use of a symbolism derived from the rational and sentimental powers of the mind, which represented the creation of all things from opposite substances by an Absolute Cause, and the realization of Spiritual Life in absolute and phenomenal spheres; while the second is external, affectional, natural, and sensualistic; being an imitator and illustrator of phenomena in the physical, the animal, and the affectional departments of Nature, under the destructive law of "Resemblance," by which opposite things are either confounded or discordantly contrasted,—that good is illustrated rather than truth,—and that a diversity, an affectionality, and an activity are introduced into Art, in the place of the unity, rationality, and repose which belong to it as a representative of Spiritual Life through Marriage,—and, finally, we are to show that while the first, as the representative of Spiritual Perfection, was characterized by Beauty and Sublimity, the second, as the representative of Spiritual Imperfection, is characterized as Beautiful, and has led to the production of the Comic, which is simply an inversion of true Art.

The antagonism between ancient art as supernatural, and modern art as natural, is an obvious and recognized fact. Even Ruskin, the exponent of modern art, has said, "All ancient art was religious, and all modern art is profane." In Grecian art, Heathen mythology, and in Roman or Mediæval art, Christian theology furnished both the inspiration and the principal subjects in all its constructions; while Modern art has been occupied in the representation of mineral, vegetable, and animal life, and in the illustration of social phenomena and affectional experiences; and these facts are so palpable that we do not see how they can be disputed. It is more difficult to show the ideal character of ancient art as opposed to the sensualistic character of modern art, because the true nature and relationships of things have been so obscured and perverted by the Fancy, that all adequate conceptions of a vital idealism, and of the nature of the Imagination and the Fancy, have been lost. As the Fancy has become the only incarnating power, her manifestations have been mistaken for those of the Imagination, which has ceased to give any vital response; and the word "Ideal" has consequently come to signify something that is fanciful and unreal, instead of signifying, as it should, the most real and substantial things. Even Winckelmann, the celebrated writer upon Greek art, supposed ideal forms to be compositions made by the selection, from a great variety of subjects, of the most beautiful features; and Ruskin supposes all the ancient ideal forms to be copies from nature, — that "Ideal Beauty" is nothing more than the most perfect specimen of any physical object, — and that even the forms of Gothic Architecture were suggested by the forms of vegetation. We have shown, however, that all legitimate Art is a representative of Christianity, Divine-Humanity, or Spiritual Life through Marriage; and represents in an external and diversified manner, extending to all the forms of life, the same ideas that are represented more internally by the original Universal Church in every sphere. It is therefore that the Catholic Church was the great patron of Art, and was originally its superintendent; all its forms having been either supervised or prescribed by her. As Architecture is constituted by a combination of mathematical and material laws and forces, it is particularly suitable as a medium for the most external representation of spiritual ideas. It has, therefore, from the earliest times, been used for this purpose; for we read in the Scriptures that the exact patterns of all things requisite for the building of the sacred Tabernacle were communicated to Moses by inspiration, and were therefore said to have been shown to him by the Lord in the Mount. We will show what we mean by the symbolism and idealism of ancient art, and the constructive power of the Imagination, by explaining the nature of Architecture, or by showing the origin of all architectural forms; and we shall produce the exact number of these primitive forms, by positing the universally recognized symbol of Spirit, the Triangle, and developing this by following the order in which, as we have shown, God becomes realized as a Tri-Personality. We shall in this way not only explain the nature of Architecture, and the nature of Idealism in Art, but illustrate mathematically the statement of Tri-Personality that we have made.

By referring to our statement of the Universal Laws of Being, it will be seen that we posit, as the ground of Existence, two opposite, indefinite, universal causes in Infinite and Finite Law; and by the combination of these, and their union through the sacrifice of finite life, obtain a conception of God as a tri-personal Creating Cause. Now, by reducing this statement to a corresponding succession of geometrical forms, as in this diagram, we produce the Triangle, the Square, the Diamond, the Arch, the Globe, and the Circle; which constitute the fundamental forms of Architecture. These forms are produced in the following order and manner. As 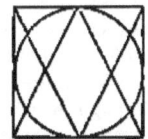 Infinite and Finite Law, from the union of which Existence or Definite Being is realized, are each threefold; by reducing these to geometrical forms, we produce two triangles. If we combine these triangles, and enclose them in one form, we produce a square, enclosing a diamond in the centre, with three triangles on each side; and this represents most perfectly the production, from Infinite and Finite Spheres of Indefinite Being, of a definite form of Absolute Existence, incarnating and representing both these indefinite principles or spheres in a natural dualistic form, in which these have not been united as one, but are held together by a definite form of the Infinite Productiveness, as a supernatural combining and manifesting power which communicates to it vitality, precisely as the indwelling Word communicates vitality to the natural man, as a light shining in darkness that comprehendeth it not; and we have already shown that this is the form in which Infinite Life must first be incarnated, constituting a natural condition of Absolute Being. If we reduce to a geometrical form the realization of the Father as Divine Life through the sacrifice of his individual life, by which he becomes at one with the Infinite Life,—that is, if we unite in one form the Square and the Triangle,—we produce the Arch. If we reduce to a geometrical form the realization of the Son as Spiritual Life through the same sacrifice of individual life, and his consequent union with the Father, we not only produce a second arch, but, by a union of these two arches, produce the Sphere or Globe, which is the symbol of Eternity, and of God as Tri-personal Creating Cause.

The Diamond is one of the most interesting forms of Architecture, for the reason that it symbolizes the Divine Activity, which communicates Life to the Soul by the combination and manifestation of the opposite laws which constitute it, and is "the Light that lighteth every man that cometh into the world;" it being for this reason, that, in the Christian order of Architecture, light is always admitted through the form of the diamond. The most perfect form of the diamond, as a representative of this idea that "God is Light," and that this light is the Life of the World, is found in one of the productions of nature,—the diamond of commerce; and we introduce a description of it here, for the purpose of supporting the statement that has here been made with regard to this form. We have shown that every department of the human constitution contains a supernatural principle through which the divine activity operates in the continuous creation, combination, and manifestation of the laws and forms through which it realizes a natural existence,—that the manifestations of this supernatural principle are representative of Spiritual Life through Marriage, or the union of opposites through voluntary sacrifice,—and that spiritual life is realized in a spiritual sphere of consciousness, through the actual sacrifice of the individual life, and the regeneration of the natural form: we may, therefore, see that both natural and spiritual life, through the natural and spiritual regeneration of the individual,—which are effected by the operation of the Divine Activity,—are represented by the Diamond; natural regeneration being represented by its form, and spiritual regeneration by its substance. Natural life, through natural regeneration, is represented by the form of the diamond, because this is octahedral, or constituted by two four-sided pyramids joined at the base: while spiritual life, through spiritual regeneration, is represented by its substance, because it is composed of pure carbon; and by this is represented an entire change of substance, from natural to spiritual, by what is termed in the Scriptures the Baptism of Fire, through which the spiritual regeneration of the soul is effected. This may be confirmed from the Scriptures, because there the Natural is represented by Wood, from which carbon is produced by the action of fire. The diamond has therefore been recognized intuitively as a legitimate symbol of Spiritual Marriage, and it was used by Dante as the symbol of spiritual regeneration. He therefore described the threshold of Paradise as "a Rock of Diamond," because, from the religious point of view from which he wrote, Salvation and Regeneration are regarded as the same.

From the description that has here been given of the origin of the primitive forms of Architecture, it will be seen that a natural condition of existence is symbolized by the form of the Square. This corresponds with the fact, already demonstrated, that the natural is dualistic, and is realized as "two and two, one against the other;" because this, reduced to a geometrical form, produces the square. It will also be found to correspond with the fact, that, in those nations who represent the natural side of thought, — that is, the incarnation of Spirit in Matter, or of the Divine in the Human, — as the Egyptians and Greeks, — Architecture is confined to the form of the square, this being surmounted by a triangle. It will also be seen that the spiritual condition of existence — spiritual regeneration — or the realization of Spiritual Life through Marriage — is symbolized by the Globe, the Diamond, and the Arch: and this will be found to correspond with the fact, that in those nations who represent the supernatural side of thought, or the union of Divine and Human, through a divine-human principle, — as the Assyrians, the Arabians, and the Romans, — Architecture is characterized by the globe, the diamond, and the arch; and the square is excluded as an essential form. This explanation of the nature of Architecture, as the most external form of Art, may serve to throw some light upon the subject of idealism in Art, or of its nature as a representative of the Spiritual, which is its legitimate and only useful office; and to show that the word "Ideal," as applied to Art, does not mean, as it has become common to suppose, the most perfect specimen or conception of any physical or natural production, but means the representation of relationships which have been ordained to exist between the permanent laws, forces, and productions of the Universe and its Creator, upon the ground that "the invisible things of Him, from the creation of the world, are clearly seen, being understood by the things that are made, even his eternal power and Godhead." It will also illustrate, in the same way that the Catholic Church does, the idea that spiritual things can, in the natural, be represented more perfectly and more extensively by the material laws, forces, forms, and manifestations of the Universe, than by the imperfect and fluctuating manifestations of the human consciousness; for the reason, that, as the individual becomes self-consciousness, he repudiates vital supernatural ideas and laws, and adopts those which are destructive, as we have shown that he must, from the operation of a universal law of existence. It was, undoubtedly, an internal impression of this fact that led many of the ancient philosophers, among whom Pythagoras was a prominent example, to assume a mathematical basis for their philosophical speculations.

In illustrating this degradation in Art, we will first refer to Architecture, Sculpture, and Philosophy; because, according to our description and classification of all the forms of Art, these are the three elements which constitute its universal individualization as body, soul, and spirit: and this decline will therefore here be found to be the most striking. In these forms of Art, we find the productions of the ancients to be so far above all that have succeeded them, that they cannot at this day even be imitated. This will not probably be disputed in Architecture, because nothing has here been originated that is not a palpable degradation of architectural form; while the attempts to imitate the sublime structures of antiquity have resulted in nothing but caricature. This fact has been recognized by Mr. Ruskin, who asserts, not only that "we have no architects," but that "the term Architecture is not so much as understood by us." He did not probably mean to include himself in the last remark, because he is particularly vehement and dogmatic upon this subject, and has invented many fanciful theories about it, without comprehending the significance of a single one of its symbolic forms. He gives the preference to the Roman or Gothic order, because it follows the form of vegetation as seen in the pointed leaf, and denounces the Grecian order, because it is opposite to this, and is founded in the form of the square. He draws a sprig with square leaves, and asks how we like the Grecian style of foliage; and contemptuously says that Greek Architecture is little more than "seven or eight equal pillars with the triangular end of a roof above them;" while Roman Architecture includes, to use his own inflated language, "shafts, and buttresses, and porches, and pinnacles, and vaultings, and towers, and other doubly and trebly multiplied magnificences of membership."

In order that we should be able to understand the degradation which has taken place in the art of Sculpture, we must first understand the position that belongs to it and the conditions that it demands; because these are what have obtained for it the rank that it holds as the highest of the Fine Arts, or Arts of Design. Now, in referring to the classification and analysis of the Arts in the psychological portion of our work, we find that, while Architecture, as the highest element in the body of Art, is representative of Universal Spiritual Laws, and their operation in realizing Tri-personality in God by the use of physical forms, and is addressed to an external, unconscious condition of the mind, which corresponds with the Catholic Church; Sculpture, as the highest element in the soul of Art, is representative of spiritual states of the consciousness by the use of natural forms and functions, and is addressed to an internal, conscious condition of the mind, which corresponds with the Protestant Church, — that, while Architecture includes three physical elements which correspond with the forms, the forces, and the growths of physical life as the symbolic ground of its representations, Sculpture includes three natural elements which correspond with the forms, the functions, and the relationships of natural life as the symbolic ground of its representations, — and that it was therefore to the Greeks, as the great exponents of the Consciousness, that the higher forms of Sculpture particularly belonged. In its legitimate forms, this Art was the product of the Imagination; and included, as its spirit, a human symbolism that was representative of the Divine: examples of this being realized in the statues of Phidias, — as its soul, an intuition of the relationships between the soul and the body, or between states of the consciousness and the individual physical condition, — and as its body, an intuitive knowledge of the relationships which have been ordained to exist between man and the mineral, the vegetable, and the animal kingdoms of Nature; relationships which are not partial and superficial, and therefore fictitious and false, as are those which are instituted by the Fancy under the destructive law of "Resemblance," but are intrinsically real and true. This external symbolism was sometimes introduced into the forms of Architecture, as an internal element, and was often used in architectural decorations: it was also used in Poetry, in Painting, and in the illumination of manuscripts; and is an element which Mr. Ruskin has absurdly termed "Grotesque," and confounded with the Comic. We may see, then, that Sculpture has attained the high rank which it holds in Art because it is the product of the Imagination, and is thus symbolical and ideal, and demands the highest and most introspective condition of the consciousness; while at the same time it demands a consciousness of physical conditions and of muscular contractions which correspond with the ideas and impressions there realized, and are necessary to embody and give expression to them: a combination of opposite states which, as we have seen, can belong only to a primitive condition of human nature. It is this imaginative insight that communicates an ideality, an intellectuality, and a repose to this Art, which represent the highest natural conditions and positions of the soul, by which it is characterized as Sublime.

Now, we cannot claim for modern Sculpture that it has realized one of these fundamental conditions, because not only is the realization of either of them now utterly impossible, but there is no belief in their ever having been realized, it being supposed that the ancients either literally copied what they saw, or made new combinations from what they saw. The moderns have failed to produce any great work in this art, because not being able to conceive they are obliged to imitate, and imitation is not possible in true art; and their failure would be more apparent if drapery, which can readily be copied, was not so often substituted for the human form. Although a knowledge of anatomy, and a knowledge, derived from observation, of the various positions of the human figure, are necessary to the sculptor, as suggestive in the formation of his conceptions, the greatest amount of such knowledge will not enable him to realize those conceptions of the particular physical condition and state of muscular contraction which are necessary to represent the internal intellectual mental position of which his work should be the incarnation, and which cannot be copied, or produced from without, but must be conceived, or produced from within. Consequently,—although the artists of the present day have been able to copy in an imperfect manner the forms of ancient art; to mould parts of the human figure from living models; and even to conceive new combinations of the several parts of figures so observed and so copied (because this decomposition and recomposition belong to the faculty of "Conception," which is the lowest constructive faculty of the Understanding, and the most generally developed of all the intellectual powers),—that high, internal, self-conscious, introspective position; that internal consciousness of corresponding physical conditions and muscular contractions; and that sense of Beauty, which we have seen to be demanded by this art, and from which it derives the elements of symmetry, of ideality, of intellectuality, of truth, and of sublimity,—are not to be found in modern sculpture. These have been succeeded by an externalism of position and of method of which the Beautiful is the highest result: and instead of the internal activity combined with external repose, which should characterize all sculpture that is not purely symbolic,—that is, which is not simply a representation of the relationships existing between the internal-natural and the physical, derived by intuition from the sense of analogy,—we find in modern sculpture attempts to express a variety and an affectional activity which belong to Painting, but are entirely inappropriate to Sculpture; while the poor imitations of humanity, which are exhibited as specimens of the beautiful, are, for the most part, wooden, disproportioned, inharmonious, and lifeless. We shall not extend our remarks upon this subject, because, if these defects in modern sculpture should not readily be recognized, all argument and all enumeration of examples would be unavailing. It will be understood, however, that these remarks apply to the external, natural school of modern art, rather than to the new, internal school that has recently commenced the development of Art from a destructive supernatural point of view, and the character of which will presently be shown.

In showing the degradation of Philosophy, by its development from within outwards,—which, as the highest form of Art, must furnish the fullest and most conclusive evidence upon the subject of its degradation,—we refer to the account that has already been given in tracing its entire history from the commencement down to the present time, because we have there shown that it furnishes a complete illustration and demonstration of the laws upon which our science is founded. We have there shown, that Philosophy has been developed, from its highest to its lowest forms, successively in three spheres,—the first being realized in the East, the second in Greece, and the last in Christian Europe; and that it has, by becoming more psychological and individual in character, and less unconsciously symbolic and representative of the highest truths relating to Being and to Creation, more and more degraded in its forms; while, at the same time, it has become more and more elevated in its position by being realized as internal, intellectual, and self-conscious. In the last period of its development, however, the degradation of Philosophy has very much exceeded that of any former period; and, besides the abundant proof that has already been given of the destructive condition into which the mind comes at the close of each philosophical development, some additional particulars remain to be noticed which have not before appeared. Besides the atheistical system of Comte, of which Lewes and Buckle are prominent exponents, which has succeeded the final development of Intellectual Philosophy in its eclectical form, another form of materialism, still more external, has been produced in the phrenological method and system founded by Dr. Gall; which was put forth as a substitute for the former method and systems of intellectual philosophy founded upon an internal observation of the facts of the consciousness. By this new theory, the Consciousness has been unwarrantably ignored and set aside as individual and partial, and therefore incompetent to discover the primitive principles of human nature from a universal point of view: although it is true that a much better reason is also given; which is, that, by observing the facts of the consciousness, only the *functions* of the mind, or the modes of its operation, are discovered, and not the *faculties* of the mind, to which are to be referred the specific manifestations of the individual; which is to a great extent true with regard to the more recent psychological inquiries. But the substitute which has been offered in Phrenology for the imperfect theories of intellectual philosophy is not only more external and material, but much less philosophical; because it substitutes the physiology of the mind for the philosophy of the mind, and includes nothing more than generalizations and classifications of the actions of individuals, based upon the most external, natural, and superficial of those very facts of the consciousness which it pretends to ignore. It therefore commenced with instituting organs for murdering, lying, stealing, quarrelling, travelling, &c., as fundamental faculties of the mind, which had been discovered, and established upon the incontestable evidence of facts, by comparing the actions or external manifestations of individuals with certain convolutions of the brain, as indicated by the form of the head, and by prominences upon the cranium. This new method, which is really valuable as leading to the collection and classification of physical phenomena related to the manifestations of the mind, has been so much abused and degraded, that any one may for a small consideration purchase what purports to be a description of his mental powers that will be a sure guide to him in selecting his occupation, and in forming his relationships with other individuals. There is, however, a still lower depth into which these investigations of the nature of the mind from an external instead of an internal point of view have led, which has been distinguished by the term "Neurology;" and which undertakes to prove, by the same incontrovertible evidence of facts, that the mind is not confined to the head, but pervades every part of the body; and that its faculties are not to be determined either by reflecting upon the facts of the consciousness, or by investigating the functions of the brain, but are to be discovered by mesmeric experiments, by which dispositions and faculties of the mind are to be found upon the surface of the body; a method the external, illegitimate, and destructive character of which cannot be exceeded. In the next place, Ethics, or Moral Philosophy, which constituted the external development of Psychology, has been succeeded by autobiographical descriptions of individual experiences, and by illustrations, in the form of fictitious narrative, of the affectional and sentimental conditions and functions of the mind. It is in this way that the relationships and duties of domestic and of social life, and even theories of political economy, of morality, and of religion, are now taught; and it is only in this form that descriptions which relate to the manifestations of the mind, or to the moral, domestic, and social qualities of human nature, can be made attractive; notwithstanding that these are superficial and deceptive productions of the Fancy, and can convey no real information upon the subjects which they profess to illustrate. This department of knowledge has thus sunk from mental analysis to mental illustration, or from a philosophy of mind to a philosophy of manners; and, while it has become easy to create any number of fictitious characters, it has become impossible to understand one that is real. The mind — having lost the power of analyzing mental states, and of comprehending the various powers of thought, of affection, and of will, by reflection in the consciousness — can only calculate how individuals, possessing certain physical characteristics and mental powers, will conduct themselves under a variety of circumstances. This class of writings, which appears under the forms of the novel and the novelette, has now become so popular and so abundant that this may be called emphatically the novel-writing and the novel-reading age; and when we contemplate the flood of literature of this most external description with which we are now inundated, proceeding from female and feminine minds, we can hardly doubt that the crisis of this latter development has nearly been reached. There is another phenomenon that should be noticed as belonging particularly to this last period of philosophical development, and which could not before have been realized, arising in the development of the destructive laws of the mind, by which an inversion of legitimate philosophical speculations is realized, and all the departments of literature become perverted; a perversion that is particularly dangerous, for the reason that it is accompanied by a personal elevation in those through whom it is realized, and a consequent elevation in their productions, which may be termed an advance from external to internal, and from material to ethereal, and which imparts to them a peculiar and deceptive charm. But as this subject would require an extensive and complicated consideration of abstract principles, which would interfere with our present object, which is to refer to things that can readily be recognized, — as philosophic manifestations have already been alluded to belonging to this particular sphere of development, — and as the analysis of Transcendentalism, which is the sphere to which these manifestations belong, will next occupy our attention, — we shall make no further allusion to it here. Having considered the degradation that has taken place in Architecture, Sculpture, and Philosophy, we will consider the minor and more external departments of Art.

The sciences and the inferior mechanic arts, being mathematical, external, and material, flourish at this period with increased vigor, for the reason that this is the material period of the soul's development. The higher subordinate arts are less depreciated than those we have just described, because they partake more of an external and affectional character. Even here, however, a decline is so evident that it can be neither overlooked nor denied. In Music, this decline is shown in the fact that it has descended from a religious and intellectual into a moral and affectional condition, — which is passing from the supernatural to the natural, and from the Sublime to the Beautiful. This may be seen in the substitution of the Opera for the Oratorio and the Mass, and in the predominance generally of the secular over the sacred style; for to such an extreme has this been carried, that it is not uncommon to hear love songs and even bacchanalian songs introduced, under disguises, into the services of the Church. It may also be seen in the popular taste, which prefers that music which is the sweetest, the most melodious, and the most affectional in character, and shows a particular fondness for "negro melodies," in which these qualities are strikingly predominant. The taste for this kind of music attends the corruption of Music as an Art; and this may be seen in the facility with which this degenerates into the Comic,—a kind of music which is destructive to musical art, and also to the human voice. In Painting, this decline cannot be denied; for where shall we find among modern painters any who can be compared with Leonardo da Vinci, Michael Angelo, or Raphael? or who that reads the history of Painting can fail to perceive the gradual decline that followed the culminating point in this art, which was attained in the labors of these three great masters? At the time in which these artists appeared, the Eastern, the Grecian, and the Roman orders of Architecture were rigidly separated, and the religious ideas symbolized by the Italians in Painting, by which Christianity was represented, existed in the most violent contrast with the religious ideas of the Greeks as symbolized by this Art, by which the Incarnation of the Divine in the Human was represented. To Michael Angelo as the exponent of the Sublime, to Raphael as the exponent of the Beautiful, and to Leonardo da Vinci as the exponent of Beauty, which unites the sublime with the beautiful, was committed the task of co-operating in the production of Eclecticism in Art, or of uniting all its elements in one great school; and although these three artists were the exponents of the sublime, of the beautiful, and of beauty in art, these three were combined in the compositions of each. Hence, when Michael Angelo was called upon by the head of the Church to construct its great Cathedral at Rome dedicated to St. Peter, he combined in his plan the Eastern, the Grecian, and the Roman orders of Architecture: and, when Raphael was called upon to decorate the palace of the Pope at Rome, on the four walls of the first room painted by him he portrayed the four antagonistic sides of human thought,—Theology, Philosophy, Poetry, and Jurisprudence; a fact which not only proclaimed the eclectical character of the school of which he was one of the founders, but also the eclectical character of the Church of Rome, and of the Pope as a true descendant of St. Peter. This school of Art is thus alluded to in Kugler's handbook of Painting as an introduction to a description of the works of the three great artists here mentioned: "All the elements which had existed apart from each other, and had composed distinct styles in the periods hitherto considered; all the qualities which had been successively developed, each to the exclusion of the rest, but which in the aggregate fulfilled the conditions of a consummate practice of Art,—were united about the beginning of the sixteenth century. This union constituted a most rare and exalted state of human culture,— an era when the divine energies of human nature were manifested in all their purity. In the master-works of this new period, we find the most elevated subjects represented in the noblest forms, with a depth of feeling never since equalled." This is the high point from which Art has fallen, even in the department of Painting, which is one of the most external of the arts, and therefore one in which degradation does not so readily appear; although it is even here so apparent and so fully acknowledged, that it is hardly necessary to describe it. It may be seen in the predominance of the Landscape over the Historical form, and even over that of legitimate Portraiture, which, as a product of the Imagination, is ideal in character,— in the extensive introduction, into its compositions, of domestic animals, with which Sublimity, which is the life of Art, can never be associated,— in the tendency to illustrate affectional experiences, and also those of common and even of vulgar life which border upon caricature, a style of art in which Wilkie was so successful, and for which he obtained the honor of Knighthood,—and, finally, this decline may be seen in the tendency to indulge in caricature, or the Comic, which is an inversion of true Art; a tendency distinctly manifested in the productions of the Dusseldorf School, which constitutes the culminating point in the external or Unitarian school of modern art. There is another sign of degradation, which will be found not only in Painting, but in every other form of modern art; and we will take a more particular notice of this, because, though it is not one of the most striking, it refers to an element in Art that it has been particularly difficult to define,— the Picturesque. This is the most external, but it is also one of the most important, elements in Art. It is realized by the Fancy, as the constructor of the body of Art, and consists of legitimate or harmonious relationships between opposite things, upon the principle of contrast, of gradation, or of unity in diversity, by which the necessary relief is given to the most prominent ideas or objects, in order that the mind may be directed towards them, and the requisite attention bestowed,— that harmonious relationships may be established between the various parts, so that its individuality shall be preserved, and one idea shall characterize the whole,— and that a proper subordination of the lower to the higher may be effected throughout. The picturesque is particularly important in pictorial art, from which its name has been derived; it being here seen, not only in the disposition of the light and shade, by which a picture is to a great extent constituted, but in the arrangement of its forms and colors, and even in the disposition of its more internal elements, by which one thing is made distinctly visible by being set off against something that is comparatively opposite and at the same time harmonious. By taking this idea as our guide, we shall be able clearly to comprehend the difference between the true and the false picturesque, which may be described as follows: The true picturesque is realized in contrasting things which are comparatively opposite, and yet harmonious, in any work, for the purpose of bringing prominently before the mind the principal elements contained in it, and binding all its parts together in a legitimate chain of relationship by which the lower are made completely subordinate to the higher for use. The false picturesque is realized in contrasting things which are opposite and at the same time discordant, or between which no legitimate relationship exists; and in making prominent those objects which should be kept subordinate, and used simply to relieve those more important, thus destroying unity and repose, which are vital elements in all Art.

That the true ground of the picturesque is contrast, has always been practically recognized, because to these contrasts the term "picturesque" has usually been applied. It is therefore rather remarkable that this ground should have been sought for in some one simple idea or element. By some writers, decay has been assumed to constitute the picturesque in Art: and Mr. Ruskin conceives it to be constituted by the sublime; distinguishing the true and the false picturesque as genuine sublimity, and "parasitic sublimity." Now, decay is often introduced into Art as a contrast to freshness and vigor, and the sublime is often introduced as a contrast to the beautiful; but neither of these constitutes the picturesque. Decay is one of the most common elements in the production of illegitimate picturesque effects, for the reason that the contrast is more extreme between life and death than between any other opposites that can be found; and it was probably the frequency of its use that led to the theory just mentioned. Thus, a decayed leaf upon a fresh branch, a dead branch upon a verdant tree, a dead tree or a ruin of some kind in a landscape, are said to be picturesque. Decay is of itself falsely picturesque, because the opposite element with which it is contrasted is readily furnished by the mind. It was probably this that led to the theory, that "universal decay" constitutes the picturesque, although it might have been suggested by the works of Turner; because in these, according to Mr. Ruskin, decay is the predominating element. When the Fancy becomes the constructor of Art, the fondness for violent contrasts, and for discordant exaggerations of all kinds, increases, because at this time it is governed by its destructive law, which includes diversity and discord. Under this influence, works of art lose their unity or individuality, and contrasts are introduced for collateral and superficial, instead of legitimate and internal, effects: and to these contrasts the term picturesque is principally applied; for unless the contrast becomes intrusive, and thus illegitimate, it is not noticed. The compositions of Raphael may not therefore seem to be picturesque, although they are highly and truly so; the greatest skill having been exercised in arranging harmonious contrasts, by which the requisite relief, as well as unity, is obtained for his subject; an art that Mr. Ruskin hypercritically ridicules, as artificial and false to nature. Pictures become striking to fanciful people in proportion to the violence of these contrasts, by which the opposite elements contained in them are exaggerated in a manner contrary to true artistic rule, and also to the legitimate proportions of nature; these pictures being perfectly analogous to those individualizations of intensified human characteristics, partaking of the nature of caricature, which we have already described as being produced by the Fancy in the departments of fictitious narrative and poetic composition, and which we find to be so peculiarly attractive at the present time. This abuse of the picturesque, then, will be found to be characteristic of modern art. In painting it may be seen — combined with the other imperfections here noticed as referable to the Fancy — in the productions of the Dusseldorf School, which is its legitimate exponent. This school has succeeded in bringing the Unitarian school of modern art to the greatest perfection, and all that belongs to the beautiful here appears in an exaggerated form. Being naturalistic in character, however, its productions become distinguished by externalism and affectionalism, and are characterized by diversity, which includes discord. This naturalism has led to a want of harmony in color, of unity in design, and of truth in perspective; and to the combination of opposite and discordant elements, by which the subject is either degraded or unduly elevated. It has led to literalness; to minute and elaborate finish; to the delineation of what is most external and affectional in human character and experience; and to what is most external in expression, separated from its internal condition or position, by which true expression is turned into gesticulation and grimace. It has led to giving prominence to what should be kept subordinate; which destroys unity or individuality, draws the attention from the idea or subject to be represented to what is contrary to it, and thus destroys that concentration and repose which are so essential to Art. Finally, it has led to the introduction of caricature, or the comic; so that, even in the most serious productions of this school, an element of caricature is often introduced, and the most successful of its pictures are those which are decidedly comic. So far has Art degenerated, that even *its idea* has been lost; and it has become common to suppose that it accomplishes its highest object in the imitation of Nature. We therefore find our public men making statements like this: "A steamer is a mightier Epic than the Iliad; and Whittemore, Jacquard, and Blanchard might laugh even Virgil, Milton, and Tasso to scorn;" and we find one of our best writers asserting, that there is no difference, in an artistic point of view, between "a litter of Pigs" and "the frescoes of Angelo."*

We might here close our description of the degradation of Art, because, from one point of view, and this the most obvious one, its greatest degradation is realized in the external or Unitarian school; but we should not in this way account for many of the phenomena which are presented by the productions of modern art. It is necessary that we should also allude to another kind of degradation that is accompanied by an elevation which has in some external respects, as in the works of Turner and Kaulbach, made an approach towards the excellence of ancient art: we mean the degradation that is realized in the Transcendental School of Art, to which the self-styled Pre-Raphaelite School belongs. It is to the ideas of this school, and not to the particular works produced by it, that we intend here to allude; because its degradation is shown in the inversion of the idealism upon which ancient art is founded, more than in the manner in which its ideal has become incarnated; and we are able to do this, because this ideal has been particularly and specifically set forth in the works of John Ruskin, who is its recognized exponent, and who has openly avowed the "steady pursuit of Naturalism, as opposed to

---

* R. W. Emerson.

Idealism." * Like all representative men, who set out to establish a new system from an internal, self-conscious point of view, Mr. Ruskin is a writer of great freshness, originality, and power; and, from the fact that he writes from an internal or transcendental region of the consciousness, many of his criticisms upon externalism in Art are noble and just. But as Transcendental Art is governed by Naturalism and Individualism, while Ancient Art represented Spiritualism and Universalism, he is unable, from this point of view, to comprehend the true nature and extent of Art, or to explain one of the symbolic representations of either Roman or Grecian Art; but is obliged to repudiate them, and to set up a new symbolism which cannot be stated, except in contradictions; and which, though stated by him simply as Naturalism, in opposition to Idealism, is a complete inversion of the legitimate symbolism of ancient art. Being governed in his thought by the destructive laws of the mind, he cannot recognize the fact, that supernatural and natural things must be represented, by all legitimate art, as vital and destructive, and therefore that, in symbolizing vital spiritual manifestations by their incarnation in the Natural, it is necessary to represent them through manifestations of Man, or Humanity; and to represent External Nature as antagonistic and destructive. He therefore does not comprehend, that it was for this reason, and not because they could not paint grasses, flowers, rocks, and trees, that landscape art was not cultivated by the ancients, or recognized as legitimate art,— that, when not used as legitimate symbolism, the external productions of Nature were but slightly indicated by the mediæval painters, as a background, relief, or contrast, to the main subject represented by them,— and that the Greeks represented the external forms of nature as presided over by Fauns and Satyrs, and other personifications, which represented the abuses of Nature, and were characterized as Evil: external forms which Mr. Ruskin has elevated above the manifestations of humanity, as constituting ideal perfection, and the highest representatives of Divinity; and abuses, which, as Fun and Satire, he has accepted as belonging to the true ideal in Art.

That Mr. Ruskin not only fails to comprehend, but repudiates, the symbolic idealism of ancient art, may be seen from the most external point of view; because he ridicules the forms of Greek Architecture, regards their religious symbolism as immoral, and

---

* "Modern Painters," vol. III. p. 848.

denies that the Imagination, or that the sense of Beauty, can be in any way connected with Pagan Art, which he terms corrupt: a reckless assertion that is contradicted by the testimony of many generations, — because he repudiates the ideal perfection in which the Apostles have been represented by the mediæval artists, and would strip them of their robes, and invest them with the rude dress and the soiled appearance of actual fishermen, — because he repudiates the ideal perfection in which the Virgin Mary has been invested by them, and would represent her as "a simple Jewish Girl, bearing the calamities of poverty, and the dishonors of inferior station, as the Carpenter's Wife;" this being what Mr. Ruskin calls demanding the truth, not knowing that naturalistic truth is spiritualistic falsehood, because "the letter killeth, but the spirit giveth life," — and because he would have Christ represented "as a living presence among us now, as in Hunt's Light of the World;" that is, as a common individual, surrounded by scenes of real instead of ideal life, bearing a lantern, and knocking at a door; instead of the historical Christ, — the veritable Son of God, — transfigured and glorified, "his face shining as the Sun, and his raiment white as the Light." This is the picture which Mr. Ruskin says "is the most perfect instance of expressional purpose, with technical power, which the world has yet produced;" and, as he assumes these to be the two great requisitions of high art, we are to conclude that this offensive caricature of the Saviour is regarded by him as fulfilling his highest conception of Idealism in art, and is one of the exceptions alluded to in the following sentence: "Of true religious ideal there exist, as yet, hardly any examples."

We will now proceed to show that the new ideal set up by Mr. Ruskin is not only naturalistic, but is the inversion of a true order of supernatural representation, which leads to the abuse of nature by the confounding of opposites through the supremacy of the destructive element; and also leads to the recognition, as a true ideal in Art, of the Comic, which is a Mephistophelian form of intellectual evil. That this ideal is a naturalistic one, may be seen from the following description of "What classes of ideas are conveyable by Art," which will be found at the commencement of his great work entitled "Modern Painters," from which most of the quotations here referred to him are taken. "I think that all the sources of pleasure, or any other good, to be derived from works of art, may be referred to five distinct heads: 1. Ideas of Power, — the perception or conception of the mental or bodily powers by which the work has been produced. 2. Ideas of Imitation, — the perception that the thing produced resembles something else. 3. Ideas of Relation, — the perception of intellectual relations in the thing produced, or in what it suggests or resembles. 4. Ideas of Truth, — the perception of faithfulness in a statement of facts by the thing produced. 5. Ideas of Beauty, — the perception of beauty, either in the thing produced, or in what it suggests or resembles. Any material object which can give us pleasure in the simple contemplation of its outward qualities without any direct and definite exertion of the intellect." In defining the meaning of the term "Ideal Beauty," he says, "Although every thing in nature is more or less beautiful, every species of object has its own kind and degree of beauty; some being in their own nature more beautiful than others, and few, if any, individuals possessing the utmost degree of beauty of which the species is capable. This utmost degree of specific beauty, necessarily co-existent with the utmost perfection of the object in other respects, is the ideal of the object." From this external and naturalistic point of view, every thing becomes inverted by the elevation of the external above the internal, and the natural above the supernatural; and consequently Mr. Ruskin places Color above Form, Painting above the other Arts, and the Landscape above all other forms: while the Venetian School, which is the great school of Color, and a naturalistic school representing the Beautiful, is regarded by him as the highest of all the mediæval schools; notwithstanding its vices were evident to him, and also the fact that it contributed more than any other to the destruction of Art, and to the corruption of the public mind. This elevation of Color is strikingly stated by him in the following passage: "Color is, more than all elements of Art, the reward of veracity of purpose. As long as you are working with Form only, you may amuse yourself with fancies; but Color is sacred, — in which you must keep to facts. The men who care for form only, may drift about in dreams of Spiritualism; but the colorist must keep to the substance." How far Mr. Ruskin has carried externalism and naturalism into his conceptions of Art, may be seen in the following description by him of what constitutes a painter, and of what he esteems to be a true ideal as opposed to the false ideal of the religious painters : "The faculties, which when a painter finds in himself he resolves to be a painter, are, I suppose, intentness of observation, and facility of imitation. The man is created an observer and an imitator; and his function is to convey knowledge to his fellow-men of such things as cannot be taught otherwise than ocularly." These faculties he supposes to have been realized to an extent unprecedented at the time of the Reformation, which he says was attended by the sudden and universal introduction of Naturalism, and the repudiation of the false ideal of the religious painters which " was trampled under foot at once by every believing and advancing Christian;" and that a true ideal was then presented to the human mind, which, had it been followed, would have produced the most beneficial results. The destruction of ancient art by the operation of Protestantism, Mr. Ruskin here regards as a vital operation; and " the inclination to copy ordinary natural objects," which he says was substituted in its place, he regards as a vital movement. He says, " This was no false instinct. It was misunderstood and misapplied; but it came at the right time, and has maintained itself through all kinds of abuse, presenting, in the recent schools of Landscape, perhaps only the first-fruits of its power. Let the reader consider what amount and kind of general knowledge might by this time have been possessed by the nations of Europe, had their painters understood and obeyed it. Suppose that all these gatherings were already in our national galleries, and that the painters of the present day were laboring to multiply them. Consider the advantages to the people; the immeasurably larger interest given to Art itself; the easy, pleasurable, and perfect knowledge conveyed by it on every subject; the far greater number of men who might be healthily and profitably occupied with it as a means of livelihood; the useful direction to myriads of inferior talents, now left fading away in misery." Whether the copying of "ordinary natural objects," or the ideal conceptions of the religious painters, constitute the legitimate province of Art; and whether the non-occupation of "myriads of inferior artists," in copying these representations, is a fact to be deplored, or a subject for congratulation, must be decided by each one for himself, according to his light.

That the modern Ideal, of which Mr. Ruskin is the exponent, is an inversion of a true order of supernatural representation, — leads to the confounding of opposite things, in which the destructive element becomes supreme, — to the demand for violent and discordant contrasts, which we have shown to constitute the false picturesque in Art, — and finally to a recognition of the Comic as a legitimate ideal in Art, — may be seen from a formal statement made by him of what he conceives to be the elements of true idealism in Art: these are, " Purist Idealism, — Naturalist Idealism, — and Grotesque Idealism." That these terms, as Mr. Ruskin understands them, include these destructive elements, we will now proceed to show. With regard to Purist Idealism, — for examples of which he refers to Fra Angelico and other of the early religious painters, and also to Stothard among the moderns, — he says, "It results from the unwillingness of men to contemplate the forms of definite evil which necessarily occur in the daily aspects of the world around them; who shrink from them as from pollution, and endeavor to create for themselves an imaginary state, in which pain and imperfection either do not exist, or exist in some edgeless and enfeebled condition. It is, however, evident that all representations of nature without evil must either be ideals of a future world, or be false ideals if they are understood to be representations of facts. They can only be classed among the branches of the true ideal, in so far as they are understood to be nothing more than expressions of the painter's personal affections or hopes. It is always childish, and necessarily precludes those who practise it from being complete masters of their art, but is beautiful in its childishness." From this statement it would appear that Purist Idealism is the only legitimate idealism recognized by Mr. Ruskin as belonging to ancient art; and therefore that Angelico and others of his school are the only true artists, separate from those who come under the definition of naturalistic or grotesque: although, if "expressions of the painter's personal affections and hopes" are to be regarded as "representations of facts," even these must, according to Mr. Ruskin's definition, be regarded as "false ideals." We suppose, from his "faint praise," that he so considers them; but, when a writer contradicts himself in one sentence, such a confounding of opposites makes it impossible to determine what he really means.

Of "Naturalist Idealism," he says, "It is the central and highest branch of ideal Art, which concerns itself simply with things as they ARE, and accepts, in all of them, alike the evil and the good;" and that art becomes ideal through the disposition of natural phenomena so that the greatest variety of these shall be combined, including a discordant contrast of opposites, which, it seems, he regards as legitimate. This, it will be seen, corresponds with the productions of the Romantic or Naturalistic schools, following the destruction of ancient Art, of which Shakspeare was the exponent in dramatic composition, and of which the forms of fictitious narrative, since then so abundant, are lower specimens; and Mr. Ruskin, therefore, alludes to the violent contrasts of Shakspeare in Prince Henry and Falstaff, Titania and Bottom, and other similar examples, as illustrations of Naturalist Idealism. He evades, however, a particular description of this his principal ideal, by taking refuge in the fact that the artist does not know how or why he produces his effects, but simply paints what is presented to his mind. We shall therefore have to refer to his description of "Vital Beauty," as illustrated in Nature upon the one hand and Man upon the other, and to his description of the productions of modern naturalistic artists, to show what Mr. Ruskin really means by "Naturalist Idealism," and that this is an inversion of the idealism of Ancient Art. As it is the legitimate province of Art to represent vital spiritual conditions and manifestations through the forms and functions of Natural Life; and as it is obliged to recognize internal and external elements which are vital and destructive, because this is the universal condition of this life; and is also obliged to represent a resurrection into Spiritual Life through the marriage of the Human with the Divine, attended by the Crucifixion of the Individual, or the sacrifice of Personal Life,— all the legitimate forms of Ancient Art are found to represent these facts. Man, as constituting the internal sphere of natural life, was made to represent vital supernatural manifestations, — Nature, as constituting the external sphere of natural life, was made to represent destructive supernatural manifestations, — while resurrection out of the natural into the spiritual was represented by the marriage of the human with the divine: these representations being made by the Pagan artists from an external and natural, and by the Christian artists from an internal and supernatural, point of view. To show the inversion of this art, therefore, in modern art, we must show that Nature is made to represent Perfection or Good, and Man to represent Imperfection or Evil: or that Nature is represented as Beautiful, and Man as Deformed: and that this representation is accompanied by an "Eclipse of Faith" from being separated from and antagonized to the Church; by which Individualism, or individual Self-Assertion, is substituted for the Sacrifice of Personal Life. Transcendental Pictorial Art is divided into external and internal schools; the first, which was founded by Turner, being devoted to Landscape: and the second, which was founded by Kaulbach, being devoted to Historical Art. As the Landscape school is the most extensive and important, and has found an able exponent in Mr. Ruskin, we will show how this relationship between Man and Nature is regarded by it, and how he has described its illustration by Turner, the founder of this school.

At the close of "Modern Painters," Mr. Ruskin recognizes this antagonism between ancient and modern Art, and supposes the truth to lie between these extremes, as may be seen from the following statement: "On each side of a right feeling in this matter, lie, as usual, two opposite errors: the first, that of caring for man only, and for the rest of the Universe little, or not at all, which, in a measure, was the error of the Greeks and Florentines; the other, that of caring for the Universe only,— for man not at all,— which, in a measure, is the error of modern science, and of the Art connecting itself with such science;" the right feeling of which he speaks being the confounding of these opposites. But in describing, at the commencement of this work, Nature upon the one hand, and Man upon the other, as constituting the elements of "Vital Beauty," Mr. Ruskin has shown us Nature as the representative of Perfection, of Good, and of consequent happiness; and Man as the representative of Imperfection, of Evil, and of consequent unhappiness; and has suggested that Man is to be redeemed from Evil by the influence of Nature in the development of his moral powers, or in exciting a principle of universal sympathy, by which he becomes at-one with it. His description of Beauty in Nature is too diffuse to be quoted from, but will be found in the twelfth and thirteenth chapters of the second volume of "Modern Painters," which treat of "Vital Beauty, Relative and Generic." We will only quote the opening of the fourteenth chapter, which treats of "Vital Beauty in Man," which will be sufficient to show the character of both statements: "Having thus passed gradually through all the orders and fields of Creation, and traversed that goodly line of God's happy creatures who 'leap not, but express a feast, where all the guests sit close, and nothing want,' without finding any deficiency which human invention might supply, nor any harm which human interference might mend, we come at last to set ourselves face to face with ourselves, expecting that in creatures made after the image of God we are to find comeliness and completion more exquisite than in the fowls of the air, and the things that pass through the paths of the sea. But behold now a sudden change from all former experience! No longer among the individuals of the race is there equality or likeness,— a distributed fairness and fixed type visible in each,— but evil diversity, and terrible stamp of various degradation: features seamed with sickness, dimmed by sensuality, convulsed by passion, pinched by poverty, shadowed by sorrow, branded with remorse; bodies consumed with sloth, broken down by labor, tortured by disease, dishonored by foul uses; intellects without power, hearts without hope, minds earthly and devilish; our bones full of the sin of our youth, the heaven revealing our iniquity, the earth rising up against us, the roots dried up beneath, and the branch cut off above. Well for us only, if, after beholding this our natural face in a glass, we desire not straightway to forget what manner of men we be. Herein there is at last something, and too much, for that short-stopping intelligence and dull perception of ours to accomplish, whether in earnest fact, or in the seeking for the outward image of Beauty, to undo the devil's work, to restore to the body the grace and the power which inherited disease has destroyed, to return to the spirit the purity, and to the intellect the grasp, that they had in Paradise."

His description of the opposition between Turner and Georgione will illustrate the same inversion, and show more particularly the loss of religious faith in transcendental art. "To the very close of his life, Turner could endure ugliness which no one else of the same sensibility could have borne with for an instant. Dead brick walls, blank square windows, old clothes, market-womanly types of humanity, — any thing fishy and muddy, like Billingsgate or Hungerford Market, had great attraction for him, — black barges, patched sails, and every possible condition of fog. You will find these tolerations and affections guiding or sustaining him to the last hour of his life; the notablest of all such endurances being that of dirt. No Venetian ever draws any thing foul; but Turner devoted picture after picture to the illustration of the effects of dinginess, smoke, soot, dust, and dusty texture; old sides of boats, dunghills, straw-yards, and all the soilings and stains of every common labor. And, more than this, he not only could endure, but enjoyed and looked for, litter, like Covent-Garden wreck after the market." "As the strength of men to Turner, to Georgione, their weakness and vileness were alone visible; they themselves unworthy or ephemeral, their work despicable or decayed. In the Venetian's eyes, all beauty depended on man's presence and pride; in Turner's, on the solitude he had left, and the humiliation he had suffered: and thus the fate and the issue of all his work were determined at once. He must be a painter of the strength of Nature; there was no beauty elsewhere than in that: he must paint also the labor and sorrow and passing away of Man; this was the great human truth visible to him. Their labor, their sorrow, and their death; ruin of all their glorious work, passing away of their thoughts and their honor, mirage of pleasure, fallacy of hope, gathering of weed on temple and step, gaining of wave on deserted strand; weeping of the mother for the children, desolate by her breathless firstborn in the streets of the city, desolate by her last sons slain among the beasts of the field. And their Death. The old Greek question again, — yet unanswered." "Religion seems to him discreditable, — discredited, — not believing in itself; putting forth authority in a cowardly way; watching how far it might be tolerated; continually shrinking, disclaiming, fencing, finessing; divided against itself, not by stormy rents, but by thin fissures, and splittings of plaster from the walls. Not to be either obeyed or combated by an ignorant but clear-sighted youth, only to be scorned. And scorned not one whit the less, though also the dome dedicated to it looms high over distant winding of the Thames, as St. Mark's campanile rose for goodly landmark over mirage of lagoon."

We feel much indebted to Mr. Ruskin for describing and illustrating so faithfully the inversion, by Transcendentalism, of the symbolism of ancient art; although this has been done unconsciously, and he has attributed the particular bent of Turner's mind and the direction of his genius to the influence of external nature and of the circumstances connected with his early life, which if true, as it is not, would not affect the question that has here been settled. This tendency, so peculiar to the transcendental mind, to make the manifestations of human nature depend upon the influence of external nature, is referable to the same inversion of order that has here been illustrated, and has fortunately led Mr. Ruskin to disclose more of the imperfections of his favorite artists than he otherwise would have done. He does this service for us again, in contrasting the genius of Bacon and Pascal, and in showing the opposite ideals realized by Shakspeare and Dante; and we will quote his description of the latter to illustrate this tendency, and also to illustrate the degradation of Unitarian Art in the region of Poetry through the influence of Naturalism; because Shakspeare, as well as Bacon, was a representative man, and combined the vices and the excellences of this school in the most intense and wonderful manner, the brilliancy of his Fancy and the pungency of his Wit being unapproached by any succeeding artist. He says, "Whatever difference, involving inferiority,

there exists between Shakspeare and Dante, in his conceptions
of the relation between this world and the next, we may partly
trace, as we did the difference between Bacon and Pascal,
to the less noble character of the scenes around him in his youth;
and admit that, although it was necessary for his special work
that he should be put, as it were, on a level with his race, on
those plains of Stratford, we should see in this a proof, instead of
a negation, of the mountain power over human intellect. For
breadth and perfectness of condescending sight, the Shaksperian
mind stands alone: but, in ascending sight, it is limited; and the
difference between these careless masques of heathen gods, or
unbelieved though mightily conceived visions of fairy, witch, or
risen spirit, and the earnest faith of Dante's vision of Paradise, is
the true measure of the different influence between the willowy
banks of Avon and the purple hills of Arno. Shakspeare is
distinguished from Dante eminently by his always dwelling on
last causes instead of first causes. Dante invariably points to the
moment of the soul's choice which fixes its fate; but Shakspeare
always leans on the force of Fate as it urges the final evil; and
dwells with infinite bitterness on the power of the wicked, and
the infinitude of the result dependent seemingly on little things."

The ground of this naturalistic ideal is to be found in the principles of "Sympathy" and "Naturalism," the external and
destructive laws of the Sentimental Nature, which, in Transcendentalism, become the ruling laws of the mind: the first demanding individual gratification from a universal point of view, and
therefore identifying the individual with every thing external to
him in which any kind of relationship or community of life can
be traced; and the other demanding the assertion of the individual from a universal point of view, and therefore demanding the
full gratification instead of the sacrifice of individual inclination,
and the full manifestation instead of the subjection of individual
thought, — as that of an absolute cause which is the "Light of
the World;" these being inversions of that repudiation of all
external things, and that individual self-sacrifice, which are demanded by the Church and represented in all legitimate Art.
That these were included in the naturalistic ideal set up by Mr.
Ruskin as a substitute for that of the ancient artists, is apparent
from his writings. A recognition of Sympathy as the ground of
all moral manifestations and of the true ideal in Art may be found
in the Chapter on "Vital Beauty" already alluded to, from which
the following is taken: "Throughout the whole organic creation,

every being in a perfect state exhibits certain appearances or evidences of happiness; and, besides, is, in its nature, its desires, its modes of nourishment, habitation, and death, illustrative or expressive of certain moral dispositions or principles. Now, first, in the keenness of the sympathy which we feel in the happiness, real or apparent, of all organic beings, and which, as we shall presently see, invariably prompts us, from the joy we have in it, to look upon those most lovely which are most happy; and, secondly, in the justness of the moral sense which rightly reads the lesson they are all intended to teach; — in our right accepting and reading of all this, consists, I say, the ultimately perfect condition of that noble theoretic faculty, which can only be fully established with respect to vital beauty. Its first perfection relating to vital beauty is the kindness and unselfish fulness of heart, which receives the utmost amount of pleasure from the happiness of all things. Only as we draw near to God, and are made in measure like unto him, can we increase this our possession of charity, of which the entire essence is in God only. Wherefore it is evident that even the ordinary exercise of this faculty implies a condition of the whole moral being in some measure right and healthy, and that to the entire exercise of it there is necessary the entire perfection of the Christian character; for he who loves not God, nor his brother, cannot love the grass beneath his feet, and the creatures that fill those spaces in the universe which he needs not, and which live not for his uses; nay, he has seldom grace to be grateful even to those that love him and serve him: while, on the other hand, none can love God nor his human brother without loving all things which his Father loves, nor without looking upon them every one as in that respect his brethren also, and perhaps worthier than he, if, in the under concords they have to fill, their part is touched more truly; so that I know not of any thing more destructive of the whole theoretic faculty, not to say of the Christian character and human intellect, than those accursed sports in which man makes of himself, cat, tiger, serpent, chætodon, and alligator in one. As we pass from those beings of whose happiness and pain we are certain, to those in which it is doubtful or only seeming, as possibly in plants, — though I would fain hold, if I might, 'the faith that every flower enjoys the air it breathes,' neither do I ever crush or gather one without some pain, — yet our feeling for them has in it more of sympathy than of actual love, as receiving from them in delight more than we can give; nevertheless, the sympathy of very lofty and sensitive minds usually reaches so far as the conception of life in the plant, and so to love, as with Shelley, of the sensitive plant, and Shakspeare always, as he has taught us in the sweet voices of Ophelia and Perdita, and Wordsworth always, as of the daffodils and the celandine; and so all other great poets, that is to say, great seers."

Now, it will be seen that this elevation of the principle of Sympathy is perfectly harmonious with the other statements with regard to Naturalistic Idealism, in which external nature is made to be the governing principle in its realization: but, in stating the transcendental idea of individual self-assertion from a universal point of view, Mr. Ruskin was obliged to deny every thing that he had before said with regard to Turnerian Art, and in stating the relation between external nature and man; for, as we have said, this ideal cannot be stated except in a contradiction. He says, "It might be thought that the tenor of the preceding chapter was in some sort adverse to my repeated statement that all great art is the expression of man's delight in God's work, not his own. But observe: he is not himself his own work; he is himself the most wonderful piece of God's workmanship extant. In this best piece not only he is bound to take delight, but cannot, in a right state of thought, take delight in any thing else, otherwise than through himself. Through himself as the sun of creation. In himself as the Light of the World. Let him stand in his due relation to other creatures, and to inanimate things,— know them all and love them, as made for him, and he for them, — and he becomes the greatest and holiest of them. But let him cast off this relation, despise and forget the less creation around him, and, instead of being the light of the world, he is a sun in space,— a fiery ball spotted with storm. All the diseases of the mind leading to fatalest ruin consist primarily in this isolation. Every form of asceticism on one side, of sensualism on the other, is an isolation of his soul or of his body; while every healthy state of nations and of individual minds consists in the unselfish presence of the human spirit everywhere, energizing over all things, speaking and living through all things. The art which is specially known as "Christian" erred by pride in its denial of the animal nature of man; and, in connection with all monkish and fanatical forms of religion, by looking always to another world instead of this. It wasted its strength in visions, and was therefore swept away by the strong truth of the naturalist art of the sixteenth century. But the naturalist art erred on the other side; denied at last the spiritual nature of man, and perished in corruption. A contemplative re-action is taking place in modern times, out of which it may be hoped a new spiritual art may be developed."

We have made these quotations from Mr. Ruskin, which we have condensed into as small a space as was possible without changing their meaning, because it is important that the two principal sources of Naturalistic Idealism here illustrated should be pointed out. We shall make no comment, supposing that the inversion of legitimate idealism, the discord between the elements which constitute this new modern ideal, and the confounding of opposite things, which have here been alluded to, although ingeniously concealed, will be sufficiently apparent. We will therefore conclude this notice of Mr. Ruskin with an account of the third and last element named by him as constituting the true ideal in Art, which is "Grotesque Idealism." It will be understood that what is called the Grotesque, in ancient art, is constituted by combinations of vegetable and animal forms, partly from nature and partly from ideal conceptions of the Imagination, which are introduced into Architecture and into illuminated manuscripts as a hieroglyphical element symbolic of religious ideas; this being, like Architecture, one of the arts which have been lost. Mr. Ruskin, however, who believes in nothing but natural productions, and does not seem to understand that any symbolism, other than that superficial one which is addressed to the Fancy, has ever existed, has adopted this element for the purpose of introducing the Comic as a true ideal in Art in the place of the sublime conceptions of the ancient painters, but particularly of Raphael, repudiating these as specimens of the false ideal in Art: and this he has done by confounding the religious symbolism termed Grotesque with the Comic; a combination that is positively monstrous. To prevent the shock which such a doctrine is calculated to give, in describing the Grotesque Ideal, he first alludes to the symbolism of the ancient artists, such as Dante and Albert Durer, under the name of "the Pathetic Grotesque;" and then proceeds to confound these legitimate and truly ideal religious symbols, which are productions of the Imagination, with the forms of "Satire and Wit," which he names "the Jesting Grotesque," and which are produced by the Fancy, when governed by its destructive law, under the influence of "Imperfection." He says, "The grotesque being not only a most forcible instrument of teaching, but a most natural manner of expression; springing as it does at once from any tendency to playfulness in minds highly comprehensive of truth; and being also one of the readiest ways in which such satire and wit as may be possessed by any inferior rank of mind can be perpetually expressed, — it becomes on all grounds desirable that what is suggested in times of play should be rightly sayable without toil; and what occurs to men of inferior power or knowledge, sayable without any high degree of skill. Hence it is an infinite good to mankind when there is full acceptance of the grotesque, slightly sketched or expressed; and, if field for such expression be frankly granted, an enormous mass of intellectual power is turned to everlasting use, which, in this present century of ours, evaporates in street-gibing or vain revelling; all the good wit and satire expiring in daily talk (like foam on wine), which in the thirteenth and fourteenth centuries had a permitted and useful expression in the arts of sculpture and illumination, like foam in chalcedony." It is probably the first time that "street-gibing and vain revelling" have been regarded as such desirable accomplishments, — that it has been supposed that such intellectual power could "be turned to everlasting use,"— or that such degraded and degrading manifestations of the Fancy have been recognized as specimens of the true ideal in Art. However ingeniously this unholy connection between the Grotesque and the Comic may have been concealed by Mr. Ruskin, the language here quoted cannot be mistaken, and establishes, in the most conclusive manner, the fact for which we have contended, — that the Comic is necessarily realized in all the forms of Art by its degradation.

From the statements which have been made for the purpose of illustrating and demonstrating the Laws of Succession, it must have become apparent, that, in the Church, in the State, in Philosophy, and in Art, changes have taken place which are in exact conformity with the universal laws of growth and development here stated; and that these changes are not confined to any particular department of natural life, but have accompanied the growth and development of all its forms from the creation of the world; because we have shown that these laws are illustrated by the primitive productions of this earth before the creation of man. The external condition of the soul that we describe as having been realized by its descent from internal to external, and from supernatural to natural, principles, as the governing powers of the thought and of the life, and which is a descent from the region of internal truth into that of external good, — although presenting a fair exterior, and appearing in useful and beautiful aspects, owing to the growth of the individual from below upwards, by which he becomes more simple, truthful, and devoted to the realization of external uses for philanthropic ends, — is the lowest point of degradation that it experiences in the whole course of its development. We say that this is the lowest point, for the reason that it is here confined to the region of natural appearances, — which are the most deceptive of all things, because they are the opposite of what they seem, — and that it here repudiates all those supernatural ideas which communicate vitality to the thought and to the life; a condition that is symbolized in the Scriptures by the "great famine in the land," and a degradation that is there symbolized by the keeping and feeding of swine by "the Prodigal Son," as we shall show in our explanation of this parable. The Bible — which is an inspired book, "written within and on the back side, sealed with seven seals," which none but Christ, as revealed in the consciousness at his second coming, can unloose — is not only brought down to the test of natural understanding and experience, and tried by the standard of natural good, but becomes degraded and neglected by being perverted to the basest uses; so that the writing upon the back side becomes obliterated by natural falsification, and a total blindness is produced to all that is representative of vital supernatural ideas.

It is true that the internal-natural condition of the soul, that has been alluded to in these statements, and which will now be separately and particularly analyzed and illustrated, is the most destructive natural condition that is ever realized by it. Although, in this condition, the individual obtains a consciousness through the highest regions of the mind and of the will, and demands an internal and real manifestation of himself that produces a reality, a simplicity, and a truthfulness in his life, that is far beyond that which is realized in a merely external condition, — he at the same time becomes consciously conceptive of the destructive laws of the mind, and applies them as the laws of his belief and life, and acts with the more external classes in carrying on a warfare against all vital ideas and institutions; and although he has, from being simply natural, become supernaturally conscious, and is consequently governed by supernatural instead of natural laws, this makes his condition still more destructive. He becomes more destructive, because the supernatural laws of which he becomes conscious, and to which he devotes himself with all the zeal of a newly-awakened religious enthusiasm, are the most destructive of all the principles of the human constitution: and nothing can exceed the violence with which he commences his attack upon all established ideas and institutions, because the religious sentiment is a ruling principle, and the most active of all the powers of the mind; and a religious development is always more violent at its commencement than at any other time, as we may learn from history.

Great natural evil must of course result as the consequence of this repudiation of all that represents a vital spiritual condition, and of this assertion of destructive sentimental laws and natural principles; because all legitimate natural production is realized through the influence of these representatives. When this sustaining influence is withdrawn, truth degenerates into falsehood, and good into evil; and the more sympathetic and externally philanthropic the individual is, the more selfish, unjust, and cruel he becomes. An experience of this kind now threatens a convulsion of society in the United States, which will sunder the ties that bind the states together, overturn the institutions of the land, and perhaps deluge the country with blood.* Neither are these evils confined to the condition and manifestations of the human constitution, but extend to all the substances and phenomena of natural existence. The disorders produced in Man are accompanied by corresponding disorders in the whole system of Nature; these being produced by a derangement of the principles which enter into the constitution of vegetable and animal life, by a change in the relative strength of the opposite elements combined in them. We already begin to experience the influence of this change, and may see that disorders in the Church, in the State, and in the manifestations of the Mind, through the predominance of the destructive over the vital principles of the human constitution, and of the natural over the supernatural element, are accompanied by corresponding disorders in the physical world; and these will continue to increase until the vital religious element again becomes the ruling power, and man, in consequence, returns to his allegiance to the vital supernatural ideas which have been externally incarnated through the Church. But the system of Naturalism which rises from the ruins of the Church must pass through a full development, and man must eat of the bitter fruits which grow upon those trees of death that have been planted by him. He needs the lesson which this worship of Falsehood will, through much suffering, impart to him, in order that his perma-

---

* This was written during the political agitation in 1854.

nent progress may be secured, and he may finally attain to the realization of spiritual knowledge and a spiritual life in God. Before these can be secured, the following predictions of the Prophet must be fulfilled: "For, behold, the Lord, the Lord of hosts, doth take away from Jerusalem and from Judah the stay and the staff, the whole stay of bread, and the whole stay of water, the mighty man, and the man of war, the judge, and the prophet, and the prudent, and the ancient, the captain of fifty, and the honorable man, and the counsellor, and the cunning artificer, and the eloquent orator. And I will give children to be their princes, and babes shall rule over them. And the people shall be oppressed, every one by another, and every one by his neighbor: the child shall behave himself proudly against the ancient, and the base against the honorable." "For Jerusalem is ruined, and Judah is fallen; because their tongue and their doings are against the Lord, to provoke the eyes of his glory."

"Because thou hast forgotten the God of thy salvation, and hast not been mindful of the rock of thy strength, therefore shalt thou plant pleasant plants, and shalt set it with strange slips; in the day shalt thou make thy plant to grow, and in the morning shalt thou make thy seed to flourish: but the harvest shall be a heap in the day of grief, and of desperate sorrow. Woe to the multitude of many people, which make a noise like the noise of the seas; and to the rushing of nations, that make a rushing like the rushing of mighty waters! The nations shall rush like the rushing of many waters; but God shall rebuke them, and they shall flee far off, and shall be chased as the chaff of the mountains before the wind, and like a rolling thing before the whirlwind. And, behold, at eveningtide trouble; and before the morning he is not. This is the portion of them that spoil us, and the lot of them that rob us."

ILLUSTRATIONS OF THE LAW OF CIRCULARITY IN

TRANSCENDENTALISM.

WE are now to describe the experiences that belong to an internal sphere of the natural consciousness; which must, for reasons already given, be realized to some extent in this atmosphere, although calculated for an ethereal one. To these experiences we give the name of Transcendentalism; because in this sphere the individual becomes internally self-conscious, and conceptive of Laws and Relationships from a supernatural point of view. Now, as these are, in the natural, dualistic, and antagonized as vital and destructive, to represent the opposition between Infinite and Finite Spheres; and as those which are vital have, in an external sphere of consciousness, been unconsciously represented in the vital forms of Society, while those which are destructive are now to be consciously conceived and applied as laws of the individual belief and life, — a universal change of condition, of position, and of manifestation, that is destructive to all the external uses which are appropriated to an external atmosphere and sphere of consciousness, must follow this introduction of the soul into an internal sphere of consciousness. The first and most external fact that presents itself to our notice, therefore, is, that as the soul advances in the realization of this higher consciousness, and becomes manifested from an internal instead of an external point of view, this advance is accompanied by a corresponding decline in those mediums through which it had been manifested in an external sphere of consciousness; and, consequently, the individual experiences the loss of external manifesting power, — finds himself without any congenial occupation, — without the power of forming for himself any consistent plan of life, or of directing himself externally in any calculated or consistent manner, — and suffering from the absence of those numerous affinities which bind him to existence, and from the want of those affectional experiences which constitute the wine of life.

In reflecting upon the differences which must necessarily exist between a material existence and the ethereal mode that is appropriate to this internal sphere of experience, we cannot escape from the conclusion, that, besides the radical change which must take place in all the relationships of life, the occupations of the individual must become essentially different, and even opposite in kind; and that those which are based upon material growths and material causes and effects, with which the individual is here principally employed, must be exchanged for others in which production is not slow and consecutive, as here, but instantaneous: because it is one of the most beautiful, as it is one of the most common, of the intuitions and recognitions of the religious sentiment, that, in spiritual and in ethereal atmospheres, external appearances corresponding with the natural productions of the earth are produced in an infinite diversity, but in greater perfection because corresponding with these atmospheres, and with higher spheres of consciousness,—that these address themselves to the mind through external senses which are inconceivably intensified and refined, and produce a corresponding delight,—and that these appearances are not there produced by the labor of man, or by any consecutive growth, as in the material order of things, but appear spontaneously as an accompaniment to the particular individual position and state, for the reason that a correspondence must exist there between internal and external things. This opposition between ethereal and material modes of existence thus becomes one of the causes of transcendental imbecility; because the individual, in coming into an internal sphere of consciousness, necessarily commences a preparation for this corresponding change in his modes of manifestation; although the principal and immediate causes are of course to be found in a decline in the power of external direction, and in the substitution of internal conceptions for external and generally recognized forms of relationship. This anti-practical character of the transcendental mind is thus described by Mr. Emerson, in a lecture upon "Transcendentalism," of which he is the principal and recognized exponent: "It is a sign of our times, conspicuous to the coarsest observer, that many intelligent and religious persons withdraw themselves from the common labors and competitions of the market and the caucus, and betake themselves to a certain solitary and critical way of living, from which no solid fruit has yet appeared to justify their separation. They hold themselves aloof: they feel the disproportion between their faculties and the work offered them; and they prefer to ramble in the country, and perish of *ennui*, to the degradation of such charities and such ambitions as the city can propose to them. They are striking work, and crying out for something worthy to do! What they do is done only because they are overpowered by the humanities that speak on all sides; and they consent to such labor as is open to them, though to their lofty dream the writing of 'Iliads' or 'Hamlets,' or the building of cities or empires, seems drudgery. With this passion for what is great and extraordinary, it cannot be wondered at that they are repelled by vulgarity and frivolity in people. They say to themselves, It is better to be alone than in bad company. And it is really a wish to be met — the wish to find society for their hope and their religion — which prompts them to shun what is called society. They feel that they are never so fit for friendship as when they have quit mankind, and taken themselves to friend.

"But their solitary and fastidious manners not only withdraw them from the conversation, but from the labors of the world: they are not good citizens, nor good members of society; unwillingly they bear their part of the public and private burthens; they do not willingly share in the public charities, in the public religious rites, in the enterprises of education, of missions, foreign or domestic, in the abolition of the slave-trade, or in the temperance society. They are inactive: they do not even like to vote. The philanthropists inquire whether Transcendentalism does not mean sloth. They had as lief hear that their friend was dead, as that he was a Transcendentalist; for then he is paralyzed, and can never do any thing for Humanity.

"On the part of these children, it is replied, that life and their faculty seem to them gifts too rich to be squandered on such trifles as you propose to them. What you call your fundamental institutions, your great and holy causes, seem to them great abuses, and, when nearly seen, paltry matters. Each 'cause,' as it is called, — say Abolition, Temperance; say Calvinism or Unitarianism, — becomes speedily a little shop, where the article, let it have been at first ever so subtle and ethereal, is now made up into portable and convenient cakes, and retailed in small quantities to suit purchasers. You make free use of these words, 'great and holy;' but few things appear to them such. Few persons have any magnificence of nature to inspire enthusiasm; and the philanthropies and charities have a certain air of quackery. As to the general course of living, and the daily employments of men, they cannot see much virtue in these, since they are parts of this vicious circle ; and, as no great ends are answered by the men, there is nothing noble in the arts by which they are maintained. Nay, they have made the experiment; and found, that from the liberal professions to the coarsest manual labor, and from the courtesies of the academy and the college to the conventions of the cotillon-room and the morning-call, there is a spirit of cowardly compromise and seeming which intimates a frightful scepticism, — a life without love, and an activity without aim. Now, we confess, and by no means happy, is our condition. If you want the aid of our labor, we ourselves stand in greater want of the labor. We are miserable with inaction ; we perish of rest and rust: but we do not like your work. Your virtuous projects, so called, do not cheer me: I know that which shall come will cheer me. If I cannot work, at least I will not lie."

This is an exceedingly graphic and beautiful, though a somewhat partial and one-sided, description of the position in this atmosphere of that class of persons who have commenced the realization of a circle of experiences belonging to the second sphere of the soul's consciousness. But Mr. Emerson seems to be much more successful in describing the phenomena than in conceiving the cause of Transcendentalism. He supposes it to be simply internalism as opposed to externalism, or idealism as opposed to materialism; and that it thus becomes manifested in all spheres and conditions of the soul, — in the Church appearing as Protestantism, in the State as Socialism, in Philosophy as Idealism, &c. He says, " This way of thinking, falling on Roman times, made Stoic philosophers ; falling on despotic times, made patriot Catos and Brutuses; falling on superstitious times, made prophets and apostles; on popish times, made protestants and ascetic monks, preachers of Faith against the preachers of Works ; on prelatical times, made Puritans and Quakers; and, falling on Unitarian and conservative times, makes the peculiar shades of Idealism which we know." As all things exist in pairs as internal and external, every thing may be said to have its transcendental side; because, as Transcendentalism originates in the realization of an internal consciousness, both with regard to the Mind and to the Soul, it is represented by all things which are relatively internal. Besides this, in every sphere of development, or circle of natural experiences, the period which precedes the re-establishment of vital supernatural ideas is relatively transcendental; an example of which we find in the period immediately preceding the coming of Christ, of which John the Baptist was the exponent; but, in such cases, we use the word in a representative, and not in a real, sense. Transcendentalism includes a growth and development of the mind and of the soul peculiar to itself, because it completes the natural development of the human constitution, preparatory to its introduction into a spiritual sphere of consciousness, and includes an internal-natural order of experiences, never before realized; in which the destructive laws of the mind are consciously conceived and applied as laws of the individual belief and life. It cannot, therefore, appear until all the phenomena belonging to the religious and moral periods in which are established forms of belief and of life representative of vital spiritual laws—and to which popery, prelacy, and puritanism belong—have been exhausted, and a way has been prepared for it by Unitarianism through the repudiation of all genuine religious forms. In order that we may obtain a more correct conception of Transcendentalism, instead of referring to the manifestations of individuals,—the knowledge of which has been acquired by observation,—we will contemplate the changes of mental condition which accompany this change from an external to an internal sphere of consciousness, and the mental states by which these manifestations are produced; so that, by penetrating the cause of these phenomena, we may discover the laws of transcendental life, and apply them in explaining the phenomena which are incident to this period of the soul's progress.

There are three principal reasons why we cannot obtain a knowledge of the nature of Transcendentalism from an external point of observation; and these will here be mentioned, that we may guard against being led into wrong conclusions with regard to it. The first is, that, in this sphere of the consciousness, two elements are to be distinguished, and two classes of individuals who correspond with these; one illustrating the internal and intellectual, and the other the external and affectional, side of Transcendentalism, which are in some respects antagonistic: the second is, that each of these classes becomes manifested under a law of contrariety, or from points of truth and of good which are opposite, so that no consistency of manifestation can be realized: and the third is, that Transcendentalism is not a continuation of the old development, but is cut off and antagonized to this as a new development in which an order of experiences perfectly opposite becomes realized, while at the same time these two opposite spheres of consciousness and orders of thought are found combined together in all the individual manifestations, which will thus be to a great extent external in character; the reason for this being, that manifestations of the mind and conditions of the consciousness depend upon a physical organization, which requires time for development before a new order of external experiences can be realized. Two kinds of disorderly manifestation will therefore have to be distinguished: one that arises in the legitimate operation of internal transcendental laws, which is principally theoretical; and another which arises in the practical application of these laws to this external condition of the individual consciousness. In illustrating the development of the mind from within outwards, we have shown that the external period of its development concludes with a descent into the individual region of Affection, and into the most external sentimental and intellectual principles; and that these become the ruling motive and directing powers, with the subjection of the intellectual to the affectional power. The change from this extreme external to an opposite internal condition of the consciousness is therefore attended at its commencement by a combination of extremes in the manifestations of individual life; and thus when the inverted ideas and relationships of Transcendentalism, charged as they are with all the force of a newly-awakened religious fanaticism,— the tendency of which is to produce an inversion of all the representatives of "Spiritualism,"—come to be combined with these external, material, and sensualistic experiences, the result is a great variety of disorderly theories, and of fanatical and destructive manifestations, which are external representations of transcendental ideas and laws. These constitute a large portion of the reform movements of the present day, in which the demand for individual liberty, not only for the individual, but for all men, without any distinction, and the clamor of unsexed and thus disorderly females for equal rights, or for freedom from subjection to the male, may be observed. The combination of these opposites is also productive of a class of writings of which "Leaves of Grass" is an exaggerated specimen; a monstrous production of the Fancy, which comes to us with the indorsement of the highest transcendental authority, illustrating the worship of the external forms and functions of Nature, which are enumerated in the most promiscuous and disorderly manner as equally entitled to veneration and admiration; reminding us of those monstrous vagaries of Hindoo superstition in which the meanest form of matter is regarded as in itself God. As Transcendentalism is the exponent of "Naturalism," is thus a worshipper of Good in the Beautiful, and is governed by the laws of diversity, partiality, and separation, it contains a tendency towards externalism, materialism, and sensualism; and, although these appear in an exalted form which corresponds in some degree with an ethereal condition of being, there is an attraction between the transcendentalist and those who are the most grossly affectional, external, and individual, because these are unconsciously governed by the same laws which Transcendentalism conceives and applies in a self-conscious manner as laws of the individual belief and life. Both become disorderly in the same direction, because Naturalism, combined with Individualism, is the common ground of activity in both, and thus both are disposed to repudiate the common external relationships of social and of domestic life; although this is done from different motives,— the first, having come down into an individual sphere of affection, from individual caprice, or natural inclination, which is destructive from an external point of view; and the second from a higher and more legitimate motive, which demands the recognition and appropriation of opposite, internal relationships as the productive laws of the individual life. Besides, as we have already said, Transcendentalism is combined in the same individual with external and sensualistic proclivities, and thus these two opposite spheres of experience become so confounded that it is impossible to separate them from an external point of view. For these reasons, we have undertaken to contemplate this subject from an internal or purely intellectual point, making use of external phenomena in the illustration of these conceptions; it being only in this way that we can separate Transcendentalism from the opposite external things which have been connected with it, and in which it must become incarnated and represented.

We have already seen, that when the soul throws off its subjection to the vital laws of the Sentimental Nature, as embodied in the representative forms of the Church and of the State, under the unconscious influence of the destructive sentimental laws, it descends into states of intellectualism and affectionalism of the most external kind, in which Good becomes the supreme principle,— a form of its development that is known as Unitarianism. We have seen, that,— though the soul has become elevated with regard to its individual life, because it has become more self-conscious, and therefore more real, — with regard to the forms of its life, as realized through the mind and through the will, it is the lowest condition into which it can come, because it completes the entire circle of experiences which are appropriate to this lower atmosphere by a development from within outwards. We have seen, that, when these have been completed, the soul commences a new circle of experiences, in an internal sphere of consciousness, from a self-conscious point of view; that is, it becomes conscious with regard to the manifestations of both the mind and the will, and internal with regard both to the principles of the mind in which its development commences, and to the quality of all the manifestations of the mind and of the will. By coming into an internal sphere of consciousness, the soul experiences a new birth, by which from external it becomes internal; and, consequently, the appropriating and constructing personal principles demand the conscious realization of internal laws and forms of truth and of good, and the mind becomes conscious from the most internal regions as a point of departure, and realizes self-conscious conceptions of relationship through its internal and intellectual receptive principles. In this conscious return to the highest regions of the mind for the laws of truth and of good by which the powers of the mind and of the will are to be developed, the affective principles become the ruling powers, and the individual comes under the government of destructive universal laws corresponding with personal individual want, instead of vital universal laws which demand the sacrifice of this want. The manner in which this is effected is as follows: In commencing a new circle of experiences under the laws of "Contrariety" and "Circularity," although the highest regions of the mind become operative, as this movement is a spiral one, instead of being a return to the unconscious and spontaneous operations of the vital intellective principles which characterized the commencement of development in an external sphere of consciousness, it is a return to the conscious operations of the destructive affective principles, by which an inversion of all the legitimate forms of truth and of good is produced.

We have already shown that the development of the individual consciousness is obtained through the influence of the Sentimental Principles, which are the governing powers of the mind, because they establish the supernatural laws of truth and of good; — that this development commences in the most external sphere of this consciousness under the superintendence of the most external Church, supported by the unconscious influence of the intellective sentimental principles, which are relatively vital, and are "Spiritualism" in the religious, and "Justice" in the moral department; — that through this Church religious Symbolic Forms and secular Institutions corresponding with these vital principles are established by supernatural agency, and that the individual is brought under subjection to these through the operation of the most external receptive sentimental principles, which are "Veneration" in the religious, and "Approbation" in the moral department, by the appropriation by the personifying principles of these external receptions, and by the application of these as governing laws of the individual life through the principle of "Direction" in the Will; — and that, in this way, the Natural becomes vitalized by the operation of a productive supernatural or representative-spiritual principle, and a harmonious combination of truth and of good incarnated in ecclesiastical and civil forms is effected; by which, natural uses, representing the spiritual marriage of good with truth, are realized. We have shown that this development of the individual in an external sphere of consciousness is continued under the superintendence of Protestantism and Unitarianism, as established in their Churches and Schools, upon the ground of Individual Liberty in both sacred and secular things: in the first, by individual interpretations of the Bible and of the State from a Trinitarian point of view, through conscious conceptions founded in intuitions from the vital sentiments of "Spiritualism" and "Justice," by which good is made subject to truth, and Religion is established as supreme; and, in the second, by interpretations of the Bible and of the State from a Unitarian point of view, by the application of individual natural thoughts and experiences realized through the unconscious influence of the destructive laws of "Naturalism" and "Sympathy," by which truth is made subject to good, and Morality is established as supreme; these interpretations being appropriated by the personifying principles, and applied as governing laws of the individual life through the principle of "Relation" in the Will; and that, by the latter, the religious doctrines and social ideas realized by the former are gradually perverted and brought under subjection to naturalistic, affectional, and sympathetic influences in the development of the mind and of the will, by which the foundations of both Church and State are gradually undermined, and prepared for dissolution.

Upon the entrance of the soul into an internal sphere of the natural consciousness, in which the experiences now being described as Transcendentalism are realized, the development of the individual is continued in a really internal and self-conscious manner by a return, under the law of Circularity, to the highest regions of the Sentiment, through which supernatural laws representing the spiritual are communicated to the consciousness; but instead of being a return to the intellective laws, which are vital, it is a return to the affective laws, which are destructive, these being "Naturalism" in the religious, and "Sympathy" in the moral department. These, therefore, become the governing laws to the individual consciousness; and the development of the soul in this sphere commences under the direction of these laws, — separated from and antagonized to the intellective laws, which alone can vitalize them, — assisted by the intellectual receptive sentimental powers, which are relatively vital, and are "Intuition" in the religious, and "Satisfaction" in the moral department. Through the operation of these internal receptive powers, under subjection to these affective laws, the individual becomes receptive of internal conceptions; and these internal realizations are appropriated by the personifying principles, as corresponding with the present want or condition of the individual from growth, and are applied as governing laws of the individual life through the principles of "Relation" and "Consciousness" in the Will. A complete emancipation of the individual from all external influences is in this way secured; and a reconstruction of all the forms of thought, and a re-organization of all the forms of life, are commenced. Now, as these affective laws are related to the opposite intellective laws, as "death against life," this development of the mind and of the individual consciousness in an internal-natural sphere must be accompanied by the perversion and inversion of all the religious symbolism and forms of thought, and of all the legitimate social principles and institutions, which have been established by supernatural influence through the operation of these vital intellective laws, and of the constructive sentimental principles, and to which the individual had before been made subject through an external, unconscious reception from the Church, and through conscious intuitions and conceptions of the religious and moral sentiments. In this way the Bible, the Church, and the State are destroyed: all the vital ideas in which these are founded are inverted, and a form representative of Absolute Falsehood is realized and established as the supreme law of the individual life. By establishing, as the only forms of Truth and of Good, internal conceptions of individual want founded upon destructive sentimental laws, which demand the subjection of the universal to the individual for personal ends, and by realizing an affinity for these in the personal constitution, two consequences result. The first is the establishment of pure Individualism upon the basis of Naturalism, by which the idea of subjection to any thing external to the individual is repudiated, and every thing not corresponding with the individual's conception of truth and of good is denounced, and its destruction demanded; while the second is the establishment of personal want as the governing law of the individual life, which is the subjection of the universal to the personal, or of the "*not me*" to the "*me;*" this being Self-worship,—the deification of the Individual through the worship of the Female Principle,—which represents the worship of Absolute Death in the form of Absolute Falsehood. And this worship of Self, or demand for self-assertion and self-gratification from a universal point of view, appears in the recognition of Feeling as the absolute law which must govern the individual, and to which all Thought must be made subservient; because the ground of this experience is simply an affinity for that which corresponds with personal want, which, as it is undefined by any intellectual law, and is confined to an apprehensive recognition which is separated from comprehension or thought, necessarily appears as the supremacy of feeling.

To show that this statement corresponds with the fact, and that the feelings are indeed now recognized as the guiding and governing laws, while the intellect is made completely subservient to them, we will quote from a transcendental writer what we presume will be responded to by every transcendentalist; this being an inversion of the commencement of Locke's "Essay on the Conduct of the Understanding:" "The last resort a man ought to have recourse to in the conduct of himself is his Understanding; for though we distinguish the faculties of the mind, and attribute the clearest conception to the Understanding as to the distinctive faculty, yet the true course of nature is, the man, which is the agent, ought to determine himself to this or to that voluntary action, upon some primitive motive in the feelings, which can never be an apparent one. No man should ever set himself about any thing upon some view or other, and thus make the effect of what he does serve him for a reason for what he does; and whatsoever faculties then he employs, the feelings, with that love which must be developed in them, ought constantly to lead; and, by the light in the Understanding, the operative powers ought only to be ruled. The will itself, how loving and disinterested soever it may be thought, must always fail, if obedient to the dictates of the Understanding. It is, therefore, of the highest concernment, that great care should be taken of the feelings, to conduct them right in the development of their faith, and in the love from which they act."

This supremacy of feeling is one of the most prominent and peculiar features of Transcendentalism, and one that is most fruitful in its results, because it releases the individual from all the restraints of law, and leads him to trust implicitly in his individual impressions, which he does not feel obliged either to account for or to defend. Transcendentalists, therefore, ignore logical demonstration, and confine themselves to affirmation and poetical illustration; asserting that their faith cannot be confined within the limits of any system, or even by any definition, for the reason that the highest truths must be felt, and cannot be described. They therefore claim to be released from all the ordinary obligations of rationality and consistency, and are completely cut off from all philosophical investigation, and from all rational communion with other minds; because, unless the conclusions arrived at are agreeable to them, no amount of evidence can reconcile them to the premises assumed. This repudiation of intellectual consistency, from a recognition of the supremacy of feeling, is forcibly illustrated by Mr. Emerson in the following manner: "Trust your emotion. In your metaphysics, you have denied personality to the Deity; yet, when the devout motions of the soul come, yield to them heart and life, though they should clothe God in shape and color. Leave your theory, as Joseph his coat in the hand of the harlot, and flee. A foolish consistency is the hobgoblin of little minds, adored by little statesmen and philosophers and divines. With consistency, a great soul has simply nothing to do. If you would be a man, speak what you think to-day, in words as hard as cannon-balls; and to-morrow speak what to-morrow thinks, in hard words again, though it contradicts every thing you said to-day. I hope in these days we have heard the last of consistency. Let the word be gazetted, and ridiculous henceforth."

In consequence of this lawless supremacy of Feeling, and repudiation of Truth as a governing principle, although the phenomena of the consciousness are more intently studied than ever before, for the reason that this is a self-conscious sphere of life, the philosophy of the human mind, which includes the intellectual and moral forms of Psychology, is more neglected than ever before; and a fanciful interpretation of individual states, or facts of the individual consciousness, takes the place of and is even mistaken for psychological truth, which is a scientific explanation of states of the consciousness, and is therefore an intellectual and not a personal experience. One reason for this, however, is, that the mind has returned to a rational region of experience, which is elevated above, and therefore leaves behind, all merely intellectual forms, except those which are representative or poetical in character: although this is a chaotic rationality, which originates in the inverted form of the Reason; and from this no vital laws of correspondence can be obtained, but only destructive laws, which the mind consciously conceives. The transcendental is an ontological period; but here the legitimate ontological position, which posits God as the infinite cause of all things, becomes reversed, and Man is posited as an infinite absolute cause, and all the circumstances of his life are made to result from "a purely self-derived activity." This is the most dangerous and destructive of all the experiences of the soul, because it leads the individual to claim divinity for his personality, and an infinite scope for its activity unrestrained by any law but that of personal individual want; which, as a spiritual principle, is infernal, and which, even in the natural, if not made subject to law, would destroy him. To illustrate this claim, we will quote from the writings of another prominent transcendentalist, Henry James: —

"God the Creator is Infinite or perfect, being sufficient unto Himself. And he is sufficient unto Himself, only because his action is self-generated, or obeys no outward end. This being the case with the Creator, and the Creature being necessarily only his Image or reflection, it follows that the creature must exhibit a like infinitude of perfection. It follows that he also must be sufficient unto himself, or exhibit a purely self-derived activity, — an activity which denies any outward motive or impulsion."

"The divine spirit in every man incessantly urges his unity with Nature and with his fellow-man, his unity with the Universe. Thus, if you regard the child before he has become morally sophisticate, or disciplined by society, you perceive that he views all things and all persons as made for his delight, and puts forth his hand with a lordly disdain of every laborious distinction of *meum* and *tuum*. Now, the child is the prophecy of the man. His ignorant innocence only typifies that wiser innocence which shall endow and render beautiful the ripe divine manhood." The inversion of truth included in this statement is particularly striking, because it is illustrated from several points of view: first, in the claim that it makes to divinity, or to infinite perfection for the soul, as an absolute cause; next, in the claim which it makes, that the individual should be exempt from all law, being "sufficient unto himself;" next, in the substitution of that destructive, personal want, which is an absorbing or accumulative principle that would make every thing one with and subject to itself,—being the most internal representative of the finite principle,—for that vital infinite force which perpetually gives without ever receiving, and is represented in Christianity by self-renunciation, which is the total sacrifice of individual property, and of personal individual want; and, finally, in the inversion of rationality, and violation of all logical consistency, by which it is characterized,—it being an inversion of this consistency to assert that man is infinite because he is created in the image of God, because it is well understood that an image is the lifeless imitation and unreal representative of something that is living and real.

Notwithstanding this destructive condition of the Soul, it is only now that it begins to obtain a relative consistency and reality; for although, while remaining in an external condition, the supernatural was represented to it from a vital point of view, in being represented it was contradicted by being incarnated in natural thought founded upon individual natural experiences of the most external description: so that the significance of this representation was not understood by it, and no corresponding individual condition was realized by it, for the reason that all its experiences were fictitious, and the opposite of what they seemed, and still were believed to be real. Having risen into an internal sphere of consciousness, the individual—although he has repudiated all the forms representative of Spiritual Life, which are appropriate to an external condition of the consciousness, and substituted inversions of these, which, instead of representing Absolute Truth, are representative of Absolute Falsehood—has gained a position which overlooks and comprehends the fictitious character of these external manifestations; and we accordingly find great unanimity, clearness, and consistency in the views of transcendentalists with regard to the unreal character of these external experiences. Nothing can be further from their vision, however, than the realities which were here represented, and the uses which these representations have been the means of realizing in the development of the individual consciousness; for, with regard to Truth, Transcendentalism is simply destructive. While the individual sees so clearly the personal condition of those who are below him, he is not merely blind to his own, but, like them, sees it through a false medium, by which it is inverted; and, while repudiating external theories and customs which are productive, would substitute internal theories and forms which are opposite to truth and to good, and which destroy the Church and the State. Although he clearly sees the want of consistency, reality, simplicity, and honesty, that is inherent in externalism in proportion to its immaturity, and also sees that the theories of the Church are contrary to the principles of natural justice, and to that benevolence from sympathy which has become to him supreme, he does not see that his own condition — being natural — is substantially the same; nor does he see, that, in discarding these rude representatives of Christianity, he has substituted theories which are still further removed from the divine justice and goodness which he seeks to recognize. Thus, when all the old landmarks in Religion, in Morality, and in Philosophy, have been swept away, what do we find substituted in their places? Why, this: that there is nothing real but action which is unrestrained by any law, and cannot therefore be comprehended within the limits of any system, — that a spiritual condition of the soul consists in "the power of self-derived action, or acting according to one's own sovereign pleasure;" a lawless idea, which, if carried out in the life, would inaugurate Chaos as a complete inversion of that Order which subjects the individual to universal law, and is the foundation of all the productive manifestations of the Universe.

An indispensible use, however, is performed by Transcendentalism, in the production of a natural form representing Absolute Falsehood, and furnishing suggestive material in its spiritual incarnation; because, until such a form has been prepared, the Spiritual Itself, which includes Absolute Falsehood as well as Absolute Truth, cannot be presented to the consciousness. This service is demanded of Transcendentalism, because it immediately precedes the Spiritual Birth of the soul, and completes its natural development by the realization of an internal order of natural experiences; and, in realizing these, the individual becomes conscious of the destructive laws of the mind, and necessarily appropriates these as the governing laws of his belief and life. This form is therefore persistently prepared by individuals under the sustaining power of Hope, which is the motive power connected with the principle of "Naturalism," in defiance of all opposition from the advocates of an external order of things, and in the face of all the discouragements arising in the disorderly and disastrous effects which are produced by the application of their theories. This opposition of externalism, however, becomes modified by the universal effect that is produced by this influx from an internal-natural sphere of life: for it may be observed, that the transcendental spirit is not confined to those individuals who have been fully developed in an external sphere of consciousness, but extends to other classes in the communities to which they belong, and indeed agitates the world, so that all become to some extent relatively transcendental; those occupying an external sphere becoming disorderly by insubordination within the old forms, and also in a destructive external manner, as seen in the manifestations of "Modern Spiritualism," which is in reality "Naturalism;" while the transcendentalist becomes disorderly by the repudiation of the old forms, and the establishment of others which are opposite. In this way, Transcendentalism is assisted in the work that has been given it to do, which is to overthrow the authority of the Bible, of the Church, and of the State, by setting up antagonistic theories and institutions established upon what it maintains to be "the higher law" which is revealed through the individual consciousness.

Notwithstanding that the inversion of all the forms of which the laws of "Spiritualism" constitute the life, which include the natural form of Christianity, is the most prominent fact that presents itself at this period of the soul's progress, it is not strange that the transcendentalists should claim, as they do, to be guided by Inspiration, and to have realized the true Christianity. Their claim to Inspiration is made plausible, from the fact that they have become thoroughly self-conscious, intuitive of laws from the supernatural region of the mind, and cognizant of the facts of the individual consciousness, — totally rejecting all external direction, and trusting implicitly in light and guidance from within; because, from the natural point of view occupied by them, this light must appear to be a true inspiration, and this guidance to be a direction from Heaven, although they are really the baleful light of an inverted sentimentalism, and the blind craving of a destructive personal want. The ground upon which the claim is made to a realization of the true Christianity

is still more plausible. Transcendentalism seems to be identified
with Christianity; first, because it would introduce man into a
new social condition, or into a state of Communism, in which an
equal distribution of property, and of all other social advantages,
is demanded; for if we regard the letter of the Scriptures, as
most are disposed to do who regard them at all, we must allow
that this is precisely the social condition that was produced by the
establishment of Christianity, as we shall have occasion presently
to show. It seems to be identified with it, next, because it substitutes an internal for an external moral code, by demanding realities instead of appearances, or an internal state corresponding
with the external condition; for according to the letter of the
Gospels, which record the life and the teaching of Christ, this
seems to be the principal object of his mission upon the earth.
But it is not more strange that Transcendentalism should be
mistaken for Christianity, than it was that John the Baptist, who
was the representative of Transcendentalism in a natural sphere,
should have been mistaken for the Christ; because, as both came
to abolish all external direction, and all external forms into which
a self-conscious life could not be infused, and as both are therefore
destructive of external and productive of internal things, there
is an external resemblance between Transcendentalism and Christianity, which may readily deceive those who are confined to an
internal-natural point of observation. Having made this general
statement of the effects which are necessarily produced by the
entrance of the soul into an internal-natural sphere of consciousness, we will proceed to describe some of the changes which take
place in the manifestations of the mind, and also of the personal
consciousness, as consequences of this primary fact. This will
enable us to account more satisfactorily for many of the phenomena which have already been noticed, and be suggestive to us
of other peculiarities of Transcendentalism.

We have said, that, in an internal sphere of natural experiences, manifestation commences in the highest departments and
regions of the mind, but in the affective and destructive, and not
in the intellective and vital, principles belonging to them. The
first region of the mind that requires to be noticed, therefore, is
the Reason ; for, although this is the spiritual region of the mind,
we are obliged to recognize a natural development of this region,
for the reason that every thing must be developed as a natural
form that is simply representative, as the condition of realizing a
spiritual consciousness, — a law that we have seen to be operative

even in the realization of Absolute Spiritual Existence. In this new awakening of the Rational Principle, however, it is its inverted, and therefore destructive, form from which the individual now becomes receptive, in which the Universal is made subject to the Personal, through an inversion of the law of Marriage. Instead of realizing metaphysical ideas based upon the law of Unity, and corresponding with the principle of "Perfection," as the foundation of ontological speculations, — which was the result of its first development, — it realizes metaphysical ideas based upon the law of Diversity, and corresponding with the principle of "Imperfection," from which this law of the mind is derived, and becomes antagonistic to all legitimate ontological theories founded in conceptions of Absolute Law, and stated in scientific forms: for although the mind has now become metaphysical, for the reason that even this inverted form of rationality must partake of that character, its metaphysics are chaotic, include the idea of absolute diversity instead of absolute order, and relate to the deification of the individual; and this will be found to correspond with what may now be observed of the manifestations of Transcendentalism. Mr. Emerson, in his lecture upon "Spiritual Laws," therefore says, "The simplicity of the Universe is very different from the simplicity of a machine. It is not that which may easily be read, but is inexhaustible. The last analysis can in no wise be made. We judge of a man's wisdom by his Hope, knowing that the perception of the inexhaustibleness of Nature is an immortal youth."

With regard to the supremacy of Personal Want as Good, which originates in the inverted form of the Reason, we find it imparting to the character a philanthropic enthusiasm, which is not practical, but theoretical, and is imbued with that universality which is characteristic of all the rational powers of the mind; but, instead of being an indication of health, this morbid inordinate philanthropy is, on the contrary, a sign of disease. In the spiritual marriage of good with truth, the desire of good is for the incarnation and manifestation of truth in use, which includes the sacrifice of the personal life for the sake of the universal, and this is therefore represented in the natural form; but, in the inverted form of the Reason, this spiritual function is reversed, and a form of truth is demanded that can be made subservient to good in the incarnation and manifestation of personal individual want, by which it becomes a destructive, instead of a productive, principle; for the consequence of this demand is, that the individual is obliged to seek for his life, or for the cause of his productiveness, in his own personal want,—for the realization of which he demands the sacrifice of all laws which are inconsistent with this object, or with the realization of universal theories of good which correspond with this want. To the realization of Natural Perfection, as conceived from this inverted point of view, and its worship as the Beautiful, the individual, therefore, now devotes himself; and thus the worship of the beautiful in nature, in which truth is made subservient to good, and a love for the beautiful in Art, so far as it is found to correspond with this inverted form of Natural Perfection, become prominent features in the manifestations of this period. It is true, that this worship of Natural Perfection, as a Beautiful Image, includes the recognition of Truth as a Universal Principle indispensable to the incarnation of Good, by which it gains an elevation and an importance that places it far above the fragmentary and superficial forms of external natural thought: and it is also true that Good has gained a corresponding elevation as a conscious, internal principle that is universally Social, instead of being personally Individual; and, in consequence of this, the individual conceptions of relationship have become elevated from affectional into sentimental experiences, while the Sentiments themselves have thrown off that subjection to external influences which before had characterized them, and become aids in the conception of the most universal truths. But it is also true, that these conceptions of relationship are based upon an inversion of the legitimate law of production, and therefore become productive of abuses instead of uses; that the sentimental manifestations are now governed by destructive, instead of vital, sentimental laws; and that the universal truths now realized correspond with these, and also with the inverted and destructive form of the Reason: so that the life of all truth, of all good, and of all use, is destroyed, and their forms are perverted to the incarnation of their opposites.

The next region of the mind to be noticed is the Sentimental; and an unusual intensity of action in this region is suggested by the fact that it is the internal region of the mind, and therefore corresponds with Transcendentalism, because this belongs to the internal-natural sphere of consciousness. We have already shown that the sentimental region is designed to establish opposite supernatural laws of relationship, which shall constitute the governing principles of all natural law and of all natural relationships, and is constituted by two opposite departments,—one containing the

Religious, and the other containing the Moral, Sentiments; the productions of which are combined and manifested through the Will as the laws of the individual belief and life. These departments are, as we have already shown, divided into opposite male and female regions, and a constructive region through which these are combined in the production of phenomena; the male region being perceptive, and the medium through which are realized the opposite laws that must be combined in production; and the female region being receptive, and the medium through which all the phenomena produced by the combination of these laws are recognized by the mind. We have also shown, that, under the laws of Contrariety and Circularity, the transcendental development commences with the action of the destructive perceptive law, combined with that of the vital receptive principle, in each department, — that the principle of "Sympathy" is the law of Self-Gratification, which is destructive because opposed to any subjection of the individual, or to the operation of any law that contradicts the individual desire, — that the principle of "Satisfaction" now becomes receptive of those internal forms of individual manifestation which have been conceived under the operation of this destructive law, and recognizes these as the laws of Good, — that the principle of "Naturalism" is the law of Self-Assertion, which is destructive because it demands the infinite extension of the Individual, — and that the principle of "Intuition" now becomes receptive of those internal forms of individual belief which have been conceived under the operation of this destructive law, and recognizes these as the laws of Truth.

With regard to the Religious Sentiments, as "Naturalism" has become the governing law in this department, and as this is antagonized to the law of "Spiritualism," upon which, as we have already seen, all the vital forms of the Church have been founded, the internal receptive principle in this department must become receptive of forms corresponding with this destructive law, and therefore antagonized to all these vital forms of the Church: and as these were representative of the spiritual marriage of good with truth, including the subjection of the individual to the universal, for universal ends and for the glory of God; so will the forms now recognized represent the inversion of this marriage, including the subjection of the universal to the individual, for personal ends and for self-glorification. In this way, the individual comes into a position realizing the worship of Self, which constitutes the religion of Transcendentalism, and leads him to affirm that "the internal of every man is God," that "God is perfect Man,"* and that "Man is Incarnate Deity."† To show that we have not here exaggerated the Anti-Christian position of Transcendentalism, and that it really includes, as we say, the worship of Self, or of personal individual want in the form of Good, and is opposite both to "the mysteries of religious faith" and to the spiritual laws which are here applied in the realization of Absolute Truth, we will quote the words of a distinguished transcendentalist,† who was so consistent in his belief, that he asserted not only the divinity of Good, but also the supremacy of the female, who is used in the religious symbolism to represent this personal individual want, which, in a spiritual sphere of consciousness, becomes the infernal tempter of the soul. After describing the sentimental manifestations in "Pietism" and "Moralism," as realized in the Protestant and Unitarian developments, he says, "Evidently, however, there was another degree of religious life, latent and waiting conditions of development in this faith, that Goodness is the indwelling life of God. Hence Transcendentalism. In the strictest sense, it is true that man is Incarnate Deity; is the Infinite Unity manifested in Finite Multiplicity. Not Jesus alone, but every spirit in human form, is Divine. True piety is to be purely one's own self; for this inmost power of life is God: the highest prayer is to put forth into beneficent action the profoundest impulse of good will; every man is a Christ in Heaven in degree as his internal inspiration and external action are harmonious; we are all mediators just in so far as the One Good, distributed through each, is re-united by the freest interchange of joyful conscious Sympathy. Let us waste no time or power on fanciful theories of a heavenly hierarchy, or impertinent investigations into the mysteries of God: our true end is to be manly,—and in that manliness to reveal, here and now, Divinity."

These manifestations represent the worship of Absolute Falsehood, which is the Unpardonable Sin. It was the realization of manifestations corresponding with these in a more external sphere, of which John the Baptist was the superintendent, which led the Saviour to say, "From the days of John the Baptist until now, the kingdom of heaven suffereth violence, and the violent take it by force. For all the prophets and the law prophesied until John." As the individual now claims to realize Divinity

---

* Henry James.   † William H. Channing.

without passing through Christianity, or without submitting to the sacrifice of the Personal for the sake of the Universal, but on the contrary claims to be the Incarnation of God, he places himself in direct opposition to God; and it is this demand to realize a spiritual position without fulfilling its conditions, or this attempt to make forcible entrance into a place for which he has not been prepared, and into which he has not been invited, that is alluded to by the Saviour in the passage just quoted, and again in the following words: "Verily, verily, I say unto you, he that entereth not by the door into the sheep-fold, but climbeth up some other way, the same is a thief and a robber." "I am the Door: by me if any man enter in, he shall be saved." It is because this spiritual theft is represented in Transcendentalism, and because this is the immediate precursor of resurrection to spiritual life or to spiritual death, as the individual shall accept or reject Christ as his Redeemer, that the Saviour was said to be crucified between two thieves, — one of whom blasphemed, and the other worshipped him; and that he said to the latter, "To-day shalt thou be with me in Paradise." It is, however, necessary that the soul should be brought into this condition of perfect Individualism and Self-Worship, which is the most extreme form of Idolatry, or of natural opposition to God, because it is the only position that can prepare it for the presentation to it of the Spiritual in the forms of Absolute Truth and Absolute Falsehood; and the only way in which a natural form representing this absolute falsehood can be prepared, as an opposite to the form representing absolute truth, which had before been prepared by the Church, — natural forms that must both be realized before any spiritual presentation can take place. This experience, which represents the Spiritual Temptation, must now be realized; because, in Transcendentalism, the soul arrives at the close of its natural experiences, which it passes through in order that the laws of Spiritual Life and of Spiritual Death, between which its choice is finally to be made, may be represented to it in the most diversified natural forms; it being necessary that it should realize a conscious experience of all these natural forms of life before the Spiritual Itself can be presented to it. At the close of Transcendentalism, therefore, the soul arrives at that turning-point in its existence, when a resurrection into the spiritual sphere of consciousness must be experienced, when it must exchange a natural for a spiritual mode of being, and when it must therefore be called upon to make a final choice between the opposite absolute causes which will then be presented to it; the ability to do which constitutes its freedom, and the doing which must result in everlasting life or in everlasting death. Of this presentation, it is therefore written, "See, I have set before thee this day life and good, and death and evil:" "therefore, choose life, that both thou and thy seed may live."

With regard to the Moral Sentiments, as "Sympathy" has become the governing law in this department, and as this is antagonized to the law of "Justice," upon which, as we have already seen, all the vital forms of the State have been founded, the internal receptive principle must become receptive of universal forms of personal want, corresponding with this destructive law of self-gratification, and therefore antagonized to all the vital institutions of society, in which the lower has been made subject to the higher for the purpose of social production, and violations of social right have been visited by retributive justice; setting up the demand for personal liberty and freedom from all the restraints and punishments of law, and ignoring all that subjection to public opinion, which, in an external sphere of consciousness, had been secured through the sentiment of "Approbation." Individual conceptions of right based upon the divinity of personal want, in the form of Good, which include freedom from all restraint by law and from all subjection to the opinions of others, the perfect equality of all individuals, and the right of each one to seek for happiness in the way most congenial to his nature, become the only laws of moral obligation by which the individual will consent to be governed. This demand for universal self-gratification constitutes the Morality of Transcendentalism; and although this does not seem to be a demand for personal gratification, but, on the contrary, appears to arise in a disinterested desire to communicate pleasure, it is only because this desire for gratification has, like the individual's conception of himself, obtained an unlimited extension, and is not therefore a demand for his own gratification merely, but for that of all who partake, or whom he imagines to partake, of his nature. So deceptive is this principle, and so far have transcendentalists been misled by this universal philanthropic manifestation, that it has been supposed by some to be a re-action from the principle of Individualism which has separated them from others, and to redeem them from the destructive influence of that isolated condition which has been realized through the operation of this separating principle. There are two principal modes in which the external element or motive power in this principle becomes manifested; one that is passive, and another that is active, in its character: the first of these is "the quality of being affected by the affection of another," this being the common definition that has been given to it; while the second of these demands that others shall be affected as the individual is affected, — this being necessary, according to our analysis of this principle, in order that the merely passive emotion excited by this principle should be changed to an active one, and the external uses of sympathy be obtained. Now, as the passive manifestation here alluded to predominates in proportion as the individual is external, and the active manifestation in proportion as he is internal, in the transcendental mind "Sympathy" becomes manifested through the sentiment of "Satisfaction," in which it becomes incarnated, in the highest active condition of which it is susceptible, while a universal character is at the same time communicated to it. Individuals do not, therefore, wait to be acted upon, but are stimulated to act upon others; they do not stop to inquire if suffering really exists, but strive to abolish those conditions in others which would produce suffering in themselves. They make no allowance, therefore, for difference in race, nature, or development; in degrees of sensibility, want, or capacity; but, in opposition to all calculations of expediency, possibility, and propriety, in defiance of the most obvious objections, and without any regard for consequences, demand that all, including both males and females, shall be placed upon a footing of equality, and be invested with an unrestrained liberty of action. Many inconvenient and ridiculous mistakes are in this way made, a great amount of sympathy is uselessly and mischievously expended, and a great deal of injustice is perpetrated by an impertinent interference with the legitimate institutions of society; which are based upon inequality, and the necessity for subjection of the lower to the higher. It is this insane attempt by individuals to make their own personal condition and wants the standard by which to measure the wants and capabilities of others, combined with a disorderly condition of the individuals themselves, that has led to most of the fanatical movements of the present day, — so destructive to the peace, the well-being, and even to the existence, of the State; movements which have been seized upon by designing individuals, and used in obtaining for themselves notoriety, wealth, distinction, or power. To illustrate these manifestations through the sentiment of "Satisfaction," and the opposition of this sentiment to that of "Approbation," we will quote from a lecture of Mr. Emerson's, upon the subject of "Self-Reliance:"—

"The populace think that your rejection of popular standards is a rejection of all standards, and mere antinomianism; and the bold sensualist will use the name of Philosophy to gild his crimes. But the law of Consciousness abides. There are two confessionals, in one or the other of which we must be shriven. You may fulfil your round of duties by clearing yourself in the direct or in the reflex way. Consider whether you have satisfied your relations to father, mother, cousin, neighbor, town, cat, and dog;— whether any of these can upbraid you. But I may also neglect this reflex standard, and absolve me to myself. I have my own stern claims and perfect circle. It denies the name of duty to many offices that are called duties. But, if I can discharge its debts, it enables me to dispense with the popular code. If any one imagines that this law is lax, let him keep its commandments one day. And truly it demands something godlike in him who has cast off the common motives of humanity, and has ventured to trust himself for a task-master. High be his heart, faithful his will, clear his sight, that he may, in good earnest, be doctrine, society, law, to himself; that a simple purpose may be to him as strong as iron necessity to others."

"Society everywhere is in conspiracy against the manhood of every one of its members. Society is a joint-stock company in which the members agree, for the better securing of his bread to each shareholder, to surrender the liberty and culture of the eater. The virtue in most request is conformity. Self-reliance is its aversion. It loves not realities, but names and customs. Whoso would be a man must be a non-conformist. He who would gather immortal palms must not be hindered by the name of goodness, but must explore if it *be* goodness. Nothing is at last sacred but the integrity of our own mind. Absolve you to yourself, and you shall have the suffrage of the world. No law can be sacred to me but that of my nature. Good and bad are but names very readily transferable to this or that; the only right is what is after my constitution; the only wrong what is against it. I shun father and mother and wife and brother when my genius calls me. I would write upon the lintels of the door-post, Whim. I hope it is something better than whim at last; but we cannot spend the day in explanation. What I must do is all that concerns me, not what the people think. This rule, equally arduous in actual and in intellectual life, may serve as the whole distinction between greatness and meanness. It is the harder because you will always find those who think they know what is your duty better than you know it. It is easy in the world to live after the world's opinion; it is easy in solitude to live after your own: but the great man is he, who, in the midst of the crowd, keeps with perfect sweetness the independence of solitude."

The next change in the manifestations of the mind to be noticed is that which is produced in the highest region of the Understanding, of which the Imagination is the constructive principle; this being also the legitimate exponent of the Reason, and the incarnator of the Supernatural. By this return to the highest regions of the mind, the Imagination, instead of the Fancy, again becomes the ruling incarnating principle; and a tone of rationality and consistency is therefore to be found pervading all the intellectual manifestations, giving harmony, repose, and elevation to his life. But, although the Imagination has again become the exponent of the Reason, the inverted form of the rational powers is now developed; and the incarnation of this is realized under the rule of the destructive law in the department of which the Imagination is the constructive power: and the consequence of this is, that the law of Diversity is regarded as the ruling law of the Universe, — all legitimate metaphysical speculations are repudiated as false interpretations of that which cannot be defined, — none but inverted relationships can be recognized, — all forms of thought representing the laws of "Spiritualism," or the vital phenomena of spiritual life, are rejected as worn-cut superstitions, and all the institutions in which these laws have been incarnated and represented are condemned as arbitrary, oppressive, and injurious to the soul, because impeding its free action and healthy development, — and even the highest aspirations of the soul only serve to direct it towards Annihilation, or absorption into the Infinite Substance, which it conceives in the inverted form of Absolute Diversity. It is true, that, through this predominance of the Imagination, a love for what is internal, abstract, universal, substantial, and real, predominates over the love of what is external, superficial, partial, and unreal or fictitious; and the mind loses that quick perception of difference, which is a separating and diversifying power belonging to the Fancy, that is essential to Talent, and is quick in proportion as it is shallow, and accurate in proportion as it is narrow, — and gains in exchange a perception of internal, instead of external, correspondences; and thus obtains an originality of conception that is allied to genius, and would, if legitimate, become productive of the most important results. But as the vital receptive faculty in this department, which is "Metaphysics," is now manifested, under the law of Contrariety, in subjection to the destructive law of "Correspondence," although the faculty of Metaphysics becomes receptive, and the Imagination becomes constructive, of theories belonging to the nature of Being, which are founded in ideas derived from the Reason, it is from the inverted form of the Reason that these are derived; by which all legitimate absolute relationships are inverted, and opposite conditions of Being, instead of being antagonized, are confounded, or seen as One; and a destructive and even chaotic condition of thought is produced with regard to the most universal relations of things. Being and Nought,—Infinite and Finite,—Subjective and Objective,—are regarded as substantially the same;—Truth is made subject to Good, and the Male to the Female Principles; —the Human and the Divine are confounded in the conception of God as "the Grand Man;" and God is even made to depend upon man for a definite consciousness;—the Personal and the Universal are so confounded, or rather the Universal is so made subject to or dependent upon the Personal, that the individual is unable to separate his personality from that of God, but believes himself to perform the functions of God as an Absolute Cause;— while Falsehood and Evil are regarded, not as real but as nominal distinctions, which represent the absence of truth and good, or a diminished quantity of these. Even Heaven and Hell are confounded, and are conceived as elements in the threefold personality of God; while Nature, as the third element, is conceived as the definite result of their combination, as we have already shown in quoting the conception of Trinity in God by Jacob Böhme, which represents a complete inversion of the Absolute Facts which we have stated as the ground of Absolute Science.

Through the predominance of the Imagination over the Fancy, the intellectual is preferred to the affectional, in music, in poetry, in painting, and in the use of language, — the analogical predominates over the logical in the forms of thought, —and the individual loses his affinity for those forms of falsehood, deformity, and indecency, which constitute the elements of Wit and the Ludicrous in an external sphere of consciousness; and gains, in exchange, an affinity for simplicity, beauty, purity, and truthfulness; but, as the Imagination has become subject to the destructive influences just mentioned, he becomes an admirer of those productions of the Fancy which are realized by the more internal affectional minds, and belong to an internal sphere of Wit and the Ludicrous; these being less gross, but more deceptive, than those belonging to an external sphere, because opposites are here more completely confounded, and the relations of things more completely inverted. Although a strong desire is felt to be made acquainted with the correspondences of things, or with symbolic representations of relationship, as the law of "Opposition," which reveals the antagonisms of Creation, and demands the subjection of the lower to the higher, is now repudiated, no legitimate relationship can be perceived, but only destructive relationships, in which the higher is made subject to the lower; and as the law of Marriage, which constitutes the vital principle of the Imagination, and represents the union of opposites through the voluntary sacrifice of individual life, has become inverted, opposites, instead of being antagonized, are confounded; and the personal, instead of being crucified for the sake of the universal, has been deified, so as to include the universal. These destructive ideas govern the individual in all his conceptions and recognitions of correspondence; and consequently real analogies are either inverted, or superseded by fanciful resemblances, by which falsehood instead of truth becomes realized.

The next change to be noticed in the manifestations of the mind, consequent upon this change from an external to an internal sphere of consciousness, is that which is produced in the Instinct, or Affectional Nature. In consequence of a return to the highest regions of the mind for the governing principles of the individual life, the Social Instincts become the governing affectional powers; but as this is a return to the affective and destructive, instead of the intellective and vital principle, as a governing law, "Sociability" becomes the governing principle in all the social manifestations which are peculiar to this period of the soul's development. Transcendentalism thus becomes distinctively a Social movement, and brings together two of the most opposite tendencies that can possibly be conceived, which are Individualism and Communism; the first completely isolating the individual from all others, and the second bringing individuals together in the most promiscuous and disorderly manner: for it cannot be denied, that these opposite tendencies do indeed constitute the two most striking peculiarities of Transcendentalism. In consequence of this change in the social governing law, a change in the whole constitution of the State is now demanded, in which the wants of every individual shall be provided for, unrestrained by any arbitrary control; and that this is a legitimate demand of Transcendentalism may be seen from several points of view. It is demanded, first, because

"Sociability" has become the governing affectional law, and the individual consequently demands a social condition, or an intercourse with other individuals, that is based upon universal personal liberty, and thus excludes the idea of subjection to any law that is contrary to the individual inclination,— although such a condition is obviously impracticable, and all attempts to realize it have therefore signally failed; for the reason, that the utmost diversity and discord exist between the wants of those who demand this association, combined with a practical imbecility in these individuals, or an incapacity for any orderly construction from a practical point of view: so that a chaotic social condition is necessarily produced, which tends to dissolution. It is demanded, next, because Personal Want, under the form of Individualism, now demands the supremacy of the individual, and thus demands self-assertion and self-gratification; and a state of communism is the only condition in which he can hope to obtain the realization of these demands, because it is the only one in which they can be recognized. Finally, it is demanded, because it is now maintained that Human Nature is Divine,— that all its tendencies are therefore legitimate and good, and calculated for the production simply of use to the individual,— and, consequently, that the free exercise of all these is necessary to his perfect development and healthy condition; because, from this point of view, the individual cannot regard the evils existing in society as being produced by the operation of these tendencies, but is obliged, although absurdly, to refer them to its vicious constitution, which, by preventing their exercise, cripples the powers of the soul, and prevents its development; these disorders being regarded as re-actions of the soul against arbitrary and unjust coercion, and as necessary to preserve it from suffocation. Communism must be demanded from this point of view, as the condition of progress and of salvation to the soul; not simply because it promises to provide for it a greater amount of enjoyment, but because it also promises to secure to it the exercise and development of all its capacities and powers, as the means of its improvement and true usefulness. Communism will therefore be found to be a legitimate transcendental want; although its realization may not always be demanded, on account of its impracticability, and may not often be attempted, because of the practical imbecility of the transcendental constitution.

There is one other fact connected with the manifestations of the Social department which remains to be noticed; and this is, that, under the operation of the law of Contrariety, "Sociability," the destructive social law, is combined in manifestation with "Friendship," the vital receptive principle, which is made subject to it; the consequence of which is, that the law of diversity is introduced into and governs the manifestations of the principle of "Friendship." Instead of demanding one friend of the same sex, which is its demand from a vital point of manifestation, this principle now demands a multitude of friends of both sexes; and this, instead of being a permanent relation, or a relation for life, as in the vital manifestation of this principle, is dependent for its durability upon the individual perception of that internal affinity from intellectual correspondence which is demanded by Transcendentalism in both social and domestic relations. The following extract from Mr. Emerson's Essay on Friendship will illustrate this fact, and will also illustrate other transcendental demands arising in the manifestation of the personal principle: "Friendship cannot subsist in its perfection, say some of those who are learned in this warm love of the heart, betwixt more than two. I please my imagination more with a circle of godlike men and women, variously related to each other, and between whom subsists a lofty intelligence." "Who hears me, who understands me, becomes mine, — a possession for all time. Nor is nature so poor but she gives me this joy several times, and thus we weave social threads of our own, a new web of relations; and, as many thoughts in succession substantiate themselves, we shall, by and by, stand in a new world of our own creation, and no longer strangers and pilgrims in a transitory globe. My friends have come to me unsought. The great God gave them to me. By oldest right, by the divine affinity of virtue with itself, I find them, or rather not I, but the Deity in me and in them derides and cancels the thick walls of individual character, relation, age, sex, circumstance, at which he usually connives, and now makes many one. High thanks I owe you, excellent lovers, who carry out the world for me to new and noble depths, and enlarge the meaning of all my thoughts. Will these, too, separate themselves from me again, or some of them? I know not, but I fear it not; for my relation to them is so pure, that we hold by simple affinity, and the Genius of my life being thus social, the same affinity will exert its energy on whomsoever is as noble as these men and women, wherever I may be."

Although the domestic and individual departments of the Affectional Nature have now become subordinate to the social, and have also lost, to a great extent, those unconscious and spontaneous manifestations which belong to an external sphere of consciousness; so far as they obtain any manifestation, it is in correspondence with some internal conception of relationship. By this, they are redeemed from a mere external and affectional condition, into one that is internal and intellectual; in which they demand a mental and social, rather than a physical and domestic, companionship; and unconscious, external forms are invested with and animated by an intellectual and self-conscious life. Although the transcendentalist believes in spontaneity as the highest mode of mental manifestation, for the reason that Feeling instead of Thought has become to him a governing principle, there is nothing that distinguishes him from the externalist more than this: that he demands the government of Law in the form of true internal relationships. Hence, although he utterly repudiates all external forms of relationship which do not find in his consciousness an internal intellectual support, he most earnestly and pertinaciously seeks to realize internal laws of relationship which shall correspond with and animate, or make living, all these external forms. But although Transcendentalism, like John the Baptist, points to the coming of that Light which is to communicate a new life to the soul, and is its immediate precursor, it is more antagonistic to this light than any thing that has preceded it; "for all the prophets and the law prophesied until John." Instead of fulfilling the Law by a realization of its spirit, it tends to overthrow and destroy it; because it repudiates all law except that which is founded in inverted relationships, and is thus the most disorderly and destructive of all things. In seeking for the internal laws which shall communicate a new life to the soul, the individual is necessarily directed, as we have already shown, to the destructive laws of the mind, which become the laws of his belief and life; and by these all legitimate relationships are inverted. With regard to the domestic relations, therefore, although the ground is taken, that, unless the form of Matrimony becomes animated by an internal life realized through the conception of a mental companionship that is productive of intellectual and social uses, the external relation becomes degrading and destructive, because it prevents the legitimate development and manifestation in production of one of the most important relationships of life, — the conception of this relationship, which it now realizes under the influence of the destructive domestic law, is a complete inversion of that which must govern all healthy intercourse between the sexes; for, although nothing more than a perfect equality of the sexes may at first be demanded, the supremacy of the female is a result which must necessarily follow the supremacy of the female, or affective, domestic law. Besides this, as "Sexuality" has become the ruling law in all the domestic manifestations, — although this has become internal in character, so that a mental instead of a physical affinity becomes the ruling attractive power, and the physical has been invested with an ethereal instead of a material charm, — diversity has been introduced into the institution of Matrimony, and "Free-Love" becomes in theory a transcendental manifestation; a theory that is carried into practice by those external individuals by whom the incarnation of transcendental laws and ideas becomes realized. The following extracts from Mr. Emerson's Essay on Love will show this fact of diversity in Love, both with regard to number and to sex, corresponding with that which we have shown to be realized in Friendship, and will also show the ethereal manner in which it is conceived by the transcendentalist: "Love is a fire, that, kindling its first embers in the narrow nook of a private bosom, caught from a wandering spark out of another private heart, glows and enlarges until it warms and beams upon multitudes of men and women, upon the universal heart of all, and so lights up the whole world and all nature with its generous fires." "Who can analyze the nameless charm which glances from one and another face and form? We are touched with emotions of tenderness and complacency; but we cannot find whereat this dainty emotion, this wandering gleam, points. It is destroyed for the imagination by any attempt to refer it to organization. Nor does it point to any relations of friendship or love known and described in society, but, as it seems to me, to a quite other and unattainable sphere, to relations of transcendent delicacy and sweetness, to what roses and violets hint and foreshow. Herein it resembles the most excellent things, which all have this rainbow character, defying all attempts at appropriation and use." In his lecture on "Swedenborg," after commenting upon his doctrine of "Conjugal Love," he says, "Of progressive souls, all loves and friendships are momentary. *Do you love me?* means, Do you see the same truth? If you do, we are happy with the same happiness: but presently one of us passes into the perception of new truth; we are divorced, and no tension in nature can hold us to each other. I know how delicious is this cup of love, — I existing for you, you existing for me: but it is a child's clinging to his toy; an attempt to eternize the fireside and nuptial chamber; to keep the picture-alphabet through which our first lessons are prettily conveyed." As the transcendentalist is a worshipper of the Female Principle, Sexual Love is regarded by him as especially divine. Swedenborg, therefore, taught that Conjugal Love is derived by the male from the female, and is "the very delight of Heaven;" and Mr. Emerson says, in the Essay on Love already quoted from, "By conversation with that which is in itself excellent, magnanimous, lowly, and just, the lover comes to a warmer love of these nobilities, and a quicker apprehension of them. Then he passes from loving them in one, to loving them in all; and so is the one beautiful soul only the door through which he enters to the society of all true and pure souls. And in beholding in many souls the traits of divine beauty, and separating in each soul that which is divine from the taint which it has contracted in the world, the lover ascends to the highest beauty, to the love and knowledge of the divinity, by steps on this ladder of created souls."

Mr. Emerson, however, in his conception of Love, does not recognize any permanent specific relationships, but, by too wide a generalization, confounds all particular forms of love; and also confounds these with the universal love, which is the love of God; while by Swedenborg these were kept distinct: so that one may be said to correspond with the external form of Transcendentalism, and the other with its chaotic and destructive result. Although transcendentalists are obliged to regard Matrimony as a union of souls which results from mental instead of physical affinity: practically, Love is realized by them, as by the externalist, through an external and not an internal attraction, and the beloved one is invested with imaginary qualities corresponding with the individual's ideal of sexual companionship. This demand for an internal affinity that is based upon a productive mental companionship, is, however, a check upon the experience of Love, because the internal and external spheres of sexual companionship are in discord; and it therefore often leads to the severance of the matrimonial relation when the external attraction has ceased to operate with a predominating power: so that marriages are more rare among the transcendentalists, and are much more liable to be dissolved, than in an external sphere of consciousness.

Even in the Individual department of affection, which is now the weakest of all, the principle of "Destruction," which is the affective law, may be seen distinctly manifested in combination with the vital receptive principle, which has become subject to it. Under the influence of this destructive law, the vital function of "Nutrition" becomes inverted, and internal are made subject to external things; a manifestation that has already been alluded to in other regions of the consciousness, in showing the degradation of Art in Transcendentalism, through the inverting operation of the destructive laws of the mind. In this department, the destructive law leads the individual to believe that the Mind is dependent for its character upon the kind of aliment that is appropriated for the sustenance of the Body; and that vegetable food and water are vital, while animal food and wine are destructive. Other manifestations of this law prejudicial to the health of the individual might be mentioned; and, as this is the executive department of the affectional nature, the higher destructive laws receive from this an external support, and obtain through it an external manifestation.

The only change that remains to be noticed in the manifestations of the human constitution, by the realization of Transcendentalism, is that which is produced in the sphere of Personal Consciousness; and this is one of the most important, because it is in this department that all things of thought and affection are combined in realizing states of Individual Consciousness, through the tri-personal form of the Will. The first change to be noticed in this sphere is that which takes place in the personifying principles. These constitute that dualistic form of the soul whose province it is to appropriate, or to make one with the individual personality, those realizations of the mind or of the general consciousness which correspond with its present individual want; and they are therefore constituted as affinities for vital and destructive laws and forms of truth and of good, which are to be combined through Individuality, or Will, in realizing a form of Individual Life. They constitute a dual universal receptive principle or form of phenomenal life; and include opposite affinities for laws and forms of life, corresponding with the Individual Want: this want being supplied by a corresponding growth and development of the mind, commencing with the highest and ending with the lowest laws and forms, first in an external, and next in an internal, sphere of consciousness. In the external sphere, the individual exists in an external, unconscious, and affectional, and therefore in a destructive, condition, — in which he requires to be restrained by, or made subject to, the vital laws of the mind, incarnated in the most external forms, in order that any orderly external manifestations of his life should be possible: and we therefore find, that, in this external sphere, the individual appropriates, in an unconscious manner, these vital forms upon the one hand, and destructive personal forms upon the other, through the operation of these personifying principles; and that it is through the conflict of these, and the subjection of the personal to the universal through the operation of a supernatural power, that Will or Individuality becomes developed in its external form, and the individual life is realized externally in an orderly condition; while, at the same time, he appears to construct his own life under the influence of selfish motives, which are the only motives from which he can consciously determine himself, in the endeavor to procure what is good for him upon the whole. Upon the transfer of the soul from an external to an internal sphere of consciousness, however, this is completely reversed. Here the individual becomes internal, self-conscious, and intellectual; and comes into a vital condition as to his personal motive: because he now desires to sacrifice the external and personal for the sake of the internal and universal, that he may be prepared for the coming of the Spiritual. He cannot, therefore, submit to the restraint of arbitrary laws, which are partial and temporary, the ground and tendency of which he does not comprehend, but demands a conscious realization of and submission to laws that are comprehensible and universal, and correspond with his own conceptions of truth and of good. But, although the personifying principles now realize an affinity for universal laws, — because it is necessary that these should now be conceived and applied in a self-conscious manner, in the development of Individuality, or Will, and in realizing a consistent form of the individual life from a universal point of view, — these are not vital, but destructive, universal laws, corresponding with personal individual want and representing the Finite, which the individual now appropriates: and by becoming subject to these laws, while he seems to sacrifice the personal for the sake of the universal, he, in fact, sacrifices the universal for the sake of the personal; because these destructive laws are made use of by the Will in the realization of personal ends from a universal point of view. By the supernatural combination and manifestation of these destructive laws and these externally vital forms, with the subjection of the vital to the destructive, Will, or Individuality, becomes developed in its internal-natural form, and the individual life is realized in a disorderly and destructive condition. We will now describe some of the effects which are produced in the Will, in its growth from below upwards, and in its development through the combination and manifestation of these destructive and vital appropriations.

The first change to be noticed in the Will is that which takes place in the principle of "Direction," through which the individual obtains an external direction of himself, by calculating all his external manifestations as means for obtaining for himself the greatest possible good upon the whole. The change which takes place in this principle, however, is not from its development, but from its decline; because, as we have already shown, natural growth and development are partial or one-sided, and therefore the growth of the higher is attended by the decadence of the lower form, and the development of the lower principle is attended by a loss of power in the higher. When the individual comes into an internal sphere of consciousness, this most external form of the Will must experience a loss of external power, and must be governed in its external manifestations more by an unconscious supernatural direction than by that conscious natural calculation which before had characterized it; so that many individuals are disposed to make a literal application of these words of our Saviour: "Take no thought for your life, what ye shall eat, or what ye shall drink; nor yet for your body, what ye shall put on;" while still more are impressed with the idea, that they are directed in all the external circumstances of their lives in a supernatural manner. This most external form of the Will, therefore, becomes to a great extent inoperative, and the individual loses his hold upon the external conditions and circumstances of life, and his power of using them, as means to ends, in the external direction of himself; so that immediate decision from the impulse of feeling, or of internal impression, becomes substituted for a calculation of causes and consequences, and a continuity of purpose. In proportion as he grows internally active, he becomes externally inactive; so that he requires to be strongly acted upon by some uncommon urgency of external circumstances, — by some strong affectional motive, which is to him a rare occurrence, — or by convictions of duty, which are suggested to him by internal conceptions of relationship, — in order that any kind of external activity should be produced. This practical imbecility has already been alluded to as one of the principal external characteristics of the transcendental mind; and we now see that this is the principal cause to which it is referable, although another cause, of course, exists in the impracticable nature of the theories which it entertains.

The next change to be noticed is the internal development of the principle of "Relation;" this being the power of the Will that presides over all the personal relationships of the individual, both natural and supernatural, and calculates means for the actualization of those laws and forms of personal relationship which have been appropriated by the personifying principles from the realizations of the general consciousness. The change which now takes place from an external to an internal manifestation of this principle, or from an external recognition and regulation to an internal conception, — which is comparatively unproductive, because founded in disorderly naturalistic ideas, which are inversions of true relationship, — is productive of effects almost as extensive, and as destructive to the external manifestations of the individual, as the change in the more external principle just mentioned. In an external sphere of the consciousness, although this principle only recognizes the most external forms of these relationships, and the most external duties which are involved in them, these are founded in legitimate supernatural ideas that communicate to them a vitality by which they become productive of use in all religious experiences, and in all religious, social, and domestic intercourse; but, by coming into an internal sphere of consciousness, these relationships are conceived from an internal point of view, and founded upon illegitimate supernatural ideas, by which they become inverted, and thus productive of abuse, instead of use. It is true, that, in an external sphere, these relationships are to a great extent fictitiously assumed and made use of by individuals for the furtherance of selfish and individual instead of legitimate ends; and that, by coming into an internal sphere, the individual avoids most of these abuses. These are avoided, first, because the individual has become simple, and thus ignores both artificiality and duplicity, and demands a true expression of himself; next, because he has lost all control over these complicated external individual relations, as well as all control over and direction of his external manifestations; and, finally, because he has also lost the power of playing a fictitious part, or of controlling the expression of himself, for the purpose of establishing permanent and temporary relationships between himself and other individuals. Much of the simplicity and sincerity which characterize this period of the soul's progress is therefore owing as much to the decline of this feminine tact or talent for intrigue and political management as it is to the demand for singleness and sincerity that is now made; because, where there is little diplomatic ability, there is little temptation, as there is little inclination, to act the politician. Neither prudence in social intercourse, nor faithfulness to external social obligations, in the performance of the more external social and domestic duties, are therefore accounted to be transcendental attributes; and, according to this statement, they could not well be so; although a singleness and purity of purpose, and a recognition of internal relationships which are less sensual and more intellectual than those belonging to an external sphere, make the power of self-control much less necessary than it is in those lower spheres of manifestation, where there is so much that needs to be concealed, and so much that requires to be restrained and directed.

The next change that requires to be noticed in the condition of the Will is that which relates to the principle of "Consciousness." In becoming internal, the individual becomes conscious from the highest natural point of the Will through the natural development of this principle, which constitutes the spiritual and vital region of Individuality. This principle of the Will corresponds with the spiritual region of the Mind, and is particularly appropriate to a spiritual sphere of the consciousness: it being through this principle that the Spiritual Itself becomes realized in the consciousness, as a perfect individuality of truth, good, and beauty, on the one hand, and as a complete inversion of this upon the other; and, through this, that the soul determines itself, under a perfect equilibrium of opposite affinities, towards Absolute Life or Absolute Death. It is the province of this principle to Individualize the Soul, and to furnish a medium through which it can contemplate its condition from a universal point of view; and thus in view not only of all the light and all the love that has been realized by it, but of all that the individual hopes to be, as well as of all that he is. By obtaining a self-conscious, introspective position, therefore, the individual is introduced into a new field of observation and reflection, and is placed in a position suitable for obtaining a true self-knowledge by self-inspection, or for contemplating the relationships existing between the opposite elements of truth and of good which constitute the sum of his individual consciousness. Although this is the spiritual region of the Will, it must, like every other spiritual power, obtain a natural development before it can become spiritually conscious; and this is particularly necessary with regard to this principle, because it is here that the soul must obtain a consciousness of itself as an individual; and it is obvious that it could not be prepared for the spiritual determination of itself, unless it was first enabled to obtain a knowledge of its entire position in view of every thing that could possibly come into its consciousness from a natural point of view. This must be obvious, because, until this highest natural position of the soul has been attained, its creation cannot be considered as completed, and it cannot therefore be regarded as an Individual; and because it cannot be prepared to act from that universal point of view that a spiritual position demands: for, according to the law of production established in this science, a universal spiritual position cannot be obtained until after a corresponding universal natural point of consciousness has been reached. From the point of view established by the principle of "Consciousness," the individual demands that all his thoughts, feelings, and actions shall be brought into subjection to the supreme laws of truth and of good which have been realized by the most internal perceptions, intuitions, and conceptions of his own mind, in order that a marriage between good and truth may here be effected, and a unity of life realized; so that the principle of "Consciousness" becomes to him a higher conscience, which constitutes the life of all moral obligation, as well as of all religious faith. But we have seen, that, in proportion as the individual becomes self-conscious from this most internal point of view, he becomes disorderly. We have seen, that, upon coming into an internal sphere of consciousness, the individual realizes affinities for destructive instead of vital laws, as the directing principles of his life; and, at the same time, becomes internally conscious from this destructive point in his mental and personal constitution: so that nothing could exceed the state of confusion that would ensue, if to this disorderly tendency was united the practical power necessary for its external manifestation. Those very individuals, who, in an external sphere of the consciousness, would have been the most conservative, for the reason that nothing could be accepted by them as materials for use in the construction of plans of life that had not been either practically tested by themselves, or derived from some persons of established authority by whom it had been, now become the most fanatical in the adoption of the most impracticable and destructive theories; because destructive naturalistic principles, the practical effects of which cannot be known, for the reason that they have never been tested, must now be appropriated by them, and applied as laws in the construction of the individual life, in the place of those which have long been known to be productive of use. Standing, as the soul now does, upon the ground of Naturalism, — fully recognizing the divinity of human nature, and thus regarding as legitimate all its impulses and aspirations, — repudiating all those vital supernatural ideas which have been realized through religious sentimentalism, and the teaching of the Bible and the Church, and depending entirely upon individual conceptions which are inversions of these ideas, as a basis for thought and a guide to action, — eschewing the idea of expediency, which, in an external sphere, prevents the errors of abstract reasoning and the irregularities of individual feeling from being carried out into ruinous experiments in the life, and ignoring all those compromises by which the opposite things necessary to all healthy natural manifestation are combined in production, — and becoming, through the supremacy of the destructive rational and sentimental laws, the worshipper of Personal Want as Good, demanding the sacrifice of all external things which do not correspond with these laws, — it insists upon applying these destructive laws universally, in the direction of the life, without regard to the ruinous consequences which are seen to be produced by them.

We have now described the sources in the principles of the Mind and of the Personal Consciousness through which the phenomena of Transcendentalism are realized; have described the manner in which these are produced; and have shown the necessity for their production. We have shown that the condition of perfect Individualism that has here been described, by which the individual is obliged to fall back upon his own personality as the only legitimate source of all motive, and upon his own conceptions of truth as the only legitimate directing power, is necessary in order that he should become a reality instead of a mere appearance, and that he should be prepared for the spiritual birth and for the reception of the spiritual from within, through a free self-determination. We have shown that this preparation can be effected only by freeing the individual from every obstruction to an independent personal manifestation of himself, in which he shall be as free from the control of arbitrary law, and from foreign influence, as he is from that of unconscious impulse; that all manifestations of affection and of thought must be consciously produced in him, — good being realized as a conscious, comprehensible experience, from the union of desire with its idea, and founded upon conceptions of relationship in which the internal and external conditions have been made comparatively harmonious; and truth being also realized as a conscious, comprehensible experience, from the union of facts of the consciousness with intuitions or conceptions which are assumed to be laws of the Reason. Now, as this is the condition of the Transcendentalist, — as he demands that all things shall be produced as conscious individual experiences, which have no reference to those of others except as they may have been suggestive, and thus have assisted him in his own self-conscious production, — he experiences a state of perfect negation in relation to all direction and influence from without, and a state of receptivity entirely passive in relation to all impressions and conceptions from within; so that his motto is, "No law can be sacred to me but that of my nature." This complete isolation of the individual, by which he becomes totally unreceptive from without and conceptive from within, constitutes that state of Virginity which must always precede a spiritual communion, conception, and birth; for the word "virgin" signifies a state of separation, isolation, or concealment. In correspondence with this, we find, that, in the account given in the Scriptures of the formation of the Israelitish Church by the communication to Jacob of a supernatural order of thought, it is said, "And Jacob *was left alone;* and there wrestled a man with him until the breaking of the day." Jesus was therefore born of a virgin, in order that this internal reception, conception, and birth from the Spiritual should be represented by the corresponding physical fact: and the presentation of the Spiritual to the Soul, and the acceptance upon the one hand of Absolute Truth, and upon the other of Absolute Falsehood, were symbolized by the Saviour in the parable of the wise and foolish Virgins who were waiting for the coming of the bridegroom; in which the wise, having provided themselves with Light, were admitted to the Marriage Supper, while the foolish, not having done so, were left in "outer darkness." These wise virgins, who, in the acceptance of absolute truth, submit to the sacrifice of individual life, or of that personal individual want which is the female element of the spiritual personality, are thus described by St. John in prophesying this spiritual presentation to the soul, and its salvation through Faith: "And I looked, and, lo, a Lamb stood on the mount Sion, and with him an hundred forty and four thousand, having his Father's name written in their foreheads." "These are they which were not defiled with women; for they are Virgins. These are they which follow the Lamb whithersoever he goeth. These were redeemed from among men, being the first-fruits unto God and to the Lamb. And in their mouth was found no guile; for they are without fault before the throne of God."

We have also shown that it is only by this return to the destructive laws of the mind, and the realization from these of forms of thought and of life by which they become incarnated, illustrated, and made comprehensible, that the individual can be prepared for the realization of a spiritual consciousness, and the consequent presentation to him of opposite absolute laws, between which his choice must be made; because the vital and destructive laws of the mind are the natural representatives to him of these absolute opposites, and the incarnation of these must therefore furnish suggestive material in the realization of this spiritual consciousness. At the same time, we have shown that this condition of the individual is not simply destructive. Although deprived of the power of external direction from a calculation of causes and consequences, and therefore unable to construct a consistent plan of life for himself that shall be adapted to the external circumstances among which he finds himself placed, he obtains, as a substitute for this, an unconscious spontaneous manifestation, and also a supernatural direction, through the most external principle of the Will; and although realizing conceptions of destructive instead of vital laws, as the ground of thought and the guide of life, the objects of this life have become more internal, more intellectual, and more correspondent to a universal and vital principle; and these are combined and manifested in a supernatural manner, so that only the requisite amount of destructive phenomena shall be produced. We shall always find a law of compensation operating to equalize the condition both of nations and of individuals, so that nothing is ever taken away without the substitution of something else which must be regarded as an equivalent. The action by contraries, which is so necessary in the natural to prevent one-sided manifestations which would be ruinous in their consequences, is perceptible in this as well as in the external sphere of the soul's consciousness; because its condition has only been reversed with regard to its internal and external positions, or to its conceptions of universal and personal forms of life. We therefore find that individuals in an external sphere, while recognizing vital institutions which correspond with vital universal laws, are governed by personal objects and motives, are deceptive in their social relations, and are philanthropic only through calculation or through subjection to some external influence; and that individuals in an internal sphere, while recognizing the most destructive ideas and opinions which are antagonistic to all the vital institutions of society, are moved in the direction of universal rather than of personal objects, are simple and truthful in their intercourse with others, and are intensely, although morbidly, philanthropic, either from choice or from an irresistible impulse.

The action by contraries here alluded to may be seen from several points of view, of which this is a prominent one: While the feelings are recognized as the supreme guide both in the belief and in the life, a demand is at the same time made for the conscious recognition of some internal law of relationship by which they are to be governed and directed. The moral powers therefore cease to act in a spontaneous, sympathetic manner in the relief of the distressed, and, in the place of this, act through internal conceptions in which internal is confounded with external want; and the individual seeks to relieve imaginary sufferings instead of those which are real: and the affectional powers cease to perform the duties which are involved in the various relations of life from a spontaneous and unconscious instinctive force, and, in the place of this, act through internal conceptions of these relationships; so that what was once performed through a spontaneous, unconscious affectional activity is now performed by the individual from a sense of fitness and the recognition of right. So far from being the result of mere feeling, therefore, or of a blind instinctive force, his actions are now characterized in the most remarkable manner as intellectual and self-conscious. This action by contraries may also be seen in this: While the individual demands gratification for all the personal wants or propensities of his nature, by which he becomes self-indulgent, he at the same time recognizes the antagonism that exists between the internal consciousness and the external condition, or between the internal and the external want; by which he becomes ascetic, because he demands the sacrifice of the external for the sake of the internal; and, although none but affective laws are recognized by him, — which cannot be made to explain to him the facts of his consciousness, because they are not orderly and constructive, but disorderly and destructive, — he continually demands the realization of the revelation of absolute universal laws by which all things shall be explained. It is true that these laws cannot be discovered by him so long as he remains in this atmosphere of naturalism, because he is here given up to "strong delusion that he should believe a lie;" but the search after them leads him into a region of thought relating to the spiritual origin of things, by which he becomes prepared for the presentation to him of "the mystery of Christ," or "the mystery of the kingdom of God," in which he will be called upon to believe, when he shall pass from this internal-natural into a spiritual sphere of consciousness.

In consequence of the impracticable and destructive character of Transcendentalism, and the self-conscious character of its experiences, these soon become exhausted, and a rapid development of this sphere of the consciousness is to be expected; and this expectation is made more certain of fulfilment by the fact, that the preaching of John the Baptist, who was the great representative of Transcendentalism, was so soon followed by the teaching of Christ. It is true, that the internal as well as the external experiences of the soul are obtained by a process of development: but as this atmosphere is not favorable to the realization of these experiences; as the destructive character of these phenomena makes it impossible that a long continuance of them should be either desirable or practicable; and as these experiences are internal and real, and therefore soon come to maturity, — they will not probably be prolonged, as have been those belonging to an external sphere, which is orderly and productive. Although the individual must be made acquainted by painful experience, in this as well as in the external sphere, with the destructive consequences of natural action, in order that he may be led to look to God as the only source of truth and of good, and as the only refuge from falsehood and evil, — the great uses of Transcendentalism are performed by bringing the soul into a state of singleness and of internal receptiveness, which prepares it for a birth into the spiritual, and a spiritual communication from within; and by the realization of natural forms representative of Absolute Falsehood, — first, in the production of internal forms, as laws of belief and of life; and, next, of external forms, as means of individual manifestation. Even these, however, cannot be realized without producing consequences the most painful to the individual, and disastrous to society; and, although Transcendentalism may not obtain sufficient power in this atmosphere to overthrow all its institutions, this is a result towards which it plainly tends.

It is impossible that so important a change in the individual as that from an external to an internal sphere of life, perfectly opposite in character, — this being from a state of bondage to one of unlimited freedom, — should be effected without struggle and sacrifice, amidst perplexity and doubt; and these troubles must originate not only in the misconceptions and persecutions of the world, which can neither understand nor tolerate him, but also in self-distrust and discontent. He will be distrustful of himself, because, as a general rule, the more self-reliance any individual possesses, the less self-complacency he enjoys, and therefore the more profound is his humility: and he will be dissatisfied with the amount and the quality of his knowledge, because he now demands that which is absolute and universal, while that to which he has attained is small in amount, and is deficient in clearness and in consistency, both of which have now become to him important requisites; while it fails to account in any satisfactory manner for the great facts of life and for the profound mystery of his being, a solution of which is now particularly demanded. Some of these troubles originate in the estimation in which he is held by others, which, with the exception of the more external and brilliant minds in which the Fancy has obtained a predominant influence, is one of great depreciation; for, although he has succeeded in freeing himself from all *externalism*, he cannot so easily free himself from the influence of the *externalists*, for the reason that "Sociability" and "Sympathy" have now come to predominate as motive powers of his mind, and he is therefore more completely identified with Humanity and bound to his kind. This constitutes an important part of his discipline: it is not sufficient that he is released from subjection to public opinion, so that his thoughts, his determinations, and his actions, may spring from the resources of his own mind and will, and thus become real, as manifestations of an individual soul: it is also necessary that the idea of being contemned and despised by others should become familiar to him, because it is only in this way that the sentiment of "Approbation" can be repudiated, and that of "Satisfaction" developed, which is of the highest importance to the development of the individual consciousness. Other afflictions originate in the feeling of helplessness, arising in the loss of external manifesting power, and in the consciousness of antagonism between himself and the externalists. In consequence of this helpless condition, and of his singleness, simplicity, and truthfulness of character, he is deprived of all the armor and of all the arms which are so necessary to security in the warfare of the world; and he consequently grows suspicious of the intentions of others towards him, and carries about with him a presentiment of unseen danger which he has not the power either of discovering, avoiding, or overcoming. Thus it comes to pass, that he who is especially dependent upon others, from greater helplessness, from the greater sociability of his nature, and from the demand that he makes for intellectual and social communion as means of expanding his feelings and elevating his thought, is driven into solitary ways of life, by the dread of being misunderstood and unjustly judged, by a want of sympathy in the world around him, and by the fear of being deceived and misrepresented. Finally, he becomes a sufferer from the nature of his own personal experiences. Self-inspection and self-culture become much more difficult and discouraging, now that the soul feels the necessity of making itself one in thought, in feeling, and in action, with its highest internal conception of duty, for the reason that the thoughts and the feelings are much more rebellious than the muscles; and it is thus much easier to obtain a consistent external manifestation under the eye of the world's applause and censure, assisted by the power of external direction, than it is, when released from all external control, to rule the intentions and wishes of the mind. It is while the individual is engaged in these fruitless attempts to produce unity of idea, of purpose, and of life, and to realize a natural perfection that shall make him like unto God, that the Spiritual Truths of the Reason, which demand the sacrifice of the individual instead of his apotheosis, are revealed to him; and it is while walking upon these unstable and conflicting waters, seeking for the Christ in his own consciousness, that he finds himself sinking in the waves, and is compelled to cry, "Lord, save me!" This account of Transcendentalism completes the description of the natural manifestations of the soul. When it has exhausted these, the Spiritual Itself must be presented to its consciousness; and a new order of experiences must commence under the operation of Absolute Law, by which its substance as well as its form will become regenerated. It also completes our illustration of the Law of Circularity, and closes our statement and illustration of the ontological laws upon which we construct Philosophy as Absolute Science.*

---

* Appendix V.

APPENDIX.

INTERPRETATIONS

OF

THE SYMBOLISM OF THE BIBLE,

AND OF

HEATHEN MYTHOLOGY,

FROM THE POINT OF

ABSOLUTE SCIENCE.

APPENDIX.

I.—PAGE 162.

THE opposition that exists between spiritual and natural spheres of intelligence is represented in the Scriptures in a variety of forms, of which we shall hereafter give an explanation. These opposite spheres are represented in Grecian Mythology under the symbolism of Jupiter and Minerva; and, although natural intelligence is there deified, the form in which it is incarnated is representative of the opposition of natural to spiritual truth. Jupiter is pictured as the King of Heaven, to represent Spiritual Truth; and he is therefore attended by an Eagle, as the bearer of his lightnings, to designate the quality of this truth; because the Eagle is the bird of Day, which soars towards and gazes upon the Sun, and builds its nest upon the highest rocks. To represent Natural Truth, the Goddess Minerva is pictured as armed with helmet, spear, and shield, to indicate its discordant, contentious, and destructive character, and is attended by an Owl to designate its external, sensuous, and negative quality; because the Owl is the bird of Night, which lives in the hollows of dead trees, shuns the light, and can see only in darkness,—being, with its enormous eyes, a caricature of Wisdom. The significance of these emblems, all of which are productions of the Imagination, will be more fully comprehended when we understand that *birds* are representative of intellectual principles,—that *beasts* are representative of affections,—that *dead trees* represent the most external forms of the Understanding, separated from the internal principles from which they subsist,—that *light, the sun, day,* represent spiritual truth, and also that natural truth which is relatively internal or masculine; while *darkness, the moon, night*, represent natural intelligence, as contrasted with spiritual truth, and also that which is relatively external or feminine, as contrasted with that which is internal or masculine, — and that *rocks* are representative of those fundamental truths which constitute the foundation of knowledge. That intelligence which is internal, abstract, and elevated, and embraces those laws or general principles which constitute the life of thought, will therefore be characteristic of masculine minds; while that which is sensuous, external, and partial, including those phenomena which are calculated for the illustration and embodiment of the former, and to which they must be united to constitute them true, living, or productive, will therefore be characteristic of feminine minds.

II. — Page 166.

THESE relationships are represented in the mythological symbolism of both the Christian and the Pagan Church. The external, unconscious, and dependent character of Good is represented in the Mosaic account of the creation of the Female out of a Rib taken from the Body of the Male while he slept. This may be seen, because the Body is the most external element of the physical constitution; and the Rib, which, with its marrow, is a representative of Truth and Good, is the most external element of the Body: so that a rib taken from the body of the Male, and formed into a Female, plainly represents the supernatural production of the most external things of truth and of good from the most internal, as a female region of consciousness separated from the most internal or male region which constitutes its vital principle; and this we shall show to be the mode of production in every department of the human constitution, and this the relationship that exists between its internal and external spheres, which are related as male and female spheres, and also as truth and good. The same relationship exists between the intellectual and affectional departments of the mind: and this may be seen, because these affectional principles, through which external good becomes realized, experience no emotion, and do not therefore become conscious, or realize any affectional condition, until objects for which they have an affinity, and with which they are therefore calculated to unite in production, are presented to them through the intellect; and it is again illustrated by the fact, that ideas of these objects constitute the intellectual and vital element in these principles. That the female principle of the soul — the production of which has here been represented by the creation of the female from the male — is relatively destructive, is represented by the fact that it was the female who was tempted by the serpent, and became the tempter of the male; and the Church, taking the letter of the Bible as a ground, therefore conceives, that, through the female, sin and death were introduced into the world; and thus accounts for the Origin of Evil.

The relationship between Truth and Good as male and female, and as vital and destructive, is also represented in Heathen Mythology by the Garden of Hesperus with its Golden Fruit. This may be seen, because Gold is a commonly recognized symbol for Good; — because this garden was occupied by four goddesses born of Night; these being named Æglé, — Brightness; Erytheia, — the Blushing; Hestia, — the Spirit of the Hearth; and Arethusa, — the Ministering; which, it will be seen, are incarnations of female characteristics; — because this fruit was guarded or presided over by the Serpent Python, whose name signifies "The Corrupter;" and was held up by the Sibyl Deiphobe, who represented Evil, because it is said that she rejected the love of Apollo, the Sun God, and, in consequence, gradually wasted away; — and, finally, because the male or vital principle in this myth was represented by Apollo, and also by Hercules, by whom the first and most external form of this dragon was destroyed, and the golden fruit redeemed from its influence.

III. — Page 245.

This most general classification of the principles of the Human Constitution, and also the form of each department contained in it, are distinctly represented in the following passage from Ecclesiasticus: "God created man of the earth, and made him after his own image. He gave him the number of his days and time, and gave him power over all things that are upon the earth. He created of him a helpmate like to himself: he gave them counsel, and a tongue, and eyes, and ears, and a heart to devise; and he filled them with the knowledge of understanding. He created in them the science of the spirit, he filled their heart with wisdom, and showed them both good and evil." * The principles here named "counsel, and a tongue, and eyes, and ears, and a heart," — and which are alluded to in the Protestant version as "the five operations of the Lord," — will be found to correspond with the five principles which constitute each of the natural and supernatural departments of the Mind, and also with the five departments which constitute the supernatural, the natural, and the personal regions of the Human Constitution: the first including the Religious and Moral Sentiments; the second, the Intellectual and Affectional Faculties; and the third, the Will; — "the Science of the Spirit," which is here said to be created in the soul, and through which is realized "the knowledge of understanding," will be seen to correspond with the Reason; because it is only through the union of Universal Laws from the Reason with the forms of the Understanding that any true knowledge can be realized, and the heart "filled with Wisdom;" — and "Good and Evil" correspond with the principles of "Perfection" and "Imperfection," which constitute the roots of the Mind, and the representatives of Infinite and Finite. The language used in this portion of the Scriptures is of course symbolic, though not used in a fanciful and fictitious manner, as in natural compositions, but according to supernatural laws of correspondence; and it is therefore only by interpreting this language from a spiritual point of view that we can obtain any knowledge of its real import. In showing the correspondence between this statement from Ecclesiasticus, and the principles of the Human Constitution as they have here been stated, we shall make use of correspondences which were revealed to or conceived by Swedenborg; for although, as the exponent of Transcendental Law, he inverted and falsified the truth, in his abnormal or somnambulic condition he became a medium for the communication of a greater number of natural analogies and supernatural correspondences than any other known individual; and, when a position is obtained which overlooks him, — a position that has been obtained by us through a conception of the Spiritual Laws of Correspondence, — these can be separated from his misapplications and inversions of true correspondence, and appropriated for use. According to Swedenborg, Counsel corresponds with faith. He says, "Counsel, of which walking is predicated, has respect to thought. In the prophetic writings, the things relating to faith are expressed by

---

* Catholic version.

walking and seeking. 'To walk' is a customary form of speaking signifying to live; as, to walk in the Law, to walk in the statutes, to walk in the truth. 'To walk' has respect properly to a way, which is of truth, consequently which is of faith, or of the doctrine of faith." According to this interpretation, then, "counsel" corresponds most perfectly with the Religious department of the mind, which is the medium for the communication of supernatural truth, and therefore of that which represents the spiritual in the natural.

Tongue signifies in the Scriptures the internal of Good, which is realized through the Moral department of the mind; and, if Counsel signifies an affinity for religious truth, Tongue must, according to our science, signify an affinity for moral good, because here the religious and moral departments are related as internal and external; and, besides this, it is the tongue that gives expression to that which the head conceives and counsels. In consequence of the fact that these departments of the Sentimental Nature are dual, and contain vital and destructive sides of Truth and of Good, which must be successively developed, opposite correspondences must necessarily be recognized. Therefore, while Swedenborg says, "Tongue corresponds with those who are in the affection of truth, and afterwards in the affection of good from truth," — which corresponds with the vital condition of the moral nature, — he also gives an opposite signification, which is this: "Tongue signifies the thirst and cupidity of perverting the truths of the word; and lapping water with the tongue signifies the falsification of the Truth." This "falsification of the truth" is produced in the development of the destructive laws of the Sentimental Nature, and consequent inversion of the laws of truth and of good, and the assertion of personal individual want as the supreme principle, which is particularly described in our analysis of Transcendentalism. This is also termed, in the Scriptures, coveting a tongue of gold, which expresses that idolatrous worship of good in the Will, or assertion of personal want as the supreme principle, just alluded to, and which represents that spiritual act of the individual, resulting in spiritual death, which is symbolized in the Scriptures in a great variety of forms, but particularly in the temptation and fall of Adam through the solicitation of the female, and in the "trespass in the accursed thing" by Achan, for which "all Israel stoned him with stones," and he and all his possessions were "burned with fire."

It is hardly necessary to say that the term "eyes" corresponds with and represents the Understanding, or intellectual department of the mind; because, in the common use of language, to see is to understand, and because no kind of knowledge can be realized except through means of the Understanding, where all Truth must become incarnated. By the term "ears" is represented, in the Scriptures, the good of the affectional principle, which is relatively female, and is therefore the good which springs from obedience. According to Swedenborg, "They who are dutiful and obedient, in another life belong to the province of the ear; yea, correspond to hearing itself." "To hear, signifies reception and perception,—the perception which is from the will of good, and thence obedience. To hearken to father and mother, signifies obedience from affection." "Ear-rings are insignia representative of obedience: consequently, they signify things actual; for to obey involves to do a thing in act. Ear-rings of Gold signify those things which appertain to simple good." It is therefore that the Golden Calf, which was set up by the Israelites as an object of idolatrous worship, and represented the worship of the external, affectional, or female principle, which corresponds with the Finite, was said to have been made from the ear-rings of the women. From all this, it will be seen, that, according to common and recognized rules of correspondence, the term "ears" signifies, as here used, the region of Instinct in the mental constitution, which is the source of the Affections, and constitutes the external sphere of Good. By "heart" is here evidently signified the Will; because these have always been extensively used as synonymous terms, and the Will has been supposed by most philosophers to be determined by some affectional want, desire, or motive power. This correspondence is also confirmed by Swedenborg, who says, "Heart corresponds to love or charity in the Will, and has relation to good or to evil, according to the predication of the subject."

IV.—PAGE 313.

THE development of the Sentimental Nature from within outwards, as it has here been described, is illustrated by the symbolic teaching upon this subject which constitutes a large portion of the Scriptures; this teaching being conveyed under some historical form, or narrative, which we designate parable, constituting such supernatural revelation a sealed book. These parables will be found to represent this development in the same dualistic form, and in the same order, as stated by us, including an individualization of the vital and destructive sides of this region of the consciousness, each of which is divided and antagonized as external and internal, and realized consecutively in forms which are known to us as Catholicism, Protestantism, Unitarianism, and Transcendentalism. In illustrating our subject from the Scriptures, which we do with the double purpose of illustrating our Science, and of showing its application in the interpretation of religious symbolism, we will take that series of the parables of our Lord which are found in the 15th chapter of the Gospel of St. Luke, including "the Lost Sheep" and "the Prodigal Son." These were addressed by him to the Jews as an answer to the complaints made by them that he held communion with "the sinners of the Gentiles," who were the disciples of John, and correspond in a more external sphere with the Transcendentalists of the present day.

We there read: "Then drew near to him all the Publicans and Sinners for to hear him. And the Pharisees and Scribes murmured, saying, This man receiveth Sinners, and eateth with them." And, before we proceed any further, this question is to be answered: Who were these Pharisees, Scribes, Publicans, and Sinners? And although it may readily be answered that the first two were Jews, and the last Gentiles, the question still arises, What is to be understood by the terms Jew and Gentile, as these are used in the Scriptures? Jew and Gentile there represent those classes which correspond with a vital and with a destructive development of the Sentimental Nature, which we have shown to be divided and antagonized by vital and destructive elements, termed, in the Scriptures, life against death, good against evil, and the godly against the sinner; and have also shown to be the supernatural region of the mind that furnishes the laws which govern the individual manifestations. Jews are there divided into external and internal portions, which are termed Scribes and Pharisees; and Gentiles are divided into external and internal portions, which are termed Publicans and Sinners. The classes who, in the Christian Dispensation, correspond with this vital sentimental development, are known to us as Catholic and Protestant; and those who correspond with this destructive development are known to us as Unitarian and Transcendental; this last denomination corresponding with the "sinners of the Gentiles," who are also termed in the Scriptures "the lost sheep of the house of Israel," to whom alone the Saviour declared that he was sent, because it was only this portion who could truly receive him; the reason for this being, that they only had realized "the fulness of the time," or that complete natural development which was necessary as a preparation for a supernatural life corresponding with Christianity; precisely as it is only those who have passed through a full development of the Supernatural, both from a vital and from a destructive point of view, who are prepared for the Spiritual Itself, or for the Second Coming of Christ.

Because the Pharisees and Scribes murmured, "He spake this parable unto them, saying, What man of you, having an hundred sheep, if he lose one of them, doth not leave the ninety and nine in the wilderness, and go after that which is lost, until he find it? And, when he hath found it, he layeth it on his shoulders, rejoicing. I say unto you, that likewise joy shall be in heaven over one sinner that repenteth, more than over ninety and nine just persons, which need no repentance."

These words of the Saviour were interpreted by the Jews as a recognition of the departure of the Gentiles from a faith to which he wished them to return; or to mean that he regarded them as lost sheep, which he was anxious to bring back into the fold of the Jewish Church; and they were therefore obliged to receive this as a justification of his course. The real meaning of this parable, however, is well understood to be opposite to this, because we know that the Church into which it was his object to bring these sinners of the Gentiles was opposite to that of the Jewish, from which they were seceders. The real meaning of the terms "publican" and "sinner" is quite as opposite to that which has been commonly applied to them; that is, that by "publicans" were meant persons of a low or common character; and by "sinners," and "lost sheep," those who had become immoral: for the term "publican" was used to denote the Unitarian, which is an aristocratic class; and the term "sinner," to denote the disciples of John the Baptist, who preached the crucifixion of all externalism, and correspond with the Transcendentalists, who are morally ascetic. The terms "publican" and "sinner" were applied to the Gentiles, because the first became disorderly by the repudiation of the vital ideas, forms, and institutions of the Church; and the second became "vile" by the realization, through an internal, self-conscious development of the destructive side of the Sentimental Nature, of inversions of these ideas as laws of the individual life, by the attempt to overthrow the forms and institutions which had been founded upon them.

We can, of course, understand these parables only by truly interpreting the symbolic language in which they are written; and, in doing this, we shall depend partly upon the suggestions of Swedenborg, and partly upon the meaning that obviously belongs to them, as seen from the point of our philosophy. By "hundred" is signified, according to Swedenborg, a Church, or "the state of the Church in general:" and we interpret this as meaning, necessarily, the most external form of the Church, which constitutes its Body, where all internal things are represented in external forms; because it is only in this most external Church that a universal form, constituting "the Church in general," is to be found; a fact that has given to it, as it appears in the Christian Dispensation, the name of Catholic or Universal. By "sheep" are here signified the members of this most external Church, or those who are subject to it, and exclusively receptive from it; and this we may know, because it was only to Peter, who was selected by Christ to be the founder of the Catholic Church, that he addressed these words: "Feed my sheep." By the "hundred sheep" is therefore signified the members of the most external Church collectively, or the condition of the Sentimental Nature while under the superintendence of this Church. The term "ninety and nine" is used to denote those in whom the destructive laws of the sentimental nature are being developed; and this may be seen because this number is representative of the greatest possible diversity, and diversity is the destructive law with reference to Truth. It is therefore that "sand," and also "dust," are used to express this destructive intellectual diversity, which is opposite to the unity of the spiritual. The term "wilderness" is used to denote the destructive condition of the Sentimental Nature, or of the Church to which these individuals belong who are being thus developed from a destructive point of view; and signifies, according to Swedenborg, "1st, The Church devastated, or in which all the truths of the Word are falsified, such as it was among the Jews at the time of the Lord's Advent; 2d, The Church in which there are no truths, because they are not possessed of the Word, such as it was among the well-disposed Gentiles in the Lord's time; and, 3d, A state of temptation, in which man is, as it were, without truths, because surrounded with evil spirits who induce temptations." By "the one sheep that was lost" is represented the soul which has left the natural condition, where it was under the control of God, and has passed into a spiritual sphere of consciousness; this being a condition of freedom in which opposite spiritual laws are presented to it, and it is compelled to choose which of these laws shall constitute its life: and this may be known, because it is only when the soul is in this condition, in which it has not only departed from the natural truths of God, but also from his jurisdiction, that the Lord could be said to "go after that which is lost," because at all other times the soul is in the hand of God, who determines all the experiences of its life under the direction of his divine providence. We are thus prepared to see, that by "going after the lost sheep" is signified the presentation of the Spiritual Itself to the soul,— that by "finding the sheep" is signified the acceptance of Absolute Truth by the soul as the law of its belief and life,—and that by "laying this sheep upon the shoulder, rejoicing," is signified the communication of Spiritual Life to the soul, which is the Atonement of Christ, by which God becomes its spiritual governor. This may be known, because by "shoulder" is represented, in the Scriptures, power, rule, or direction, as thus: "And the government shall be upon his shoulder." We can now understand why there is more joy in heaven over the one sinner that repenteth, than over ninety and nine just persons who need no repentance. It is because the one has been redeemed, and added to the angels of heaven, while the ninety and nine have not yet been prepared for a spiritual birth; for, although these are here called "just persons," the justice here referred to is natural and representative, and not spiritual and real. Although, "touching the righteousness which is in the law," the Jewish Scribes and Pharisees were "blameless," they were the furthest removed from the possibility of realizing the law of spiritual life, and they therefore rejected the Saviour. Being whole, they did not need a physician; while those "sinners of the Gentiles," who had inverted the vital natural representatives of spiritual life, and become disorderly, destructive, and naturally diseased, were prepared to be restored to a vital spiritual condition by the great Physician of the Soul. The Lord also addressed to these Scribes and Pharisees another parable, which is that of the Prodigal Son, the significance of which is precisely the same, as was also the effect intended to be produced; the only difference being, that one relates to the position and action of the Lord with reference to the Soul, and the other to the position and action of the Soul with reference to the Lord.

"And he said, A certain man had two sons; and the younger of them said to his father, Father, give me the portion of goods that falleth to me. And he divided unto them his living. And, not many days after, the younger son gathered all together, and took his journey into a far country, and there wasted his substance with riotous living. And, when he had spent all, there arose a mighty famine in that land; and he began to be in want. And he went and joined himself to a citizen of that country; and he sent him into the fields to feed swine. And he would fain have filled his belly with the husks that the swine did eat; and no man gave unto him. And, when he came to himself, he said, How many hired servants of my father's have bread enough and to spare, and I perish with hunger! I will arise and go to my father, and will say unto him, Father, I have sinned against heaven and before thee, and am no more worthy to be called thy son: make me as one of thy hired servants. And he arose, and came to his father. But, when he was yet a great way off, his father saw him, and had compassion, and ran, and fell on his neck, and kissed him. And the son said unto him, Father, I have sinned against Heaven, and in thy sight, and am no more worthy to be called thy son. But the father said to his servants, Bring forth the best robe, and put it on him; and put a ring on his hand, and shoes on his feet: and bring hither the fatted calf, and kill it; and let us eat, and be merry: for this my son was dead, and is alive again; he was lost, and is found. And they began to be merry. Now his elder son was in the field; and, as he came and drew nigh to the house, he heard music and dancing. And he called one of the servants, and asked what these things meant. And he said unto him, Thy brother is come; and thy father hath killed the fatted calf, because he hath received him safe and sound. And he was angry, and would not go in: therefore came his father out, and entreated him. And he, answering, said to his father, Lo, these many years do I serve thee, neither transgressed I at any time thy commandment; and yet thou never gavest me a kid, that I might make merry with my friends: but as soon as this thy son was come, which hath devoured thy living with harlots, thou hast killed for him the fatted calf. And he said unto his son, Son, thou art ever with me, and all that I have is thine. It was meet that we should make merry, and be glad: for this thy brother was dead, and is alive again; and was lost, and is found."

According to Swedenborg, "Man, in the Word, signifies intelligence and wisdom derived from the Word, and this is the Church in him." This, however, is an external definition, which does not recognize the medium in the individual through which the Church becomes realized in him. As a more internal definition, we say, By Man, in the Scriptures, is signified the Supernatural Principle, or Region of Consciousness, which constitutes the Church in him; it being for this reason that the Prophets were called Sons of Man. Now, as this supernatural principle realizes two distinct conditions of development, — the first being unconscious and simply receptive, and therefore demanding a stationary condition of the individual; and the second being conscious and conceptive, and therefore demanding a changing and progressive condition of the individual, corresponding with the development of his mind from within outwards, — we conceive that by the two sons of a certain man are signified these opposite states: the first of these corresponding with the most external Church, which the elder son always represents, this being in the Christian dispensation the Catholic Church; while the second corresponds with Protestantism, Unitarianism, and Transcendentalism. That this conception is correct will be shown by interpreting the symbolic language in which this parable is written; and it is particularly important to understand this division, because a large portion of both the Old and the New Testament is occupied in representing these various states of the human consciousness.

This being the ground of representation here adopted, the action of this dramatic parable commences with a representation of the Protestant movement, which is the first independent, self-conscious manifestation of the sentimental nature. This is represented by a demand of the younger son, that he should be endowed with his portion of the property of his father; and nothing can be more complete than the correspondence between this demand of the younger son, and his departure from his father's house, taking with him as a personal possession the portion of his father's goods which "falleth to him," and that departure from the Catholic Church, and that partial but conscious conception of supernatural truth, which attended the establishment of Protestantism, — in which the Church was constructed upon the ground of theological conception combined with the recognition of individual inspiration and internal direction in the interpretation of the Scriptures, the conception of truth, and the direction of the life. The events which followed this departure of the younger son will be found to represent the succession of phenomena which has been realized in the consciousness consequent upon this establishment of conscious internal individual direction, in the place of unconscious external direction from the Catholic Church. The next change represented in this parable is that from Protestantism to Unitarianism; and this is represented by the "far country," into which the younger son took his journey. This correspondence is an obvious one; because this change from Protestantism to Unitarianism is from a supernatural to a natural order of thought and experience, which are the most distant from each other. The process of this change is represented by the wasting, in this far country, of the younger son's substance with riotous living; and this correspondence plainly represents the gradual decay of the belief in vital supernatural ideas, and that final repudiation of these ideas which attended the establishment of Unitarianism; a wasting of substantial things, or of the means of support to the soul, that was truly said by the elder son to be a devouring with "harlots," because these supernatural ideas are representations of the spiritual marriage, and the term "harlot" is therefore used in the Scriptures to symbolize the destruction of these ideas. These results are also represented by "the mighty famine in the land" which immediately followed this wasting of the young man's substance, and plainly represents the full development of Unitarianism, by which a total destruction of vital supernatural significance in the representative forms of Society, of the Scriptures, and of the Church, is accomplished by their repudiation, or by an interpretation from a naturalistic point of view, by which all their vitality is destroyed.

The next change represented in this parable is that from Unitarianism to Transcendentalism; by which, internal individual conceptions of the destructive supernatural laws are established as the only governing laws of the belief and of the life, — all vital forms of truth, of good, and of use, are repudiated, — and destructive forms, which are inversions of these, are established in their place. This is represented by the fact, that the younger son went and joined himself to a citizen of that country, by whom he was sent into the fields to feed swine. This is shown from the character of the citizen who employed him, — from his occupation, as a feeder of swine, — and from the fact, that "he would fain have filled his belly with the husks that the swine did eat." As Cities represent "the interiors of the natural mind, and the doctrinals of the Church,"* a citizen of that far country into which the

---

* "Dictionary of Correspondences."

prodigal had gone must represent the internal conception of the law of "Naturalism," which is the destructive religious law, upon which the doctrines of Transcendentalism are founded, and which compels the individual to teach these doctrines. It is therefore said, that "he sent him into the fields to feed swine;" because "Field signifies whatever respects doctrine;"* — "to feed is to teach;"* — and "Swine signifies those who love natural and not spiritual riches;"* or, rather, those who love inversions of vital supernatural truths, who are the transcendentalists. That "swine" represents this most destructive natural condition may be known, because "To eat the flesh of swine signifies to appropriate infernal evils;"* and because it is written, that Christ permitted the devils, at their request, to enter into a herd of swine. The last representation of this transcendental condition is the desire to fill the belly with husks which the swine do eat; and this correspondence may be seen, because "Husks are an inferior kind of vegetable, that none but the swine will eat;" while "The Belly"*— which the prodigal would fill with these husks — "signifies the interior understanding, — those things which are nearest to the earth, — and also natural good;"* and by "the interior understanding" is represented the internal-natural, or transcendental, sphere of consciousness; while by "those things which are nearest to the earth" is signified what is opposite to heaven or to supernatural truth, and is the inversion of this truth realized in Transcendentalism in a form representative of Absolute Falsehood, which is conceived and appropriated by the individual as the law of his belief and life. In correspondence with this, Swedenborg says, "Walking upon the belly to the earth signifies being infected and imbued with infernal falses;" and, after the temptation and fall of Adam, God said to the Serpent, "Because thou hast done this, thou art cursed above all cattle, and above every beast of the field: upon thy belly shalt thou go, and dust shalt thou eat, all the days of thy life."

The next change represented by this parable is the transition from a natural to a spiritual sphere of consciousness, in which opposite spiritual laws are presented to the individual, and he is obliged to choose which of these shall become the law of his new spiritual existence. This change is represented by the statement that the prodigal "came to himself." When the soul becomes spiritual and real, — that is, when the individual comes to him-

---

* "Dictionary of Correspondences."

self, — he comes into this dual spiritual consciousness, because he is constituted by a dual affinity for these opposite spiritual laws: one being the Love of God, or an affinity for Infinite Law, which demands the sacrifice of Personal Life; and the other being the Love of Self, or an affinity for Finite Law, which demands self-assertion, and the realization of Personal Life as an Absolute Cause. That this spiritual position of the soul is here represented, and also the choice by it of a vital law, may be known, because it is here written, "When he came to himself, he said, How many hired servants of my father's have bread enough and to spare, and I perish with hunger! I will arise and go to my father, and will say unto him, Father, I have sinned against heaven and before thee, and am no more worthy to be called thy son: make me as one of thy hired servants. And he arose, and came to his father." This may be known, first, because "To arise, is to be elevated from a state of evil to a state of good;" * and this is realized by the individual, when, coming into a spiritual sphere of consciousness, he rejects Absolute Falsehood, and accepts Absolute Truth, as the law of his life, — next, because the prodigal determines to go to his Father, who is here the representative of this Truth, for the purpose of obtaining Bread; for the want of which he was starving, and which is used in the Scriptures to symbolize this Truth, as we may know from the words of Christ upon which the Sacrament of the Eucharist is founded, — and, finally, because he desires to become one of his father's hired servants, by which is represented the fact that he has abandoned all claim to an absolute personality, or to be an absolute cause, and desires to become dependent upon God for all things; this being the act of self-renunciation which is included in the spiritual act of Faith.

It may also be known from the subsequent events in this narrative, — the meeting of the Father and the Son, — the repentant condition of the Prodigal, — putting upon him the best robe, a ring upon his hand, and shoes upon his feet, — the anger of the elder son, — and the killing and eating the fatted calf. By the meeting of the Father and the Son is represented the communication to and acceptance by the Soul of Absolute Truth, through which it realizes Salvation; and this may be known, because at this meeting the Father "fell on his neck, and kissed him:" for, in the language of correspondence, "the Neck signifies influx,

---

* "Dictionary of Correspondences."

und the communication of interior and exterior principles, and consequent conjunction;" and "to kiss, signifies unition, or conjunction from affection, and also initiation, and acknowledgment;"* and, from these correspondences, it will be seen that Spiritual Marriage, or the marriage of the Soul to God, is here represented. By the repentant state of the prodigal, and the relinquishment by him of his right to be called a son, is represented that act of spiritual self-renunciation, or that acknowledgment of personal opposition to God from the total depravity of the personal principle, which must accompany an act of Justifying Faith. By putting upon the prodigal "the best robe," and by "putting a ring upon his hand, and shoes upon his feet," is signified the spiritual regeneration of the mind, of the heart, and of the will: "the best Robe" is the "marriage garment," or the "garment without a seam," which signifies the universal form of Truth realized in the regeneration of the Mind; the Ring upon the hand signifies that Love of God, or that personal affinity for spiritual truth which is realized through the regeneration of the heart, or of the personal principle; and the Shoes upon the feet signify the consequent regeneration of Individuality, or Will, through the operation of this truth, so that he becomes a medium for the manifestation of the Will of God.

By the anger of the elder son at the return of his brother, and his unwillingness to participate in the festivities occasioned by this return, is signified the natural condition, antagonistic to the spiritual, in which is the Church of which he is the symbol; and also the fact, that, although she is the most perfect external representative of Christianity, she is the farthest removed from the possibility of its realization, and is the most hostile to its form, — which was shown by the rejection and crucifixion of Christ by the Jews, notwithstanding that Moses had testified of him, and they were expecting him. That the elder son represents the most external Church, may be known, because it is said that he "was in the field;" and Swedenborg says, "Field signifies the good of life, wherein are to be implanted the things appertaining to faith, *i.e.*, the spiritual truths of the Church," which corresponds with what is known to be the character of the most external Church. The words of the Father — "Son, thou art ever with me, and all that I have is thine" — are therefore to be understood simply as a recognition of the permanence and per-

---

* "Dictionary of Correspondences."

section of this Church, as the most external representative of Christianity, in which are contained universal representatives of spiritual life adapted to all the manifestations of the human constitution. They are in correspondence with other allusions to this Church,—such as, " the just, who need no repentance," and " the whole, who need no physician ; " and are to be understood in a representative, and not in a literal sense, which is opposite to the truth. That the relation between the elder and the younger son is here correctly stated, is shown by this : that the former was subject to an external direction exclusively, while the latter had thrown off this subjection, and had given himself up to an internal direction in feeling and in thought. This is shown by the words of the former, who says, " Lo, these many years do I serve thee, neither transgressed I at any time thy commandment ; " and by the actions of the latter, who " took his journey into a far country, and there wasted his substance with riotous living," or " with harlots ; " because we have shown that the first represents passing from the legitimate representations of spiritual life to individual conceptions which are opposite, and that the second represents the conception and appropriation of the destructive laws of the Sentimental Nature, which are opposite to marriage, as the laws of the individual belief and life. It is also shown by this : that the elder son was not allowed to eat "of a Kid," while for the younger son " the fatted calf was killed." This may be seen, because " Kid signifies the truth of the Church,"*— "To eat denotes communication, conjunction, and appropriation," * or to make one-with by conscious individual appropriation ; so that to eat of a Kid would represent the realization of Protestantism, and was therefore denied to the elder son,—"Calf signifies the affection for knowing divine truth,"—and " fatted Calf signifies those who are filled with knowledges of things true and good from the affection of knowing them : " * therefore, eating of the fatted calf evidently represents an individual condition corresponding with this definition, which is realized in spiritual regeneration, here represented as experienced by the younger son.

---

* " Dictionary of Correspondences."

V.—PAGE 416.

WE will illustrate this account of the development of the Mind from within outwards, and growth of the Individual from below upwards, by an explanation of the history of Job, which is found in the Jewish Scriptures; because it is the most comprehensive of those parables or symbolic compositions found in the Scriptures which represent the development of the Soul through the operation of the Sentimental Nature, and it is therefore particularly appropriate as an illustration of the full development of the human consciousness that has just been described; although this parable illustrates not only this natural growth and development, but also the birth of the Soul into the Spiritual, its Salvation through Faith, and its regeneration into a form of Divine-Humanity. In explaining this parable, we shall point out some of the mistakes which were made by Swedenborg in interpreting its symbolic language,—mistakes which arose in his false position, and in the fact that the idea represented by the Protestant doctrine of Justification by Faith is also represented in this parable; for Swedenborg, being more violently opposed to this than to any other doctrine of Christianity, excepting perhaps Tri-Personality, could not recognize any correspondences which plainly favored it, or allow the record to be of divine authority. He therefore says, "The book of Job is an ancient book, wherein, indeed, is contained an internal sense, but not in series, or in regular connected order; and the spiritual sense there collected from correspondences does not treat concerning the holy things of heaven and the Church, like the spiritual sense in the Prophets." It will clearly be shown, however, in the explanation now to be given, that a "regular connected order" is here astonishingly perfect, this dramatic parable being particularly consecutive and regularly progressive; and that it does, in the most complete and remarkable manner, "treat of the holy things of heaven and the Church, like the spiritual sense in the Prophets;" the series of experiences here represented corresponding most perfectly with those represented in the parables of our Saviour, as already explained; both being intended to represent the entire history of the Soul, or its birth by blood, by water, and by spirit. The story commences thus: "There was a man in the land of Uz, whose name was Job; and that man was perfect and upright, and one that feared

God, and eschewed evil. And there were born unto him seven sons and three daughters. His substance also was seven thousand sheep, and three thousand camels, and five hundred yoke of oxen, and five hundred she-asses, and a very great household; so that this man was the greatest of all the men of the east."

Now, as the development of the soul through the operation of the sentimental nature is represented by the story of Job, the experiences with which this story commences represent those which belong to the most external Church, — corresponding with the Jewish and also with the Catholic Church, — and by his great household are represented the communicants or members of this Church; these being synonymous with the "hundred sheep," with the "elder son," with the "steward of the rich man," and other similar symbolic individualizations, a great number of which could be enumerated, but which we, of course, have no time now to explain; and we shall find that the kind of property possessed by Job will, when explained, show this to be the fact. It will be readily understood that by the "sons and the daughters of Job" are signified the Truth and Good of the Church, because these are the most common correspondences of the Bible: and that truth and good corresponding with the spiritual are meant to be represented, may be known from the numbers; because seven is always used to represent what is spiritual, intellectually considered, and three to denote the good which corresponds with it. This truth and this good we again find represented more externally and more definitely by the other possessions of Job; these being sheep, camels, oxen, and she-asses, which represent those supernatural forms of truth and of good, a knowledge of which this Church dispenses to its members, and which are received by them through the operation of the religious and moral sentiments: the "sheep" and "camels" representing the truth and good which belong or have reference to a Supernatural order of thought and of experience, and are received through the Religious Sentiments; while the "oxen" and "she-asses" represent the truth and good which belong to a Natural order of thought and of experience, and are received through the operation of the Moral Sentiments. In the enumeration of these possessions, it will therefore be seen that the term "thousands" is applied to those things, which, according to this explanation, are referable to a supernatural, while "hundreds" are applied to those which are referable to a natural, order, because belonging to a lower numerical region: so that, according to the explanations here given, "seven thousand sheep" distinctly represent truths of a supernatural order; "three thousand camels," forms representative of external worship, which is supernatural good; "five hundred yoke of oxen," the truths of natural good; and "five hundred she-asses," the affections for these truths, or forms of good corresponding with them. Having considered the nature of these possessions, and shown that they were intended to represent the sum of those things for which the individual is dependent upon the most external Church, we will proceed to consider the experiences of Job, and show that these were intended to represent the changes which take place in the sentimental experiences of the individual.

The first of these changes is represented by the destruction of certain of the possessions of Job; and the first calamity that befell him is thus related: "The Oxen were ploughing, and the Asses feeding beside them: and the Sabeans fell upon them, and took them away; yea, they have slain the servants with the edge of the sword; and I only am escaped alone to tell thee." Now, we have shown that by "oxen" are represented the truths of natural good, and that by "she-asses" are represented the forms of good corresponding with them: and this is shown by the fact that the Oxen were ploughing, and the Asses feeding beside them; because to "Plough is to implant truth in good,"* and to feed beside any thing represents affection for it and reception from it. It will therefore readily be seen, that taking them away, and destroying those who were attending upon them, represents the first effect of Protestantism in the Church, which was the separation of good from truth as natural and antagonistic to the Spiritual. That this destruction of the possessions of Job really represents a reformation of the Church, or the change from an external to an internal Church, may be seen, because, in the purification of the Temple by Christ, the first things driven out were the Oxen and Sheep, and the latter of these come next in this destruction of the possessions of Job. The second calamity that befell Job is thus related: "While he was yet speaking, there came also another, and said, The fire of God is fallen from heaven, and hath burned up the Sheep, and the servants, and consumed them; and I only am escaped to tell thee." Now, we have already shown that by "sheep" is represented the reception of religious truth from the most external Church, by whom no private judgment with regard to these truths is tolerated. We shall therefore see, because nothing can

---

* "Dictionary of Correspondences."

be more striking or appropriate than this correspondence, that by "the fire from heaven which burned up the sheep" so soon after the removal of the oxen is represented in the most perfect manner that vivid individual intuition of religious truth, or that internal realization by individuals of this truth, which, in the establishment of the Protestant Church, not only takes the place of external reception from the Catholic Church, but establishes a more internal system that is opposite to and destructive of the comparatively external truths so received. The third calamity which befell Job is thus related: "While he was yet speaking, there came also another, and said, The Chaldeans made out three bands, and fell upon the camels, and have carried them away; yea, and slain the servants with the edge of the sword; and I only am escaped alone to tell thee." Now, by "camels" is represented, as we have seen, external worship, which is supernatural good, and which is rendered to the Church by its members as religious service: and although it is not necessary that we should be able to see why camels were chosen to represent this fact, because we see that they were thus chosen, the appropriateness of this symbol may be seen from the facts, that the camel has been formed to bear heavy burthens, and has been provided with an internal apparatus that will contain water sufficient to sustain it for a long period; and we all know the intimate relation that exists between water and the sentimental principle. It will therefore be seen that the third and last result which was realized in the establishment of the Protestant Church is here represented, which is an entire separation from the most external Church, including the complete separation of truth from good, and the repudiation of all its naturalistic beliefs, of all its symbolic forms representing spiritual truth, and of all its ceremonial and discipline representing spiritual good. The next calamity that befell Job, and which concludes the first act of this sacred drama, is thus related: "While he was yet speaking, there came also another, and said, Thy sons and thy daughters were eating, and drinking wine, in their eldest brother's house; and behold, there came a great wind from the wilderness, and smote the four corners of the house, and it fell upon the young men, and they are dead; and I only am escaped alone to tell thee." Now, as the sons of Job represent, as we have seen, the religious truths of the Church, two questions arise: first, What is the particular form of religious truth which is here represented as being destroyed? and, next, By what, and how, has this destruction been effected? The answer to the first of these will be found in the fact, that the children of Job "were eating, and drinking wine, in their eldest brother's house," because "Elder Brother signifies the internal Church," * and we have already shown that this is the Protestant Church. The condition of this Church is shown by the fact, that the house, in which these children were, had four corners,—that is, was square; because, as we have already shown that the square, which is constituted by "two and two, one against the other," is the representative of a natural form and condition, it becomes evident, that a naturalistic condition of the Church is here represented,—a condition that is produced by the perversion of its doctrines, by which it is prepared for dissolution. The second of these questions is answered by the fact, that this house was destroyed by a "great wind from the wilderness," which "smote the four corners of the house;" because—having shown that "wilderness" signifies "the Church devastated, or in which all the truths of the word have been falsified," and that "four corners" represent a naturalistic condition—"a great wind from the wilderness" must signify here a force destructive to all the vital religious truths of the Church, and the "smiting of the corners of the house" must signify that Naturalism was the cause of its destruction. As all the possessions of Job have now been destroyed, with the exception of his three daughters, the fact here represented evidently is the substitution of Moral Good for the Religious Truth of the Church. We may therefore see that the first act of this drama closes by representing the establishment of Unitarianism.

The second act in this sacred dramatic parable opens with the introduction of Job into a new order of experiences, which are symbolized in the following most comprehensive manner: "So Satan went forth from the presence of the Lord, and smote Job with sore boils from the sole of his foot unto his crown. And he took him a potsherd to scrape himself withal; and he sat down among the ashes." Now, by "Satan going forth from the presence of the Lord to afflict Job," three things are most distinctly represented: first, that these afflictions, or that these experiences, were to be produced by the operation of an evil and destructive natural principle; next, that they were to be produced by the permission, and under the superintendence, of God, or of Divine Providence; and, lastly, that they were to be produced under the law of Necessity, or by what is termed in the Church the pre-ordination of

---

* "Dictionary of Correspondences."

God. Having seen what was the general character of these experiences, we will next consider the psychological character of the facts which were intended here to be represented by "the boils of Job," by "the scraping himself with a potsherd," and by "his sitting down among the ashes;" and show the relation these bear to the sentimental condition of the individual.

According to Swedenborg, by "boils" are signified "interior evils and falses destructive of goodness and truth;" but, although these boils are produced by the operation of destructive internal principles, they do not represent these principles. Swedenborg has here confounded these external appearances with the cause of them; and he has therefore given the same signification to "boils," and to the "potsherd" with which these impurities were removed. The "boils of Job, from the sole of his foot unto his crown," represent the entire expulsion of externalism from the consciousness, through the realization of a new internal life; or the effects which result from the demand of Transcendentalism, that an internal and real shall be substituted for an external and unreal condition of the life and of the consciousness. It is therefore that Job is described as scraping himself with a potsherd, because the internal conceptions of truth and of good which, in Transcendentalism, become laws of the belief and of the life, and by which this externalism is removed, are, as we have seen, inversions of supernatural truth and good; and we find that "potter's vessel," which is synonymous with "potsherd," is explained by Swedenborg to mean "the falses which are in the natural man, or the things of self-derived intelligence," which is a correct definition of these conceptions. The "ashes which Job sat down among" represent the entire destruction of all externalism by this fire of Naturalism. This phenomenon is a perfect counterpart to the burning of the Sheep by the fire of God, already explained; because in both cases it is the destruction of external forms through the intuition and internal conception of sentimental laws, — in one case from the vital, and in the other from the destructive, side of the Sentimental Nature. Swedenborg, who does not distinguish between natural and spiritual spheres, says, "Ashes signifies what is condemned, because the fire from which they are derived signifies infernal love." This definition seems to be an unmeaning one, because ashes do not come from fire, but from something opposite to it which the fire has destroyed: that the fire was infernal would not therefore make the ashes to be condemned; for, even if "ashes" represent what is condemned, it could not be said to be condemned because it was burned, but rather to be burned because it was condemned. As in the case of "boils," Swedenborg has here confounded the cause with the effect; by which, correspondence is made chaotic: and this is not a simple inadvertence, but corresponds with the central principle of his system, which confounds opposites, instead of separating them, and producing a legitimate union between them. Both "ashes" and "dust" are used in the sacred symbolism to represent what is relatively dead, and therefore corresponds with the Finite, because they represent absolute diversity, separation, or disorganization. To the Transcendentalist, all external things are therefore seen as Ashes; while, to the Spiritualist, all transcendental things are seen as Dust. We may now see that this final condition to which Job has been reduced by the power of Satan is a perfect representation of the transcendental condition of the human consciousness that has just been described, and which immediately precedes the spiritual birth of the soul, or its introduction into a spiritual sphere of consciousness. We have shown that these experiences of Job — that is, "the sore boils from the sole of his foot unto his crown," the "scraping himself with a potsherd," and the "sitting down among the ashes" — were intended to represent the experiences of Transcendentalism; and, if the symbolic language used in this parable has been correctly interpreted, this must be acknowledged. We are not, however, confined to this evidence. This general statement of the experiences of Job is followed by a more particular and internal one, which represents the preparation of the soul for the spiritual birth, the presentation to it of the Spiritual, and its salvation through an act of faith. In this statement, Job appears as a personification of the Church, — in which character he bewails the changes in its condition, and contemptuously describes its enemies, — and also appears as a personification of Transcendentalism, by which the Church has been destroyed; and, although this double representation makes the form of this narrative somewhat contradictory, it also makes it more peculiar, interesting, and complete.

This narrative commences with a dialogue between Job and three former friends, who come to him for the purpose of saying that his afflictions have been sent as a punishment for his sins, or for his theological unbelief, self-assertion, and worship of good; these friends being the representatives of those states of religious consciousness through which he had passed. Although a volume might be written upon the correspondences contained in this dialogue, so profuse is it in details, we can make but a short extract from it. This, however, will be sufficient to show that the experiences of Transcendentalism are here represented, and also that the original condition of Job illustrates the primitive and most external Church, from which individuals are receptive of all the forms of belief and of life. It will also represent the fact, that this receptive condition of the individual has been succeeded by one entirely opposite; which, although higher from a personal point of view, is disorderly, and destructive to all the vital external forms established by the Church, — a change that includes the transition from a belief in human free-agency to a belief in divine predestination, and from a belief in human depravity to a belief in the divinity of human nature; and also includes self-assertion, self-glorification, self-sanctification, and the worship of good; all of which, as we have already shown, are experiences of Transcendentalism. From this position, Job is represented as pleading his cause with God, maintaining the purity and uprightness of his ways, and complaining that he had been afflicted by divine power without just cause. As a personification of the primitive Church, he says, —

"Oh that I were as in months past, as in the days when God preserved me; when his candle shined upon my head, and when by his light I walked through darkness; as I was in the days of my youth, when the secret of God was upon my tabernacle; when the Almighty was yet with me; when my children were about me; when I went out to the gate through the city; when I prepared my seat in the street! The young men saw me, and hid themselves; and the aged arose, and stood up. The princes refrained talking, and laid their hand on their mouth. The nobles held their peace, and their tongue cleaved to the roof of their mouth. When the ear heard me, then it blessed me; and, when the eye saw me, it gave witness to me; because I delivered the poor that cried, and the fatherless, and him that had none to help him. The blessing of him that was ready to perish came upon me; and I caused the widow's heart to sing for joy. I put on righteousness, and it clothed me: my judgment was as a robe and a diadem. I was eyes to the blind, and feet was I to the lame. I was a father to the poor; and the cause which I knew not I searched out. And I brake the jaws of the wicked, and plucked the spoil out of their teeth. Unto me men gave ear, and waited, and kept silence at my counsel. After my words they spake not again; and my speech dropped upon them. And they waited for me as for the rain; and they opened their mouth wide as for the latter rain. I chose out their way, and sat chief, and dwelt as a king in the army, and as one that comforteth the mourners."

From this, which is a perfect description of the primitive and most external Church at the time of its greatest supremacy and power both in temporal and spiritual things, Job passes to a description of the discordant naturalistic manifestations of the Sentimental Nature, destructive to the Church, which result from the operation of the destructive sentimental laws. He says, "But now they that are younger than I have me in derision, whose fathers I would have disdained to have set with the dogs of my flock. Yea, whereto might the strength of their hands profit me, in whom old age was perished? For want and famine they were solitary; fleeing into the wilderness in former time desolate and waste. Who cut up mallows by bushes, and juniper-roots for their meat. They were driven forth from among men (they cried after them as after a thief), to dwell in the cliffs of the valleys, in the caves of the earth, and in the rocks. Among the bushes they brayed; under the nettles they were gathered together. They were children of fools, yea, children of base men: they were viler than the earth. And now am I their song; yea, I am their byword. They abhor me, they flee far from me, and spare not to spit in my face. Because he hath loosed my cord, and afflicted me, they have also let loose the bridle before me. Upon my right hand rise the youth; they push away my feet, and they raise up against me the ways of their destruction. They mar my path; they set forward my calamity; they have no helper. They came upon me as a wide breaking-in of waters: in the desolation they rolled themselves upon me."

These correspondences most distinctly represent the repudiation and inversion of Supernatural Truth by the operation of the destructive sentimental laws, which is realized in the development of the mind from within outwards, as it has here been described. This may be seen by interpreting a few of the symbolic terms here used. "Want and famine" represent the destruction of vital supernatural ideas, and consequent want of faith in the supernatural truths of the Church, as we have already shown in interpreting "the Prodigal Son." The "wilderness," into which these enemies of Job were driven, and which produces "nettles" instead of grass, represents "the Church devastated, or in which all the truths of the word have been falsified," as we have already shown. "A wide-spread breaking-in of waters" represents the inundation of the Church by supernatural falsities, which are inversions of supernatural truths. This corresponds with the destruction of the world by Water, or by the flood, which represented a total destruction of vital supernatural ideas in the Church, from which all other things are sustained, and the substitution of inversions of these, by which all vital forms are destroyed,— necessitating the reconstruction of all things upon a vital supernatural basis. According to Swedenborg, "By ' a fool' is signified he who is in falses and evils from the love of self, consequently from self-derived intelligence." We may therefore suppose, that by the "children of fools" are here represented those who realize internal conceptions of destructive supernatural laws. These are here said to be "viler than the earth," because while the Earth represents the natural region of the Mind, including the Understanding and Instinct, which is destructive to supernatural thought, and is therefore relatively vile, these laws are destructive to vital natural thought, and are therefore "viler than the earth." The manifestations of the understanding being corrupted by the operation of these laws, instead of being represented by the "horse," which is the legitimate symbol of the Understanding, are here represented by the discordant braying of asses "gathered together under the nettles," which are, as we have seen, a growth of the "wilderness."

After this representation of the desolation of the Church from the operation of destructive supernatural laws, Job appears as the personification of Transcendentalism, and thus laments the desolate condition to which he has been reduced, defends the uprightness of his ways, and under the belief in Fate, or in a divine predestination, accuses God of injustice: "And now my soul is poured out upon me; the days of affliction have taken hold upon me. By the great force of my disease is my garment changed : it bindeth me about as the collar of my coat. He hath cast me into the mire, and I am become like dust and ashes. I cry unto thee, and thou dost not hear me : I stand up, and thou regardest me not. Thou art become cruel to me : with thy strong hand thou opposest thyself against me. Did I not weep for him that was in trouble? Was not my soul grieved for the poor? When I looked for good, then evil came unto me; and when I waited for light, there came darkness. My soul is weary of my life : I will speak in the bitterness of my soul. I will say unto God, Do not condemn me : show me wherefore thou contendest with me : is it

APPENDIX.

good unto thee that thou shouldst oppress, that thou shouldst despise the work of thine hands, and shine upon the counsel of the wicked? Hast thou eyes of flesh? or seest thou as man seeth? Are thy days as the days of man? Are thy years as man's days, that thou inquirest after mine iniquity, and searchest after my sin? Thou knowest that I am not wicked; and there is none that can deliver me out of thine hand. Thine hands have made me, and fashioned me together round about; yet thou dost destroy me. My face is foul with weeping, and on my eye-lids is the shadow of death; not for any injustice in mine hands: also my prayer is pure. Behold, I cry out of wrong, but I am not heard: I cry aloud, but there is no judgment. He has fenced up my way that I cannot pass, and he hath set darkness in my paths. He hath stripped me of my glory, and taken the crown from my head. He hath destroyed me on every side, and I am gone; and mine hope hath he removed like a tree. He hath also kindled his wrath against me, and he counteth me unto him as one of his enemies. He hath put my brethren far from me, and mine acquaintance are verily estranged from me. My kinsfolk have failed, and my familiar friends have forgotten me. Yea, young children despised me: I arose, and they spake against me. All my inward friends abhorred me; and they whom I loved are turned against me.

"Oh that I knew where I might find him! that I might come even to his seat! I would order my cause before him, and fill my mouth with arguments. I would know the words which he would answer me, and understand what he would say unto me. Will he plead against me with his great power? No; but he would put strength in me. There the righteous might dispute with him; so should I be delivered for ever from my judge. Behold, I go forward, but he is not there; and backward, but I cannot perceive him; on the left hand, where he doth work, but I cannot behold him: he hideth himself on the right hand, that I cannot see him. But he knoweth the way that I take: when he hath tried me, I shall come forth as gold. My foot hath held his steps: his way have I kept, and not declined. Neither have I gone back from the commandment of his lips: I have esteemed the words of his mouth more than my necessary food. All the while my breath is in me, and the spirit of God is in my nostrils, my lips shall not speak wickedness, nor my tongue utter deceit. God forbid that I should justify you: till I die I will not remove my integrity from me. My righteousness I hold fast, and will not let it go:

my heart shall not reproach me so long as I live. Let mine enemy be as the wicked, and he that riseth up against me as the unrighteous. Let me be weighed in an even balance, that God may know mine integrity. Behold, my desire is that the Almighty would answer me, and that mine adversary had written a book. Surely I would take it upon my shoulder, and bind it as a crown to me. I would declare unto him the number of my steps; as a prince would I go near him."

Nothing could more completely represent that belief in absolute necessity and the divinity of human nature, and that self-assertion and self-worship, which we have seen to be incidental to the realization of Transcendentalism, than this defence of himself by Job. One more fact, however, remains to be noticed in showing the correspondence between these experiences of Job and those of Transcendentalism. We have shown that the development of the Soul in an internal-natural or transcendental sphere of consciousness is designed to accomplish two principal objects: one being the realization of an internal and self-conscious condition and position, which must precede the communication to it of a spiritual consciousness; and the other being the realization of a natural form representative of Absolute Falsehood, which, together with Absolute Truth, will be presented to the soul from within, when it shall be transferred from a natural to a spiritual sphere of perception, by which presentation is realized the spiritual temptation. Now, the first of these, which includes the destruction of all externalism in the belief and in the life, and the complete realization of Individualism, is represented by the "sitting-down of Job among the ashes;" while the second is represented by the solicitation of the wife of Job, which immediately followed this concluding act, that he should "curse God, and die." It will be seen that this is perfectly analogous to the temptation of Adam by his wife in Paradise. In both cases, the female represents that incarnation and individualization of personal individual want, by means of the destructive laws of the Sentimental Nature, which is realized at the close of the natural development, and becomes productive of the worship of good in the beautiful; this being that natural representation of the worship of Absolute Falsehood which must be realized in the mind before the Spiritual can be revealed to the consciousness. We have now shown that the second act in this sacred drama closes with a representation of the complete establishment of Transcendentalism; a fact that is suggested by the concluding sentence, which is this: "So these three men ceased to answer Job, because he was righteous in his own eyes."

The third and last act in this drama presents Job in still another character, in which he realizes a series of experiences representing the introduction of the soul into a spiritual sphere of consciousness. We here read: "Then was kindled the wrath of Elihu, the son of Barachel the Buzite, of the kindred of Ram: against Job was his wrath kindled, because he justified himself rather than God. Also against his three friends was his wrath kindled, because they had found no answer, and yet had condemned Job." The statement made to Job by Elihu represents the presentation of Spiritual Truth, and thus the introduction of the soul into a spiritual sphere of consciousness; and we may see this from several points of view. It may be seen, because he repudiates the claim of Job to spiritual perfection, which is opposite to the acknowledgment of sin demanded by Spiritual Truth; and also repudiates the theological friends of Job, who had condemned him for the same fault; because, if Job could not be condemned from their religious point of view, it must be from a spiritual point, there being no other from which he could be condemned; and this is, therefore, next in the order of realization. A really spiritual statement could not, of course, be made before the Spiritual Itself had been incarnated in Flesh, but only one representing the spiritual in that natural, unconscious, and symbolic manner which constitutes the body of supernatural representation: and, although many of the arguments of Elihu are similar to those put forth by the theological friends of Job whom he condemns, this is fully accounted for by the fact, that the sentimental theology of the Church represents, while it contradicts, the same ideas which are afterwards realized in a spiritual sphere of consciousness; a fact that will be demonstrated in our theological system. It may also be seen, because Elihu announces himself as coming "in God's stead," saying, "The spirit of God hath made me, and the breath of the Almighty hath given me life:" and because he immediately precedes, in this narrative, the actual communication, to the consciousness of Job, of Spiritual Life: for, as soon as Elihu had ceased speaking, "the Lord Himself answered Job out of the Whirlwind." This latter fact represents not merely the presentation to the consciousness of the Spiritual, because this was done by the communication of Elihu; but that reception of and submission to Spiritual Truth, which is realized through an act of Faith. We may know this, because the term "whirlwind," which, in the physical world, is produced by the union of two opposite atmospheres, by which a circular motion, and thus a perfect equilibrium, is produced with reference to direction or force, is used in the symbolic language of the Scriptures to represent the consciousness of two opposite absolute principles or laws, by which a perfect equilibrium is realized in the Will, and thus a perfect freedom of volition secured; and therefore "God speaking to Job out of the whirlwind" represents a divine communication resulting from spiritual choice. That an act of Faith through which the soul becomes justified, sanctified, and united to God through regeneration, is represented by this fact, may be seen, because an immediate and entire change of mind and of heart was evidently wrought in him: and instead of defending himself, and urging his claim to wisdom and to goodness, he makes that acknowledgment of total ignorance, depravity, and dependence, which we shall show to be included in this spiritual act. In replying to the Lord, he therefore says, "Behold, I am vile: what shall I answer thee? I will lay mine hand upon my mouth. Once have I spoken; but I will not answer: yea, twice; but I will proceed no further. I know that thou canst do every thing, and that no thought can be withholden from thee. Who is he that hideth counsel without knowledge? Therefore have I uttered that I understood not; things too wonderful for me, which I knew not. I have heard of thee by the hearing of the ear; but now mine eye seeth thee. Wherefore I abhor myself, and repent in dust and ashes."

It is therefore said that Job was accepted of the Lord, and also that "the Lord gave Job twice as much as he had before;" by which the spiritual regeneration of the Soul is represented, it being thus written: "For he had fourteen thousand Sheep, and six thousand Camels, and a thousand yoke of Oxen, and a thousand She-Asses. He had also seven Sons and three Daughters." "And the Lord said to Eliphaz the Temanite, My wrath is kindled against thee, and against thy two friends; for ye have not spoken of me the thing that is right, as my servant Job hath. Therefore take unto you now seven bullocks and seven rams, and go to my servant Job, and offer up for yourselves a burnt-offering; and my servant Job shall pray for you: for him will I accept."

These supernatural and spiritual phenomena were also represented by the Pagans from a natural point of view, an example of which we will give by an interpretation of the myth of Cupid and Psyche; although, from the corruptions which have been introduced into these ancient myths, the representation is not so perfect as that which we find in the Scriptures. The substance of this narrative appears to be this: Cupid, the God of Love, having become enamoured of the earth-born Psyche, caused her to be confined in a strong tower, from which she could not depart; where he visited her, but could not be seen by her because his visits were made in the night. In the process of time, the curiosity of Psyche was awakened by whispers that her spiritual partner was an evil demon; and she consequently became desirous to see him, and, if this report should prove to be true, to destroy him. Cupid having fallen into a profound slumber, she improved this opportunity; and having provided herself with a Light, and armed herself with a destructive weapon, she sought the now sleeping deity with this desire and intent. In the eagerness of her curiosity, she applied the light so near to his person, that some drops of the burning fluid fell upon him, and he awoke. So confounded was she by the light which beamed from his eyes, that she dropped the knife, intended for his destruction, upon herself, inflicting a wound which produced her death; upon which, she was conveyed by Cupid to heaven, to enjoy Spiritual Life through marriage with him.

In this history is condensed a representation of the natural and spiritual experiences of the soul, through which it is prepared for, and finally realizes, a resurrection into Spiritual Life. By Cupid is represented the Spiritual concealed under the form of a Supernatural Revelation, which the mind cannot recognize through Sight, but only imperfectly recognize through Feeling,— which it cannot comprehend through the rational powers of the mind, but only apprehend through religious sentiment,— and which is communicated in some form to every individual through the religious department of the mind. By Psyche is represented the Soul. By the strong tower, within which Psyche was confined, is represented the Church: and this may be seen, because it is precisely so, that the soul is confined within the limits of the Church, to which it becomes subject during the periods of its immaturity and dependence, and is preserved by becoming receptive from her as the supernatural representative of the Spiritual; and because, like Psyche, the soul cannot, at this time, obtain any knowledge of the spiritual through sight, or comprehension through the Reason, but only of its external natural representative through feeling, or through sentimental apprehensive recognition.

By the curiosity of Psyche being excited by whispers of detraction against Cupid is represented the commencement of that loss of faith in the most external Church, and of that determination to realize supernatural knowledge from a self-conscious, comprehensive point of view, which ends in the establishment of Protestantism. By the slumber of Cupid is represented the total obscuration of supernatural truth in the mind, or loss of supernatural perception; and thus that disbelief in supernatural truths, and belief in natural appearances opposite and destructive to them, which are realized in Unitarianism through the unconscious operation of "Naturalism" and "Sympathy," — the destructive sentimental laws. By the light which was procured by Psyche to guide her to the presence of her former supernatural companion, that she might destroy him, is represented that intuition and internal conception of these destructive supernatural laws, which are realized in Transcendentalism as the guide of the individual, and as the law of his belief and life, and are opposite and destructive to all the forms and beliefs of the Church. By the destructive weapon with which she armed herself for his destruction is represented the conception that is realized in Transcendentalism of the inverted and destructive form of the Reason, which corresponds with the destructive sentimental laws, — is an inversion of, and therefore opposite to, vital universal laws, — and is therefore destructive to the life of supernatural truth; constituting a suitable ground for the construction of an antichristian church. By the application of light so near to the person of Cupid is represented that close investigation of truth from the universal and rational point of view which is realized in Transcendentalism through the suggestions of the destructive sentimental laws, in which these inverted universal laws of the Reason become incarnated, and which must precede the spiritual birth of the soul, because it is this most internal position of the individual in relation to truth that prepares him for the presentation of the Spiritual Itself. The burning drops which fell upon the person of Cupid, and awoke him, represent that full natural development of the soul which necessitates its introduction into a spiritual sphere of consciousness. By the awakening of Cupid is represented the presentation of the Spiritual to the consciousness of the soul; by the self-destruction of Psyche through the influence of the beaming eyes of Cupid is represented that act of self-renunciation, or sacrifice of the personal life, which is consequent upon the reception of Absolute Truth by the soul as its life; and by the resurrection of Psyche, and her marriage with Cupid in heaven, is represented that realization of Spiritual Life, through Marriage, which is consequent upon an act of Justifying Faith.

This myth is an illustration of the fact, stated in our analysis of Transcendentalism, that, before the Spiritual can be revealed to the consciousness, the individual must necessarily become conceptive of the destructive rational and sentimental laws as his only guide in the conception of truth and of good, and as the only laws of his belief and life; and, consequently, that he must become hostile to all vital rational and supernatural truths, which are representative of Spiritual Life, and to all the institutions which have been founded upon them, or in which they have been incarnated; and, therefore, that it is always while warring against this truth and these institutions, that the Spiritual Itself is revealed to the consciousness of the individual, and he becomes receptive of and subject to it, realizing Spiritual Life through Marriage. This sudden change from a violent opposition to supernatural truth, to the reception of, and submission to, the Spiritual Itself, — of which this truth is the representative, — as the law of individual belief and life, is a prominent theme in the Scriptures of both the Old and the New Testament, for the reason that it represents the only free act of the soul from a vital spiritual point of view. The most perfect representation of this fact is found in the account given in the New Testament of the Conversion of Saul. We there read, that while "yet breathing out threatenings and slaughter against the disciples of the Lord," and while journeying towards Damascus with hostile intent, "suddenly there shone round about him a light from heaven; and, falling on the ground, he heard a voice saying unto him, Saul, Saul, why persecutest thou me?" By "journeying towards Damascus" is represented that return to the rational and supernatural ground of things which is incidental to the realization of Transcendentalism; because it was Damascus "from which came Eber, or the Hebrew Nation," and "to them were committed the oracles of God," because they came of the supernatural race or stock. By "the light from heaven which shone round about him" is clearly represented the presentation of the Spiritual Itself to the consciousness; and by "falling on the ground"—which translation we take from the Catholic Bible, as the true interpretation—is signified spiritual worship in the Will. This latter fact may be known, because "to fall prostrate signifies humiliation, reception, and acknowledgment;" and by "ground" is signified the

Soul,—the Individual Principle,—or Man in the most universal sense, and thus as a church. In correspondence with this, Swedenborg says, "Ground, in a universal sense, signifies the Church, and the man of the church in particular. In the Word, by 'ground' is everywhere signified somewhat relating to the Church: hence also is derived the name of Man, or Adam, which is ground. When man is regenerated, he is no longer called earth, but ground, because celestial seeds are implanted therein." That the "spiritual worship in the Will" here represented was the worship of Absolute Truth, and thus that "falling on the ground" here represents the immediate conversion of Saul to Christianity through an act of Faith, may be known, because he heard the reproaches of the Saviour, and said, "Lord, what wilt thou have me to do?" This is shown by the blindness of Saul for three days,—which signified the entire removal from the mind of his destructive natural beliefs, because "natural sight is that of the eye," and "three signifies what is full from beginning to end,"—and by the fact, that, at the end of that time, a new sight was given to him, and "straightway he preached Christ in the synagogues, that he is the Son of God."

END OF VOL. I.

Boston: Printed by John Wilson and Son.

www.ingramcontent.com/pod-product-compliance
Lightning Source LLC
Chambersburg PA
CBHW021426300426
44114CB00010B/671